Beyond Rationality

How and why do people make political decisions? This book is the first to present a unified framework of the Behavioral Political Science paradigm. BPS presents a range of psychological approaches to understanding political decision-making. The integration of these approaches with Rational Choice Theory provides students with a comprehensible paradigm for understanding current political events around the world. Presented in nontechnical language and enlivened with a wealth of real-world examples, this is an ideal core text for a one-semester courses in political science, American government, political psychology, or political behavior. It can also supplement a course in international relations or public policy.

Alex Mintz is Former Provost and Director of the Program on Political Psychology and Decision Making (POPDM) at IDC Herzliya in Israel.

Nicholas A. Valentino is Professor of Political Science and Research Professor in the Institute for Social Research at the University of Michigan.

Carly Wayne is Assistant Professor of Political Science at Washington University in Saint Louis.

Beyond Rationality

Behavioral Political Science in the 21st Century

ALEX MINTZ
IDC Herzliya

NICHOLAS A. VALENTINO
University of Michigan

CARLY WAYNE
Washington University in St. Louis

CAMBRIDGE
UNIVERSITY PRESS

University Printing House, Cambridge CB2 8BS, United Kingdom

One Liberty Plaza, 20th Floor, New York, NY 10006, USA

477 Williamstown Road, Port Melbourne, VIC 3207, Australia

314–321, 3rd Floor, Plot 3, Splendor Forum, Jasola District Centre,
New Delhi – 110025, India

103 Penang Road, #05–06/07, Visioncrest Commercial, Singapore 238467

Cambridge University Press is part of the University of Cambridge.

It furthers the University's mission by disseminating knowledge in the pursuit of
education, learning, and research at the highest international levels of excellence.

www.cambridge.org
Information on this title: www.cambridge.org/9781316516355
DOI: 10.1017/9781009029827

© Alex Mintz, Nicholas A. Valentino, Carly Wayne 2022

First published 2022

Printed in the United Kingdom by TJ Books Limited, Padstow Cornwall

A catalogue record for this publication is available from the British Library.

Library of Congress Cataloging-in-Publication Data
Names: Mintz, Alex, 1953– author. | Valentino, Nicholas A., author. | Wayne, Carly, author.
Title: Beyond rationality : behavioral political science in the 21st century / Alex Mintz, Nicholas A.
Valentino, Carly Wayne.
Description: Cambridge ; New York, NY : Cambridge University Press, 2022. | Includes bibliographical
references and index.
Identifiers: LCCN 2021008472 (print) | LCCN 2021008473 (ebook) | ISBN 9781316516355
(hardback) | ISBN 9781009029827 (ebook)
Subjects: LCSH: Behaviorism (Political science) – United States. | Rational choice theory. | Human
behavior models. | United States – Politics and government – 2009–2017. | United States – Politics and
government – 2017– | BISAC: POLITICAL SCIENCE / American Government / General | POLITICAL
SCIENCE / American Government / General
Classification: LCC JA74.5 .M56 2022 (print) | LCC JA74.5 (ebook) | DDC 320.97301/9–dc23
LC record available at https://lccn.loc.gov/2021008472
LC ebook record available at https://lccn.loc.gov/2021008473

ISBN 978-1-316-51635-5 Hardback
ISBN 978-1-009-01485-4 Paperback

To my late parents, George and Charlotte Mintz, who aspired for a better world.

Alex Mintz

To Dominic and Catherine Valentino, my first and best teachers.

Nicholas A. Valentino

To Ben Mansfeld, whose love and support empowers me always.

Carly Wayne

Contents

Figures

Table

Boxes

Acknowledgments

The authors thank Eldad Tal-Shir and Samantha Goldstein for their invaluable research assistance and Charles Taber for advice during the early stages of this project.

Living in Interesting Times

How Behavioral Political Science Can Help Us Understand the Current Political Moment

> ... a man hears what he wants to hear
> and disregards the rest.
>
> Simon and Garfunkel, "The Boxer"

The 2020 election was full of surprises, following four years of unusual politics in the United States. Pollsters underestimated President Trump's support, for the second time, and a larger share of eligible voters cast ballots than in any election in over 100 years. Prior to the election, President Trump began to question mail-in voting and the systems put in place to count votes during the COVID-19 pandemic. In the days and weeks following the election, the President refused to accept the outcome, and his team filed what most legal experts considered to be weak lawsuits in multiple states to overturn the outcome of an election that had been overseen by Republicans, Democrats, and Independents around the country.

By December 2020, many Republican leaders began to publicly worry that the President's effort to delegitimize the outcome of the election he lost by more than seven million votes might backfire, as some conservative voters in Georgia even declared a boycott of the Senate runoff elections that would determine control of that powerful legislative body. Many attorneys refused to argue the cases in front of judges, and some firms withdrew their support in the middle of the process out of fear their reputations would be harmed. The lawsuits were quickly dismissed, even by conservative judges Trump himself had appointed, including the three newest justices on the Supreme Court. By a week after the election, polls showed the majority of Americans believed Trump had lost the election, but many Trump supporters simply refused to accept the result. President Trump's unwillingness to concede and publicly accept Joe Biden's win merely extended the news cycle. One might say, and many did, that these events were "unprecedented" in American history. Unfortunately, several of these tactics were extensions of those deployed in the previous election, and in the intervening years.

The 2016 US presidential campaign had already overturned conventional wisdom from start to finish. While predictive models based on long-run economic and political trends suggested a competitive race, few predicted Donald Trump could win. Well-regarded theories about how primaries work, and which sorts of candidates are likely to navigate them successfully, suggested an experienced Republican party insider would likely emerge. Trump succeeded despite – or perhaps because of – boorish rhetoric toward a large number of groups including the disabled, Gold Star families, Muslims and other religious minorities, Mexicans, immigrants in general, women, world leaders, sitting federal judges, and the mainstream media.[1] Trump veered from other historical norms as well, refusing to release his tax returns and threatening to jail his Democratic opponent, Hillary Clinton. He was also dramatically outspent by Clinton. In the end, his victory seemed inconsistent with any number of theories about how candidates win elections in America.

In short, the 2016 and 2020 elections, and many examples and headlines in between, showed that elites, let alone most lay citizens, often behave in ways that deviate from the predictions of rational choice theory (RCT), when it comes to the political arena. However, these strategies can be easily explained by assumptions that are derived from behavioral political science (BPS). The behavioral forces springing from Trump's personality, his willingness to take huge risks when faced with electoral defeat, the effect of his framing tactics on his supporters, and the powerful influence of outrage as a catalyst for risk taking are all places we might look to explain many of these political outcomes. But before we even get to 2020, we might wonder how could such a nontraditional candidate, with few partisan ties and no experience in government or military service, win the highest office in the land in the first place?

In this book, we introduce and use the *Behavioral Political Science* paradigm. This approach can help us understand not only politics in the United States in this historical moment, but also the politics of other countries and in other times. Behavioral Political Science can explain behavior that violates the rules often assumed by a dominant approach to political behavior, rational choice theory.

DEFINING BEHAVIORAL POLITICAL SCIENCE

The most important claim in the book is that a set of ideas from psychology, economics, political science, and communication studies can be combined in a simple way to greatly enhance our understanding of politics. These approaches, which we refer to collectively as Behavioral Political Science or BPS, can help explain the many deviations we see in political attitudes, political decision-making, and political behavior that are often predicted from the dominant, alternative approach to understanding politics, RCT.

What is BPS? One way to define the paradigm is in the negative, carefully listing features that it does *not* include. Therefore, BPS might simply be considered any approach *that does not adopt classical rational choice assumptions about how individuals make decisions.* An even stronger definition, however, is positive: *BPS is an umbrella framework that consists of various intellectual schools that consider the cognitive constraints and diverse motivations that structure human decision-making in the political realm.*

And in fact, BPS does encapsulate a broad and increasingly rich set of research programs that test and modify traditional assumptions about the processes and motivations structuring political decision-making, including: (1) the role, use, and influence of heuristics and cognitive biases on decision-making; (2) the effects of message framing on political attitudes; (3) institutional factors and the psychology of group decision-making in policy formation; (4) the role of emotions in political behavior; (5) individual differences in preferences stemming from personality, values, and norms; and (6) the importance of motivation and identity in information processing and reasoning, among other areas of research. A common thread connecting these diverse research programs is that humans regularly fail to live up to at least some of the classical assumptions of RCT.

The field of Political Psychology consists of various independent and interrelated research programs, theories, and models about the role of psychology in politics and the psychological effects of political events and decisions. Behavioral Political Science integrates many of these approaches into *one* overarching, comprehensive theoretical framework about what motivates decision makers and how they process information on the way to making political choices. At its core, the approach foregrounds heuristics and bounded rationality, and recognizes humans' susceptibility to framing, nudging, motivated reasoning, and other cognitive biases. It integrates a host of motivations that people pursue in politics beyond material self-interest. As such, BPS represents a clear alternative to RCT.

Indeed, scholars have known for some time that political actors often violate many of the core assumptions of rational choice models. The late Herbert Simon, a political scientist and Nobel laureate in Economics, noted more than fifty years ago that we often cannot, and almost always do not, collect and systematically process *all* the information relevant to the decisions we face in the political domain. Simon discovered the concept of *bounded rationality* – one of the key schools of BPS. He was one of the first to systematically consider ways in which standard assumptions underlying RCT fail to capture the processing *abilities* and *motivations* of real people struggling to make choices about candidates, policies, and political actions.

Importantly, however, these deviations from rationality often occur in predictable ways. Exciting new approaches converge around a small and manageable number of modifications to RCT assumptions that can be incorporated into both formal and informal models of political decision-making. Such modifications can greatly enhance our ability to understand heretofore puzzling behavior. In other words, BPS helps systematically investigate the origin, diversity, and heterogeneity of political preferences. It clarifies the imperfect ways in which individuals process information in order to translate these diverse preferences into attitudes and behavior. In this book, we present a framework for understanding the contributions that BPS approaches have made to our understanding of political phenomena. Our central argument is that incorporating empirically grounded BPS assumptions with the formal logical rigor that has typically characterized RCT can significantly improve our understanding of a wide range of political phenomena.

Theories of democracy, and indeed all of politics, begin with two crucial assumptions about the world that are rarely stated and, unfortunately, often do not hold: (1) There must exist a *shared reality* among the governed, and (2) This shared reality must be *tied reasonably closely* to that which actually happens. In other words, most citizens, regardless of their upbringing or partisan viewpoints, must agree about what has happened in the world, and this shared understanding must be reasonably close to actual events.

These two assumptions are necessary in a democracy in order for citizens to hold elected officials accountable for their promises and their behavior once in office. Citizens must more or less agree on what was promised, and whether the promise was kept. The same argument can be made for nondemocratic regimes, though the key stakeholders might differ (e.g., they might be other political elites rather than the public writ large). So, regardless of regime type, both the rulers and the ruled must have some minimally valid sense of what is happening in the world. These pictures in our heads about what has happened and who is responsible can then guide behavior, whether at the ballot box or in the street. Theories of international conflict also assume some shared and credible information about the state of nature as leaders decide whether to go to war or negotiate peace. These assumptions of shared and valid mental pictures about the real world are so obvious that they often go unmentioned. Unfortunately, these assumptions underlying RCT are often incorrect. This book is about how politics works under such conditions. Before delving into the BPS paradigm in more depth, we first begin with a few examples that illustrate the importance of the approach for understanding the current political moment.

FAKE NEWS

The phenomenon of "fake news" is a primary example. The explosive growth in the number of users of social networks, including such tools as Facebook, Twitter, and Instagram, have enabled millions who were previously unable to participate in the public debate to create and distribute both real and fake news to tens of millions of internet readers around the world. Indeed, in his farewell speech, President Obama warned that fake news constituted a threat to democracy. "Increasingly," Obama said, "we become so secure in our bubbles that we start accepting only information, whether it's true or not, that fits our opinions, instead of basing our opinions on the evidence that is out there." The unmooring of the daily news from events of the real world would create obvious problems for democratic citizens in their attempt to objectively and systematically arrive at good decisions. Examples abound in the current moment, particularly in the wake of the January 6, 2021, attack on the US Capitol, spurred in large part by false claims about election fraud and the proliferation of conspiracy theories by groups like "Q-Anon."

False beliefs and conspiracy theories were not unique to 2020, however. The 2016 US presidential election was notable not only for Trump's surprising victory, but because of the emergence of *fake news*. Conspiracy theories on the fringes of the partisan blogosphere have been common for some time, but in 2016 they began to find their way into mainstream conversations about the candidates, a phenomenon that only accelerated during the COVID-19 crisis and the 2020 presidential campaign. These stories often vaulted onto the front-page in mainstream outlets, which then repeated misleading statements even when they were easily refuted. A few specific examples are helpful to illustrate how this type of "pseudo-reality" can be created.

Pizzagate

During the 2016 campaign, a story circulated on right-wing websites accusing Hillary Clinton and John Podesta, one of Clinton's top aides, of running a child sex ring out of a popular pizza joint in the Washington, DC, area.[2] This fictitious claim began with WikiLeaks' release of emails hacked from Podesta's account in October 2016. Posters on far-right wing message boards began fabricating false connections between the word "pizza," found in some personal and work-related emails between Podesta and his brother, and child pornography. Then a link was made to a specific pizzeria named Comet Ping Pong, because the owner was friends with Democratic party operatives. The story then spread virally on popular social media platforms like Facebook and Twitter, with increasingly outlandish details added each day. Before long, this wildly false and gruesome tale of child rape and torture in the basement of the pizza joint (which does not have a basement) had been shared and viewed hundreds of thousands of times around the country and, indeed, the world. The story was even propagated by individuals with close connections to the Trump campaign, such as Michael Flynn Jr., the son of former Trump National Security Advisor Michael Flynn, who on November 2 tweeted "U decide – NYPD Blows Whistle on New Hillary Emails: Money Laundering, Sex Crimes with Children, etc. MUST READ!"

Did anyone take this fanciful story seriously? It would appear so. On December 4, 2016, an armed man travelled from North Carolina to the restaurant in order to, in his words, "self-investigate" the story. While in the restaurant, he fired multiple shots from an AR-15 assault rifle through the door of a broom closet he thought led to the nonexistent basement. Fortunately, no one was injured. Beyond this dramatic and frightening example, many others were at least *unsure* about the veracity of the story. A national poll taken in the immediate aftermath suggested 9 percent of Americans believed that Hillary Clinton was "connected to a child sex ring being run out of a pizzeria in Washington DC," and nearly 20 percent more were unsure whether the story was true or not.[3] *In just over a month, a story was fabricated and deployed through social media that left nearly 30 percent of Americans either believing or being unsure about a patently fake news story.* The man who opened fire at the pizza shop later told the *New York Times* that he was a regular listener to the right-wing show *InfoWars* and had acted because host Alex Jones told listeners to personally investigate the claims. Eventually Alex Jones apologized for his provocation, admitting that his actions put the pizzeria's owner and many other innocent people at risk. This was not the first time the popular conservative talk radio host had promoted false stories. Jones also gave substantial airtime to a story claiming the massacre of twenty school children and six teachers at Sandy Hook Elementary school in Connecticut was fabricated by gun control enthusiasts.[4] He also promoted another fabricated story that the attacks on 9/11 were carried out by the US government in order to boost domestic support for the war in Iraq.[5] Needless to say, misinformation is both commonplace and consequential.

One of the first to recognize that the pictures in our heads rarely match the world as it really exists was Walter Lippmann, a journalist and communication theorist of the early twentieth century. He posited that citizens do not react directly to events in the real world, but instead respond to a world mostly imagined. In his time, there were plenty of examples of people reacting to events imagined to be true but which bore almost no resemblance to that which was real. He opens his 1922 book *Public Opinion* with a story about happenings on a little island in early September, 1914, populated by a small number of French, English, and German citizens who had not heard news from Europe since the last steamship brought the newspapers a few months earlier. They had not heard that WWI had begun in late July. "For six strange weeks, they had acted as if they were friends, when in fact they were enemies" (Lippmann 1920, p. 3). This example, if it can be generalized to a global social media system rife with misinformation, demonstrates that a fundamental lack of shared reality may have profound political consequences.

These mental pictures, which Lippmann labelled the "pseudo-environment," emerged from bits of public information, news images, televised speeches, and soundbites captured in unique combination by each person's mind. The pseudo-environment is affected by the pace of the news cycle, which in the previous example was once quite glacial, but also by habits of our own mind: What our stereotypes tell us must be true. Lippmann guessed that these imagined worlds were what triggered our behavior, and this is where a lot of interesting politics emerged. Lippmann's guess, one that has held up surprisingly well for nearly 100 years now, was that the explanation for most puzzles in the political world could be found in "one common factor":

The insertion between man and his environment of a pseudo-environment. To that pseudo-environment his behavior is a response; but because it *is* behavior, the consequences, if they are acts, operate not in the pseudo-environment where the behavior is stimulated, but in the real environment where action eventuates. If the behavior is not a practical act, but what we call roughly thought and emotion, it may be a long time before there is any noticeable break in the texture of the fictitious world. (Lippmann 1920, p. 10)

In addition to a shared view of reality, it also matters how closely the pseudo-environment hews to the real world. Citizens need access to new and credible information in order to systematically evaluate political alternatives and make the best choices among candidates, parties, and issues.

False or misleading information that alters the public's perceptions, choices, and behavior may, to use the Founders' words, produce a system that *fails* to establish justice, insure domestic tranquility, provide for the common defense, promote the general welfare, and secure the blessings of liberty. For example, following the 2016 election in the United States, and despite the empirical fact that Hillary Clinton won the popular vote by almost three million ballots cast, only 52 percent of Republicans believed this was true. Even after Biden won the popular vote by more than seven million votes in 2020, and captured 306 Electoral College votes in the process, many Trump supporters refused to accept the outcome. Dozens of failed lawsuits in swing state courtrooms were thrown out summarily.

These false beliefs have consequences. The insistence that the election had been stolen led to the riot at the Capitol that killed at least five and injured more than a hundred. At the same time, encouraged by politicians who undermined faith in the country's own medical experts, many Americans insisted to pollsters they would not vaccinate themselves against COVID-19, risking severe illness and even death. This stubborn refusal to accept reality was not simply a Republican problem, of course. Democrats also believe false claims about Republicans, and reject favorable information about the opposition that is demonstrably true.[6] How does this happen, and how can we understand the public's behavior as a result? Behavioral Political Science has some answers.

Election Results

The 2020 and 2016 elections also demonstrated that political *elites* could behave in ways that violate rational choice assumptions. For example, when high-ranking US intelligence officials presented credible proof Russia had attempted to influence the outcome of the 2016 election, Trump replied, "I mean, it could be Russia, but it could also be China. It could also be lots of other people. It also could be somebody sitting on their bed that weighs 400 pounds, OK? You don't know who broke into the DNC." He also questioned the validity of the election tally itself, claiming that widespread voter fraud by illegal immigrants explained why he had lost the popular vote. This pattern repeated following the 2020 election.

In both cases, Trump seemed to reject demonstrable facts because they contradicted the narrative that his electoral college victory represented the will of the majority of Americans. In the former case, Trump committed a *type II* error – not believing something that actually happened (e.g., Russia interfering in the election). In the latter case, it was a *type I* error – believing something that actually did not happen (e.g., large numbers of illegal immigrants voting). To explain this behavior, one needs to consult BPS approaches about framing, priming, and nudging, among others. For example, Trump's claims are consistent with BPS assumptions about how complex internal motivations such as preserving self-esteem impact information processing (see Chapter 8).

The current political moment is challenging for any standard explanation of elite or mass behavior. At the very least, it seems that credible and consensually accepted political information is harder to come by than during the previous media era, when the "Big 3" broadcast outlets -NBC, ABC, and CBS- dominated the US nightly news environment. On the elite side, many of the decisions of the Trump administration seemed to undermine its public image and strategic goals. Needless to say, the available information is not just incomplete, it is sometimes fabricated, and when strategic elites exhibit incoherent and inconsistent policy preferences, democratic accountability breaks down. In this moment, we need new tools for understanding how citizens, leaders, parties, institutions, and states behave. This book is an attempt to organize and explicate such tools under the BPS umbrella to understand a wide variety of puzzling political phenomena.

The COVID-19 Crisis

During the 2020 COVID-19 crisis in the United States, the president often downplayed the pandemic and its medical implications, while refusing to encourage the public to wear masks, advocate mass social distancing, or order lockdowns in communities experiencing high rates of infection.

President Trump's resistance to masks and social distancing during the COVID-19 pandemic, even in the face of overwhelming evidence that these efforts reduce infections, can be explained by rational choice models. However, there is no doubt that BPS can greatly enrich rational choice explanations by highlighting the underlying psychological factors shaping Trump's motivations and actions. Moreover, BPS also unpacks the cognitive processes en route to these decisions. For example, using a two-phase poliheuristic calculation (see Chapter 5), it can be shown that the president first rejected policy alternatives such as a national lockdown because they were likely to damage his reputation in the short run. Only then did he choose from among the "surviving alternative" strategies – such as downplaying the pandemic even in the face of more than 300,000 COVID-19 related deaths by late 2020 – to maximize his net gain (his benefits minus costs). Many pundits from both sides of the aisle believe Trump could have saved thousands of lives, and easily won reelection, if he had taken COVID-19 much more seriously.

Furthermore, Trump and members of his administration extensively used another BPS concept, framing, in order to distract from the danger of the disease by referring to it as the "Chinese Virus," and claiming that rival Joe Biden "caves to the pandemic." As we will show in this book, a host of explanations that belong to the BPS paradigm that can explain this type of behavior and enrich our understanding of politics.

WHAT THIS BOOK IS ABOUT

At one level, this is a book about a theoretical framework, BPS, that consists of several research programs, and centers around a simple but timeless question: In politics, why do both elites and the mass public often make decisions that, from the outside, seem to undermine their own interests? At another level, the book is about what we term "beyond rationality" – the contemporary political moment– where such questions seem much more pressing than usual.

In recent decades, the world economy has grown substantially, unemployment in many developed countries is at historic lows, inflation is under control, life expectancy is up, infant mortality down, and over a billion people have been lifted out of poverty. At least until the upheaval of the COVID-19 pandemic, the United States economy had recovered from the 2007 housing crisis and subsequent recession. By November, 2018, unemployment sank to 3.7 percent, lower than the unemployment rate prior to the recession.[7] In many ways, people around the world have been substantially better off than they were just twenty years ago.

Nonetheless, over the same period, far-right populist parties in Europe have gone from fringe to powerful minority, and some even control ruling coalitions. Far-left parties in countries like Venezuela have also captured power. In June of 2016, the British people shocked the world, and most political experts, by voting to withdraw from the European Union. Then, in November of that same year, Donald J. Trump was elected. He and the Republican House majority immediately began to dismantle the Affordable Care Act (ACA), roll back environmental protections, and threaten international trade agreements whose benefits economists had touted for years. These momentous policy shifts were unexpected in part because they had no simple or obvious catalyst: In the absence of a severe economic downturn or military threat, why would so many people, in so many democracies, vote to put such progress at risk? Furthermore, the people taking the risks often appeared to have the most to lose. In the case of the ACA, most estimates of the negative impact of repeal fell squarely on those areas of the country that had voted most enthusiastically for Trump. In France, support for the far-right anti-immigrant party was strongest in economically vulnerable, rural areas with few immigrants, and weak in places like Paris where most of the terrorist attacks had actually occurred.

Why would publics endorse such drastic shifts in policy when, on average and compared to many other historical moments, things were going well? Why would large segments of society choose candidates who explicitly endorse policies that would make them materially less well off? This book organizes several approaches that can help explain the Trump phenomenon and other dramatic and puzzling political trends. Our goal is the same as most of political science: to understand human political behavior. To do so, we present the BPS framework. By integrating insights from behavioral models with rational choice models of decision-making, we think we can better explain political decisions and behavior than either model can alone.

For instance, one key puzzle springing from RCT that BPS helps to solve involves the meager ability of most humans to calculate the best political alternative in many common situations. One of the main problems that leaders encounter in international affairs is the daunting task of incorporating all relevant details available about their nation's strategic situation into a decision to wage war or negotiate peace with hostile adversaries. Scholars have repeatedly found that, to navigate such choices, leaders focus on a very narrow set of alternatives and dimensions while using rules of thumb and cognitive heuristics – decision-making short-cuts (Chapter 3). Often, these heuristics can help individuals optimize decisions when time is itself a valuable resource. However, in some situations, these same heuristics lead individuals to make mistakes. One famous example of how these shortcuts can impact choice was articulated by Kahneman and Tversky (1979) in *Prospect Theory*, which describes how individual decisions are affected by whether a choice is presented, relatively speaking, as a loss versus a gain. Specifically, humans' aversion to loss is far more powerful than their desire for identically sized gains (Kahneman & Tversky 1979), and this is critical to the decisions of leaders, groups, and coalitions (Levy 1996).

This theory undercuts another key assumption from RCT – that a person's preferences in the political world, say between one policy and another, are not affected by "framing effects"– trivial differences in the way those policy alternatives are described. However, prospect theory, and a large body of other work, has shown this assumption to be invalid. For instance, the way the media frame a problem, prime certain decision criteria over others, and trigger specific emotional reactions can profoundly affect the process whereby people formulate their preferences and then translate them into political behaviors (Nincic 1997).

Framing effects appear over and over in the political world (as we will describe in Chapter 4). For example, when news media describe a rally by a local hate group as a blatant display of racism, citizens are justifiably far less supportive of the group's right to demonstrate than when the same rally is described as a triumph of freedom of speech (Nelson, Oxley & Clawson 1997). The group is the same in either case, and an individual's trade-off between free speech and public safety is assumed to be fixed. How can such minor changes in frames so dramatically shift opinion? BPS argues that this is because the *ways a message is conveyed,* not just what information the message contains, systematically affect how people react to that information.

These framing effects – and other cognitive and information processing biases – are common not only among lay citizens. The dynamics of information processing in the realm of gains versus losses also affect elite decisions as important as whether a state goes to war or bargains for peace (McDermott 2001). For example, a *poliheuristic* bias leads decision makers to exclude some alternatives from consideration when faced with negative implications on a political dimension, even if these alternatives might offer a better solution (Chapter 5). Cognitive biases also emerge in group settings, such as leader–advisor interactions, where social dynamics influence decisions quite profoundly. For example, symptoms of *groupthink* and *polythink* may result in the manipulation of information, censorship of criticism, and overly restricted choice options (Janis 1982; Mintz & Wayne 2016). Given these nearly universal tendencies, it is easy to see how leaders might make suboptimal decisions for themselves and their countries. And if highly motivated, politically sophisticated leaders can make these types of mistakes, then most lay citizens also certainly could.

Another contribution of BPS is to break down the traditional distinction between reason and emotion in decision-making (Chapter 6). Rational choice models of behavior typically assume that reason and emotion stand at opposite ends of a decision-making spectrum, but work in BPS has demonstrated that emotions can be a double-edged sword for political reasoning. On the one hand, they can, at times, bias information processing and negatively affect individuals' ability to engage in cold calculation of the best choices to maximize their self-interest. However, often, emotions are in fact central to helping individuals maximize their utility and may also actively shape individuals' preferences. Factoring emotions into people's utility calculations can thus help us better appreciate a broader concept of utility than simple material self-interest and more accurately portray the ways in which individuals make decisions and engage in political behavior.

Along these lines, work in BPS has also begun to question RCT assumptions about how people formulate preferences – and how this might vary over time and across individuals. For example, individual personality, moral values, and societal norms have all been found to impact political choice, often above and beyond material considerations (Chapter 7).[8] This finding is similar to another branch of BPS called motivated reasoning theory (Chapter 8), whereby individuals possess not only accuracy motives (e.g., wanting to make the "right" decisions), but also directional ones that align with their preexisting beliefs or group identities. Leaders, for example, may discount information that contradicts their preferred course of action (Levy 1997), leading to a wishful-thinking bias in foreign policy decision-making. Partisans may choose to believe rhetoric that validates the policy positions of their partisan group (Republicans or Democrats) even in the face of evidence to the contrary (Redlawsk 2002) in order to maintain a positive group- (and self-) image.

Despite the steady stream of evidence that many rational choice assumptions do not reflect the reality of how individuals make decisions, RCT is very influential across subfields of political science: American politics, comparative politics, international relations, political economy, and public policy and administration. There are good reasons for this. Rational choice approaches offer a relatively straightforward and parsimonious approach to understanding political phenomena, as we explain in more detail in Chapter 2. However, it is not only possible to integrate findings from behavioral studies into these decision-making models, doing so may drastically improve their explanatory power and predictive validity.

Like RCT, BPS is a generic framework for understanding political phenomena in the domestic and international arenas and, so, is broadly relevant across political science subfields (see Figure 1.1). To use Thomas Kuhn's terminology, BPS changes the study of politics not by discounting the power of rational choice approaches, but rather by identifying the specific assumptions underlying rational choice models of politics, empirically examining them, and revising them to provide a more complete, accurate explanation of human behavior. Therefore, while BPS is a stand-alone paradigm, it also complements and augments RCT.

We argue that BPS augments and improves standard rational choice models in two distinct ways: First, it methodically examines the (in)ability of actors to process information necessary to maximize utilities. Second, it more fully explores the diversity of political motivation – the ground from which political preferences spring.

THE TWO DIMENSIONS OF BEHAVIORAL DECISION-MAKING:
ABILITIES AND MOTIVATIONS

We organize this framework along these two main dimensions of distinction between the RCT and BPS schools. First, each approach makes very different assumptions about the

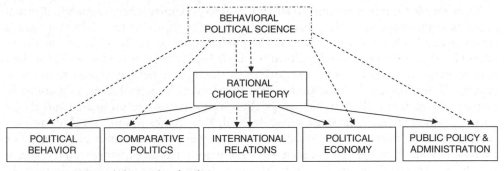

FIGURE 1.1 **BPS and the study of politics**
BPS is an umbrella framework that consists of various intellectual schools that consider the cognitive constraints and diverse motivations that structure human decision-making in the political realm. It does not replace RCT, but substantially expands our understanding by improving assumptions about human cognitive abilities and motivations in the political realm.

abilities political actors possess as they process information and make decisions. RCT often assumes people have strongly ordered preferences about many states of the world – they know what they like, and they know how to weigh what they like on one dimension versus all criteria relevant to a given decision. But we know this is a very challenging task indeed. It is the problem of knowing not only how much you like one kind of fruit at the store, but also being able to weigh that preference against the price, and then to make that comparison for all the other fruits available. Only then can you truly get the best value (a task known as optimizing).

Furthermore, a critical component of the RCT tradition is to recognize that many political decisions are *strategic* in nature: in order to get what we want we often have to understand what *others want* simultaneously. This is an even harder calculation. It would be like adding to the aforementioned shopping task a concern that some fruits are so desirable that the store might run out of stock before we can get to them. If so, we might be tempted to pick our second-best option out of concern for getting nothing at all. This puzzle is a *game-theoretic* problem that involves other people, rather than the *decision-theoretic* one that characterizes the lone shopper choosing the best value at the store.

BPS recognizes that humans are *suboptimal information processors*, whose behavior is influenced by a wide range of factors such as cognitive and information processing limitations, group dynamics, world views, misperceptions, emotions, and framing effects, not often considered by RCT. This recognition challenges both game-theoretic and decision-theoretic problems, because people are often unable to meet the cognitive demands assumed by many of these models. Throughout this book, we will review several important ways in which decision-making *processes* differ from the expected utility calculations specified in RCT.

A second major distinction involves *motivations*. Several approaches in the BPS tradition identify very different motivations for human decision-making compared to those often invoked by RCT. The sources of our varied motivations and goals – the very preferences we hold so dear and rarely question – have not traditionally received much attention in RCT. Instead, RCT simply takes preferences as given. Nonetheless, it seems obvious that improving our understanding about what motivates preferences could lead to better predictions in utility maximization models.

So, what are the things we care about and want to maximize when we make a decision in politics? Put more formally, what goes into the utility function that drives a person's choices? Are leaders most interested in the public good, or are they driven mostly to maximize their own power and political survival? Do lay citizens care most about their narrow material interests, or are they driven by the need to belong to important social groups? Work in the BPS tradition has discovered fairly large violations of a common assumption in many RCT models, that elites and citizens are motivated mostly by narrow individual, material self-interest. Instead, BPS studies found that elites and lay citizens alike often seem willing to sacrifice such goals in order to protect the groups they cherish. In some cases, people are even willing to wholly sacrifice their personal material well-being, or even their very lives, simply to punish out-groups who violate deeply held norms. Suicide bombers are a prime, yet extreme, example. The approaches discussed in this book attempt to explain where such motivations come from and how they vary, even in terms of our evolution as a social species.

We therefore organize BPS in these two categories: the *processes and abilities* of individuals to make decisions on the one hand, and the *motivations and goals* (e.g., preferences) we hold dear on the other. The psychological insights derived from research on decision-making processes can help explain how citizens and their leaders often act "as if" they are rational *despite* limits in their ability to engage in the kind of reasoning assumed by RCT, as well as the ways they fall short of the RCT ideal. Meanwhile, research on the psychology of human beings' complex goals and motivations can provide a deeper understanding of the origins of political preferences and help improve the predictive ability of our theoretical models.

DIVERSITY OF TOPICS AND METHODS OF BPS

Before we move on to a detailed discussion of the ability and motivation dimensions of distinction, we must emphasize that the *substantive topics* these approaches can help to explain are quite diverse. Some puzzles involve individual decisions by lay citizens as they enter the voting booth. Others focus on the behavior of legislators as they propose laws and attempt to shepherd them through Congress or parliament. We often find counterintuitive behavior at the group level too, in protest actions, social movements, and violent rebellions. Still other puzzles involve the military decisions of nation-states. Regardless of the substantive focus and level of analysis (e.g., individual, group, or state-level), BPS can help better understand, explain, and even predict political phenomena. These goals are shared by the RCT approach as well. The two approaches are thus compatible in many ways and understanding them both will be mutually beneficial for the scientific study of politics.

We provide a basic introduction to RCT in Chapter 2, highlighting its advantages and key limitations. In the rest of the book, however, we focus on the advantages of BPS approaches for understanding politics. Specifically, we illuminate how BPS approaches can help explain the causal process whereby individuals formulate preferences and then translate these preferences into political decisions. Indeed, one of the primary strengths of the BPS approach is that it unpacks the cognitive processes leading to decisions; not just pointing to what has been decided, but *how and why*.

We will also point out throughout the book how BPS exhibits a diverse and pluralistic array and scope of methodological orientations. Indeed, there is nothing inherent in the approach that suggests BPS theories can only be tested experimentally. Likewise, though rational choice theorists have long relied on formal modeling as an important methodological tool, RCT scholars have increasingly adopted a variety of methods (case studies, observational studies, and experiments). As such, we see both BPS and RCT as *approaches* to understanding political phenomena that make different assumptions about how and why people make decisions. Experimental methods and formal modeling, in contrast, are *methods* that can be employed to test theories from both BPS and RCT traditions.

BPS researchers are, nonetheless, perhaps best known for employing experimental studies in their research. Various techniques for running experiments have been designed. Before the advent of computers, the random assignment process was performed by hand and survey responses were often provided using paper-and-pencil (this is, of course, still common practice in many places). In addition, samples often consisted of university undergraduates enrolled in introductory classes in psychology or political science. Over the past few decades, however, major technological advances in personal computing and hand-held communication devices like cell phones have led to innovative research designs and sampling. We can now test hypotheses using sophisticated and realistic political stimuli, generate responses privately from participants on their own computers at home, and more easily utilize nationally representative samples. All these methodological advances have greatly increased the quality and theoretical reach of BPS approaches. Experimental methods in BPS also take many forms, including lab experiments with sophisticated computer interfaces that can track everything from information processing to eye movements, survey experiments, field experiments, "natural" experiments, and even studies using medical technology such as fMRIs, hormone levels, skin conductance, and more to test the biological underpinnings of political phenomena.

However, research in the BPS tradition expands beyond experiments and generally consists of four main methodological approaches: experimental, observational, case study, and, increasingly, formal modeling. Statistically, BPS scholars have embraced new, sophisticated tools of empirical analysis to tease out causal effects from large observational studies. For example, scholars have utilized research designs such as regression discontinuity, synthetic controls, statistical matching on observables, agent-based simulation models, content analysis of archival material, and more, in order to make causal arguments when researchers are unable (for ethical or practical reasons) to run a classical experiment.

Qualitative analysis using case studies and comparative case studies are also common. This method can involve the analysis of a single case at one moment in time (e.g., the US decision to attack Iraq in 1991), one case over time (presidential decisions on the use of force), and comparative case studies (the importance of race in US elections across states). Case studies often use process tracing to investigate the causal mechanisms undergirding political behavior and can be particularly valuable when studying elite decision-making and the cognitive mechanisms guiding their thinking, since access to political leaders can often present a challenge (Bennett & Checkel 2014). Other qualitative methods such as interviews and focus groups have also been used by BPS researchers.

Formal models have historically been less common in BPS. However, in the past decade, they have increasingly been used in the process of theory construction and hypothesis generation (e.g., Acharya, Blackwell & Sen 2018; Bendor, Kumar & Siegel 2010; Feddersen, Gailmard, & Sandroni 2009; Little 2019; Minozzi 2013; Penn 2008;

Wayne 2019; Woon 2012). As we have said already, the precise specification of assumptions and deployment of logic in deriving predictions is a foundational pillar of the scientific method and is a key advantage of what social scientists refer to as *formal theory*. We contend that the logical rigor and precision of this method – which has primarily been used to test rational choice theories of politics – can also be used to test BPS theories that make *different* assumptions about the ability and motivation of individuals to make political decisions. Indeed, we believe that the use of formal theory as a method for deriving predictions could potentially be put to greater use by BPS scholars. Put plainly, there is nothing inherent in behavioral approaches that is incompatible with the precision and deductive rigor gained using formal methods.

Indeed, economists have developed various equilibria solutions for game theoretic models that address the limitations on human processing abilities discovered by behavioral researchers. For instance, in *quantal response equilibria* (McKelvey & Palfrey 1995), individuals are assumed to make errors in selecting their optimal strategies, errors that affect the modal outcomes of strategic interaction. In *self-confirming equilibria* (Fudenberg & Levine 1993), players' strategies are best responses to their *beliefs* about other players and, because of that, they may never observe behavior that contradicts their beliefs, even if such "off-equilibrium path" beliefs (e.g., beliefs about things that never end up happening) are incorrect. When actors have different beliefs and conjectures about each other, using this type of equilibrium concept may be better suited than the traditional Nash equilibrium commonly used in solving game-theoretic models (Lupia, Levine & Zharinova 2010). In *cognitive hierarchy equilibria* (Camerer, Ho & Chong 2004), players naively believe that their strategy must be the best or most sophisticated – that is, that other players will make a variety of mistakes in choosing their strategy, but that they never will. These and other mathematical applications demonstrate that both RCT and BPS researchers conduct rigorous, deductive work on human decision-making and behavior.

In recent years, web analytic techniques, machine learning, and social network analyses have become highly relevant to BPS research as well. These big data and machine-learning methods allow researchers to uncover patterns of information acquisition and decision-making, and even perhaps to influence real world outcomes. For example, in both the 2016 and 2020 US presidential elections, both parties attempted to harness the power of big data to develop psychological profiles of millions of Americans based on their consumer and online behavior.[9] Sentiment analysis can be used to assess not only voters' evaluations of candidates (Tumasjan et al. 2010), but also their propensity to vote, their attitudes about policy alternatives, and their interest in politics more broadly (Ceron et al. 2014). These approaches are just gaining a foothold, but they offer promise for exploring the variety of psychological biases and constraints that dictate how voters and leaders translate new information into political decisions.

ORGANIZATION OF THE BOOK

This book is organized broadly into two sections, each focusing on a primary dimension of tension between the assumptions of the dominant paradigm, RCT, and work in BPS: cognitive processes and abilities and goals and motivations. In other words, BPS augments RCT both by adding new factors to our understanding of what *motivates* individual behavior and by demonstrating that people's *ability* to process information departs from the maximizing and holistic assessment of information assumed in most RCT models. Rather, individuals use heuristics that may lead to biases, are sensitive to framing, have difficulty assessing risk, are influenced by emotions, and engage in motivated reasoning – all of which may influence political behavior and outcomes. Figure 1.2 displays various BPS critiques within these "abilities" versus "motivations" domains. In Chapter 2, we will review in some detail what the assumptions of RCT are. We briefly discuss the history of thought about human rationality and its benefits for studying politics at the individual, elite, and nation-state levels. The next six chapters of the book then describe the various schools of BPS and how their findings may augment or modify core assumptions of the Rational Choice approach.

Ability Critiques

Heuristics, Cognitive Biases, and Bounded Rationality

In Chapter 3, we discuss *bounded* rationality, exploring the concepts of cognitive satisficing, the use of heuristics (shortcuts) in decision-making, and the impact of various cognitive biases on decision-making. This work examines the standard RCT assumptions about human cognitive *processes and ability* to optimize utility. In classical RCT, human beings are assumed to have near infinite processing capabilities, analyzing the components of every potential choice and integrating all available information seamlessly together to formulate an expected utility calculation (i.e., how good a given choice is). Based on these calculations, an individual will then be able to discern which choice offers the highest expected utility and, so, will choose that option. A modification of that assumption is Simon's notion of *bounded rationality*, which recognizes limitless processing capacity is *not* possible. Rather, individuals are thought to be susceptible to a host of different limits on their cognitive abilities, relying instead on a variety of

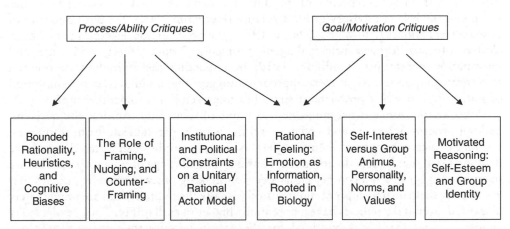

FIGURE I.2 **Scheme of the book**
The book is organized around two overlapping and complementary ways in which BPS improves our understanding of politics. The first half of the book focuses on insights about limitations on human cognitive processes and abilities, represented by the first four boxes in the bottom row. The last half takes on new perspectives about the origins of human goals and motivation in the political domain, represented by the last three boxes.

16

heuristics to make decisions.[10] Chapter 3 outlines many of these heuristics and biases, and their implications for our understanding of politics, in depth.

Framing Effects

In Chapter 4, we continue our discussion of biases. We review two major conceptual definitions of framing effects. The first is based simply on changes in the salience of specific judgment considerations and can often occur very subtly and outside conscious awareness. Prospect theory (Chapter 3) is one dominant example of this type of phenomenon (Kahneman & Tversky 1979). Another example springs from a new literature from Behavioral Economics on *nudging* – very subtle differences in the way information is presented can dramatically alter a wide range of citizen choices and behavior. A second type of framing is based on how well a message tells a convincing story, highlighting what considerations are most important on a given issue. When these different narrative frames are successful, they can alter how we understand social problems and whom we hold responsible for fixing them. Understanding how elite frames of political issues affect the trade-offs citizens make between cognitive efficiency and interest maximization is a primary focus of work on this type of framing, as the effects in terms of policy support and electoral choice can be quite large. Chapter 4 explores the impact of both of these types of frames, with numerous examples of how these frames alter individual decision-making.

Group Processes in Policy-Making

In Chapter 5, we turn to look at elite decision-making and the ways in which governmental decisions are often constrained by institutional or bureaucratic structures, including the tendency to make decisions using advisory groups. *Bureaucratic Politics* theories emphasize the ways in which the structure of the government can change incentives of officials and affect the implementation of policies. Importantly, this may result in behavior that is *individually* rational, but suboptimal from the perspective of the state. For example, work in this tradition has examined the role of advisory group structure (Hermann 2001), the push and pull of bureaucratic politics (Allison & Zelikow 1971), the poliheuristic, electoral concerns of elected officials (e.g., a principal-agent problem) (Mintz 2004), and time and information constraints (Lindblom 1959) in impacting the formation of optimal governmental policies. All of these approaches suggest that a unitary-actor assumption of state policy may be a problematic simplification, even if it is sometimes useful.

Poliheuristic theory is one important example of work that explores the decision-making process of leaders and voters – and the ways it may deviate from traditional rational choice assumptions (Mintz 2004). Numerous studies using this theory have demonstrated that leaders do not in fact consider the full range of policy options before them but engage in a noncompensatory decision-making process whereby policies that are bad for them on one important dimension (usually the political one) are immediately discarded, even if the policies have a potentially higher overall utility. Thus, leaders may choose policies that are suboptimal for the nation because they are advantageous politically – a fundamental principal-agent problem that is not addressed in models that treat the state as a unitary actor. Group-based models of decision-making such as groupthink and polythink (Janis 1982; Mintz & Wayne 2016) also demonstrate the way in which government decisions can appear to deviate from the policy choices that a rational, unitary actor model would predict.

ᅟ
ᅟ

ᅟ
ᅟ
ᅟᅟ
ᅟ

ᅟ

Emotional Factors

In Chapter 6, we review the role of emotion in political cognition and behavior. Researchers from a variety of fields including psychology, political science, and economics have begun to notice how emotions profoundly shape the ways people learn, think, and act. We discuss some of the most important ways in which emotions affect political cognition and behavior, including at the biological and neurological level. Since the time of the ancient Greeks, philosophers have believed emotions represented an impediment to good judgment, rational thinking, and sound policy-making. One of the most important and counterintuitive conclusions in this new area of research is that our emotions are critical for normal social interaction and political decision-making. In other words, we would be incapable of rational and sound judgment without our emotions, even when they are intensely and passionately felt. Indeed, many emotional reactions are just as likely to protect citizens from manipulation as they are to increase their vulnerability to charismatic leaders. The importance of emotions in human decision-making thus constitutes both a process *and* motivation critique of RCT – emotions impact not just *how* we make decisions, but also *why* we make them.

Motivation Critiques

Personality Differences, Norms, and Values

Chapter 7 is concerned with the origin of preferences, examining the role of personality differences, norms, and values in impacting individuals' preferences. Rational choice theories often leave the origins of preferences – and their striking heterogeneity – largely unexamined. Yet, understanding where preferences come from is crucial for building explanatory models of political behavior. The "individual differences" research tradition in BPS seek to address this issue, directly investigating what motivates individuals to hold the beliefs they do and act the way they act. This emphasis on the psychological causal mechanisms lying between exposure to information and the resultant behavior is a particular strength of the BPS approach. The chapter focuses on the role of these individual differences between people (e.g., personality types) on individuals' unique preferences at both the mass and elite level. We also explore the role of societal norms, group-based symbolic attitudes, morals, and values in shaping and constraining individual preferences.

Motivated Reasoning

Chapter 8 explores how people react to new information and what motivations impact its processing. Under classical RCT assumptions, people are expected to evaluate claims objectively, update their prior beliefs in the direction of the new information, and change their attitudes and behavior accordingly. It turns out this often doesn't happen, and that presents a puzzle for RCT. So, what does happen when people receive new, credible information suggesting their beliefs are incorrect, and that they should change their policy opinions, candidate choices, or political actions as a result? Most of the time they do nothing at all. Actually, not entirely nothing. People often work hard to ignore, counterargue, and reject the new information so that they do not need to change their opinions, choices, and behavior. This somewhat broad set of phenomena has become recognized as *motivated reasoning*, an idea with profound implications for debates about almost every phenomenon we study in political science.

Most importantly for this book, motivated reasoning often seems to violate several of the basic assumptions of RCT. Specifically, how can we maximize our own interests if we do not update our beliefs in accordance with credible new information? If your preferred candidate is revealed to have taken positions on issues that you disagree with, and you simply ignore that fact, how can representative democracy really work? We will review many of the important insights and implications of motivated reasoning theory, which represents one of the most forceful challenges to RCT assumptions about reasoning. We will also highlight the universal power of *group identity and personal self-esteem* to impact human motivation. Individuals are shown to be primarily concerned with maintaining a positive self-image and group-image rather than material personal gain. As such, motivated reasoning helps reduce *cognitive dissonance*, and this process has profound consequences for political phenomena such as intergroup conflict.

We conclude in Chapter 9, arguing that BPS approaches can provide insights to policy-makers just as Behavioral Economics frequently does. Indeed, we show that in some countries it already has had an impact on public policy. We also make the point that BPS can enrich our understanding of politics by not only improving assumptions about human decision-making capability and motivation, but also by explaining the psychological processes that underlie political behavior. One way to think about BPS is as an exploration of human decision-making rules that might ultimately improve RCT explanations and predictions of political phenomena. BPS could do this, for example, by explaining the conditions under which people will be driven by RCT assumptions and when they will not. In this chapter, we also explore some of the limitations of the BPS approach, highlighting the potential difficulties of incorporating more complex behavioral assumptions into formal theories of politics. We also discuss the kinds of policy questions BPS is best suited to address and areas in which an RCT paradigm may be more helpful.

IMPLICATIONS

Understanding the distinct strengths and weaknesses of RCT versus BPS approaches to political phenomena is important for several reasons. One of the key reasons is that improving our explanations of political behavior can and should help us design better public policies for fixing some of the most important problems people face around the world. For example, understanding why countries go to war can help us design military strategies and foreign policy approaches that reduce the ravages of armed conflict, civil disputes, and genocide. Understanding why individuals choose to participate in politics, in both violent and nonviolent ways, is crucial to building enduring democracies.

The importance of behavioral approaches to our understanding of politics has begun to gain traction outside the academy as well. For example, former US President Barack Obama issued an executive order in 2015 insisting that the government put insights from the social and behavioral sciences to better use in policy-making on behalf of the American people.[11] The executive order begins with the claim that "a growing body of evidence demonstrates that behavioral science insights – research findings from fields such as Behavioral Economics and psychology about how people make decisions and act on them – can be used to design government policies to better serve the American people." We agree completely. Readers should take this opportunity to explore various approaches and best practices to improve the way our government, and those around the world, serve citizens' interests. We hope this book is a step in that direction.

2

The Rational Actor Model of Political Decision-Making

Prior to election day, pollsters in the United States attempt to predict the outcomes in states around the country. Their challenge is to get an unbiased estimate of the population's preference for one candidate over another. Once a manageable challenge, estimating what choices a population will make is increasingly difficult due to a variety of factors, including low response rates. Even more troubling is that, since 2016, polling estimates have systematically underestimated support for Republican candidates in many states. It also seems more difficult in the current moment to estimate who will actually turn out to vote on Election Day. Turnout likelihood is a multiplier that increases the weight some voters have on the estimate and decreases the weight of those whom pollsters suspect will stay home. We call this element of election prediction the *likely voter model*.

In both the 2016 and 2020 elections, pollsters actually did a pretty good job of estimating the national public's preferences. The final average polling expectation for the popular vote margin in 2016 was that Clinton would win by a few percentage points representing millions of votes, and that is exactly what happened. In 2020, the final average pre-election polls predicted Biden would win by about 7.5 per cent of the popular vote, whereas he won by 4.5 per cent. This was a much larger error than in 2016, but less consequential since Biden also won the Electoral College.

What the pollsters got wrong more significantly, and systematically in both elections, were predictions in several battleground states like Wisconsin, Pennsylvania, Michigan, North Carolina, and Florida. In these states, the polls all dramatically overestimated the support Clinton would garner on Election Day, and those states instead handed Trump a relatively easy victory in 2016 in the Electoral College. These errors were even larger in many states in 2020, leading to surprising GOP victories in the House of Representatives and several Senate races.

While there are several potentially important explanations for these polling errors, a lot of attention has focused on the "likely voter models" mentioned previously. These models estimate the chance that voters, regardless of their preferences, will actually show up to the polls. The likely voter models in 2016 got it wrong in key battlegrounds: people who had not been expected to turn out – less educated, lower income, rural white voters – turned out in record numbers. Moreover, many voters who expressed very strong opposition to Trump, and who turned out to vote just as the likely voter model predicted they would, actually left the presidential ballot blank and only voted in races down the ballot. In Michigan, for example, nearly 100,000 of these *underballots* were cast, outpacing by perhaps a factor of ten Trump's margin of victory in that key battleground state. One suspected explanation? Enthusiastic supporters of Clinton's primary opponent, Bernie Sanders, protested loudly on social media that they could never support Hillary Clinton, and would in fact leave the presidential ballot blank instead.[1]

This specific behavior, undervoting (leaving candidate choice blank) in specific races once a voter is already at the ballot box, poses a significant challenge for existing rational choice explanations of voter behavior. Indeed, the act of voting itself poses a significant question for RCT theories of politics. Given how unlikely it is that a single vote will change the outcome of an election with even thousands of voters, let alone tens of millions, why do people bother to vote? We will review this so-called *paradox of voting*, as it one of the foremost rational choice puzzles that Behavioral Political Science (BPS) can help to solve. Second, once the obstacles to voting have been overcome and an individual shows up to the polls, why would they then skip the highest election on the ballot? While the act of voting might be considered expressive and therefore carry some social rewards that figure in rational accounts, existing RCT models are not concerned with expressive behavior *inside* the voting booth, especially since vote choices are secret. In other words, a voter does not gain any social benefit from voting for a specific candidate – as they could simply claim that they voted for any option that was socially desirable. If Sanders' primary supporters wanted to tell their friends they left the ballot blank they could have done so, even if they actually voted for Clinton. Third, why would those who preferred a candidate *more liberal* than Clinton turn out to vote and then leave their ballot blank, thereby increasing the likelihood that the far more conservative Trump would be elected?[2]

In contrast, prior to the presidential election of 2020, former Vice President Joe Biden's lead over President Trump was significantly higher compared to Hillary Clinton's in most of these battleground states. Many pundits expected the result to be much clearer. Biden received 7 million more votes than President Trump, a substantially larger margin than Clinton received in 2016 (who won the popular vote by 2.9 million), and captured almost the same number of electoral college votes as Trump did in his 2016 victory (306 for Biden, 304 for Trump). However, Trump, once again, systematically over-performed his polls in a swath of battleground states, including Wisconsin, Michigan, Pennsylvania, and others. Trump seemed to do substantially better among groups one would have expected to go for Biden even more than they had for Clinton: Latinos in Florida and south Texas, and African American men. The reasons for these polling misses remain a matter of debate, but they might have something to do with basic distrust among some Republicans for the polling firms that attempt to measure public sentiments.[3] If even some Republicans will not answer a pollster's call, estimates of Republican support will be systematically biased downward. Unfortunately, there are no simple statistical fixes for this kind of *unit nonresponse* bias. Other hypotheses point to mistakes in how pollsters predicted who constituted a "likely voter" in their samples. Indeed, in the 2020 election, both sides proved adept at mobilizing voters. President Trump received more than 74 million votes in 2020, the second-highest total ever for a presidential candidate, trailing only Joe Biden, who received 81 million votes. Record high turnout may have disrupted the factors pollsters traditionally rely upon to predict who will vote. In any case, these errors suggest that our efforts to understand voting behavior based on simple assumptions about material interests, at the individual or group level, may not suffice.

In other words, BPS helps us solve some fascinating puzzles like the paradox of voting. But first let's review the basic premises and strengths of RCT and think about why it has been so influential in political science to date.

WHY IS RATIONAL CHOICE SO DOMINANT IN THE STUDY OF POLITICS?

Many political science textbooks focus almost entirely on RCT models of important political phenomena. The reason the rational choice tradition has achieved such prominence is because it employs rigorous, parsimonious, and logical rules of theory construction: First it posits basic assumptions that describe the preferences people hold, then it posits assumptions about how people translate those preferences into behavioral strategies, given constraints based on the environment and other actors' choices (a game theoretic model). Then it makes predictions about the observable outcomes to which these strategies will lead. In other words, conventional models are based on deductive assumptions of actor *rationality* and *structural determinacy*.

According to RCT, political phenomena are the result of individuals' or states' rational action in response to the structural features of a strategic interaction. If the predictions fail, it is because we failed to accurately map key elements of the strategic picture, or one or more assumptions about the actors' preferences was false. The benefit of this approach is that we can subsequently modify our assumptions and build a better deductive theory.

The formal logical approach for theory building often utilized by RCT scholars is useful, as it helps researchers be very clear about their assumptions and use deductive reasoning to arrive at predictions about political outcomes. As you will read in the following pages, while BPS challenges many of RCT's standard assumptions about the types of preferences people try to maximize and how exactly they go about doing so, it does not dismiss the need for building theory on precise, logical, falsifiable foundations. But *valid* assumptions about human decision-making are paramount. Understanding both the limitations of human information processing and the dominant motivations behind human preferences can improve predictions. Therefore, we argue that the two approaches should be viewed as complementary rather than contradictory.

For example, RCT models often – though not exclusively – assume people are driven to maximize material self-interest. However, BPS approaches have revealed a host of other motivating factors for individuals: emotional satisfaction, noncompensatory political considerations, altruism, values, norms, in-group identity, out-group animus, and more. To be sure, RCT models have begun to accept and integrate these nonmaterial motivations into their work, and we will review some of these throughout the book. However, the incorporation of these so-called nonstandard assumptions into formal RCT models is still rather rare.

Essentially, in terms of both process and motivation, people fall short of the rational ideal: they rely on heuristics (Chapter 3), are sensitive to framing (Chapter 4), make decisions in group settings that may exhibit unique decision-making processes (Chapter 5), are driven by emotions (Chapter 6), have a variety of nonmaterial preferences (Chapter 7), and are plagued by motivated reasoning (Chapter 8). While rational choice theorists tend to believe these processes may still allow individuals to behave "as if" they are rational, behavioral political scientists are somewhat less optimistic. Furthermore, while standard RCT models suggest individuals engage systematically with information in their environment to arrive at decisions, BPS finds people often do not attempt to hold their beliefs up to the world to determine if they are correct.

Thus, as you will see at the end of this chapter, BPS diverges from and augments RCT in two critical ways: (1) it is process oriented and (2) it incorporates known psychological limits into models of political behavior and political decision-making. In other words, BPS helps to explain how and why people deviate from common assumptions in RCT accounts.

So, what exactly are these common assumptions about preferences and processes often invoked by RCT with which BPS takes issue? We focus on the following: self-interest, material preferences, and a systematic process for translating those preferences into behavior.

COMMON ASSUMPTIONS IN THE RATIONAL CHOICE MODEL

Let's first review the strengths of rational choice modeling as a method of inquiry. Its most important contribution is its insistence upon clearly stated assumptions and the use of rigorous logic to derive predictions about human behavior. The very idea that one could study politics using the scientific method, just as one could study the motion of heavenly bodies or the chemical properties of the world around us, reshaped what are now known as social sciences during the twentieth century. The notion that deductive theories of human political interaction could be proposed, based on a small number of very clear assumptions about what people care about when they make decisions in the public sphere, was revolutionary.

The roots of this idea came from philosophers like Auguste Comte in the late 1800s. He insisted that government institutions, elites' decisions, and even mass movements could be studied scientifically – by collecting and evaluating systematic observations in order to "test" hypotheses drawn deductively from theories, or laws, of *social physics*. He argued observation was critical for explaining the behavior of individuals and societies, not just chemicals and heavenly bodies. Why was this idea so controversial for its time? Critics railed that the existence of simple, immutable laws underlying the basic functions of society would eliminate the possibility of free will in human decisions. Comte's famous book, *Course of Positive Philosophy* (1853), was especially threatening to theologians, who felt scientific positivism[4] was incompatible with an omnipotent deity whose mind could never be known by mere mortals. Further upsetting church leaders, Comte described three stages of societal intellectual development, with religious and metaphysical thinking ranking below positivist-deductive approaches.

Using the basic tenets of the scientific method – observation, experimentation, comparison, and control – Comte believed not only that we could better understand human behavior, but that we could also build better government institutions. This normative goal drew fire from liberal thinkers of the age such as Herbert Spencer. Spencer was fascinated by positivism and the notion that the scientific method could be used to understand human systems, but rejected the idea that this could help with the kind of social engineering Comte imagined. Interestingly, it was Spencer (1898) who coined the term "survival of the fittest" to describe the outcome of competition within and between human societies. At the heart of Spencer's theory was the assumption – similar to the one proposed by Darwin in his theory of evolution – that people were self-interested first and foremost in order to stay alive and reproduce. Spencer's evolutionary sociology was built on the same assumption about human nature that the rational choice approach would soon adopt: people are motivated mostly by the need for safety, security, and economic prosperity.

Thus, the first assumption of most rational choice theories is that people are *self-interested*. In fact, the idea that individual self-interest and personal gain are ubiquitous human motivations has very ancient roots. Even before Spencer's time, the notion that human decisions begin with a calculation of personal costs and benefits was dominant. Beginning with ancient Greek philosophy and reigning nearly uncontested through the late twentieth century, theories of human behavior were grounded in three significant assumptions about our basic nature. First, people are instinctually *selfish*. This means we make decisions that help us reach our *individual* goals, rather than focusing on what might help others whose welfare is unrelated to our own.

Sometimes this assumption is taken to mean that *altruism* – any act that is costly for one person but benefits another – is impossible. While this particular implication of the rationality assumption has filled many volumes in philosophy, law, and political theory, rational choice models preclude altruism only under very strict definitions. We could, for instance, observe actions that appear altruistic if material returns are present but not easily identifiable. Indeed, prominent work in evolutionary psychology suggests that reciprocal altruism (in both people and animals) may develop over time due to natural selection processes (Trivers 1971). For example, the trait of "heroism," whereby individuals sacrifice their lives in battle to protect their group, may be selected for over time, as groups with more "heroes" in their ranks would be more likely to survive (Smirnov et al. 2007). Still, the less direct, material, and quantifiable the personal benefits of a particular choice are, the less likely they are to influence decisions, according to standard rational choice models.

A related common assumption in many RCT models is that people are *materialistic*. That is, we are powerfully motivated to maximize material wealth (Friedman & Savage 1948). Of course, wealth is not necessarily an end in itself. Many people are driven to amass wealth and other resources so that they can afford things that make them and their loved ones happy and avoid pain and suffering. Materialism, therefore, indirectly encompasses a wide range of other types of goals: we need wealth to protect and help those close to us, for example, because we are happy when our loved ones are safe and secure. Or we can use wealth to express ourselves in a variety of ways, both artistic and political.

While the focus on material wealth maximization may be consistent with other interests, it is still restrictive, and not necessarily applicable to many political decisions. It assumes people will first make choices that have a good chance of improving their material conditions and economic opportunities or otherwise securing their personal safety and well-being. Ultimately, therefore, we maximize wealth for reasons that can be traced back to our individual needs. As we will discuss throughout the book, but especially in Chapter 7, people often do not seem to be trying to maximize their material self-interest – directly or indirectly – when making political decisions. Instead, many studies have found that more symbolic attachments – attitudes about groups, religious or moral principles, and social norms and values – predict what people choose when it comes to politics. This is one of the major contributions of the BPS paradigm.

Of course, there is nothing inherent in RCT that mandates the assumption that people are narrowly focused on material well-being rather than broader psychological tastes and interests. First, as mentioned previously, assuming very narrow motivations like individual material wealth maximization is often justified with the argument that the benefits of many nonmaterial goals (self-esteem, respect from one's peers, the satisfaction of helping others) can only be achieved if one has discretionary material resources and time to spend on these activities. Moreover, it is challenging to measure subjective psychological states like the satisfaction that comes from helping others, or having high self-esteem, or gaining respect from one's peers, as compared to the immediate, individual, material benefits of a choice. As a result, using material preferences as the default may serve as a useful heuristic, or a convenient jumping-off point for understanding human behavior before incorporating more complex psychological payoffs and preferences. And, indeed, in response to the concerns raised by behavioralists about the myopic focus on material self-interest, a growing number of rational choice studies have incorporated less tangible motivations into their models. In other words, the conceptual definition of self-interest has been broadened to include nonmaterial, less immediate, or group-based benefits.

In theory, the RCT approach can stretch to accommodate *any* dimension on which individuals order their preferences, including psychological ones, even when these rationales are not explicitly included in the theory. Indeed, the most basic formulation of RCT is simply that *individuals have preferences and act in ways that will best position them to achieve those aims, given the constraints of the environment.* For example, RCT models may specify a given preference ordering for an actor (e.g., the USA prefers to ally with the UK over many other countries), but will usually leave the specific rationales for these preferences purposefully open-ended (e.g., the UK could present a material benefit by opening access to the rest of the European Union market, or a symbolic one, given that the USA has a greater cultural affinity with the UK). However, one underlying assumption of this decision to "black box" the origin of the preference ordering by RCT is that these rationales are, essentially, *interchangeable* and do not meaningfully alter the strategic interaction. BPS approaches question this idea. The debate about these two core RCT assumptions – individual self-interest and materialism – thus continues to rage, and for good reason. We will review these discussions in some detail throughout the book.

The second common assumption in RCT is that humans are *procedurally rational*. Rational individuals hold preferences that are *complete* and *transitive*. The "completeness" assumption states that if we must choose between three alternatives, we will know our ranking of any pair of them. In politics, for example, this would mean an individual would be able to express preferences between any two pairs of policies that might receive government funding. We might wonder if citizens would prefer to spend more money on infrastructure, education, or tax cuts. Those with *complete* preferences would know something about each policy priority and be able to rank any two pairs ("Do you want to spend more money on infrastructure or education? On education or national defense? On infrastructure or national defense?").

Procedural rationality also implies that an individual's preferences are *transitive*. Transitive preferences are logically ordered. If a person prefers spending on infrastructure over education, and they also prefer spending on education over national defense, then they will prefer spending on infrastructure over national defense. Violations of transitivity can lead to devastating consequences for individuals and for society. Imagine the voter we just described is given a choice between a candidate who will pursue infrastructure spending and one who will prioritize education. According to their stated preferences, the voter chooses the candidate who says they will spend more on infrastructure. But then another candidate who prioritizes national defense joins the race. Transitivity would lead the voter to stick with their original choice. But what if the voter prefers spending on national defense over infrastructure, in violation of transitivity? Without transitive preferences, another candidate could come along and topple this second candidate by promising spending on education, and the first candidate could return to win by offering more spending on infrastructure. The voter, at that point, has contradicted themselves because their preferences are *cyclical*. In this situation, elections would lead to highly unstable policy-making and the notion of democratic accountability would break down.

Here we can refer back to our initial example. In the presidential election of 2016, voters who strongly preferred Bernie Sanders over Hillary Clinton because she was too moderate, should have liked Trump even less. Once their choice was between Clinton and Trump, they should have turned out and supported the candidate whose proposals hewed more closely to their policy preferences. In the end, however, many Sanders supports seem to have abstained from voting for president entirely, even though they voted in other contests. This helped their least favorite candidate for president win. After the election, these voters were in a position that would not typically have been predicted by the standard assumption of transitive voting preferences.

In 2020 we witnessed similar puzzles. Latino voters in several cities, for example, appear to have supported Trump in larger numbers than they had in 2016, despite the harsh anti-immigrant policies that had been put in place and which may have negatively impacted their group and their communities. BPS can help us understand the variety of motivations that result in these voting patterns.

Strict procedural rationality also implies that once we have decided what we want, we hold and manipulate *all* the relevant information in our minds in order to calculate and then single-mindedly pursue the choice that maximizes our interests. In other words, not only do we have clear preferences, but we are able to act in ways that maximize the chance of getting what we want, subject to constraints in the world.[5] In its most superficial form, this assumption seems to insist that human brains are perfectly functioning and highly powerful computers. For example, to hold elected officials accountable, citizens must evaluate their performance not just on the most salient dimensions of performance, but on *every* dimension of performance valued by the individual. Further, they must be able to think counterfactually about what *would have happened* if another candidate had been elected, in order to estimate whether the official had exceeded or fallen short of expectations. This was reportedly of concern to many participants in surveys and focus groups conducted during the 2020 Democratic party primaries, because it was hard to know exactly what policies they would have pursued, and whether they would have been more or less successful than Biden in the general election. If each citizen fails to consider every dimension of performance, and to compare that to what would have happened under the opponent's administration, they would not be able to choose the candidate best for them. The assumption that humans can and do undertake these massive computational tasks has been subject to substantial empirical scrutiny.

The formal definition of procedural rationality is captured by *Bayes' rule*, which we will briefly describe next. Our intent in giving a brief primer here is to highlight how BPS approaches may help us better understand why people sometimes appear unable or unwilling to meet the procedural standards often assumed to be driving reactions to new information in our environments.

Bayesian Updating as the Process Underlying Rational Decision-Making

As we have discussed, one of the central assumptions of a procedural interpretation of RCT states that individuals process new information relevant to their decision and update their beliefs efficiently so that they will always give themselves the best chance to achieve their goals. This process of receiving new information and using it to improve the quality of one's future decisions is referred to as *Bayesian updating*. At the heart of the Bayesian concept of learning are two simple assumptions that are consistent with the general rules we have already discussed. First, people must be able to estimate their chances of "success" whenever they make a decision, where success is defined as the outcome that leaves them closer to their goal than any alternative choice. Second, people must use relevant previous experiences to update and refine their guess, or in the language of Bayes, to estimate the *conditional probabilities* associated with the consequences of a given choice. In some cases, calculating this conditional probability is easy – individuals realize they are more likely to, say, be the victim of a shark attack if they go in the ocean often than if they never set foot in the water. In other situations, understanding the exact implications of conditional probability is a lot trickier. Let's think of a simple example that is often used to teach the concept: What is the probability of having a relatively rare disease (e.g., cancer) after receiving a positive test result? For the purposes of this example:

- *Assume that only 1% of women at age forty who participate in a routine mammography test have breast cancer.*
- *Assume also that exactly 80% of women who have breast cancer will get positive mammograms (20% will get a false negative).*
- *But 9.6% of women of women who don't have breast cancer will also get positive mammograms (e.g., a false positive).*

A woman of this age had a positive mammography in a routine screening. What is the probability that she actually has breast cancer? It turns out that most people, including doctors and other medical professionals who have every incentive to get the answer right, answer this question incorrectly. Research found that only 15% of doctors get anywhere near the right answer (Casscells et al. 1978; Eddy & Clanton 1982; Gigerenzer & Hoffrage 1995). So how would one calculate the right answer? It is actually quite simple. If only 1% of forty-year-old women have cancer, and 80% of those will receive a positive test, that is 0.8% of all women (80% of 1% is 0.8%). Let's call these results "true" positives. But the problem also states that 9.5% of women who *do not* have cancer will get a positive result (9.6% of 99% is 9.5%). These are the "false positive" cases that are so critical in determining the quality of the new information provided. To get the new "updated" estimate of one's risk for having cancer based on a positive screening, you need to find the share of all people with positive test results who actually have the disease. That quantity is simply the proportion of "true" positive results (0.8%) among the sum of "true" and "false" positives (0.8% + 9.5% = 10.3%). The answer is 0.8% divided by 10.3%, which equals 7.8%. In other words, before performing the test a woman has a 1% chance of having cancer – this is the "base rate" of cancer in the population of 40-year-old women. With a positive test, that chance increases *to only* *7.8%*! In other words, getting a positive test for breast cancer does not mean you have cancer. Far from it, without any other information, over 90% of those with a positive result from a test like the one described do not have the disease.

Of course, in one respect the information the test provided was quite informative. Imagine how important it would be to know if your chance of having a potentially deadly disease is almost *eight times higher* than the average woman in your age cohort. However, if this were a gamble in Vegas, it would still make sense for the patient to bet against having cancer in this situation.[6] This is what most people fail to grasp: One can improve one's understanding of the state of the world quite a bit (you are now eight times more likely to have the disease than you were before the test), but you may also still be quite unlikely to have the disease.

So, what do doctors think? On average, doctors in this situation guess that this patient's chance of having cancer is ten times higher than it actually is, between 70 and 80 percent! This is a huge error that carries real psychological and physical implications, not to mention potentially massive health-care costs for unnecessary treatments with potentially dangerous side effects. If medical experts are so prone to make this mistake, even when their own careers and the health of their patients depend on getting the right answer, it calls into question common assumptions about our ability to be fully procedurally rational in the Bayesian sense. Box 2.1 contains the simple algebra necessary to apply Bayes' rule in any circumstance.

But why don't we just give everyone the test? Yes, the additional information it provides is small, but isn't any new information better than none at all? The answer is *not necessarily*, because information is expensive. It would cost tens of millions of dollars and thousands of hours for medical professionals to provide tests for this and every other potentially deadly disease to everyone in the population. Those resources must come from somewhere, and the overall budget for medical care is limited. Should policy-makers choose to test everyone for this one rare disease if that meant forgoing efforts to fight other deadly diseases? Moreover, treating women for cancer that *do not* *actually have cancer* is also very expensive – both to society and individual patients. The cost of the new information, therefore, needs to be known even before we start. Indeed, the 2015 decision by the American Cancer Society to raise the recommended age at which routine mammography screening should begin (from 40 to 45) was made in part due to these concerns about false positive diagnoses causing undue psychological distress and costly, painful medical intervention.[7] These kinds of information costs are a critical feature of most policy decisions we make and recognizing that fact is a critical feature of any theory of decision-making.

COUNTERING MAJOR TERRORIST ATTACKS: A BAYES EXAMPLE

Let's now apply Bayes' rule to politics. As was pointed out in our previous example, in order to make any potentially costly political decision, people need to correctly estimate their chances of success under different conditions. This is often very challenging for political leaders, because they usually have only a small number of historical examples upon which to establish prior probabilities. For example, let's imagine that the president wanted to stop a major terrorist attack on some specific day in the future. Major terrorist attacks in the United States are very rare, occurring less than once every several years. On any given day, one might estimate the chance of a significant attack on American soil to

---

Box 2.1: Simple calculation of Bayes' rule

Formally, Bayes rule is calculated as follows. The first thing to be sure about is our baseline information, otherwise known as the prior probabilities or "base rates" associated with the outcomes we are interested in. The second category contains the new probabilities we arrive at after updating our initial knowledge. These are called the *conditional probabilities*. Bayes discovered the relationship between these prior probabilities and conditional probabilities is as follows:

$$P(A|B) = \frac{p(A)p(B|A)}{p(A)p(B|A) + p(\sim A)p(B|\sim A)},$$

where P(A) and P(~A) are the *prior probabilities* of A and of ~A (read as "*not* A") occurring. In our medical example, P(A) is the probability of having cancer before you get the screening (1%) and P(~A) is the probability that you do not (99%). P(B|A) is the *conditional probability* of a positive test result *given* that you have the disease (80%), the *true* positive rate. P(B|~A) is the conditional probability of a positive test given that you *do not have* the disease (9.6%). This is the *false* positive rate. P(A|B) is the actual quantity of interest: the probability that one has cancer *given* a positive test result. Using this formula, we can use simple arithmetic to produce the same result we discussed previously:

$$P(cancer|positive test) = \frac{(.01)*(.80)}{(.01)*(.80) + (.99)*(.096)} = \frac{.008}{.10304} = 7.77\%.$$

We can also use this basic formula to calculate the probability that a person does NOT have cancer given that she has received a negative test. We know that 99% of women in the age cohort *do not* have cancer. Since 9.6% of those will nonetheless receive a positive test, that means 9.6% * 99% = 9.5% of women without cancer will receive a positive test (a false positive) and 90.5% of those without cancer will receive a negative test (a true negative). But 20% of the 1% with cancer will *also* receive a negative test (a *false* negative). Combining those two prior probabilities means 90.5% + 0.2% = 90.7% of those tested will receive a negative test result. Now when we apply Bayes' formula we get 90.5% / 90.7% = 99.8%. So, this means your chance of *not* having cancer upon getting a negative result drops from 1% to 0.2%. This reduction may also seem impressive, since your chance of having the disease was reduced by 80% after receiving the new information, but it does not completely eliminate the risk of cancer. Before and after the test, of course, your chance of having cancer is very low.

---

be far less than 1 percent. Let's say it is 1 out of 1000 (a 0.1 percent risk). Now let's say that the president could vastly expand the intelligence agencies consisting of thousands of agents and expensive surveillance technology as well as using sophisticated technology to monitor and search social networks, spanning the globe searching for terrorists, hoping to uncover plots before they come to fruition. This vast surveillance network will intercept terrorist communications most days of the year. Next let's make the optimistic guess that when an attack is imminent, our alarm system has a 60 percent chance of catching it. This would be an excellent positive detection rate since actual attacks are so rare. Unfortunately, many suspicious communications sound just like others which were not associated with an attack. Those intercepts are equivalent to the "false positive" results we discussed in the medical example. Let's imagine that 1 out of 100 days, the information gathered is so convincing that the system sounds a false alarm (a false positive percentage of 1 percent). Now let's imagine our surveillance network sounds the alarm indicating there will be an attack tomorrow. What is the chance an attack will actually occur?

The prior probability of an attack is very small: 0.001, and even then, our network will catch it only 60% of the time. Using the formula described previously,[8] we can calculate that the chance of an actual attack on that day is still only 5.67%. In other words, before the alarm sounded, there was a 0.1% chance that an attack would occur on that day. After the alarm, the estimated risk is elevated to about 6%.

Once again, we are faced with a glass-half-full versus glass-half-empty scenario. On the one hand, we now know that the likelihood of an attack is nearly *57 times higher* tomorrow than we knew before. However, that likelihood is still so small that we would be wrong almost 95 out of 100 times. And sending police or military resources in every such instance would quickly use up our country's entire security budget, leaving nothing for pursuing more common and potentially deadly types of crime or natural disaster.

Finally, we must remember how expensive it is to build and maintain the surveillance network. One estimate based on information gleaned from documents released by Edward Snowden places the cost of the anti-terrorism spy network at $52 billion per year.[9] This money could be spent on other national defense programs, measures to deter terrorism, or on domestic social welfare. These costs must be weighed against the advantage produced from the surveillance, compared to what would happen if we used our best guess without surveillance. Note also that our enemies can increase the cost (or decrease the benefit) of surveillance by making their communications about attacks as noisy and secure as possible. By all accounts, this was something that al-Qaeda did extremely successfully in the lead-up to the 9/11 attacks, sending multiple "false threats" in the weeks prior to 9/11. Indeed, the level of threats led former CIA Director George Tenet to report to the 9/11 Commission that the entire system was "blinking red," making it difficult to discern which, if any, threat was real.

Given all these trade-offs, many have argued that elected leaders continuing to pursue such costly counterterrorism measures are irrational because they funnel resources away from more effective counterterrorism and crime-intervention strategies (see, e.g., Mueller & Stewart 2012). On the other hand, presidents may believe that the public is not able to apply Bayes' rule in order to see how inefficient such a counterterrorism policy could be and so they would risk a backlash to efforts to roll back these kinds of national security programs. Instead, they might assume the public responds via one of many biased information processes we will discuss later, such as dramatically overestimating risks or responding to irrelevant factors. Or perhaps they themselves engage in these same biased information processing tendencies!

Now, some might argue that preferring costly responses to disrupting terrorist violence is indeed rational, given a certain set of preferences. For example, perhaps people are overwhelmingly concerned with loss of life, and so care less about expanding social welfare programs than they do about preventing even one death from terrorism. However, this requires very strict assumptions about individuals' preferences. For example, even in Israel, a country that has suffered more terrorist attacks per capita than nearly any other developed country in the world, the total number of civilians killed in any kind of terrorist violence between 1950 and 2015 was 2,538.[10] This includes 122 foreign civilians killed on Israeli soil. This is a nontrivial number, particularly given Israel's relatively small population (~9.2 million citizens). However, to place this number in context, consider that, in that same time period, *more than ten times* that number of Israelis died in fatal car accidents.[11] Needless to say, even in Israel, the risk of dying in a terrorist attack is far lower than dying in a car accident (Kahneman 2011).

It is, of course, impossible to know how many attacks *would have occurred* – if Israel had not spent as much money on counterterrorism. More, most likely. This is called the counterfactual, imagining the state of the world that would have happened if one policy was altered while everything else remained the same. Creating believable counterfactuals is tricky business. What if, for example, improving road infrastructure led people to drive faster, increasing traffic fatalities? Still, to justify this level of spending on terrorism rather than infrastructure, counterterrorism programs must be ten times better at preventing attacks than road projects are at preventing accidents. Policy-makers make such trade-offs all the time, whether they know they are doing so or not.

Thus, to help explain why governments spend so much money on counterterrorist measures and people hold such priorities, it might be helpful to account for the psychological biases that alter citizens' utility calculations. For example, individuals may overestimate the risk of terrorism because of the availability heuristic, whereby individuals make judgments concerning the frequency of an event based on how many similar instances are recalled (Tversky & Kahneman 1973). Another possibility is that people simple weigh types of death differently: a death from terrorism somehow "costs" more than an automobile-related fatality, perhaps because the former elicits strong preferences for vengeance and retribution, while the latter does not (Wayne 2019). Thus, the preference for high counterterror spending could be explained either by nonmaterial preferences (Friedman 2019; Wayne 2019) or by biases in the way individuals assess the frequency (and high risk) of different types of events (Kahneman 2011). Another possibility, often invoked by scholars of terrorism, is that fears about future attacks prompt citizens to endorse these expensive security measures that may or may not be effective (Sinclair & Antonius 2013). While plausible, fear is not always at the root of such popular support. Instead, anger and moral outrage in the wake of terrorist violence may engender support for retributive violence from the public (Liberman & Skitka 2019; Fisk, Merolla & Ramos 2019; Wayne 2019).

SO, ARE CITIZENS REALLY BAYESIAN?

At one level this is a silly question, since Bayes' rule at its root simply dictates that people respond to information in their environment in a sensible and logical way. In order to survive, any living species must, at least on average, correctly identify and react to threats and opportunities in the environment. Still, the assumption that humans engage in a very systematic, even mathematically precise, *procedure* for arriving at each decision they make has always been a controversial part of RCT (Zagare 1990). How could people really collect *all* relevant information about each alternative, appropriately weigh each bit, and then correctly calculate which alternative will maximize one's welfare? To vote for president, for example, one must have enough reliable information to make a good guess about how each candidate will perform on a variety of issues, giving each comparison its proper weight based on how important it is, and then combining these estimates into a summary decision about which candidate is best overall. The best evidence we have about how voters actually come to their decisions in the voting booth strongly deviates from this narrative. In fact, the vast majority of democratic citizens seem unwilling or unable to perform any of these steps even when making decisions of significant importance.

This defense of the typical voter – that he operates "as if" he is fully rational, despite limited interest or ability to process the available information that would make him *fully* rational – is pervasive. First, it is important to point out that the "as-if rational" explanation is in fact a behavioral approach – called *bounded rationality* – which we detail at length in Chapter 3. However, though BPS theorists often use the term bounded rationality to explain *deviations* from RCT predictions of politics, RCT uses the idea of as-if rational behavior to explain how models that assume full rationality can nonetheless *still* be predictively valid, even if the underlying assumption of Bayesian processing is not met.

Examples of this approach abound. Lupia and McCubbins (1998) argue that if information processing is costly then voters may be completely rational to ignore available information and, instead, use shortcuts to make voting decisions. And these shortcuts may in fact be quite effective: those with access to very basic information about otherwise obscure policy issues (such as changes to insurance law) approximate fully rational voters (Lupia 1994). The literature on retrospective voting (Key 1966; Fiorina 1981) likewise assumes citizens need only perform relatively simple calculations in order to make the best choice at the ballot box: Am I better off today than I was before the incumbent under elected? If yes, voters should reward the incumbent, under the assumption that what held true in the past will hold true in the future. If not, voters should give the challenger a chance to pursue different policies.[12] This simple decision rule, rather than the identity concerns often cited by behavioral researchers, may help explain the development of partisanship over time (Bendor, Kumar & Siegel 2010).

However, these defenses of citizen rationality do not account for the possibility of *systematic* errors in information processing that bias decision-making in a specific direction. In other words, if errors were random – some pulling voters in one direction and others in the opposite direction – then the idea that mistakes will essentially wash out and lead to as-if rational decision-making, even if the process itself is not wholly rational, is plausible. Behavioral theorists contend, however, that these errors *are* systematic – for example, voters consistently seem to blame leaders for events that are clearly outside the leaders' control (Achen & Bartels 2017; Healy, Malhotra & Mo 2010). It is these systematic processing errors that behavioral theorists contend lead to objectively worse voting decisions on average (see, e.g., Huber, Hill & Lenz 2012; Lau & Redlawsk 2001) than would be expected in the RCT framework.

Whether or not voter irrationality leads to objectively worse outcomes *for democracy* is another question, however. For example, Ashworth and Bueno de Mesquita (2014) have suggested that voter irrationality may not always reduce democratic performance. The reason for this is that elections are fundamentally strategic interactions between voters and elected officials. In other words, if politicians *know* voters are irrational, they can adjust their behavior to take advantage, and the accountability of democratic institutions will decline. As Ashworth and Bueno de Mesquita (2014) show, this leads to mixed results in terms of maximizing voter welfare. For instance, a prevalence of informed voters might lead more extreme leaders to temporarily masquerade as moderates (assuming the typical voter is moderate). This might benefit voters in the short term, as they would get more moderate policies than they otherwise might. But in the long term, this pandering could undermine accountability, as voters would be unable to distinguish true moderates from extremists. Once the electoral incentives for that extreme politician to pretend to be moderate go away – say, a president in his second term and therefore no longer concerned about reelection – they could pursue policies at odds with the majority's preferences (see also Ashworth, Bueno de Mesquita & Friedenberg 2018).

As this example demonstrates, an important strength RCT brings to our understanding of politics is the rigorous focus on the implications of *strategic interaction* in political settings. Namely, individual preferences and processing abilities matter, but we must also consider how *two or more* actors understand each other's preferences and abilities in order to predict their behavior. With these basic assumptions and a commitment to deductive theorizing of strategic interactions, RCT has made great progress across political science subfields. Rational choice models have been dedicated fruitfully to understanding political decision-making by legislators, economic and military interactions between states, mass decision-making, voting, protest movements, and on and on.

However, this book's central conjecture is that, given what we know about human psychology, these approaches are incomplete and may lead to faulty explanations of political behavior. Pairing the deductive rigor and focus on strategic interactions from RCT with the insights from BPS about a range of human psychological constraints and motivations can thus greatly enrich our understanding of a wide variety of political phenomena.

LIMITATIONS OF THE RATIONAL CHOICE APPROACH

In the rest of this chapter, we outline the areas in which rational choice approaches have fallen short. First, we focus on understanding where our preferences come from in the first place, as mentioned previously. At its root, rational choice approaches are not designed to explain *why* we value some things over others. Another way to put this is to say our likes and dislikes are fixed and *exogenous* in the rational choice approach. This is the reason economists insist that there is *no accounting for taste*. Some people prefer oatmeal raisin cookies and others like chocolate chip. Most RCT models begin with these preferences, and then evaluate strategies people use to maximize the chance of getting their favorite cookie. BPS researchers, on the other hand, would try to figure out how any individual could formulate a preference for oatmeal raisin cookies over chocolate chip in the first place.

As we have already discussed, in interrogating the origins of political preferences, BPS researchers have found that people often fail to maximize material wealth. They often sacrifice personal material well-being and personal security for other types of utility, such as self-esteem, family time, group acceptance, or professional respect. These alternative forms of utility are not only difficult to quantify, they may also run directly counter to the maximization of material wealth. This is one simple way in which "Economic Man" might fall down: he (or she) is often not so focused on economic well-being at all.

Second, RCT assumes that individuals engage in a holistic decision-making process that leads them to the best outcomes. However, even by the less stringent assumptions of "instrumental rationality" previously outlined, citizens often fall far short of this ideal. It is a simple matter to document the public's difficulty in processing available information in order to formulate policy preferences. For example, most people do not hold anything near correct beliefs about the racial and ethnic makeup of their own nation (Sigelman & Niemi 2001; Wong 2007). One study found that when asked what percentage of the United States' population was African American in the mid-1990s (the correct answer was 12.1 percent at that time), many Americans vastly overestimated the share of the African-American population. Indeed, only 15 percent of Americans guessed anywhere between 6 and 18 percent (Nadeau, Niemi & Levine 1993). Similar errors abound in estimates of the size of the immigrant population (Herda 2010).

The arithmetic necessary to get these answers correct is quite simple, having only to do with understanding how proportions work, and possessing enough information to make even somewhat accurate guesses. This is an important point: RCT does not require individuals to be omniscient and know *everything*, but it does require that individuals use all *available* information to make the best decision. However, people frequently don't seem to use even the most readily available information. And these errors are politically consequential: for example, those who overestimate the size of the immigrant population are much more likely to oppose open immigration policies (Sides & Citrin 2007). When it comes to more difficult mathematical concepts – risks and rewards – and when getting the right answer depends upon accurately manipulating those quantities in the mind, one can imagine that nearly all citizens fail. Even political elites, with greater experience and knowledge, often have a difficult time accurately assessing, processing, and incorporating the vast amount of available information into their decision-making processes.

In summary, BPS suggests that these assumptions prominent in RCT – (1) material, self-interested preferences, and (2) holistic information processing and Bayesian updating – can be unrealistic in many situations. One purpose of this book is to review several specific ways in which these assumptions seem to fail, and then to think about the implications of those findings for our explanations of political phenomena. It is important to note, however, that the simplicity of the assumptions underlying rational choice models are also their greatest analytical strength. When fundamental assumptions about human needs and capabilities are made plain and simple, we can make clear and logical predictions about how people will behave in a wide range of political domains. We can then compare these predictions against the real world, and see if our assumptions were correct, or if we need to modify them. One key challenge for BPS has been to coalesce around a manageable, concrete set of *different* assumptions that do a better job. This book aims to highlight what this new set of assumptions might be.

We will, therefore, review a range of questions in political science that have been addressed by the Rational Choice approach and then, we think, improved upon by BPS. These include why individuals would participate in politics in the first place and which candidates they would vote for once at the ballot box. We will also review theories in international relations that use the rational actor approach to explain why countries decide to go to war, when they cooperate economically and when they put up barriers (tariffs and quotas) against other nations, and even when political leaders decide to use violence against their own citizens.

As we will show, studies in the rational actor tradition immediately discovered significant contradictions between predictions and actual behavior. Meanwhile, scholarship in psychology and other fields began to cast doubts on whether the aforementioned rationality assumptions are met by many citizens or their leaders.

Let's take another current example in American politics. During his first presidential campaign in 2016, candidate Trump insisted on deporting undocumented workers in the United States, claiming they were prone to commit crime and take away jobs from US workers. Trump even proposed publishing a list of crimes committed by immigrants and insisted US citizens should send in stories about such crimes that would be published on an online central clearinghouse.[13] The first problem with all this is that there is a large body of evidence suggesting immigrants, both legal and illegal, are significantly *less* likely to commit crimes than native US citizens of similar socioeconomic status. Even research by the conservative CATO Institute corroborates these findings.[14] Second, one would need to consider how much it would cost to arrest and deport every individual living in the United States illegally. The best guess is it would be very expensive, and so we need to consider what other budget priorities we would be willing to give up. Third, deporting undocumented workers might not improve wages or employment in the United States, given that the last time such a policy was tried, under Kennedy in the 1960s, it had no effect.[15] Moreover, far more US blue-collar jobs have been lost to automation (e.g., the use of robotic machinery) than to immigrant workers taking jobs at lower wages.[16] Of course, the real economic impact of Trump's hostile immigration policies are nearly impossible to calculate for the average voter.

What was not hard to guess, however, was how attacking outsiders made many Americans feel. The vilification of immigrants was a successful political strategy precisely because voters could not calculate the real impact of these policies, either to their own pocketbooks or even to that of the nation. Psychological motivations, including those surrounding emotions and identity, thus were likely a prominent driver of both Trump's rhetoric and its reception among the American voting public.

Clearly, the burden for holding elected officials accountable to our interests on any given issue, let alone every one that matters, is large. But, unfortunately, it gets even worse! Before we can choose a candidate who represents our interests, we first need to turn out to vote. As you will see from the next section, even understanding that decision has been very challenging for RCT.

EARLY APPLICATIONS OF RATIONAL CHOICE MODELS TO EXPLANATIONS OF POLITICAL BEHAVIOR

Anthony Downs (1957) first deployed rational actor models to explain the political behavior of average citizens, particularly why an individual would choose to participate in politics in the first place, and which candidates they would choose in the voting booth. From the beginning, a central paradox has plagued these models: Given how unlikely it is for a single citizen to influence the outcome of elections in any large constituency, why would they participate at all?

We have discussed the common assumptions of RCT at length earlier, so only a brief reprise is necessary here. To put it simply, a rational actor would only bother to expend the time, energy, and financial resources required to participate in politics if the potential benefits that accrue from such an effort would outweigh the costs. The classic equation goes as follows:

$$R = P(B) - C,$$

where R is the reward from voting, P is the probability that one's participation will change the outcome of an election to a candidate that is preferred, B is the benefit one would achieve if one's preferred candidate wins, and C represents the total costs of voting such as the time and expense associated with going to the polls. A little reflection reveals that in large societies, this equation would predict that no rational individual should vote. The probability that any individual would, on his or her own, decide an election in a society with a large population is exceedingly small. Therefore, even if the potential benefits (B) of having your preferred candidate beat his opponent were quite large, it is hard to imagine how the product of P*B could be larger than the costs (C). So why, then, do so many millions of people turn out to vote in elections so often?

Downs himself recognized that something in the model must be missing, and so he began to speculate about forces which have preoccupied political psychologists ever since. In the case of electoral participation, rational choice models began to build a quantity representing the intrinsic value people placed on participation that was separate from the benefits that would accrue from tilting the outcome in one's favor into their equations. Riker and Ordeshook (1968) labeled it the "D" term, and it captured the value people placed on exercising their civic duty to vote in elections, even if their candidate was guaranteed to lose. This is a prime example of a rational choice model that attempts to incorporate nonmaterial preferences into the expected utility calculations of its actors. The modified voting calculus was as follows:

$$R = P(B) - C + D.$$

Obviously as civic duty (D) increases, so would turnout. But this solution to the paradox was less than satisfying for some because it simply pushed the question one step further back. Why would people intrinsically value a costly activity that had no chance of affecting an election outcome? One solution to the voting paradox is offered by Aldrich (1993), who points out that voting itself is a very low-cost, low-benefit activity. It is not, therefore, the best place to expect rational behavior because "mistakes" like voting when you cannot affect the outcome are nearly costless, since the time and energy it takes to vote is often minimal.[17] Others (e.g., Morton 1991) have pointed out that individuals identify as members of large social groups and as such they may view their single voting act as an act of group identity and solidarity; rather than one out of hundreds of millions, one might think they represent millions of other citizens when they go to the polls. Of course, even then, the individual would be foolish to believe their vote had a significant chance of affecting the outcome. Since the act of voting is private, no one would know who turned out and who did not, let alone which candidate was chosen in the voting booth. Since one vote would almost never tip an election from one candidate to another, one would still predict very low turnout rates among strictly rational voters.

There is a second puzzle in the voting literature that RCT also has trouble explaining: Once citizens decide to vote, how do they choose a candidate? Downs was interested in this question as well, building a model of voter choice to explain why people would choose one candidate over another once they overcame the obstacles to showing up to the polls in the first place. Rational citizens would first evaluate each party platform and identify which was closest to his or her ideal point. They would also figure out how far away the opposing party was on the issues, so that they could calculate the differential benefit of having the preferred candidate (who represented that party) win. This "party differential" is critical for the rational approach to vote choice, and it implies that citizens are frequently monitoring the environment to determine which party they would prefer based on the difference in utility they would receive from one versus the other party holding office.

Many were surprised when the first systematic surveys of the American public described voters who were quite unable to identify many details about the issue positions of the parties (Campbell et al. 1960) or to express coherent ideologies linking issues together in any consistent way (Converse 1964). Further, the evidence seemed to suggest that partisan identifications were something far more powerful than summaries for the issue positions citizens held. Instead, they seemed to act as "perceptual filters" that actually caused individuals to change their own issue positions. The impact of party identification on beliefs and issue positions violated the basic assumption of rational choice models of voting, and indeed seemed to violate basic assumptions about representation in democratic theory. How could democratic representation even be possible if voters were led to their issue positions by the partisan elites they identified with? In such a world, new information demonstrating that a voter had chosen the wrong party for their interests would be rejected. The individual would continue to support his or her party even thought it was no longer in his or her interest to do so.

One set of answers to this challenge to the basic assumptions of the rational choice model of citizen choice – in addition to the bounded rationality approaches highlighted earlier – is that *individual* voters may often get it wrong, but when preferences are aggregated across the entire electorate, the polity as a whole seems to react rationally to new information. For example, Page and Shapiro (1992) suggest that individuals may make errors about which party would be best, but that these errors are more or less random in nature. If so, they would cancel out in the aggregate, leading the whole system to be more or less rational in reaction to new information. Another approach suggests that, even if many citizens are not informed and fail to respond to new information appropriately, the most attentive citizens would serve as a rational anchor for the public as a whole, pushing the "public mood" in the right direction (Erikson et al. 2002; Stimson et al. 1995).

Still, these attempts to save the concept of rational voting through aggregation do not address a host of questions and concerns. Are these errors in judgment really "random" across individuals? Can the most interested really be expected to hold the same issue positions as those less informed? The answer to those questions, it seems, is often a resounding "no." Policy outputs seem to shift considerably when all citizens are informed, and mistakes do not tend to cancel out over the entire citizenry (Althaus 2003; Bartels 1996; Gilens 2001). Indeed, citizens, for the most part, appear to choose their candidates on the basis of social identities much more than on candidates' policy positions (Achen & Bartels 2017). Thus, among average citizens at least, it appears that their political behavior falls well short of the rational ideal, meaning that other tools of analysis are needed to better understand mass political behavior.

RATIONAL ACTOR MODELS IN INTERNATIONAL RELATIONS

While RCT approaches to the study of mass political behavior have been frequently challenged, the approach remains dominant in international relations theory. Theorists studying world politics have often assumed that leaders, as a highly motivated and politically sophisticated subset of the population, would be less susceptible to "nonrational" political thinking than average citizens. As a result, some have argued that departures from the assumptions of Economic Man might be smaller among these capable and motivated elites. Thus, while behavioral approaches to mass political behavior began in earnest in the 1950s with seminal work by scholars such as Bernard Berelson, Philip Converse, Robert Dahl, Paul Lazarsfeld, the behavioral turn in international relations came later, spurred on by work by Robert Jervis (1976) on perceptions and misperceptions in international relations and Kahneman and Tversky's (1979) work on prospect theory (see Chapter 3).[18] Prior to this work, international relations theories in the rational choice tradition sprang from two major camps: structural theories and bargaining theories.

Structural theories of international relations posit that stable features of the international system determine state action (e.g. Mearsheimer 1995; Waltz 2000). For example, whether a system is unipolar – with one very powerful state (Jervis 2009), bipolar – with two balanced state actors (Waltz 1964), or multipolar – with multiple states vying for influence (Christensen and Snyder 1997), fundamentally constrains the policy options a given leader can pursue. If so, no matter who the leader of a particular country is, they would ultimately make the same foreign policy choices. The relative *anarchy* of the entire international system – the lack of a third-party enforcer to effectively define or punish lawbreakers – governs all diplomacy and conflict between states. Given an anarchic system, states can never be sure of the intention of other states, which are all primarily concerned with their own survival, and must act accordingly (Waltz 2010). According to structural theorists, it is this *rational* uncertainty that leads to conflict (Waltz 2010). These theories were particularly prominent and popular during the Cold War. For example, popular concepts such as "mutually assured destruction" (MAD) and "balance of terror" relied on the fundamental stability of a bipolar system dominated by the United States and the Soviet Union. As long as both states were rational actors who prioritized their own existence, nuclear weapons would never actually be used because each state's nuclear capability balanced the other out.

Bargaining theories also emphasize the primacy of decisions based on the simple assumptions of RCT and the important role of uncertainty in the international arena. However, these theorists take an additional step, arguing that leaders attempt to leverage the structural characteristics of the system to their advantage. Bargaining theories, like realist theories, typically treat states as unitary actors, with the leader acting as the true representative of the state's interests.[19] These so-called billiard-ball models of international relations assume that the political push-and-pull within each state is of less significance to state policy than is the overarching interest of the state writ large (Fearon 1995). In other words, the preferences of a given leader, the bureaucracy and the citizenry are assumed, for simplicity, to be identical. It is this general interest that is thought to primarily guide leaders' strategies on the international stage. They build up reputations (Sartori 2002), create alliances (Morrow 1993), use costly signals of intent (Fearon 1994; 1997), arm themselves (Morrow 1993), and create international legal systems (Koh et al. 1997) in an effort to achieve diplomatic victories and avoid costly wars.

For example, in 2012, President Obama publicly proclaimed that the Syrian government's use of chemical weapons against their citizens in the ongoing civil war would be a "red line" that would require US intervention. According to bargaining theory, this was a costly public signal with significant potential audience costs if Obama were to back down – the United States would lose its reputation and either the American public opinion would judge him harshly or the Syrian government would no longer respond to US entreaties in the future. In the RCT framework, this red line should have engendered audience costs that rendered it too difficult for the president to back down. This is not what happened in the Syria case, however: President Obama backed down and there were no consequences for Syrian President Assad's aggression including the use of chemical weapons on his own citizens.

Many of President Trump's decisions also seem to confound standard RCT theories of presidential behavior. For example, his numerous policy flip-flops on a variety of issues often left both allies and adversaries wondering what his real priorities were. Take, for example, President Trump's decision to tell the Russian Foreign Minister and Russian Ambassador to the United States in May 2017 about highly classified information provided by Israel about an ISIS plot to blow up airlines with bombs hidden in laptops. In addition to potentially undermining national security and the US intelligence relationship with a close ally, it also triggered several days' worth of harsh and negative coverage of the administration, and of Trump, in particular. Such behavior seemed not to be the product of cost-benefit, rational, and careful calculation. Experts all over the world suggested no benefits would accrue to the United States for revealing this information. Instead, this was likely a simple case of bragging by the US president, perhaps due to individual self-esteem considerations. Such behavior would not be predictable under most standard rational accounts of elite behavior when the stakes are so high. With its emphasis on the effect of emotions in decision-making, bounded rationality, the use of heuristics, and other biases in leader psychology, we think BPS approaches may be better equipped to explain and predict these dynamics.

In other words, though RCT models of international relations have helped political scientists understand a great deal about the contexts in which states and leaders make policy choices, they also make strong simplifying assumptions about the basis of human decision-making. These assumptions are often required in order to solve the complex game-theoretic math in many of these models. However, those same assumptions often go unexamined empirically. When they turn out to be incorrect, the model will fail to predict policy outcomes.

EXPERIMENTAL CHALLENGES TO RATIONAL CHOICE ASSUMPTIONS IN IR

Recent work in international relations (IR) has revived the BPS approach, building on earlier research that experimentally tested core assumptions of popular rational choice models in international relations.[20] This new research in the behavioral IR tradition uses experimental methods to unpack the black box of decision-making to better understand the complexity of international state behavior (Mintz 2007). Specifically, behavioral models of IR explore the micro-foundations underpinning state behavior – an analytic strategy where one "explains outcomes at the aggregate level via dynamics at a lower level" (Kertzer 2017, p. 83). This approach to international relations emphasizes the need to test assumptions about micro-level mechanisms posited by rational choice theories. For example, one of the prominent theories of international relations discussed previously, structural realism, relies on untested micro-level assumptions about how leaders respond to threat, fear, and uncertainty (Kertzer 2017). In the real world, these forces cannot be manipulated by the researcher, only observed *in situ*. Experimental methods, with their emphasis on control, measurement, and internal validity would be a powerful methodological tool for exploring the causal impact of these forces, at least on average citizens in the lab (Kertzer 2017).

In the rational choice tradition, models of political behavior are typically designed as multiplayer games in which each player can choose from a set of different potential behaviors that can lead to different outcomes with different payoffs or values. However, the outcomes of a player's chosen strategies, the payoffs they will ultimately receive, depend on the behavior of other players in the game. The metaphor most often invoked is the game of chess – the quality of your move depends on what you assume the other player will do next.[21]

Rational players choose strategies that maximize their likely payoff. So, for example, if a player's status quo payoff is 0 points and they need to decide whether to threaten another state or stay out of the fray, they will have to take into account the payoffs for all the potential outcomes as well as the probabilities that each outcome will occur when choosing which path to pursue (threatening, or staying out and maintaining the status quo). For instance, imagine a player (A) makes a threat, and there is a 90 percent chance that the other player (B) will respond to that threat. If so, a war breaks out where the first player must pay 10 points. However, there is a 10 percent chance that Player B will simply cave and just give up the 10 points to Player A. What should the rational Player A choose? They would choose *not* to threaten. This is because the expected utility for threatening is, $(-10*0.9)+(10*0.1)=-8$, while the payoff for not threatening is the status quo of 0 points. The equilibrium outcome, the one that happens when everyone makes the correct calculation and behaves accordingly, would then be that Player A never threatens and so Player B never has to respond.

Note that if this equilibrium held, we could never observe a correlation between threats and war commencement, since there would be no threats. But, of course, that is not proof that threats are irrelevant to the onset of wars! This makes fraught the sole reliance on observational evidence to test any causal theory in international relations or any other part of political science. We often do not get to observe variation in important variables because people behave strategically. For example, wars are all examples of deterrence *failure*, but not all "non-wars" are examples of deterrence *success*: In many of these non-war cases, the states probably had no interest in fighting in the first place. This conundrum makes it difficult to use observational methods in order to study the factors that make deterrence successful. Again, this is why experiments can be so helpful.

However, when RCT models are tested experimentally on subjects in the lab, the results often stray off the equilibrium path, meaning that subjects choose strategies that *do not* appear to optimize the preferences assumed at the beginning. For example, a series of experimental studies by Tingley and Walter (2011a; 2011b) found that experimental subjects often do not play international relations games according to the assumptions posed by prominent rational choice models. One highly influential theory in IR is the idea of reputation as an important component of bargaining and credibility. In other words, if a state has a reputation for following through on the things they say, and vigorously defending their interests, this will put them in a better bargaining position down the road, as other states will be more likely to believe them. So, if State A wants to deter State B from attacking an ally, the leader of State A might claim that it is willing to go to war to defend that ally. This claim will be much more credible and, therefore, effective if State A has a history of following through on these types of threats and going to war in similar situations.

Rational choice theorists have developed a game that models this interaction. According to the predictions of the model, strategic actors should invest significant resources in building a reputation for being strong *early* in order to reap the benefits later, even if it costs them in the short term. Later in the conflict, when there are fewer future opportunities to capitalize on a strong reputation, one would assume less investment in reputation. One of Tingley and Walter's experiments (2011a) set out to test this model. The subjects in their experimental study, however, seemed to have it backwards: they would underinvest in their reputation early, and then overinvest in their reputation later (Tingley & Walter 2011a). Why would this happen? The authors suggest it may be because of heterogeneity of preferences – some individuals may care less about future payoffs than they do about immediate benefits. Moreover, limitations in cognitive ability may mean that different individuals realize the benefits of reputation only in later stages of the game when, ironically, it matters less. Of course, a common critique of this type of experimental work is that it is not conducted with the actual political leaders as subjects, and they would play the game quite differently than the average citizen (typically, undergraduate students). While this is an important concern, similar studies that have actually been conducted *on political leaders* have found that politicians are often just as subject to these anomalies as non-politicians: "they exhibit a stronger tendency to escalate commitment when facing sunk costs, they adhere more to policy choices that are presented as the status-quo, their risk calculus is strongly subject to framing effects, and they exhibit distinct future time discounting preferences" (Sheffer et al. 2018, p. 302).

Another case where empirical studies have failed to confirm basic assumptions underlying RCT is with the impact of strategic communication. An influential theory in international relations has to do with the ways in which states signal their intentions to other states. How can State A convince State B that it is strong (and able to withstand an attack) when State B knows that State A has an incentive to *pretend* to be stronger than it is? This dilemma is called the paradox of persuasion – states have an incentive to misrepresent their true capabilities or intentions in order to gain an advantage. This kind of misrepresentation is often referred to as "cheap talk." Cheap talk is a message that is costless to send. However, precisely because it is costless, everyone has an incentive to use it. If it costs nothing to say, "I am strong," everyone will say it and so the message will tell us nothing about our adversary's true type. This situation is referred to as a pooling strategy – fundamentally different types of actors (strong and weak) do the same thing and, thus, pool together.

So how can rational adversaries *credibly* signal their type in order to influence the behavior of other actors? Well, there is really only one way, according to rational choice theories: Send a "costly signal" (Farrell & Rabin 1996). By definition, costly signals require the messenger to give up something of value. Examples include spending money on troops or military technology ("sinking costs") (Fearon 1997) or making public proclamations that put a state's reputation on the line ("tying hands") (Fearon 1997) or "building audience costs" (Fearon 1994). These strategies will be taken more seriously, because weak states would not want to pay these costs if, ultimately, they would be forced to back down. Rational choice theorists have spent a great deal of time formally modeling these ideas. In these models, State B's behavior should only be modified if it receives some kind of costly signal from State A that enables State B to learn something about State A's type. Cheap talk shouldn't work.

Tingley and Walter (2011b) test this proposition experimentally using what is called "an entry deterrence game." This game consists of two players, a challenger and a defender. The defender wants to prevent the challenger from entering and therefore threatening his hold on power. Of course, the challenger wants to enter in order to take the defender's power. In their experiment, Tingley and Walter (2011b) made one significant alteration – they allowed the defender to issue a costless verbal threat privately to the attacker, prior to his decision on whether to enter or not. Remember, based on the previous discussion, this costless signal should *not* have had a significant impact on the resulting strategies either player took, because the defender had an incentive to lie about retaliating against a potential challenger and incurred no costs for doing so. Any threat would have been pooling and would thus not have enabled the attacker to learn anything regarding his type and relative resoluteness.

However, Tingley and Walter found that cheap talk *did* substantially alter the outcome of the game. Attackers were significantly more likely to back down when a verbal threat was issued and, when they did not, defenders were significantly more likely to fight, even if that choice was costlier than backing down and allowing the challenger to enter the game. In other words, people in these studies perceived cheap talk as informative and changed their behavior as a result (Tingley & Walter 2011b). In explaining this result, Tingley and Walter stress that these differences may spring from a misunderstanding about how the game should be played, "misinterpreting the instructions, or simply playing irrationally for different idiosyncratic reasons," allowing them to be manipulated by others who understand the game better (2011b, p. 1009). The authors also suggest that the willingness to lie may itself serve as a separating strategy – honest defenders don't lie and don't defend when it is not worth it, whereas liars would use cheap talk and would defend, even if it didn't pay.

Finally, it is not just undergraduate students who behave this way. Hall and Yarhi-Milo (2012) found that *political leaders'* impressions of the sincerity of other leaders' promises also influenced their foreign policy choice, even without the use of costly signaling, suggesting that, though the Tingley and Walter experiments were not conducted with actual leaders, leaders may behave similarly. These are only a few examples in a growing body of behavioral IR scholarship that tests and modifies key assumptions common in rational choice models of IR – how preferences are formed, how beliefs change, and how decision-making processes are biased (Hafner-Burton et al. 2017; Mintz 2007).

Though traditional rational choice models of IR do allow for variation in preferences, and can be stretched to include "nonstandard" preferences including, for example, morals and norms, the central focus of most of these models is not preference heterogeneity, but the role of system level structures and information in shaping behavior (Hafner-Burton et al. 2017). Moreover, even when allowed to vary, these preferences are still assumed to be symmetrical, such that both players assess risk and time discounts similarly, and are self-interested rather than social in nature (Hafner-Burton et al. 2017). BPS approaches dig further into both the origin and heterogeneity of preferences, emphasizing the nuanced impact of emotions (Chapter 6), the way norms, values, and personality (Chapter 7) constrain preferences, and the prevalence of group rather than self-oriented goals (Chapter 8) in decision-making.

RCT also makes strong assumptions regarding the ways in which beliefs change in the presence of uncertainty or in response to new information. However, as described, this Bayesian mode of belief formation and updating is very intensive from a cognitive standpoint, and a growing accumulation of experimental evidence now suggests that even political sophisticates and elites fail to meet this high standard when making strategic decisions. While we might expect that an average citizen would not possess the time, energy, or information required to engage in Bayesian updating of their beliefs, we certainly expect our leaders to do so. Thus, understanding how incorrect beliefs are generated and then persist among elites, even in the wake of contradictory evidence, is a primary theoretical challenge for behavioral IR theorists.

Finally, other strands of Behavioral IR look at the actual decision-making process, questioning not only the heterogeneous *motivations* of political elites that shape their strategic behavior, but also the *ability* (or inability) of political leaders to make the types of utility-maximizing decisions hypothesized by rational choice theorists, despite their increased political sophistication and experience. BPS approaches to this puzzle have alternatively examined the role of cognitive biases (Chapter 3), framing effects (Chapter 4), institutional or group pathologies (Chapter 5), and emotions (Chapter 6) in decision-making processes to explain why such a highly motivated, politically sophisticated subset of individuals could still be so prone to holding persistent, incorrect beliefs. Collectively, this work explores how various information-process pathologies (at both the individual and group level) may lead to systematic deviations from rational choice assumptions regarding preference completeness, transitivity, and insensitivity to irrelevant alternatives.

FORMAL MODELING: A TOOL FOR BOTH RCT AND BPS APPROACHES TO POLITICS

As we suggested at the beginning of this chapter, BPS does not preclude the use of formal approaches to understanding politics. The strength of the formal approach, often used by rational choice theorists, derives from its insistence on clear, logical, and formal statements about the way concepts are related in a causal explanation. They state assumptions clearly, and then use rigorous logic to arrive at predictions about how people should behave given those assumptions. If behavior in the real-world deviates from those predictions, one must reject the original assumptions and adopt others. The approach is general, and it values parsimony; explaining political phenomena with a few clear assumptions is preferred. Most importantly, perhaps, the process of formally stating all of one's assumptions and the relationships between concepts in a causal model often reveals inconsistencies and contradictions that had been present all along in more informal theorizing. The point is that formalizing a theory, in and of itself, is an important step on the road to explanation and does not mandate any particular assumptions about human cognition and decision-making. Though formal models are typically associated with RCT assumptions about human behavior, formal models are a tool that could be applied using different BPS assumptions as well.

Improving our assumptions about what motivates people and how they translate those motivations into actions is the shared goal of all social science, regardless of the methods any particular scholar employs. As a result, throughout this book, we will emphasize the ways in which behavioral, psychological assumptions can improve our understanding of politics, synthesizing the empirical findings from behavioral research to clarify how these findings might warrant a modification of the assumptions built into formal models of political decision-making.

Of course, incorporating modified behavioral assumptions into formal models of politics is not simple. And, indeed, the common rejoinder from Rational Choice Theorists to this push to modify standard assumptions is that their choice to focus on the strategic environment (e.g., a rationalist choice) rather than the attributes of the individual (e.g., a behavioral choice) is a strategic "research bet" in which they make simplifying assumptions, black-boxing certain complications of political decision-making, to create a tractable mode (Powell 2017).[22] Such models, though imperfect, can often predict political outcomes quite well. However, we contend that the choice to focus *either* on individual decisions *or* the strategic environment is, in fact, artificial. Incorporating BPS insights regarding the complex structure of agents' preferences and the flawed ways in which they process information into models of the strategic environment can increase our ability as researchers to both explain *and* predict political outcomes. Indeed, in response to growing evidence regarding citizens' nonstandard preferences and bounded rationality, game theorists working in the rational choice tradition have incorporated these findings into their models, with fruitful results.

There are several promising examples of research that incorporate BPS assumptions about preferences or processing abilities, while also engaging in the deductive rigor and formalization of assumptions for which rational choice approaches are well known. For example, work by Smith and Stam's (2004) on bargaining and war incorporates the assumption of "non-common priors" (e.g., differing beliefs at the outset of an interaction) into their game theoretical model of the bargaining process of war to better understand why, in the real world, we frequently observe leaders whose beliefs do not seem to converge (i.e., become the same) once all private information has been revealed. This structure allows the model to emphasize the importance of learning and how actors' distinct conceptual beliefs about the world can impact the likelihood of conflict, in additional to traditional rational considerations of credibility and incentives to misrepresent (Smith & Stam 2004). William Minozzi's (2013) work incorporating beliefs as an *endogenous* rather than exogenous feature of a strategic interaction is another example of formal work that incorporates more realistic assumptions about the preferences motivating beliefs, beyond objective probabilities. This idea, that beliefs can be endogenous to preferences, is crucial for understanding how individuals might evaluate information and learn about the world. For instance, Little (2019) formally considers how the tension between accuracy motives and directional motives – which are central to the theory of motivated reasoning (see Chapter 8) – impact belief formation. He demonstrates how the presence of directional motives on a small set of core beliefs (e.g., I want to believe that I am a smart person) can lead individuals to distort their beliefs about a host of other, related beliefs over which they otherwise do not possess any type of directional motive (e.g., the test I failed was poorly designed). In other words, the desire to maximize sometimes opposing informational goals (accuracy and directional) can explain why individuals hold what seem to be implausible views about a variety of issues.

Other formal work has begun to incorporate behavioral assumptions about preferences as well. For example, Acharya, Blackwell, and Sen (2018) explore how the causal arrow does not always flow from preferences to action, but, in fact, from action to preferences. In other words, the choices an individual makes can change their preferences. Feddersen, Gailmard, and Sandroni (2009) examine the importance of moral (rather than material) values in voting; Penn (2009) considers how citizens might take into account not only short-term self-interest, but long-term "farsighted" goals in their voting. In other work, Penn (2008) investigates how the design of institutions *themselves* could induce changes in identity, which, in turn, alter citizens' preferences and views toward the state. The burgeoning work on retrospective voting (Bendor, Kumar & Siegel 2010; Woon 2012) provides another example of formal research that incorporates behavioral assumptions to better explain and predict real-world outcomes. In this literature, voters punish or sanction elected officials for past performance, even if that performance will not affect *future* utility.

Likewise, the field of Behavioral Economics has also incorporated some of the insights from psychology and BPS reviewed in this book. Much of the behavioral modeling tradition in political science builds on similar efforts taken on in Behavioral Economics, including, for example, research by Gul & Pesendorfer that incorporates a variety of behavioral preferences into formal economic models, including low self-control (Gul & Pesendorfer 2001; 2004), interest in the *intentions* of other people's behavior (Gul & Pesendorfer 2016), and limited cognitive abilities (Gul, Pesendorfer & Strzalecki 2017). We see this type of research as an excellent development for social science more broadly, and would hope even more integration between economics, psychology, and political science can occur in the future.

THE NEED FOR BEHAVIORAL POLITICAL SCIENCE

Our hope is that the previous discussion has clarified the assumptions embedded in the RCT approach, a perspective that has risen to prominence in political science over the last several decades. As we mentioned in the introduction, RCT has been questioned mostly on the grounds that humans either do not have the *ability* or the *motivation* to meet the information-processing standards necessary to arrive at the correct decision in all but the simplest of situations relevant to politics. These central assumptions – that people are comprehensive and efficient utility maximizers with primarily self-interested, material aims – have seemed at odds with empirical findings across all subfields of political science. Empirical BPS findings on individual preferences and decision-making processes, therefore, greatly improve our understanding of politics. In the next chapter, we will begin our exploration of the BPS approach, focusing on the typical features of human information processing and reasoning.

3

The Limits of Human Information Processing

Bounded Rationality, Heuristics, and Biases

In the previous chapter, we described some of the core assumptions RCT makes when analyzing human behavior – that individuals generally have self-interested, material motivations and process information in ways that allow them to choose strategies that will maximize their utility, given these preferences. However, in study after study of political decision-making, people do not seem to meet the high standards of motivation and ability in information seeking and processing (e.g., Jones 1994). Rather, people appear to be only *boundedly* rational – using cognitive short-cuts and rules-of-thumb to make decisions when it would be too complicated or time-consuming to gather complete information about all possible alternatives.

Importantly, as we discuss in Chapter 2, some theorists actually accept the idea that, because information is costly, people will not process all available information, but, rather, will take shortcuts to make quicker decisions, given time constraints. However, in general, when rational choice theorists invoke this idea, they still tend to assume that these decision-making shortcuts lead to decisions that are "as-if" rational – that people would reach the same outcome even if they had analyzed every component of the decision in depth. BPS scholars, on the other hand, have demonstrated the ways in which this is often *not* the case – where this type of heuristic processing leads to biases and sub-optimal decision-making. These challenges form the basis of the *bounded rationality* school of political science, whereby scholars have questioned individuals' ability to make fully informed decisions, pointing out the systematic biases and errors human beings make in their judgments and decisions.

When deciding how to vote or which policies to endorse, people rarely possess the information they need in order to compare multiple alternatives on more than one dimension. In most campaign matchups, especially those involving nonincumbents, voters know relatively little about the experience, skill, and policy views of either candidate, let alone both. And even when people do hold more detailed information, they find it difficult to combine, compare, and weigh all of it in order to come to conclusions that would maximize the quality of the outcome. Under these difficult conditions, is there really any way voters can make decisions better than they would simply by randomly guessing? The answer is "yes": better decisions, but typically, not perfect ones.

In other words, researchers studying bounded rationality have found that it is not that people are "irrational," but that they use shortcuts in systematic, predictable ways. Specifically, cognitive biases caused by our tendency to rely on *heuristics* – coarse rules of thumb that sacrifice some decision-making accuracy for a corresponding increase in simplicity and speed – cause specific deviations from the complete and perfect information processing and decision-making ideals originally posited by RCT. There are several important dimensions of biases, when "human decision behavior systematically deviates from (or is biased when compared to) a normative model that is assumed to be the optimal way to make the decision under investigation" (Sage & Palmer 1990, 227–229). We can then use our understanding of the predictable patterns of these biases to understand, forecast, and potentially improve, future decision-making.

THE IDEA OF BOUNDED RATIONALITY

One of the first to consider the way that cognitive biases might violate the "utility maximization" approach of RCT was Herbert Simon. In his revolutionary paper, "A Behavioral Model of Rational Choice," published in 1955 in the *Quarterly Journal of Economics*, he suggested that human nature as prescribed by *Economic Man* was "in need of fairly drastic revision" (p. 99). He focused on the problem of human computing power, recognizing that rather than being powerful computational machines with unlimited storage capacity, humans must make important decisions with very limited information and less than advanced mathematical skills. So how do they go about that?

Simon (1955) suggested that, most of the time, people would "*satisfice*" rather than "*optimize*." While optimizing requires individuals to behave in ways that net them the *best possible* outcome, satisficing simply requires that individuals choose courses of actions that net them an outcome that is *good enough*. Collecting information about one's alternatives is costly in terms of time and sometimes money. In order to figure out whether the two-dollar apple is really twice as good as the one-dollar apple, one would need to know about both varieties, the farms on which they were grown, the timing of the harvest, the weather, how long they keep fresh, and perhaps many other bits of information. If one were very serious, one might even buy an agricultural newspaper to read about how different apple orchards did that year. Now let's imagine this person valued her time at one dollar per hour, and the newspaper cost another dollar. If she were only making this choice once, it would not make much sense to invest a lot of time doing research collecting information about which apple is better. The research itself could cost more than the product. Instead, she might simply say, "I choose the least expensive apple as long as it is just good enough." In other words, she might first decide on some *acceptability threshold* in any given decision and stop collecting new information as soon as such an option is available. If both apples met her minimum threshold, she would purchase the less expensive one. If neither did, she would keep sampling apples until that threshold was reached.

Simon's revision of RCT assumptions, based on the recognition that information seeking is costly, opened the door to explanations for a whole host of phenomena. These ideas are captured under the heading of *limited* or *bounded* rationality. But exactly how limited is limited? While RCT tends to assume these limitations nonetheless lead to the "right" decision most of the time, BPS studies have found that, when it comes to our information and computing power, human decision-making is very limited indeed. Biases related to information scarcity or limits on human computational ability have been discovered throughout politics, and these shed light on many unsolved puzzles. Examples abound: Political participation seems higher than expected in large electorates where the personal cost of voting outweighs any chance of affecting the outcome; trivial changes in the way an argument is *framed* can dramatically alter policy choices even when outcomes are identical; prejudice and racism have a very large effect on policy views, even at the expense of individual material interests;[1] emotional processes which precede conscious awareness seem to have a very large impact on the ultimate choices that are made.

So, these biases in cognitive processing exist. But can we overcome them if we are knowledgeable or motivated enough? The American Founding Fathers hoped so. They structured institutions so that elected leaders would be those better suited to resisting these biases that seemed to plague the average citizen. However, we now know that expertise or experience does not significantly reduce the impact of bounded rationality on political decisions. Studies conducted on leaders have found that the same psychological processes that influence mass decision-making also influence the behavior of public officials (e.g., Sheffer et al. 2018), which could have devastating consequences for the conditions of millions of people around the world. For example, in the field of International Relations, bounded rationality and the satisficing principle help to explain the decision to use force (Ostrom and Job 1986; James and Oneal 1991). Leaders strive to achieve a "good enough" outcome rather than evaluating all the available alternatives on all dimensions in a holistic manner (Bendor 2010).

The behavior of candidates during the 2020 US presidential campaign can be interpreted using the bounded rationality–heuristic framework. During the vice-presidential debate of 2020, Senator Kamala Harris called the response to the COVID-19 virus, "the greatest failure of any presidential administration," attempting to boost the country's attention to this issue. Vice President Pence, in contrast, focused on the economy and economic issues such as taxes, in an attempt to draw attention away from COVID-19.

During the presidential campaign of 2016, one might recall that candidate Donald Trump referred to the NATO alliance as "obsolete."[2] At the time, Trump focused largely on the financial-economic dimension of the alliances – his claim that alliance members were not contributing their fair share to fund the alliance – but not on other advantages that the alliance provides. In this regard, his view may fit the bounded rationality approach (rather than procedural rationality), as it appeared to be based on limited information and, as such, was a satisficing choice.

Following President Assad's chemical attack against his own people in April 2017, and Russia's support of the Assad regime, President Trump changed his mind on NATO, calling the alliance important.[3] Perhaps this new view was based on an assessment of multiple dimensions, such as the military advantage NATO might provide in deterring aggression, countering a potential Russian response, and so on. The president admitted that his revised estimate was due to new information he received – that NATO does indeed fight terrorism. Importantly, this information was available prior to the election, but was simply not used by Trump in forming his initial view on this issue. This is important because RCT does not require decision-makers to be omniscient, but it does require them to process all relevant, available information to make a maximizing decision. In other words, the revised view appears to have been the result of additional information Trump sought out only once he became president. BPS, with its focus on framing and priming, contributes to our understanding of such behavior.

HEURISTICS

While Simon's satisficing idea gives us the architecture to think about a more manageable cognitive process for making decisions, it does not give us much guidance about what *types* of information will be used most often. The answer to that question is *heuristics*. These are shortcuts or rules of thumb we use to process information to try and make the best possible guess. As a result, heuristics often influence our decisions. Factors such as the party affiliations of each candidate, testimonies from trusted leaders or experts, and reactions to the performance of the incumbent can all serve as important heuristics for voters. Heuristics can be quite helpful to the average citizen. They help individuals make decisions quickly while preserving cognitive effort. In this sense, heuristics are often *adaptive*. For example, they may help citizens acquire enough information about complicated electoral alternatives to make a decision that may get them very close to the best alternative.

The 2020 and 2016 presidential election campaigns in the United States provide numerous examples of the use and importance of heuristics. In 2020, Trump repeatedly referred to his opponent as "sleepy Joe" to portray him as old and ineffective. The president also called COVID-19, "the Chinese flu" to both distance his administration from the pandemic and put the blame on China for the virus. In 2016, Hillary Clinton's opponents highlighting her use of State Department emails on her personal server served as a heuristic in judging her trustworthiness and character, regardless of whether this behavior actually put the nation at risk, whether it was legal, or even if other officials from both parties had done the same thing. A complete survey of information regarding the decision to use a private server for government email may have resulted in a different conclusion about Clinton's character in general. Similarly, Trump's comments about women served as a heuristic for many voters, leading many to withdraw their support even though he had hired and promoted many women in his businesses. On the other hand, turning to "positive" heuristics, Trump's campaign slogan, "Make America Great Again" may have reminded many voters of times when the economy was rapidly expanding, jobs were plentiful, and families could afford to live comfortably on a single income. Whether promises to return such economic bounty can be delivered by candidates are less important once they get voters to focus on them. Hillary Clinton's emphasis on "qualifications" also served as an important heuristic in the minds of many voters with regard to her general level of competence for the presidency.

Indeed, most campaign slogans and thirty-second commercials capitalize on the power of heuristics: highlighting a certain aspect of the opposing candidate in a negative way, or portraying the sponsor positively using simple phrases, visual symbols, and music. In voting, the simple affective heuristic – "I don't like that guy" or "She seems like a good person" – is a very powerful predictor of voting decisions. One does not need an elaborate, informed, or detailed model to predict which candidate will win most of the time. This basic likeability heuristic (Brady & Sniderman 1985) challenges many common RCT assumptions about the basis of preferences, since whether a candidate is likeable might not have much to do with how well they design and implement policies that maximize the public good, but it does provide a simpler and more parsimonious explanation for why people do or do not vote for a certain candidate. In order for this decision rule to be "rational" from a material standpoint, likeability would have to be valued above all other dimensions on which a candidate could be judged. This is often not the case.

Another good example of bounded rationality comes in the form of ballot initiatives: statewide elections where a specific policy change is put to the voters directly. In 1988, California voters were presented with a complicated set of policies attempting to solve the problem of skyrocketing automobile insurance rates. Auto insurance companies, of course, had their interests in keeping rates relatively high, while consumer activist groups preferred lower rates. A third group, the trial lawyers in the state, had every incentive to avoid simplifying the laws so that their services would continue to be in demand. The initiatives on the ballot that year were large in number (five in total) and thick with complicated details that even many elites with a stake in the outcomes had difficulty understanding. Despite this level of difficulty and complication, many citizens did seem to figure out how to vote in ways that were consistent with their interests as consumers; Lupia (1994) discovered that less-informed citizens could approximate the behavior of their (scarce) fully informed compatriots in this situation by using a heuristic. Those who lacked detailed "encyclopedic" knowledge about each alternative could simply use a shortcut: what was the insurance industry's position on a given option? If the insurance industry supported the rule change, most voters correctly assumed that the rule change would be in favor of the insurance industry and not in favor of the average citizen. As such, voters who knew just that one fact were able to choose the option best for consumers, and not for the insurance companies! As this example demonstrates, the use of heuristics does not *always* lead to objectively worse decision-making. In fact, research shows that sophisticated voters may be even more likely to use heuristics in a way that leads them to the "correct" political decisions for them (Lau & Redlawsk 2001).

The use of heuristics is also not limited to the masses. In governmental budgeting decisions, the common practice of using the principle of "fair share" in allocations to various governmental programs and the use of "incremental spending," are just two examples of heuristics in public administration and public policy.[4] In foreign policy, President Obama's realization that a majority of the public (and Congress) opposed the use of force in Syria in September 2013, despite President Assad's use of chemical weapons against his own citizens, may have served as a heuristic that influenced the president's decision not to intervene. In other words, it was sufficient for President Obama to know that there was opposition in Congress and the public to intervention in Syria to reject this policy alternative. Another reason may have been the president's reliance on the common rule of thumb of avoiding casualties to US forces. This may have increased the preference for an air campaign over boots on the ground, even though ground troops are often more successful in securing policy objectives, and so, could have led to an overall higher utility, though at the risk of troop losses.

There are many fascinating examples of how our brains make quick decisions, even about important political matters, based on very limited information. One set of experiments has even demonstrated that people can correctly predict the outcome of elections between candidates they have never heard of before, after viewing pictures of candidate faces for less than one second (Ballew & Todorov 2007). Presumably people use attractiveness cues to correctly guess who is most electable. This suggests that, while civics classes often insist that good democratic citizens carefully learn and consider all the issue positions, ideology, personality traits, and experiential strengths and weaknesses of each candidate in every election, the typical process for selecting candidates may be much simpler, for better or worse.

THE POTENTIAL COSTS OF HEURISTIC THINKING

Of course, just because we often use heuristics does not mean they always lead us to the "correct" choice. In fact, heuristics often lead to biases that cause us to miss choices that would make us better off. For example, our well-known tendency to stereotype individuals based on superficial, outward appearances or group membership can cause a lot of damage, and not only to those who are unfairly judged. In an evolutionary sense, this tendency to stereotype may have developed because it was helpful for the survival of small and vulnerable tribal groups in the distant past (Craemer 2008; Kurzban, Tooby & Cosmides 2001). Thousands of years ago, recognizing who was and was not a member of one's own tribe may have been a matter of life and death. Economists have developed the term "statistical discrimination" (Arrow 1973; Phelps 1972) to explain individuals' tendency to stereotype: people, acting in an environment with imperfect and limited information, will guess about the likelihood that, say, someone is going to rob them, based on what they know about the base likelihood that people of different skin colors commit theft.[5] The problem, of course, is that people are often *wrong* about these base rate probabilities – they make mistakes in how they apply Bayes' rule[6] and, as a result, *overestimate* the likelihood that someone from another group will commit a crime.

The debate on the connection between illegal immigration and crime is an important example. In February 2017, President Trump established the Victims of Immigration Crime Engagement (VOICE) office within the Department of Homeland Security. This office ostensibly set up to "serve the needs of crime victims and their families who have been affected by crimes committed by individuals with a nexus to immigration"[7] and reflected President Trump's concern about the prevalence of violent crime committed by illegal immigrants. For example, in a 2019 speech, Trump insisted that "in the last two years, ICE officers made 266,000 arrests of aliens with criminal records including those charged or convicted of 100,000 assaults, 30,000 sex crimes, and 4,000 violent killings."[8] He used these statistics to bolster his subsequent claim that "over the years, thousands of Americans have been brutally killed by those who illegally entered our country and thousands more lives will be lost if we don't act right now." Many Americans seemed to agree with him: a 2019 Quinnipiac poll found that nearly 30 percent of Americans believed that undocumented immigrants were more likely to commit crimes than citizens.[9] However, the claim was simply not true: immigrants, illegal or otherwise, commit crimes at *lower rates* than citizens.[10] Why then do so many citizens, along with President Trump, believe illegal immigrants present such a high crime risk?

Many may be making a classic inferential error in interpreting probabilities. Essentially, they look at these raw crime numbers cited by Trump and, because they seem large, assume that illegal immigrants must be committing a large share of total crime. The problem with this assumption is that, in order to actually assess whether illegal immigrants are more likely to commit crimes than citizens, you need to compare the ratio of immigrants who commit violent crimes to the ratio of *non*-immigrants who do. Using data only on crimes committed *by immigrants* in order to assess the likelihood that someone will commit a crime leaves out a crucial piece of information – the likelihood that a non-immigrant will commit a crime. So, while stereotypes are a way for people to make quick assessments about another individual with minimal effort, stereotyping is, unfortunately, often wrong, not just from a moral standpoint, but a factual one, and can destroy relationships and compromises that might otherwise have produced substantial future benefits.

Many other common heuristics and biases can also have large political consequences. For example, negotiations are often characterized by the *reactive devaluation* bias (Maoz et al. 2002), whereby a preferred proposal is devalued simply because it gets proposed by an adversary.[11] This bias occurs when people use the following heuristic: since my enemy does not want what is best for me, any offer they make must not be in my best interest, even if I would have made that choice prior to the bargaining session. This heuristic also induces bias, however, in circumstances when enemies in fact share an interest in making peace, and their offers genuinely reflect those interests. It is easy to see how a bias that leads people to reject desirable offers can undermine their welfare. In one study, for example, researchers found that Israeli Jews devalued an Israeli-authored peace plan when they thought it was authored by Palestinians, even though the proposal offered the exact same compromises (Maoz et al. 2002). Such a bias makes reaching international agreement much more challenging.

Another important bias is the *fundamental attribution error*, caused when individuals rely on a heuristic that attributes others' negative actions to stable personality characteristics rather than to situational constraints, but their own negative actions to the specifics of the situation (Jones & Harris 1967). When someone cuts us off in traffic, our first reaction is to conclude that the other driver is rude, inconsiderate, and impatient by nature rather than that they were forced to do so by some external factor: What if they were rushing to the hospital, for example, to see a dying family member? However, when *we* cut someone off in traffic, it is because we had a very good reason to do so and therefore our behavior does not reveal a flaw in our character! In politics, this bias means that leaders are likely to systematically underestimate the situational constraints impacting others. For example, during the Cold War, leaders in the United States and the USSR deemed the other side's military and diplomatic maneuvers as evidence of aggression rather than as a result of internal electoral calculations or bureaucratic constraints (or even as a response to their own previous behavior toward the adversary).

In the years leading up to the 2003 Iraq War, for example, something similar occurred in the US government's assessment of Saddam Hussein's intentions. Saddam's refusal to openly state that he did not possess weapons of mass destruction (WMDs) or to provide full transparency to international inspectors led the Bush administration to conclude that Saddam most likely *did* possess WMDs and had malign intentions regarding what to do with them. However, after the US invasion it was discovered that Saddam did not in fact possess WMDs. This left a puzzle – why wouldn't he have just admitted that Iraq did not have WMDs to avoid a US invasion? The answer was likely Iraq's ongoing tensions with neighbor Iran – if Saddam had publicly admitted that he had given up his WMDs, it would have left his regime vulnerable to aggression from their hostile neighbor and the West by insinuating weakness. In short, Saddam faced situational constraints that led him to act as if he *did* possess weapons of mass destruction, making his intentions toward the United States appear more aggressive than they likely were. This tendency to attribute the negative behavior of others to internal characteristics rather than situational constraints can cause leaders to adopt more hawkish policy stances than they otherwise might (Kahneman & Renshon 2007).

Cognitive biases may also play a role in helping states achieve "strategic surprise" at the outset of a war or conflict. John Lewis Gaddis (2002) defines a surprise strategy as one in which "force is used in an unexpected way at an unexpected time against an unexpected target, with a view to trying to achieve what more conventional methods of warfare cannot." Numerous historical and contemporary cases of strategic surprise are a by-product of miscalculations, errors in judgment, and cognitive biases in decision-making. Uri Bar-Joseph and Jack Levy (2009), for example, have identified and discussed some of the biases and factors that can lead to strategic surprises. They focus on having "too much information" that can shape the decision on the one hand, and "not enough information" on the other hand as playing a role in a surprise, as well as strategic deception, motivated and unmotivated biases, small group dynamics, and organizational behavior in explaining historical surprises such as Barbarossa, the Arab-Israeli Yom Kippur War of 1973, the October 2002 US national intelligence estimate, and Operation Iraqi Freedom. According to Gaddis (2002), errors and biases such as the assumption of incapability on the part of a rival led to a discount of probability in the strategic surprises at Pearl Harbor and in 9/11. According to Janis (1982), groupthink (see Chapter 5) was responsible for some of these fiascos. Mintz and Wayne (2016) have shown that polythink, another important group dynamic, affected some pre-9/11 decisions (see Chapter 5). By departing from the unitary actor assumption (e.g., that the state acts *as if* it were one individual) and the maximizing principles of rational choice, BPS can provide a more complete explanation of strategic surprise, thus contributing to a better understanding of this important phenomenon.

Errors in judgment may also be caused by another cognitive bias labeled *optimistic overconfidence*. Individuals are often overconfident in their own abilities, prospects and control over their future (Kahneman & Renshon 2007; Taylor & Brown 1988). For example, knowing that 50 percent of marriages in the United States end in divorce, each of us should know that – all else equal – our chance of getting divorced is approximately 50%. However, most newlyweds believe that *their* odds of getting divorced are much lower. This false optimism impacts several different kinds of judgments: individuals overestimate the amount of control they have to affect outcomes in their own lives (*illusion of control*); ignore contrary evidence or negative consequences (*wishful thinking*), are excessively confident that they know the truth (*overprecision, false estimation of confidence intervals*), and assume they are "better than average" on a host of dimensions (*better-than-average effect*).

In politics, overconfidence manifests in many ways. For example, during the 2016 presidential campaign, there was optimistic overconfidence among Hillary Clinton's supporters that she would win the election. This widespread bias was fueled by public opinion polls that consistently placed her probability of victory above 75%. On the one hand, the polls underestimated Trump support, potentially due to nonresponse bias whereby Trump supporters were more likely to ignore pollsters or to lie about their voting preferences.[12] However, even when the polls were *not* that far off – for example, the 538 poll aggregator site estimated that Trump had at least a 30 percent likelihood of victory – people seemed to erroneously assume that, because all the polls gave Trump a lower chance than Clinton that meant that Trump had *no* chance. In other words, "people [mistook] having a large volume of polling data for eliminating uncertainty."[13] One consequence of this overconfidence among Clinton supporters may have been at least marginally lower turnout among Democratic voters in the swing states where she was expected to win comfortably. These differential mobilization rates among Democratic and Republican voters may have been enough to turn the tide for Trump.

In the realm of national security decision-making, foreign policy-making, and crisis diplomacy, the optimistic overconfidence bias could potentially have devastating consequences, leading rival states into war and bloodshed. Indeed, many of the cognitive biases researchers have identified likely lead political elites to behave in a more *hawkish* way toward foreign adversaries than they otherwise might, increasing the risk of conflict. Kahneman and Renshon (2007) catalogued a list of cognitive biases discovered in forty years of psychological research and found that nearly all of them would be likely to favor a more hawkish perspective "than an objective observer would deem appropriate" on issues of war and peace (Kahneman & Renshon 2007, p. 79). Negative emotions such as anger or fear (see Chapter 6) may further exacerbate these biases, increasing views of the adversary as hostile, for example, or prematurely rejecting peace overtures as insincere or misinterpreting ambiguous actions as aggressive and threatening. Table 3.1 summarizes some of these biases, explaining the specific ways in which they may increase the likelihood and severity of international conflict.

Examples of these biases in war-and-peace decisions abound. Rival states on the brink of war have been shown to commonly make "estimates of their chances of winning sum[ming] to more than 100 percent – for example, both think they have more than a 50 percent chance of winning" (Johnson 2009, p. 4). This overconfidence means that

TABLE 3.1 *List of hawkish biases identified in foreign policy decision-making*

Bias	Primary Effect in Conflict Situations
Positive Illusions	Biased overconfidence raises the probability of violent conflict occurring and of deadlock in negotiations (when the parties overestimate their bargaining position or ability)
FAE	Perceive hostile actions of adversaries as due to unchanging, dispositional factors and discount the role of contextual factors; neglect the effects of one's own hostility on the behavior of adversaries
Illusion of Transparency	Ignore how one's actions are likely to be perceived by others, resulting in behavior that is likely to provoke aggression or hostility
Endowment Effect/Loss Aversion	Induces an aversion to making concessions and a reluctance to accept objectively "fair" exchanges
Risk Seeking in Losses	Reluctance to settle, prolongation of conflict
Pseudo-Certainty	Lowers probability of concessions if there is a potential that those concessions might advantage an opponent in a possible future conflict and concurrently raises the probability of conflict occurring by adopting a worst-case scenario of the other's intentions
Reactive Devaluation	Unconscious devaluation of offers, concessions or plans suggested by rivals or adversaries makes it difficult to reach agreement

Source: Renshon & Kahneman (2017).

leaders *overestimate* their odds of military victory, which, in turn, can lead them to prematurely end bargaining and launch a preemptive military strike against their adversary (Johnson 2009). If both sides are overconfident, this problem becomes further compounded. Interestingly, "mutual optimism" is actually an oft-cited RCT explanation for war. According to RCT models, mutual optimism causes war by leading rational state leaders to deliberately risk war in order to either reveal one's credibility (e.g., a costly signal) or obtain better peace terms (e.g., the risk-return tradeoff) (Slantchev & Tarar 2011). However, these models do not interrogate where the incorrect beliefs originate – why are *both* states confident about their prospect of victory when, by definition, only one state can be correct in that assessment? BPS researchers argue that the origin of this overconfidence is a product of biases stemming from limitations in human information processing.

Biases do not only affect the decision to *start* a conflict; they persist during and after conflict as well. For example, once leaders start a war, they often find it difficult to end, even when it is going poorly. This is partially due to a *sensitivity to sunk costs bias*, whereby individuals rationalize subsequent decisions based on costs already paid. This can increase the *path dependence* of policy-making (e.g., the dependence of future decisions on past decisions and action). No future action can recover the costs in human lives or time spent. However, individuals do in fact seem to consider these costs in their decision-making, assessing them as "wasteful" if they do not accomplish the original objective. Waiting in a long line can have this quality. After thirty minutes of waiting to purchase an item at a store, you may feel it is not really worth any additional wait time, however, you reason, "I might as well wait longer because I have already waited this long – if I don't, all of that previous time will have been wasted." That decision would be inherently irrational; the time has been wasted regardless of whichever future action is taken. This example is innocuous, but, in politics, the costs are often far higher. For example, President Johnson insisted on continuing the escalation of the Vietnam War through 1967, despite the growing signs that the invasion was unlikely to be successful. His decision is often attributed to a sunk cost bias – if the United States had pulled out and accepted defeat, then what did the deaths of some 8,400 US serviceman between 1957–1966 mean? They would have been lost "in vain." Ultimately, the United States did pull out of Vietnam in 1975, after more than 48,000 additional US soldiers and many more Vietnamese were killed.[14] Clearly, sensitivity to sunk costs can have enormous political – and human – consequences.

People are also subject to a bias known as *naïve realism*. This is the belief that we perceive reality objectively, but anyone who disagrees with us is uninformed, biased, or irrational (Ward et al. 1997). This is also referred to as the *blind spot bias*, that is, recognizing biases in others, but not in oneself (Pronin, Gilovich & Ross 2004). One example is the well-known tendency of Democrats and Republicans in the United States is to assume members of the other party simply do not understand policies well enough to pick the candidate that is best for the country or even for themselves. This was evident in the 2016 and 2020 campaigns on both sides, with some Democrats seemed especially prone to imply those white working-class voters who would vote for Trump were ignorant and "voting against their interests."[15] This tendency to write off the views of others as misinformed can stifle otherwise productive conversations about politics between citizens and may reduce the space for compromise among political elites, contributing to political polarization. Naïve realism can also lead to *confirmation bias*, whereby individuals seek out evidence that confirms their pre-existing views but reject evidence that potentially disconfirms them (see Chapter 8).

Of course, these are not the only cognitive biases that have important consequences for political phenomena. Other biases include things like frame blindness, shooting from the hip, preference over preference, and plunging in, to name a few. *Frame blindness* is defined as "setting out to solve the wrong problem because your framework causes you to overlook attractive options or lose sight of important objectives" (Forman & Selly 2001, p. 4). *Shooting from the hip* is defined as "trying to keep straight in your head all the information relating to the decision rather than relying on a systematic procedure" (p. 4). *Preference over preference* occurs when the decision-maker has a clear preference for a course of action that affects his reasoning regarding choices.[16] *Plunging in* refers to when people rush to make decisions without fully considering their goals in advance (p. 4). Trump's ban on immigration from seven Muslim majority countries, issued just days after he took office, is one example of plunging in. The directive was issued with little consideration of the potential legal challenges to the ban at both the state and federal level. Consequentially, the policy was blocked by the courts, causing chaos and confusion in airports around the country. A newly formulated ban was then introduced to get around the court's concerns, although it too was blocked shortly thereafter.

The prevalence of these and other biases among both average citizens and political elites causes important problems for major theories of international relations that depend on the mutual, rational assessment of the costs and benefits of conflict by adversarial states. Deterrence theory is an important example. As former National Security Advisor Henry Kissinger pointed out in the 1950s, the very concept of deterrence is as much a psychological phenomenon as it is a military-strategic one, because its basic logic requires preventing actions "through fear of punishment or retribution" (Mearsheimer 2017). In short, deterrence works when an adversary believes that, if they pursue a certain course of action, the punishment they receive will outweigh the benefit.[17] As such, their fear of reprisal would lead them *not* to take the action. However, because deterrence is fundamentally about *beliefs*, perceptions and misperceptions of intentions and capabilities, miscalculations, biases in evaluation, emotions, and the way situations are framed to policy-makers can all affect success or failure. Indeed, misperceptions regarding an adversary's intentions is one of the central mechanisms behind *spiral theories of deterrence*: states seeking to maintain their own security may *seem* like they are in fact aggressive, meaning that leaders will incorrectly assume opponents with "status quo" preferences are aggressively expansionist, leading to a spiral of arms building and threats that increasingly risks a catastrophic conflict (Goldgeier & Tetlock 2001; Jervis 1976).

Thus, Robert Jervis (1976) and other pioneering BPS researchers recognized that while international anarchy may create the security dilemma – that, because there is no international army to forcibly maintain order,[18] every state is fundamentally insecure – biases in how leaders process information to determine adversary intentions make this situation even *worse*. In short, individuals, including state leaders, will tend to process information in a "top-down" fashion, whereby, rather than information affecting their beliefs, their beliefs will affect how they view information. This means that, "once a person develops an image of the other – especially a hostile image of the other – ambiguous and discrepant information will be assimilated to that image" (Jervis 1976, p. 68). In this way, the specific image a leader assigns to another state – whether that of an enemy, ally, colony, and so on – will structure the foreign policy strategy a leader chooses in dealing with that state (Hermann & Fischerkeller 1995) and this image will be incredibly resistant to change (Jervis 1976). Research on the psychological foundations of deterrence thus demonstrates how the BPS approach can *augment* rational choice approaches to understanding how deterrence works – the strategic dilemma created by anarchy is still central and incentives to preserve reputations for resolve still exist, but psychological biases in information processing make these challenges *more difficult*, rendering deterrence less stable and more prone to escalatory spirals than it otherwise might be. Modifying rational choice models with more accurate assumptions about the limits and biases inherent in human psychology can thus help explain deterrence success and failure better than by using RCT models alone.

THE KENNEDY–NIXON DEBATE

Biases and heuristics play a central role in domestic politics and elections as well. One oft-cited example of the power of visual versus verbal information to alter the perceived character and competence of a candidate comes from the 1960 presidential campaign. This is often called the *halo effect* or *physical attractiveness stereotype*, whereby people assume that physically attractive individuals are more likely to have other socially desirable traits (such as intelligence, competence, courage, etc.). When Richard Nixon debated John F. Kennedy in the late stages of the campaign, Nixon was reportedly suffering from an illness and refused to allow makeup artists to do their normal pre-television preparation for on-air personalities. During the debate, Nixon was visibly uncomfortable, sweating, and less composed than he would normally have been. In surveys following the debate, television viewers evaluated Nixon more negatively, claiming he was untrustworthy (Kraus 1996). Radio listeners felt very differently, believing he had won the debate on substantive policy grounds. The visual cues that night, having very little to do with Nixon's underlying character or intentions, led some to discount the hard policy distinctions revealed by the candidates during the debate. The distinct power of visual versus audio cues is one example of the power of *thin slicing* (Ambady & Rosenthal 1992), the human brain's bias to quickly elaborate up from very scant pieces of information in the environment to make important political decisions. This tendency might obviously have quite devastating consequences for democratic citizens to elect those best able to represent them. These effects may even mean we can simply be tricked by attractiveness or other irrelevant characteristics. And indeed, a host of experimental work in the years since the Nixon–Kennedy debate has demonstrated the power of visual cues (such as attractiveness) to alter attitudes toward political candidates (see, e.g., Todorov et al. 2005).

THE PENTAGON COGNITIVE BIASES STUDY

Another example of biases affecting decision-making was reported in a 2006 study of Pentagon officials and high-ranking military officers on which technologies to adopt in order to combat terrorism.[19] Conducted at the National Defense University of the United States, with respect to how to best combat terrorism, the study demonstrated the widespread existence of cognitive biases even among top military brass. The study presented officers with a decision problem and scenario that required them to select among four counter-terrorism measures:[20]

1. Border Crossing Sensors: Introduce environmental monitors that can trace whether chemical or biological weapons have been set off. Using EPA monitoring stations, these monitors sample the air for traces of chemical and biological toxins.
2. Environmental Monitors: Introduce sensors that can be used at border crossings in order to detect whether terrorists are attempting to smuggle chemical or biological weapons into the country.
3. Local Emergency Responders: Provide local emergency responders with radio-logical detection equipment.
4. Do Nothing: Decide not to proceed with implementing any particular system at this time.

The study, by Mintz et al. (2006) which utilized the Decision Board information board simulator for tracing cognitive processes of decision-making (Mintz et al. 1997), showed that officers had a "preference over preference" bias – where a decision-maker has a clear ex ante preference for one potential option, regardless of its relative utility – for "Doing Something" as a compared to the "Do Nothing option." As a result, they "locked in" on a certain alternative (e.g., border sensors) before they even accessed critical information about the option which they had ex ante decided against (Do Nothing), and evaluated the financial consequences of their decision less than the military and political consequences of their decision. The study also showed, consistent with the Bounded Rationality/heuristics school, that officers accessed only part of the information en route to their final decision (Mintz, Redd & Vedlitz 2006). In other words, officers typically preferred to do something, even if that was costlier than doing nothing, and, once they had chosen an option (often without accessing all relevant information), they became convinced that choice was optimal, even in the face of new information that suggested it may not have been. The officers were not maximizing utility. They did not select the alternative which had the highest net gain (i.e., the alternative with the highest total benefit minus total costs), which would have been Do Nothing in this case. Instead, most were clearly employing a "satisficing" strategy which was consistent with the predictions of the BPS approach.

MENTAL ACCOUNTING IN POLITICS

Mental accounting is another kind of cognitive bias. It occurs when people think of money differently depending on where it came from or what it is allocated for (Thaler 2008). What we know about this bias comes mostly from a field called Behavioral Finance, but it carries substantial implications for politics. The model focuses "on the mental coding of combinations of gains and losses using the prospect theory value function" (Thaler 1999).[21] There are three interrelated components to mental accounting. As described by Kivetz (1999, p. 250):

The first component captures how outcomes are framed and experienced. For instance, compared to money earned through hard work, an equivalent amount that is won in a lottery may be perceived as unexpected, less serious, and valueless (e.g., O'Curry 1999). The second component of mental accounting involves the assignment of activities to mental accounts. Specifically, consumers tend to label both resources and consumption, and group them into accounts such as regular income versus windfall gains and necessary consumption (e.g., paying utility bills) versus hedonic (e.g., a cruise vacation). Moreover, consumers have systematic preferences for matching certain mental accounts, such as when they prefer to pay for luxurious consumption with "windfall gains" (e.g., Thaler 1985). Finally, the third component concerns the frequency with which mental accounts are evaluated (e.g., daily, weekly, yearly) and whether they are defined narrowly or broadly. This might suggest, for example, that consumers who "balance" their accounts every week, as opposed to once a month, are more likely to spend lottery winnings on luxuries during the same week the money was won than a week later.

Voters and leaders alike use this type of mental arithmetic. They code gains and losses separately, placing them in different mental "accounts." Thaler (1985, 2008) explains that segregation and integration of gains and losses "can be performed in four ways: (a) segregate gains, (b) integrate losses, (c) cancel losses against larger gains, (d) segregate 'silver linings.'" In politics, voters may approve or disapprove separately how the president is handing the COVID-19 pandemic, the economy, foreign affairs vis-à-vis China or Russia, and so on. They then often aggregate these different dimensions into a general approval rating by placing much different weights on different achievements. Leaders may do the same thing. In other words, leaders do not frame their achievement as a whole, but keep separate "central accounts," one for achievements concerning the economy, another for achievements concerning foreign policy, etc. In turn, these accounts are aggregated via the currency of public approval.

THE 2016 REPUBLICAN PRIMARIES AS A CASE STUDY OF SATISFICING DECISION RULES

As we describe previously, heuristics are often used by citizens in deciding whom to vote for in democratic elections. These heuristics are often caused by decision rules that are "non-holistic" – decision-making processes that do not consider all the relevant information and dimensions of a given choice. The 2016 US Republican primaries provide a good example of how these decision rules can work in practice.

Seventeen candidates competed for the GOP nomination in the primaries of 2016. It is reasonable to assume that most voters could not have examined the complete policy positions, records, ideology, and personalities of each contender. Instead, most voters likely used heuristics to make their choice, evaluating the candidates based on several decision criteria, including dimensions such as: ideology, ability to handle the economy, ability to create jobs and bring jobs back to the United States, issue areas such as immigration or terrorism, and general election electability. In analyzing voter strategies for making their decision in 2016, we examine potential decision rules that rely on the many heuristics described above. The presence of a massive primary field for president was, of course, repeated four years later on the Democratic side, leading to similar decision-making dynamics for voters in that primary contest.

Maximizing vs. Satisficing

As pointed out in Chapter 2, rational decision makers attempt to *maximize* their total benefits minus their total costs, thereby selecting the alternative that has the highest net gain. However, individuals do not always reach this maximizing ideal and instead, frequently utilize a *satisficing decision rule* in which they search only until they find an alternative that is "good enough," but not necessarily best. Since information costs are high, decision makers evaluate the possible alternatives and accept the first one that meets a certain minimum threshold. This strategy is much less cognitively demanding than the "fully rational" version of utility maximization.

For example, according to the maximizing decision rule, those who chose Donald Trump did so because he scored the highest combined score on most or all possible evaluative dimensions (economy, jobs, immigration, counterterrorism), compared to other candidates. In other words, Trump's aggregate score – electability, the economy, jobs, ideology, foreign policy – was higher than the corresponding score of any other GOP candidate participating in these primaries, despite the fact that he may have had relatively lower scores on other important dimensions (such as political decorum). As we noted, this very broad and encompassing form of utility maximization is not that common, given the cognitive constraints of most citizens.

According to a satisficing decision rule, on the other hand, a voter will support a candidate who is simply "good enough" but not necessarily "the best." Thus, in the 2016 GOP primaries example, Donald Trump may simply have been the candidate who was acceptable on a few attributes that were easy to see, even if he fell short on others. He emphasized themes that were highly salient and appealing to the conservative primary electorate: immigration restriction, curtailing trade agreements with countries that he deemed unfair to the United States, and continuing to fight terrorism abroad. These policies all had a simple thread in common: They appealed to citizens who felt they, and therefore "America," were being taken advantage of.

Trump's simple, symbolic solution to the nation's problems in 2016 was to Make America Great *Again* (emphasis ours). The policy proposals ultimately springing from this particular rhetoric – building a wall on the US-Mexico border, imposing a temporary ban on immigration from many Muslim-majority countries, enacting harsher detention policies at the southern border that led to separations of families – would have little impact on the daily lives of his most ardent supporters. Nonetheless, it appealed to their sense of group-based grievance, and by dominating the Republican primary field on this dimension he was hugely successful among rank and file Republican primary voters. This focus on a limited range of information to make a decision is referred to as a non-holistic search.

Non-Holistic Search

Satisficing decision rules are often consistent with a *non-holistic search*. Significant cognitive limitations affect the search for information by individuals (voters, leaders, bureaucrats, protesters, etc.). Holistic searching involves a review of *all* the relevant information for deciding on a course of action – all potential alternatives, dimensions of the decision, potential implications of the decision, and the weights (i.e., importance level) assigned to each cost-benefit trade-off associated with the decision. This process is very thorough, but also very costly (in terms of time and effort). Thus, frequently, individuals resort to a non-holistic search. When utilizing a non-holistic search, the decision-maker instead reviews, consistent with bounded rationality, only part of the information, using the minimal amount of information they deem necessary to make an educated choice. Thus, citizens utilizing non-holistic searches – a much more common form of decision-making, particularly in voting and elections, than holistic searches – often rely on the use of such rules of thumb, and other simplifying cognitive shortcuts that enable them to make a decision without accessing and evaluating all the potential information related to the decision. In other words, voters will often engage in a trade-off of speed versus accuracy. In presidential campaigns supporters of either candidate typically focus on a few prominent reasons to vote for either of them, rather than on the entire range of issues and opinions.

Order-Sensitive vs. Order-Insensitive Search

From a traditional, rational choice perspective, the order of information presented or processed should not affect the choice. This is known as the *invariance assumption*. However, research in BPS has shown that the sequence (the order of presentation or accessing of information) can be incredibly important in shaping people's decisions. Both the sequence of dimensions and the order of potential alternatives affect our decisions (Redd 2002). Because individuals frequently do not engage in complete information search, their choice may depend critically on where in the set they started their review.[22] If you are buying a used car and only have time to compare deals at five dealerships, the price at the sixth will not enter into your decision calculus, even if it would have been the best buy. In the presidential campaign of 2016, many candidates may have been viable if the Republican electorate had been able to consider their platforms carefully. The fact that the field was so large, however, meant that voters could not even see them all on the same debate stage. Those relegated to lower status news events would have had even less opportunity to make the cut of those considered by citizens with limited time and cognitive energy. The Democratic Party surely noticed this, and many believe their own winnowing process in 2020, which began with well over twenty candidates, also suffered from this problem.

Alternative-Based vs. Dimension-Based Search

The way information is presented and accessed also affects individual (and group) choices. Decision-makers can base their search for information on either alternatives (the different potential choices), or on dimensions (the different components of each alternative). For example, an alternative-based search for political candidates would begin with an evaluation of a given candidate on dimensions before moving on to the next candidate. In contrast, a dimension-based search would evaluate candidates on a single dimension – say, ideology – before proceeding to the next dimension – say, job creation.

Note that if citizens were fully rational, the result of these two strategies would be identical: You would either sum a candidate's scores for each dimension or sum the dimension scores for each candidate, with the same aggregate outcome emerging either way. However, it is easy to see how satisficing could profoundly change outcomes depending on whether people compare across dimensions or across entire choice options. Imagine one Republican voter in 2016 engaged in a dimension-based search. They might compare all candidates first according to who would best address immigration, then trade, and then job creation.

Now imagine a second voter using an alternative-based search. This voter would sum scores on a long list of dimensions for the first candidate before moving on to the second. In this process, lower-salience candidates would be unlikely to make the cut, simply because the voter never got to that candidate to see where they stood. In this process, candidates with lower name recognition or less financial support would be severely disadvantaged. In either case, the information that the voter could use is *available*, but the total amount of information they are willing to consider is constrained. Depending on the type of search process they use, the outcome could be very different. Understanding the dominant search process utilized by cognitive satisficers is an important avenue of research for both BPS and RCT scholars.

Compensatory vs. Non-Compensatory Patterns

A decision-making model can also be either *compensatory* or *non-compensatory*. In the traditional *compensatory* model, a low score on one dimension of an alternative can be compensated for by a high score on another dimension. This is a common assumption in traditional RCT where the best choice is the one that produces the highest net score. For example, if a Republican voter in 2016 were interested in the candidacy of Jeb Bush, a lower score on his expressed view on immigration may be compensated for with a high score on his experience in office.

In contrast, a *non-compensatory* search means that if an alternative has a low score on one dimension, then no other score along another dimension/s can compensate. For example, if Jeb Bush were seen as weak on immigration in 2016, many conservative voters might have decided he was simply unqualified for president based on that one dimension, despite his experience in office relative to Trump, and/or despite positive scores on other dimensions. The non-compensatory approach is non-additive and relies on cognitive shortcuts or heuristics, because not all information will be reviewed. The non-compensatory model is also dimension-based. The decision-making process is simplified as decision-makers eliminate alternatives that do not meet a certain threshold using one, or a few, criteria.

Non-compensatory models are typically non-holistic and satisficing, in that not all alternatives will be considered before an acceptable solution is found. It has been suggested that non-compensatory, rather than compensatory models, are used when the decision is more complex or complicated because they are simply cognitively easier for decision-makers to deal with (Brannick & Brannick 1989; Einhorn 1970, 1971; Johnson & Meyer 1984; Payne 1976). The idea behind the non-compensatory model is to quickly eliminate alternatives and simplify the information search and evaluation phases of the decision process (Payne 1976, 384; Payne, Bettman & Johnson 1988, 534). This process of eliminating options quickly based on a non-compensatory process can utilize several different decision rules.

These satisficing methods of information processing – non-holistic search, order dependent information acquisition, dimension-based processing, and non-compensatory rules – profoundly alter decision-making. demonstrating the large role information processing routines can have on political outcomes, including elections. So how do individuals make decisions in the face of these constraints? In the following, we review some specific voting rules that follow a basic logic of cognitive satisficing and apply them to the 2016 Republican primary.

HEURISTIC VOTING RULES

Lexicographic Voting Rule

According to the lexicographic decision rule (Payne, Bettman & Johnson 1988), voters will select among the candidates based solely on the dimension (criterion) *most important to them*. Low or high scores on other dimensions will not affect the ultimate decision. For example, in the 2016 GOP primaries, voters who were primarily concerned with reversing a faltering economy might have selected Trump because of his success in business. Others who were most concerned with electability might have voted for Jeb Bush, because he was well-known and had won several elections before. In contrast, voters who selected conservative ideology as the dimension they were going to base their decision on might have voted for Gingrich or Rubio, who scored much higher on that dimension than Trump. Importantly, for both types of voters, the candidate's low or high scores on other, less important dimensions would be *irrelevant* to their ultimate choice. Thus, the lexicographic voting rule is an example of dimension-based thinking, non-holistic search, and non-compensatory patterns of decision-making.

Elimination by Aspects (EBA) Voting Rule

According to the EBA decision rule (Tversky 1972), voters will eliminate alternatives *sequentially* based on dimensions they judge to be important, in a descending order. High scores on one key dimension are very important, but scores on other dimensions will factor in as well. Rather than just voting based on who has the highest score on the most critical dimension (as in lexicographic voting), voters will first eliminate only those that have an unacceptable score on their critical dimension. Then, voters will proceed down the list of dimensions, eliminating other candidates that have negative scores on secondary key dimensions. Thus, if they rank conservative ideology as most important, followed by immigration, and then electability, they will first eliminate candidates from consideration if they are not conservative enough, then they will remove from consideration candidates who they believe are soft on immigration, and then candidates who are unlikely to defeat the Democratic nominee in the general election.

Consider the following example, based on the 2016 GOP primaries: Voters did not select Ron Paul because of his large "deviation" from traditional conservative ideology. They removed Gingrich from consideration as they sensed he could not win the general election. Voters may have ended up voting for Trump based on this elimination voting rule, despite their concerns about his personal behavior toward women, because that was not one of the most important dimensions of their vote choice. Other voters may have had different preference orderings over the dimensions. For example, voters who ranked conservative ideology first, then electability would have eliminated Trump from consideration, as they did not like his position on a host of conservative issues, and then Gingrich, based on his low chances of electability. These voters would most likely have chosen Jeb Bush or Marco Rubio. As such, the EBA rule is also an important example of how decision-making can be altered by these bounded rationality information processing patterns and sequences.

Conjunctive Voting Rule (CON)

Under the CON decision rule, the decision-maker sets a minimum acceptable value for each dimension of the decision. An alternative is rejected if it fails to exceed any minimum value, even if its overall sum is highest. The conjunctive decision rule is different from the lexicographic or disjunctive one, as it requires the alternative to be above a minimum value on *all* dimensions, not just the most important one.

Thus, in the 2016 GOP primaries example, for a candidate to be acceptable, based on the conjunctive voting rule, he or she needed to be acceptable above a minimum value on all dimensions (for example, conservative ideology, ability to handle the economy, create jobs, have a good chance to defeat Hillary Clinton, and so on). A candidate that did not receive a high enough score on any of these dimensions was eliminated from the choice set.

Poliheuristic Voting Rule

According to the poliheuristic two-step voting decision rule (see Chapter 5), voters first eliminate alternatives (candidates) from consideration based on a non-compensatory rule and then select among remaining candidates based on a maximizing decision rule. In other words, political candidates are first considered on a crucial, non-compromising dimension, for example, likelihood to beat their political opponent in the general election. If a candidate scores negatively on this dimension, s/he will be automatically discarded based on this rule, even if, in all other respects (dimensions), this candidate scores very highly. After this first stage, the different choices will then be evaluated based on a more traditional utility-maximizing strategy or a lexicographic choice.

In the 2016 GOP primaries, many GOP voters may not have considered Paul, Walker, Graham, and Jindal (for example) as being able to win the national election. They were "removed" from consideration. In the second phase, voters selected among the remaining candidates based on their ideology, ability to handle the economy, and other remaining criteria of importance. Other voters who felt that Washington outsider was a non-compensatory dimension would have immediately eliminated candidates that served in the US capital, and then chose one of the remaining options. Perceived electability as a non-compensatory dimension for some voters re-emerged as an important issue in the 2020 Democratic primary, with Joe Biden as the primary beneficiary of this heuristic. Poliheuristic theory thus demonstrates the critical importance of non-compensatory patterns of thinking in impacting political preferences.

CONCLUSION

In this chapter, we discussed the bounded rationality approach to decision-making and introduced the idea of heuristic thinking and processing, explaining how this type of information processing can lead to biases and errors in political decision-making. We illustrated these concepts and theories using several examples and case studies from domestic and international politics, including the Kennedy–Nixon debate and the Pentagon cognitive biases study. Finally, we discussed various voting rules and illustrated how these different rules, all of which are examples of satisficing rather than maximizing decision-making, can shape the choice of a candidate, as was evident in the 2016 and 2020 elections. These concepts, models and examples demonstrate significant deviations from rational choice predictions and explanations regarding the process by which individuals make political decisions. In particular, theories of bounded rationality and use of heuristics fundamentally question the *ability* of individuals to process information in ways that maximize their utility.

Our understanding of the use and influence of heuristics in all sorts of political decisions thus challenges aspects of RCT predictions regarding individual reasoning and learning. Importantly, however, heuristic processing also leads to a predictable set of biases that can be incorporated into decision-making models to better explain and predict political outcomes. Namely, many biases, including those described in this chapter, tend to lead individuals to be *less* trusting of out-groups and *more* hawkish in conflict settings than they otherwise might be (Kahneman & Renshon 2007). Incorporating this distrust or hawkishness into formal (or informal) models of intergroup conflict could yield important insights on human behavior. For instance, one might observe different outcomes if individuals assign different probabilities to the likelihood that an in- versus out-group member carries through on a promise, or if past *negative* actions by an opponent are incorporated more readily into Bayesian updating than past *positive* actions. In voting too, the use of heuristic decision rules can help explain why citizens appear to possess non-transitive preferences: for example, some voters in Georgia in 2020 insisted their party should boycott the Senate runoff elections because state Republican officials had not allowed Trump to undermine the certification of Joe Biden's victory there, which would, of course, harm their preferred candidates. Citizens may not vote holistically, using a wide variety of ideological and policy preferences, but rather they could employ decision shortcuts focused on a single dimension (such as perceived likability). Incorporating BPS assumptions about decision-making ability into formal models of strategic choice can thus yield important dividends in our understanding of political outcomes.

4

What You Say May Matter Less Than How You Say It

The Role of Framing in Political Communication Effects

Since Aristotle, philosophers have discussed the powerful impact that elite rhetorical *frames* may have on the way publics react to and understand the political world. Aristotle's definition of framing, which he labeled *atechnoi*, involved the features of the situation outside of the speaker's control that might be invoked, challenged, or described in order to maximize persuasive power. When presenting a case to a jury, for example, it is up to the attorney to bring in facts in just the right order, each with the proper weight, to create a narrative most consistent with the interests of the client. The facts cannot be changed, and thus certainly constrain persuasive arguments, but they are by no means utterly binding and universally understood.

Marcus Tullius Cicero, a Roman politician and attorney, is widely recognized as a pioneer in the techniques of framing, which he developed into the theory of *statis*. The theory laid out several specific techniques for orators to present a set of facts in the way that would benefit them most. An example of such a technique is the redefinition of an event: "Yes, our country invaded yours, but not to forcibly acquire land. We only wanted to secure the (new) border from incursions by criminals from your side." Cicero's successful defense of murderers and villains in ancient Rome seemed to vindicate his theory of oratory based on framing, at least to many of his contemporaries.

Needless to say, political elites have been using rhetorical tactics that fall under the broad definition of framing to advance their positions since ancient times. Opponents and rivals then use counter-framing strategies to thwart such attempts. In campaigns and elections, political actors use a variety of framing tactics to get elected. In the international arena, leaders utilize these tools to mobilize public support for their policies, to market peace and war, to tarnish their rivals in the international system and to crush domestic opposition. The conviction that framing is a powerful persuasive tool for political elites in both democratic and non-democratic regimes is widely held and, in many ways, contradicts rational choice models of decision-making. Because frames do not change the underlying dimensions of a choice – the facts of the case – they should not affect our decisions, at least not according to RCT. Still, they often do and this sensitivity to framing is an important example extending our discussion of cognitive biases in Chapter 3. In the following pages, we define framing, explore the impact of framing on political decision-making, and discuss how its effects lead us to question basic assumptions in many rational choice models of behavior.

Framing has been defined in several ways by scholars in a variety of fields (see, e.g., Berinsky & Kinder 2006; Druckman 2001; Gamson & Modigliani 1987; Nelson, Clawson & Oxley 1997; Neuner 2018; Price & Tewksbury 1997). Specifically, several dimensions of information provision – the way elites raise and discuss important public affairs topics – have been shown to influence how individuals make decisions, and we will discuss many of those distinct framing dimensions in this chapter. The conceptual ambiguity associated with framing is not often viewed as a strength, since it leads one to wonder if there is any media effect that falls outside its boundaries. This unfortunate state of affairs led Entman (1993) to label framing a "fractured paradigm." Needless to say, this wide variety of definitions renders the framing concept a blunt tool at best for understanding political decision-making.

We will first discuss prospect theory, which provides an explanation for human decision-making that relies heavily on the framing concept in interaction with known limitations of human cognition. Next, we will review other major, but distinct, definitions of framing, and the psychological processes that are presumed to undergird each one. Researchers are still debating which definition of framing is correct, so we will describe the distinctions between these various definitions and provide real world political examples of framing effects that fall into each of these major categories that BPS scholars have considered. Finally, we will review what research tells us about the *limits* of framing: how powerful (or not) framing by political elites can be for altering public opinion about political issues.

PROSPECT THEORY AND THE FRAMING OF RISKY CHOICE

Prospect theory is one of the most influential BPS theories of decision-making, pioneered by psychologists Daniel Kahneman & Amos Tversky. In prospect theory, framing refers to the superficial features of a message that, critically, *do not change the fundamental argument in any substantive way*, but instead draw attention to different anchor points – the reference from which individuals start their deliberation about an issue (Kahneman & Tversky 1979, 1984). In particular, prospect theory focuses on the way a message might subtly shift the listener's focus from the realm of *losses* to that of *gains* or vice versa. When this sort of frame shifts, people's willingness to take risks dramatically changes. Further, as we will review in the following, this bias occurs *even when the two situations are substantively identical*, differing only in trivial ways in which the problem is being described. Prospect theory and its emphasis on the way people assess gains versus losses is one of the most important discoveries in psychology and Behavioral Economics and its application and extension to the political domain is one of the key contributions of BPS. Avoiding a loss, after all, can also be presented as a gain, depending on the reference point. One additional feature of this discussion to note is that prospect theory has led to the discovery of several additional cognitive biases of the sort we discussed in Chapter 3.

Prospect theory is one of the most important discoveries of several basic limitations of human mental processing and their effect on decision-making. It represents a serious challenge for traditional rational-choice approaches to understanding both elite and mass political behavior. Kahneman and Tversky (1979) demonstrated that very simple changes in a message can fundamentally alter individuals' decisions. Loss aversion is central to prospect theory, and in study after study, researchers have found that people typically weigh losses over two times more heavily than gains (Camerer 1995): the pain of losing $20 on the subway is greater than the pleasure of finding $40! Consequently, people take larger risks to avoid losses than they do to make equally sized gains.

This oversensitivity to losses relative to gains violates common assumptions in rational choice models that rely on expected utility theory (EUT).[1] For example, the *invariance assumption* insists that distinct but mathematically equivalent representations of the same choices should produce the same outcomes (Levy 1992). Relatedly, the *independence of irrelevant alternatives* states that the only factors that should influence a rational individual's choice between two options, say A and B, will be features of those two options. Introducing additional alternatives or information not directly relevant to the value of A or B should not matter, because they will not change the expected utilities of either choice. The logic goes as follows: According to EUT, people weigh what they think they will get from each possible choice and multiply that times the probability the particular outcome will occur. Then they add up all those quantities, from all the possible outcomes of each strategy, and choose the one with the highest value. According to EUT, a rational person would not change how much they value an outcome based on something so trivial as whether it is described as reducing a loss versus augmenting a gain (see Levy 1997 for an excellent review), since these two states of the world are identical. Why would it matter whether you thought of $20 as a rebate for a purchase you already made or a bonus toward a future purchase? It is the same amount of money in your pocket either way. In the real world, however, this simple framing manipulation influences people quite profoundly.

Let's review a more detailed example to see how it works. For example, imagine respondents must choose between a 95 percent chance of winning $10,000 (and a 5 percent chance of winning nothing) or a simple cash prize of $9,000. Which would you choose? According to Expected Utility theory, one should pick the option with a 95 percent chance of winning $10,000. Remember the expected value of a choice is the product of the outcome times its probability. Thus, the expected utility of the first option is higher (10,000 * 0.95 = 9,500) than the expected utility of the second option (9,000 * 1 = 9,000). However, prospect theory would predict that many people prefer the certain $9,000 to a 95 percent chance of winning $10,000. In contrast, when a choice is framed as a potential *loss* (rather than a potential gain), preferences shift dramatically. If given the choice between a 95 percent chance of *losing* $10,000 or a 100 percent chance of losing $9,000, prospect theory contends that more will seek to avoid the sure loss and thus choose the first option, even though they will, on average, lose more money than if they took the sure bet.

One explanation for loss aversion is called the *endowment effect*: people ascribe higher value to a given item *simply because they already possess it*. Another way to think of this is that "losses hurt more than equal gains please" (McDermott 2004). Because of this bias, simply changing the *reference point* that individuals use (e.g., the benchmark against which they evaluate an alternative) fundamentally alters their preference. The framing of choices, then, dramatically impacts the outcome any time an alternative can be thought of as either a loss or a gain. Figure 4.1 graphically depicts this phenomenon.

Applied to politics, loss aversion implies that people tend to be more cautious when they perceive the nation to be in a safe economic/social/military position with much to lose. On the other hand, they are more likely to take potentially large risks when they perceive the nation to be facing large economic/social/military losses (McDermott 2004). For example, the circumstances immediately following the attacks of

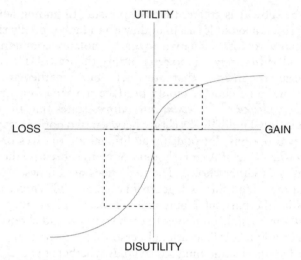

FIGURE 4.1 **Graphical depiction of prospect theory value function**
Prospect theory, introduced by Kahneman and Tversky (1979) discovered that, contrary to a core assumption of rational choice models, people are influenced by the domain they are in. The figure here describes the observed relationship between changes in perceived utility based on whether the identical outcome is framed as a loss or a gain. The perceived change in utility for an option framed as a gain (like saving more lives) is smaller than the change in utility for the same option framed as a loss (losing fewer lives). People are, in other words, more willing to take a risk in order to avoid a loss than they are to increase a gain of the same size.

September 11, 2001, were ripe for taking military risks. Many Americans believed their country was facing large losses from future terrorist attacks on a grand scale. President Bush and many others argued that something had to be done to prevent these losses, even if that something carried great risks for even more suffering. The costs of the actual policy choice, invading Afghanistan without a clear exit strategy in place and then attacking Iraq without firm evidence that Saddam Hussein was involved in the 9/11 attacks or that his regime possessed weapons of mass destruction, illustrates the profound effect of loss-aversion and risk-acceptance bias. From a leadership perspective, prospect theory implies that a leader will be inclined to take riskier measures to avoid a loss (of territory, lives, money, etc.) than they would be to make equally large potential gains. For example, Jimmy Carter's very risky, ultimately disastrous attempt to rescue American hostages held in Tehran for nearly a year right before the 1980 presidential election could be seen as risk-taking behavior to avoid a loss (McDermott 2004).

In contrast, President George H. W. Bush's decision not to march on to Baghdad following the easy defeat of Saddam Hussein's army in Kuwait during the 1991 Gulf War is a prime illustration of risk aversion in the domain of gain (McDermott 2004; Mintz and Geva 1997). According to this theory, President Bush Sr., who enjoyed an unprecedented 89 percent approval rating at the end of the Gulf War, was in the domain of gains and accordingly did not want to risk his popularity with a risky maneuver in Iraq. Contrast this with the situation his son, George W. Bush, found himself in after 9/11, after the loss of 3,000 lives and the destruction of iconic financial buildings and government structures. Though the objective military context was similar (e.g., US military superiority and a desire to overthrow Saddam Hussein's regime), the shift in the domain from gain to loss maps onto the distinct policy decisions that followed (e.g., the United States stopped short of removing Hussein in 1991, but then strove to do so in 2003, and was ultimately successful).

Prospect theory also suggests a variety of additional cognitive biases – *representativeness*, *availability*, and *anchoring* – that, once engaged by a message frame, affect decision-making. *Representativeness* is an error whereby individuals assume that the probability of an object or event belonging to a specific category is based on their similarity to other objects in that category, ignoring the "base rate likelihood" (Bar-Hillel 1980) of an event's occurrence. For example, if a student at a university is described as enjoying math and studying all the time, people may overestimate the likelihood that the student is an engineer, even if engineering students represent a very small percentage of students with such skills.

The implications of the representativeness bias for politics are very important (see Locksley, Hepburn & Ortiz 1982). Take, for example, the challenges inherent in counterinsurgency-style warfare. If a soldier in Iraq sees a bearded young man in traditional Islamic garb approaching him with his hands in his pockets, that soldier must quickly decide – is this a nonviolent civilian or an insurgent about to attack? The representativeness bias suggests that the soldier will overestimate the odds that the man is an insurgent based simply on how well the target seems to represent the negatively valenced group, *even if the actual percentage of insurgents in the area is very low* and there is no other *a priori* reason to assume the individual is engaged in terrorism. Similar challenges are present in domestic contexts, such as policing. Unfortunately, police are often more likely to view African-American men as threats, regardless of their actual behavior. The Black Lives Matter movement has evolved in large part as a reaction to the tragedies such problematic biases can cause. This tendency to ignore low base rates when presented with someone who otherwise seems to "represent" a category of people or actions can lead to negative consequences – including self-fulfilling processes that radicalize members of these communities and contribute to a vicious circle of brutality, popular uprisings, and recrimination.

The second cognitive bias identified in prospect theory, *availability*, relates to the presumed relative frequency individuals assign to events or objects. Namely, individuals are likely to assume that memorable events happen more frequently than non-memorable events, even though the latter category is much larger almost by definition as a result of the cognitive limitations of memory. So, for example, panic over the 2014 Ebola outbreak in West Africa triggered great concern among Americans about the possibility of the virus spreading to the United States. With the October 2014 report of an Ebola patient in Texas – and his subsequent transmission of the disease to at least two of his nurses – as many as four in ten Americans reported being "very" or "somewhat" worried that they or a family member would contract the disease. The dangers of the common cold or flu, on the other hand, are rarely discussed by the public and news media – despite the fact that between 12,000 and 56,000 Americans die of influenza each year according to the Center for Disease Control.[2] While the risk of the common flu virus is far more common, Ebola is more memorable due to its gory symptoms and rapid onset. These features cause people to inflate the disease's frequency and overestimate risk. So why does this matter? For one, the Ebola panic came at a significant cost: The United States government spent millions on potentially unnecessary security measures such as international flight bans from certain African nations in an attempt to pacify the public's inflated fears. On the other hand, the COVID-19 pandemic has illustrated the opposite problem – because the prognosis for young individuals is quite good (e.g., most have mild symptoms) and because those who do succumb to the illness have done so largely outside of the public eye – many individuals around the world have *underestimated* its relative risk, with devastating consequences.

Anchoring is another important bias identified by prospect theory. Anchoring suggests that individuals primed with a certain idea or value, even one completely irrelevant to the task at hand, may fail to properly ignore that information when conducting a second task. This is because individuals tend to fixate on the first piece of information they hear about a subject, failing to update their opinions when given subsequent contradictory information (Tversky & Kahneman 1974). For example, in diplomacy and international negotiations, it is well established that whichever party makes the first offer will obtain a better outcome (Galinsky & Mussweiler 2001). In other words, the side that makes the first offer often ends up with a settlement much closer to their ideal point than the other side, even though moving first should carry no special value given the availability of unlimited counteroffers. This is because subsequent negotiators will use the original offer as an anchor or a reference point for bargaining, which will typically be closer to the ideal point of whoever proposed that number in the first place. In other words, the outcome of a negotiation between someone with an ideal point of 0 and another person with an ideal point of 10,000 will be lower than 5,000 if the first person moves first, and higher than 5,000 if the second person moves first (Galinsky & Mussweiler 2001).

The importance of anchoring is revealed often in politics. For example, President Trump enjoyed widespread support among his supporters to repeal Obamacare in part because he focused heavily on the program's cost. His plan, he claimed, would cost much less. However, once the CBO released a study projecting that 24 million Americans would lose their health insurance if Obamacare were repealed, the program became much more popular. This move in public support for the law can be explained by a change in the anchor point – where people once compared Trump's campaign promise to replace Obamacare to the "high cost" anchor, they subsequently compared it to a world in which they had no coverage at all.

Another important example is the idea of offers in a prisoner exchange. In 2011, kidnapped Israeli soldier Gilad Shalit was released from Hamas' custody back to Israel in exchange for more than 1,000 Palestinian prisoners held by Israel, many of whom had been sentenced to life in prison for planning or perpetrating terrorist attacks against Israeli civilians. A host of political reasons contributed to this shocking disparity in the exchange, but it is notable that the final exchange was almost the same as the initial offer made by Hamas nearly six years earlier in 2006 – 1,000 Palestinian prisoners in exchange for Gilad Shalit.[3] The negotiating teams anchored around this initial number and there was very little deviation from it, even years later. This deal came at a steep cost to Israel: many members of Hamas who sat in Israeli prisons and were released in the Shalit deal became leaders of the military wing of Hamas and several Israelis were later killed by those released in this deal.[4]

The effect of being in a domain of gain (leading) versus in the domain of loss (trailing) has important effects in sports as well. For example, every athlete knows that when their team is trailing near the end of the game, they are expected to take risks, whereas if the team is leading, they should be risk-averse, keeping the ball close. At the most basic level, this is rational. It makes sense for a team about to lose a game to go for "Hail-Mary" plays that offer them a chance, however small, to regain the lead and win.

The nonrational aspect of this is when individuals or teams pursue this strategy *too early*. For example, in basketball, a trailing team that is poor at three-point shots might begin to shoot such low-probability shots too early in the game in order to quickly make up their deficit, or to foul players on the opposing team to stop the clock, when the best strategy at that point would be to continue to run their standard, more successful playbook. In contrast, a leading team might decide to "play the clock" with safe plays rather than taking some risk to increase the lead. The key point, however, is that these domains of gain and loss may cause individuals to choose strategies that are *suboptimal*: they become *too* cautious or *too* risky such that they actually lose utility.

Since the late 1970s, prospect theory has been explored and tested in hundreds of different social, economic, and political contexts. At its core, prospect theory has deeply questioned the assumptions held by rational choice scholars that (1) individuals possess consistent utility maximizing preferences, and that (2) they are able to make optimal choices that maximize these preferences.

THE ART OF POLITICAL MARKETING

This does not mean that risk-taking or risk-avoidant behaviors are always suboptimal, however. For example, during political campaigns, the effect of believing one's side is headed for defeat often profoundly affects strategy compared to those who feel they have a lead – and a correct assessment of these probabilities may help candidates choose the best strategy to fit their current polling numbers. For example, trailing candidates such as President Trump in the 2020 presidential campaign, will often adopt riskier strategies to erase a deficit in the polls. Risks of this sort include the use of controversial negative ads and overspending campaign resources. Those leading in the polls, in contrast, generally make more cautious moves such as trying to "look presidential," avoiding debates, focusing only on less risky or controversial issues, and avoiding negative advertising for fear of a backlash. Of course, the problem arises when candidates *over-correct* based on these domains, becoming too risk-averse or risk-taking, such that they actually lose ground against their opponents.

The Republican primary for the 2016 presidential election offers one example. Early on in the primaries, Donald Trump became a surprising dark horse candidate, whose poll numbers were steadily rising, particularly after the first Republican debate. In the lead-up to the second debate, this meant that Donald Trump was in the domain of *gain*, while other candidates were in the domain of *loss*. As such, in the second GOP debate, virtually all the other presidential candidates attacked him. CNN pointed out that "Trump faced a barrage of attacks from a field of contenders clearly more prepared, and eager, to take on the brash billionaire. Those who pulled punches in the last debate – like Scott Walker and Jeb Bush – didn't hesitate to tackle Trump, *eager to regain their faltering standings in the polls*" (emphasis is ours).[5] This strategy did partially work, at least temporarily. By all accounts, Trump lost that debate: 31 percent of viewers said Trump was the loser while 51 percent said his opponent Carly Fiorina was the winner, and his expected vote total dropped suddenly from 32 percent to 24 percent.[6] However, the other candidates, in choosing to mainly attack Trump were also not able to spend enough time setting themselves up as the best choice.

On the other hand, Trump, who was in the domain of gain at the time, chose a risk-averse strategy in the debate. After seeing his poll numbers steadily increase over the weeks prior to the debate, Trump attempted to appear "presidential," taking few risks in order to avoid costly mistakes. However, this style did not play to Trump's electoral strengths and caused him to lose ground to his opponents. In line with prospect theory, Trump chose to play it safe while in the lead, while other candidates took risks attacking his suitability for office. In 2020, when trailing badly in the polls, Trump used a highly combative and disruptive strategy in his first debate with Biden. It didn't go well, as most news outlets described his behavior as rude and un-presidential. However, the strategic choice was understandable when seen through the lens of prospect theory as a risky attempt to avoid electoral losses.

There are many other instances of behavioral change under loss versus gain contexts in other elections around the world. For example, when Israeli Prime Minister Benjamin Netanyahu was behind in the polls prior to the 2015 Israeli election, he used social networks and other political marketing channels on the day of the election to scare voters, stating that the leftist, foreign, nonprofit PACs were driving Arab voters to the polls by the thousands. And in Turkey, President Recep Tayyip Erdogan called for snap elections in August 2015 after the June election resulted in a hung parliament.[7] He repeatedly warned the Turks that the Kurds were gaining power and influence. This strategy was risky, as the relatively strong racial appeals had a high potential to backfire. However, ultimately, these strategies paid off for both leaders, helping them to secure re-election. These examples demonstrate that the change to risk-acceptant behavior in the face of potential losses can, in fact, be beneficial in many cases.

This approach can also help us better understand elite decisions about the use of force. Essentially, the use of diversionary tactics in the face of domestic difficulties may be due to leaders becoming risk-acceptant when they perceive themselves to be in the domain of loss due to a deteriorating political or economic situation. While leaders who are doing well at the polls and expect to win an election (domain of gain) will be risk-averse and refrain from using force, leaders in the domain of loss, concerned about re-election may be more apt to engage in these types of "wag the dog" tactics. Expected utility theory is not sensitive to this type of perceptual anchoring by a leader: a leader is thought to simply choose the outcome with the highest absolute value regardless of whether that would "reduce losses" or "increase (equivalent) gains."

Prospect theory can help explain several historic foreign policy choices as well, such as the United States' continued involvement in the Vietnam War following Nixon's election in 1969. By 1969, prospects for victory in the war were very small; however, President Nixon nonetheless increased investment in the war, rather than pulling forces out. This is likely because Nixon (and the American people) were in the domain of loss, concerned about losing a stalemated war that had initially been marketed as a swift victory. As a result, Nixon continued to sacrifice lives and money even when victory was unachievable. In this way, loss aversion motivates the sunk-costs bias discussed in Chapter 3.

Prospect theory can also explain outcomes in the domestic policy domain. For example, the Republican Party's repeated efforts to repeal the Affordable Care Act in the face of growing popular support for the law follows the same basic logic. Congressional Republicans admitted that they were operating in the realm of loss – they had made a promise to repeal Obamacare and had failed several times. They were worried about further damage to their reputation as a party, so they persisted in their attempts at repeal even when they knew they did not have the votes, had not adequately vetted the costs of the alternate legislation, and – crucially – even after they realized that the majority of the public opposed the effort. Republicans may have been risking *greater* electoral losses by continuing the repeal effort.

On the other hand, voters in red states became much more pro-ACA as soon as Trump was elected, and the prospect of a full repeal became concrete. These citizens were suddenly operating in the realm of *gains*. Many valued their newly won health insurance over an uncertain alternative. These dynamics made it harder for Congress to justify repealing the ACA, but Republican elites still tried, since they were operating in the realm of losses (e.g., loss of face and reputation, given their previous statements). BPS can thus improve our understanding of elite decision-making by incorporating psychological explanations and predictions based on deviations from the reference points of leaders.

FRAMING FROM OTHER PERSPECTIVES

Because the semantic content of the message is logically identical across frames in the experiments used to test prospect theory, Druckman (2001) labels this body of work "equivalency framing." The effect of frames from this perspective are driven by changes in the accessibility of some information or thinking strategies inside the mind. The large effects demonstrated in the experiments designed to test prospect theory, Kahneman (2003) concludes, must be due to the alteration of the salience of specific reference points, often called cognitive *anchors*. When one anchor (e.g., loss) is accessible in memory as a result of the frame of the message, behavior will shift toward risk acceptance. When another is salient (e.g., gains), risk aversion will dominate behavior.

This definition of framing – as a very simple manipulation of the cognitive accessibility of particular considerations in memory – has been found in other research as well. Iyengar (1991) invokes accessibility bias to help understand the powerful effects of two common news media frames: *episodic* versus *thematic*. In an episodic frame, the news focuses on specific individuals, events, or cases in order to illustrate the more abstract issue a story addresses. When crime is covered, for example, a specific criminal act in a particular part of town would be the focus of the episodic frame. On the other hand, thematic frames place a problem in a broad and general context, mostly free of specific examples or people. A story about changes in crime statistics over time, for example, would be considered thematic. Iyengar (1991) finds that when crime is covered episodically, which it most often is, people make much different attributions of responsibility for the problem than when they see a thematic story on the same topic. In the episodic case, they assign blame to the individual and do not consider the possibility that, for example, larger structural factors, such as a poor national economy, may have made crime more likely. The thematic frame, in contrast, leads to attributions of responsibility at the *system* level, causing individuals to blame government or society at large for the very same problem. This simple framing device, changing the accessibility of individual versus broad national considerations related to a specific issue, can quite powerfully change public opinion.

A second major definition of framing is, however, quite distinct from the one described previously. *Narrative framing* refers to the particular way a message weaves facts together, the way it lays out a persuasive story about why a particular event happened, who is to blame for a problem, and who should be responsible for fixing it. Notice how this narrative-based definition of framing is much more general than the one based simply on the accessibility of specific pieces of information like a reference point for a given policy. In the news business, we might consider a frame to be the "hook" for a story about a given topic. Gamson and Modigliani (1987) originally proposed the definition and described frames as "a central organizing idea or story line that provides meaning to an unfolding strip of events, weaving a connection among them" (p. 143). Druckman (2001) refers to these as *emphasis* frames, because they alter critical information in a story that leads people to think about completely different considerations when making up their minds.

Gamson and Modigliani's basic definition is consistent with cognitive psychological accounts of the way people understand and remember issues when they are presented in the form of a good story (Berinsky & Kinder 2006). For example, in a story about the KKK's plan to march in a given town, a journalist might emphasize either the mental trauma these rallies may cause among historically victimized communities, or threats to public safety, or citizens' rights to free speech. Perhaps not surprisingly, this emphasis matters a great deal in influencing public support or opposition to the rally (Nelson, Clawson & Oxley 1997). Neuner (2018) extends this logic to argue that frames in the news can become frames in the mind, altering the way people organize new information about a topic such that they come to understand the same issue very differently than they once had.

Note that the psychological mechanism underlying this type of framing effect is very different than the cognitive accessibility mechanism discussed previously. Rather than a simple, automatic consequence of information accessibility, narrative framing effects of this type are probably the result of more conscious processes. Nelson, Clawson, and Oxley (1997), for example, find that the impact of the different frames involving the KKK story depend not simply on how cognitively accessible specific information is in memory, but on how consciously *important* that information is when a person makes up their mind. This distinction is also consistent with Price and Tewksbury's (1997) account. They argue framing is about the conscious *applicability* of information rather than its automatic accessibility in memory. Beyond simply being available for use in making up one's mind, the frame must also convince the citizen that the information is important for the decision being made. From a rational choice perspective, this type of framing may be thought of as an attempt to change the weight an individual assigns to a given decision criterion, thereby reweighting the different components of an expected utility calculation about an issue. As a result, the extent to which these framing effects lead to "rational" versus "irrational" outcomes depends a great deal on whether people are consciously engaging with the argument or are guided unconsciously from one anchor to another.

If all this is true, elite frames can obviously have a profound effect on the public's understanding of important social problems and its support for particular policy solutions. If the problem at the heart of unemployment is framed as the decision of individuals to go out and get a job or stay home and collect unemployment, then the public might be much less generous about paying higher taxes in order to build a generous social safety net. If, on the other hand, larger economic forces related to decisions about international trade and monetary policy are framed as having led corporations to cut jobs and put people out of a job, then support for unemployment benefits might increase, even if citizens recognize that both factors are important.

ELITE FRAMING EFFECTS IN INTERNATIONAL RELATIONS

Framing effects are not just a topic of academic theorizing. Political leaders from democracies and nondemocracies alike seem to know that message framing matters. When crafting messages for their constituents, elites carefully choose frames in order to enhance support for their policies. Leaders typically frame their preferred policies to highlight benefits and downplay costs (Mintz & DeRouen 2010). Notice how this approach draws on the accessibility mechanism described previously. For example, in President Obama's Executive Order of September 2015, government agencies were asked to improve "how information is presented to consumers, borrowers, program beneficiaries, and other individuals, whether as directly conveyed by the agency, or in setting standards for the presentation of information, by considering how the content, format, timing, and medium affects comprehension and action by individuals, as appropriate."[8] In other words, it is not necessarily the *content* of the message that the administration is concerned with changing, but the way in which it is presented, in order to make it easier for citizens to remember (and use) the information to improve their access to government services.

Many other specific framing techniques focus on how new arguments change the salience of specific judgment criteria. Among the most common framing tactics in leaders' policy messaging, for example, are *spinning, diversionary tactics, revolving framing, threat framing*, and the *salami tactic* (Mintz & DeRouen 2010). Mental accounting is also often used to simplify and frame preferred policies and actions, while segregating gains from losses. Nudging is another technique from Behavioral Economics that relies on this framing logic and is highly applicable to politics. We review a few of these in the following pages.

The technique referred to as *spinning*, for example, works simply via the repetition of a particular perspective over and over again with the intention of leading the populous to change how seriously they view a problem that might otherwise damage a leader's reputation. Thus, for example, repeated claims by President Trump that COVID-19 was not very deadly, that it would quickly disappear, and that he had experienced very mild symptoms when he contracted the disease seem to have persuaded millions not to protect themselves by social distancing and wearing a mask. Some observers even went as far as claiming that, "the President obsesses with dominating Covid" in an attempt to "look manly" (*Washington Post*, October 7, 2020). Spinning the disease as minor, and insisting that he had overcome it with personal strength tied to his masculinity, has been cited as one reason for the observed gender-gap in mask wearing during the pandemic (Capraro & Barcelo 2020).

Trump's reference in summer and fall 2016 to the use of a private email account by Democratic presidential candidate Hillary Clinton for State Department–related work was designed partially to keep the issue on the table during the campaign. It framed the public's discussion around her (lack of) trustworthiness, and drew attention away from Clinton's experience and accomplishments as Secretary of State. This news emphasis kept Clinton on the defensive throughout most of the campaign and obscured her strengths vis-à-vis her rivals. In a mostly unsuccessful counter-framing effort, former President Bill Clinton blamed the GOP and the Press for their deliberate emphasis on the email issue.[9] As this example demonstrates, frames are most effective when political strategists, politicians, or other leaders emphasize a particular consideration as a way of understanding an issue, and this alters the way the public attributes blame and credit in that domain. For example, one study demonstrated that the simple and persistent media emphasis on Hilary Clinton's email server during the 2016 election led many Americans to focus their attention on that simple frame, whereas they maintained no such successful focus on a single scandal when it came to Trump (Bode et al. 2020).

Another example of spinning occurred in the debate over crowd sizes at the Trump inauguration in January 2017. Whereas aerial and TV photos showed that there were fewer spectators at Trump's inauguration than at either of Obama's inauguration events, the president contradicted it. His advisor, Kelly-Anne Conway, insisted that the Trump administration was entitled to express "alternative facts" about the crowd size. Similarly, the president debated Hillary Clinton's win of the popular vote. The counter-frame the president used was that he would have won the popular vote if votes by illegal immigrants had been excluded from the tally (although, of course, there was no evidence that illegal immigrants cast votes at all). This counter-frame was an attempt to establish a popular mandate by Trump in order to govern.

Another prominent framing technique used by presidents is the use of *diversionary tactics*. Presidents often use force abroad in an effort to distract public attention from domestic problems (e.g., Ostrom & Job 1986). Rooted in the "rally around the flag" effect (Mueller 1973) – a short-term boost in presidential approval ratings following the use of force – is the hypothesis that "presidents sometimes use force in an effort to reverse declining approval ratings" (quoted in Brulé & Mintz 2006; also see DeRouen 1995; Morgan & Bickers 1992) or divert attention from deteriorating economic conditions (e.g., DeRouen 2000; Fordham 1998). The use of diversionary tactics is thus a framing technique that assumes the public has limited attention and can be distracted from one issue when a new issue surfaces or is highlighted by elites.

Revolving framing refers to the rapid introduction of different frames in order to identify the frame that will work best. A leader changes the frame (e.g., the key reason for the policy action), in the hope that one frame will be popular and can then be highlighted subsequently. For example, in the 1991 Gulf War, the Bush administration introduced a series of very different frames for their decision to get involved (see Mintz & Redd 2003), claiming the war was, alternatively, "about oil, about Iraq's possession of chemical weapons and effort to achieve a nuclear weapon, about the threat Hussein poses to his other neighbors, and about the need to establish a new world order in the wake of the Cold War" (Drew 1991, 81). In contrast, *threat framing* simply highlights the danger in a situation, action, or in some instances, inaction. In international affairs, state leaders often use threat framing to mobilize support or to signal resolve to their opponents. For example, doing nothing vis-à-vis Russia's moves in the Ukraine was portrayed by opponents of the Obama administration as a threat. Using the *salami tactic*, policy-makers set a new reference point in each key step in the negotiation process. In other word, each "salami slice" incrementally and gradually moves the negotiator closer to his or her goal, as we will show later in the case study of the Iran nuclear deal.

Sensitivity to framing can lead to results that are inconsistent with predictions of RCT. Namely, framing and priming can divert attention from a key issue and elevate another to the forefront of the public debate or highlight different aspects of the same issue for voters. According to the consistency assumption of RCT, unless *new* information is introduced, an individual should not shift the relative weight they place on one dimension or the other of a decision – but framing and priming effects can lead to exactly this outcome. In the following, we go into more details on some of these important types of framing, providing more extensive examples of the use of frames in international relations and in the domestic political arena.

NUDGING

Nudging is one of the most prominent recent developments in the study of Behavioral Economics with its impact on individual choice and behavior. The general idea is that a subtle behavioral "nudge" can significantly alter future choices without any overt mandate or direct manipulation from the receiver's point of view (Thaler & Sunstein 2008). The definition of a nudge begins with the assumption that there is no such thing as a neutral design for choosing between a set of alternatives. All choices are framed in some way. The second assumption is that small and apparently insignificant decisions in how these choices are framed can lead to very large changes in outcomes down the road. Third, all choices are influenced by the often-imperceptible design elements selected by *choice architects*. A choice architect, according to Thaler and Sunstein, is an individual who structures or packages alternatives in a way that pushes the target audience toward one outcome over another, and therefore, has a powerful opportunity "for organizing the context in which people make decisions" (Thaler & Sunstein 2008, p. 3). In short, choices are framed; these subtle frames have important implications for behavior; and, as a result, the individual designing the frame has a powerful ability to affect individual choice.

So, what is a nudge? In the abstract, a nudge is: "any aspect of the choice architecture that alters people's behavior in a predictable way without forbidding any options or significantly changing their economic incentives. To count as a mere nudge, the intervention must be easy and cheap to avoid. Nudges are not mandates. Putting fruit at eye level counts as a nudge. Banning junk food does not" (Thaler & Sunstein 2008, p. 8).

There are plenty of examples of nudges having powerful effects on consumer behavior. For example, companies can substantially increase profits by circulating the smell of cooked food in their stores. Even personal decisions about savings and finance are powerfully influenced by nudges. Workplace 401(k)'s, for example, experience much higher rates of participation when they insist that workers *opt out* of savings plans when they begin a new job rather than *opt in*. Expected Utility theory would predict that savings behavior would be driven solely by calculating needs in retirement minus the current value of that money. However, research on nudging finds that *lifetime* saving behavior is profoundly affected by whether a person must take ten minutes to opt into a program rather than opt out.

In another example, Ariely and Jones (2008) describe a nudge from *The Economist* magazine, where they offer three potential purchase options: (1) digital only ($59), (2) print only ($125), or (3) print + digital ($125). The catch is that, of course, it seems frivolous to offer the print only option when its price makes it strictly inferior to the print +digital offer. No rational person would select it, so why bother offering it? However, the researchers found that when only the digital only versus print+digital options were presented, consumers were much more likely to prefer the cheaper digital-only option. Adding the strictly inferior print only option actually made the print+digital option look *more* attractive, leading more people to prefer it. Thus, by including an objectively inferior choice in the choice set, *The Economist* could actually nudge people into spending more money on their subscription than they otherwise would.

Why do these nudges work so well? The effectiveness of nudges is consistent with Simon's ideas about bounded rationality. It recognizes that searching for the best alternative is time consuming and potentially costly, and that this cost must be built into the calculation associated with the total utility of the final choice. Making a particularly reasonable choice less difficult to find, therefore, can dramatically increase its likelihood of selection when the chooser is using a "satisficing" rather than "optimizing" strategy.

Do "nudges" work as techniques by which policy-makers influence the behavior of large populations? The answer seems to be yes. Consider reducing the average energy consumption of households around the country in order to reduce carbon emissions that nearly every climate scientist in the world insists are driving up the mean level of thermal energy in our oceans and atmosphere. One (unrealistic) way would be to convince governments around the world to pass laws that would penalize individuals for consuming too much electricity. This option would almost surely fail, since such laws would be highly unpopular, and each country would rightly insist that they should not have to reduce emissions unless all other countries also did so – a classic collective action problem. But what about simply putting a smiley face on the electricity bill of every consumer who used less than average electricity for that month, or informing consumers when they used less energy than their neighbors? These interventions have been shown to substantially reduce domestic energy use without any politically infeasible legislative mandates (Thaler & Sunstein 2008).

In the most normatively hopeful sense, therefore, choice architects in the policy domain may be able to steer public behavior in ways that could solve large-scale collective action problems and lead to better outcomes for the entire planet. According to Thaler and Sunstein (2008), we can use nudges to "influence choices in a way that will make choosers better off, as judged by themselves" (p. 5).

However, nudges can also have unintended negative consequences. The notion that policy-makers can change the public's behavior outside their awareness also seems normatively problematic and manipulative to some observers. Shouldn't we as citizens have the right to know exactly how and why our choices are being framed in a particular way? And if we do not agree with the goals that are being maximized, even if those goals can be demonstrated to be positive for the planet, don't individuals in a free society still have the right to refuse to participate? This is a fascinating philosophical debate outside the scope of the current discussion. Citizens must take up these questions now and in the future. For example, President Trump signed a bill in 2017 to allow broadband companies to collect sensitive information from their customers in order to create targeted advertisements. Under the previous policy, customers were prompted to give permission for the use of such data. Americans now must "opt out" of the status quo to protect their privacy, rather than "opt in" to a policy that collects their sensitive information. According to the theory of nudging, this should lead to a dramatic reduction in the privacy of the average American's online behavior, even though they are technically still allowed to opt-out of this surveillance by their internet provider.

Nudging and framing are indeed powerful. This also means they will be a tool both sides of a debate will use (Chong & Druckman 2007; Sniderman & Theriault 2004). Thus, often, citizens are presented with *competing* frames on issues that they then must reconcile. For example, when competing partisan elites attempt to frame an issue in terms that reflect well on them and poorly on their opposition, what is the result? As one might guess, competing frames often do happen, but the strength of an opposing frame is important (Druckman 2004). When given two frames, one of which reflects an individual's preexisting preferences and values, a strong counter-frame can pull the individual some distance from their previous position compared to when the counter-frame is very weak. In other words, while elites do attempt to neutralize the opposition frames and inoculate their own constituents from the potentially persuasive impact of those messages, they will not always succeed. Thus, while framing can be powerful, its effects are by no means unlimited. The constraints of the competitive partisan environment substantially limit, but do not eliminate the power of elite decisions about how to talk about important issues of the day. An illuminating example of this competitive framing environment comes from the 2015 negotiations regarding nuclear weapons in Iran.

FRAMING AND COUNTER-FRAMING IN THE IRAN NUCLEAR DEAL DEBATE: A CASE STUDY

In July 2015, the P5+1 (the five permanent members of the United Nations Security Council: China, France, Russia, the United Kingdom, the United States, plus Germany), and the European Union, signed an agreement with the Islamic Republic of Iran, known as the Joint Comprehensive Plan of Action (JCPOA). The Iran nuclear deal led to a fierce political debate in the United States, where Congress was supposed to vote on the agreement by mid-September 2015. This immediately triggered framing and counter-framing campaigns by both the Obama administration and those opposed to the deal.

President Obama and Secretary of State Kerry framed the debate as a simple dichotomous choice: an agreement or war. This frame may have been intended to generate public anxiety, since polls showed that Americans wanted to avoid yet another costly war in the Middle East. Opponents of the deal emphasized, in contrast, several other options, including heavier sanctions on Iran and renegotiating an even better deal, among others. Another framing tactic used by the Obama administration pointed to short-term benefits while downplaying potential long-term costs and challenges. For example, the administration claimed that the breakout time for Iran to become nuclear was now two months, whereas under the agreement it would be at least one year. Republicans and other opponents of the deal highlighted, in contrast, long-term challenges while ignoring short-term benefits. They claimed, for example, that the agreement would allow Iran to pursue nuclear weapons legally after ten years and that Iran would at that point have the capability to develop the weapons even if they abided by the agreement in the interim. Both sides may have been correct, but they emphasized different facts (and time horizons) while downplaying others.

In addition, advocates and opponents also used different reference points for the deal. Opponents claimed that any acceptable agreement must enable verification of Iranian nuclear and military facilities "anywhere, anytime," which Obama's deal did not guarantee. Supporters argued, in contrast, that the proposed agreement would, in fact, provide unprecedented verification in Iran's nuclear facilities, and that no nation would ever commit to unlimited and unfettered foreign inspections of its military facilities and bases.

Both sides also used *thematic framing* tactics. President Obama claimed the deal deliberately and necessarily focused only on Iran's nuclear program, because expanding the discussion to other aspects of Iran's internal or regional politics would prevent a compromise. Opponents insisted, in contrast, that the United States should not sign any agreement that left out such critical issues as Iran's human rights violations or support for terrorist groups in Syria, Lebanon, Iraq, Lebanon, and Yemen.

There was also evidence of *revolving framing* by administration officials – the rapid cycling through justifications for a policy in order to see which one appealed most to the public in this case. Thus, then–Secretary of State John Kerry first claimed that rejection of the agreement with Iran would lead to war, then that it would lead to the weakening of the United States in the international arena, then that it would weaken the US dollar, and finally that it would cause isolation of the United States. In a speech on September 2, 2015, Secretary Kerry criticized lawmakers opposed to the Iran nuclear deal, claiming that the United States would "pay an immeasurable price" on the world stage, if the deal was blocked,[10] framing the outcome as a loss if the agreement would not be signed and as a gain if it would be reached.

The framework of the P5+1 agreement with Iran over its nuclear program is also an example of a gain vs. loss framing. The White House and State Department framed the consequences of the agreement as *a significant reduction in capabilities* (smaller number of centrifuges, 97 percent decrease in nuclear material, etc.), and the prevention of war. In contrast, Israel, Saudi Arabia, other Gulf States, and many Republications in Congress focused on what capabilities Iran *would retain*: Iran's centrifuges, facilities, and R&D know-how and capabilities for a nuclear program that would be kept under the agreement.

Elite framing of the consequences of signing and not signing the deal are evident in distinct characterizations of the same conversations. For example, both the White House and Israeli government released descriptions of an April 2015 Obama–Netanyahu phone call, following the announcement of the framework for agreement on the Iran nuclear program. According to the White House, President Obama called Prime Minister Netanyahu from Air Force One to discuss the JCPOA regarding Iran's nuclear program:

The President emphasized that, while nothing is agreed until everything is, the framework represents significant progress towards a lasting, comprehensive solution that cuts off all of Iran's pathways to a bomb and verifiably ensures the peaceful nature of Iran's nuclear program going forward. He underscored that progress on the nuclear issue in no way diminishes our concerns with respect to Iran's sponsorship of terrorism and threats towards Israel and emphasized that the United States remains steadfast in our commitment to the security of Israel. The President told the Prime Minister that he has directed his national security team to increase consultations with the new Israeli government about how we can further strengthen our long-term security cooperation with Israel and remain vigilant in countering Iran's threats.[11]

In contrast, the version that came out of Jerusalem, communicated by the Prime Minister's media adviser, highlighted Netanyahu's opposition to the deal: "Prime Minister Benjamin Netanyahu spoke to US President Barack Obama this evening and expressed Israel's strong opposition to the framework agreement with Iran which poses a grave danger to Israel, the region and the world." Prime Minister Netanyahu also stated that:

A deal based on this framework would threaten the survival of Israel. Just two days ago, Iran said that 'The destruction of Israel is non-negotiable,' and in these fateful days Iran is accelerating the arming of its terror proxies to attack Israel. This deal would legitimize Iran's nuclear program, bolster Iran's economy, and increase Iran's aggression and terror throughout the Middle East and beyond. Such a deal would not block Iran's path to the bomb. It would pave it. It would increase the risks of nuclear proliferation in the region and the risks of a horrific war. The alternative is standing firm and increasing the pressure on Iran until a better deal is achieved.[12]

Both sides also used the gain vs. loss framing to make their point. Whereas opponents claimed that more sanctions would have brought more concessions from Iran on the nuclear negotiations, supporters of the agreement claimed that they were barely able to hold the international sanction regime against Iran intact, and warned that the sanctions would crumble should Congress vote to disapprove the deal.

The US fact sheet of the April 2015 Framework, as well as Harvard University's Belfer Center translation of Iran's fact sheet,[13] was particularly interesting, revealing very significant differences between how Iran and the United States presented the same agreement to their respective publics. This was done to bolster their position toward the negotiation on a final agreement and to calm their domestic skeptics, rivals, and the general public. It is fair to say that both the reference point and the framing of the agreement's parameters and results were very different in Washington and Teheran.

President Obama and his team framed and "sold" the agreement as cutting off all paths of Iran to a nuclear bomb. Opponents ridiculed this claim by pointing out that the agreement allowed Iran to maintain its infrastructure for developing a nuclear program with a weak verification regime. For example, opponents pointed out that the Iranians would collect and present their own samples of materials from the Parchin nuclear site – a claim later denied by the International Atomic Energy Agency (IAEA).

In essence, opponents framed the agreement in terms of what Iran gained or, at least, was allowed to keep, while supporters emphasized the parts of the agreement that forced Iran to compromise or give up certain activities. While the precise effects of these framing efforts are unclear, we do know elites were characterizing the same events in very different ways, in the hopes of persuading their publics.

For example, President Obama claimed that Iran's Supreme Leader Khamenei's assertion that all economic sanctions on Iran would be lifted immediately did not correspond to the actual text of the deal. In a speech at American University, Obama claimed: "It's those hardliners [in Iran] chanting 'death to America' who have been most opposed to the deal . . .. They're making common cause with the Republican Caucus."[14] Essentially, Republicans in Congress were lumped in with the Revolutionary Guards in Tehran. The other rhetorical/framing tactic the President used was "to equate opposition to his deal with a vote for war in Iraq in 2003 and a lust for war generally."[15]

The Obama administration marketed the agreement by highlighting its benefits and pointing to the danger of rejecting the deal. The President then claimed in a speech at the UN General Assembly (September 2015) that by signing the agreement, a potential war was prevented, and the world was therefore safer. In highlighting the benefits of the deal, however, the White House hardly mentioned that Iran's Revolutionary Guards would get billions in cash. In remarks countering Senator Bob Corker's claim that Kerry was "fleeced" by the Iranians on the nuclear deal, the Secretary of State, who tried to counter-frame opposition to the deal, said that disapproval would provide a "big green light for Iran to continue its nuclear program."[16] He also said it would lead to war. President Obama used counter-framing tactics, while criticizing Senator John McCain (R-Arizona), for "giving the supreme leader of Iran the benefit of the doubt" while accusing the US officials of "spinning negotiations."[17] Obama stated that "it needs to stop," thus setting a reference point that Republican critics of a potential deal should not cross.

In contrast, Republicans in Congress and the Israeli government lobbied against the deal, counter-framing Obama's position. Leaders of the Gulf States, including Saudi Arabia quietly and privately voiced their concern about a nuclear Iran. Meanwhile, in a speech in the UN General Assembly in Fall 2015, Israeli Prime Minister Benjamin Netanyahu claimed that "Iran will not morph from a 'rapacious tiger into a kitten.'"[18] This counter-framing campaign included ads in major newspapers and on the air, numerous briefings with members of Congress, lobbying, etc. However, President Obama needed only one-third of members of Senate or House to approve the deal and consequently prevailed. Opponents of the bill also used the reference point that inspections in Iran were supposed to be "anywhere, anytime," to highlight significant deviations from this and justify their opposition to this agreement. This helped them emphasize the shortcomings of the final deal and shape the political and public debate.

Opponents also criticized the deal for failing to address *other* issues the United States had with the country of Iran. The negotiations with Iran on the nuclear deal can thus also be seen as an excellent example of mental accounting in international negotiations. Whereas the United States acknowledged Iran's aggression in the Middle East (in Syria, Lebanon, Yemen, Gaza, and its role in Iraq), the White House insisted that the negotiation and the agreement would only be about the nuclear program, not about other important issues such as the four Americans in prison in Iran at that time, Iran's human rights policy, and its record supporting terrorism or support for the Assad regime in Syria and the Hezbollah organization in Lebanon. In other words, each of these issues was separated into different "accounts," rather than as part of one negotiating package – something opponents of the agreement harshly critiqued.

As discussed earlier in this chapter, however, framing is less effective when competing frames vie for the public's attention, as this competition can limit the impact of any one narrative on how citizens will view an issue. However, in autocracies, a competitive political and media environment is largely absent. Thus, in regimes like Iran, where citizens have less access to competing viewpoints, counter-frames, and perspectives, elite narrative frames may be even more powerful.

The view from Iran:

Iran is an important case study for this idea. And, indeed, Iranian leaders engaged in framing of the Iran deal as a win for their country. Setting an important (and new) reference point for the final deal, the Supreme Leader of Iran said immediately after the framework on the Iran nuclear deal was announced, that Iran would not allow outside inspections of Iran's military sites (even though the UN, the United States and Israel all suspected Iran conducted tests related to nuclear weapon development in these bases). Thus, the announcement by the Supreme Leader cleverly framed the negotiation by "moving" it from Iran agreeing to foreign inspection of its nuclear sites to not allowing foreign inspectors of its nonnuclear, military sites.

An adviser to the Iranian Supreme Leader Ali Khamenei called continued American threats of a military option against Iran "laughable." Brigadier General Mohammad Ali Asoudi, Khamenei's representative in the Revolutionary Guards, said "President Barack Obama's insistence that Iran could still be confronted militarily should it shirk its obligations under the nuclear deal had become a joke" to Iranian officials based on the Fars news agency.[19] Another tactic used by the Iranian Revolutionary Guards to garner public support and hide/cover their agreement to the deal was to claim that they would deal a "crushing defeat" to the Americans if the United States used force against Iran.[20] Specifically, the commander of the IRGC boasted of his nation's "immense power" and said it possessed "very advanced technologies" to repel any threats to the Islamic Republic.[21]

Moreover, Iran's supreme leader, Ayatollah Ali Khamenei challenged key elements of the framework nuclear deal with the United States and other world powers after the framework announcement, as did the commander of Iran's powerful and influential Revolutionary Guards and other conservative leaders in Iran. Trying to put a nice face on these threats, President Obama said,[22] "even a guy with a title supreme leader has to be concerned about his own constituencies." President Obama explained that Iran's leader was "trying to protect his political standing in his own country." The president said there might be ways of structuring the deal that "satisfy their pride, their optics, their politics, but meet our core practical objectives." Obama also said he is not surprised that Iranian leaders frame the agreement "in a way that protects their political position."

The Iranians used these framing tactics in a sophisticated way: the framing effort was not intended only for domestic political purposes and was not targeted only to the Iranian people. It also served as a new reference point in the negotiation for the final deal. Indeed, throughout their negotiations with the United States over their nuclear program, Iran demonstrated a clear understanding of how effective framing tactics could shift political negotiations and outcomes. The Iranian negotiators thus used the *salami tactic* in their negotiation with the P5+1+EU: Iran first agreed on April 2nd, 2015, in Lausanne Switzerland on the general terms of an agreement. This framework agreement is known as the "Declaration of Principles." It set a new starting point for the Iranian negotiation team in the subsequent round of negotiation: removing sanctions on Iran in exchange for a ten-to-fifteen-year halt on their nuclear program. Iran's leaders then swiftly publicized their interpretation of the Lausanne temporary deal. Their position was very different from the one published by the United States: The Iranian negotiations used the Framework as a starting point for the negotiation, and indeed made significant gains in the final deal, the JCPOA, as compared with the original, Lausanne document.

President Trump's Withdrawal from the Iran Nuclear Deal

The debate over the 2015 Iran nuclear deal offers a great example of framing and counter-framing tactics used by Obama administration officials and opponents of the deal, both inside the United States and in Iran, Europe, and the Middle East. This deal also received renewed attention during the 2016 presidential campaign, when then–GOP candidate Donald Trump repeatedly promised to tear up the nuclear agreement with Iran on his first day in office, declaring it "the worst agreement ever negotiated."[23] This renewed debate over the deal was also marked by competitive framing efforts by opponents and proponents of the agreement until Trump, withdrew the United States from the deal in 2018.

Compared to the Obama administration, the Trump administration used very different frames to describe this deal, Iranian intentions, the Iranian regime, and its actions in the Middle East. Specifically, Trump officials framed the deal as paving the way for Iran to become a nuclear power, support terrorist organizations, and threaten Israel, the United States, and other US allies in the region, while virtually never mentioning potential merits of the deal. Thus, in sharp contrast to Obama, Trump reversed the perception of the expected utility for the United States in pursuing the deal: there were no benefits to this deal according to Trump and his key advisors, only very substantial costs. By using this security frame and engaging in rhetoric about Iran's threat to US interests and global stability, the Trump administration placed the United States and its allies in the domain of loss vis-à-vis the Iran nuclear program signed by his predecessor. Another tactic the Trump administration used to discredit the 2015 deal was to expand its scope rhetorically. These conditions included Iran's testing of ballistic missiles; its support of Hezbollah and Islamic Jihad, and of forces fighting against the regimes of Bahrain and Yemen; and Iran's support of anti-American, pro-Iranian insurgency in Iraq. As he promised in the campaign, Trump then withdrew from the deal.

By declaring during the campaign and repeatedly during his tenure in office that the Iran nuclear deal was "the worst ever negotiated," President Trump had essentially set *a new reference point* compared to Obama and Kerry's view of the Iran's deal, and outlined a path leading to the cancellation of the deal, which was difficult not to follow through on. By expanding and changing the mix of nuclear and nonnuclear demands on Iran, the Trump administration also had an easier time demonstrating that Iran had violated the deal than by just focusing on the nuclear elements of the agreement, which Iran appeared largely to have kept. Thus, just as elite rhetorical framing was critical in passing the original deal, framing by the administration played a central role in successfully marketing the decision to later withdraw from the deal. Of course, in the presidential campaign of 2020, the Iran deal again became a campaign issue, as former Vice President Joe Biden, repeatedly promised that he would re-join the agreement.

CONCLUSION

Our main goal in this chapter was to discuss an idea that is intuitive to many: the way an issue is presented, even more than any concrete facts about that issue, can substantially affect opinions. We have discussed equivalency frames, narrative frames, framing and counter-framing tactics, spinning and priming, and provided several examples of how rhetorical framing can be used in politics, including during the negotiations leading to the nuclear agreement with Iran and the subsequent reversal of this decision. The chapter also discusses nudging – a framing-related concept used in Behavioral Economics but rarely in political science.

But what does the prevalence of all these BPS effects mean for the RCT framework? Sensitivity to different types of highlighted frames reflects the relatively limited attention the average citizen pays to politics – being exposed to different narratives constitutes the bulk of information the average person learns about a given issue. Narrative frames then lead individuals to change their beliefs about what is most important regarding the event. The outsized influence that narrative frames play in attitude formation still suggests citizens are often engaging in relatively shallow processing when forming their political attitudes about issues. In short, citizens seem to use framing information sent by elites as a cognitive shortcut to avoid thinking hard and collecting new information, making them quite vulnerable to these strategic framing tactics.

What is even more vexing for RCT than these narrative framing effects, however, is the sensitivity of individuals to the equivalency frames highlighted earlier – that is, framing a decision in terms of the potential costs rather than gains, even when the actual outcome is *identical* in either case, still leads people to dramatically change their decisions. This is the key finding of prospect theory: that what should be considered irrelevant information to a given choice situation strongly affects the preferences of citizens and elites alike when presented differently. So, while many of the definitions of framing that have appeared in the literature can simply be interpreted as a rational reaction to new information in the environment or a reweighting of different dimensions of a given policy choice, these more-trivial changes to frames present a greater challenge for traditional RCT models of decision-making. We suggest, however, that these BPS findings can fruitfully augment RCT models, while systematically incorporating these biases in human cognition.

5

The Limitations of the Unitary Actor Model of Government

Thus far, we have emphasized the role of psychological processes in individual decision-making – whether it be the masses or political elites. However, in national security decision-making, foreign economic policy, bargaining and negotiations, and many other domestic and international issues, we often think not in terms of individuals, but in terms of states. For example, Germany invaded Poland on September 1st, 1939, to begin World War II. During the Cold War, the Soviet Union placed missiles in Cuba. From 1955 to 1975, the United States waged war in Vietnam. In 2018, America initiated a trade dispute with China. These statements imply that entire countries make unitary, intentional foreign policy choices. But what exactly does it mean to say that a country *chose* a course of action? A country does not have thoughts or emotions and, as such, does not hold singular attitudes that drive its decisions. When the United States *does* something – pursues a peace agreement, gets involved in conflict, engages in trade relations – it means individuals in the government form attitudes and engage in some interaction that leads them to a particular course of action, which they then entrust other individuals in other parts of the government to carry out. Those whose job is to implement the policy must decide how that should be done, and even sometimes whether it *can* be done. What can BPS tell us about these complex processes – and how individual and group biases and motivations aggregate to affect the policy of a state?

Think about the decision by the state to go to war, and how to fight it. Thousands of people had to work together for the United States to launch wars in Afghanistan and Iraq in 2002 and 2003. Intelligence and military officials from various departments – the CIA, FBI, State, Defense, and other departments – had to collect and analyze information to advise the president. The president had to choose whether to invade and, in many cases, garner necessary support from other elected officials such as those in Congress. The military had to formulate a plan and issue orders to its soldiers, who had to carry out these plans. In other words, "going to war" is a complicated sequence of events carried out by a large number of individuals, each with their own preferences, biases, and predispositions. It seems plausible to assume that the details of any international conflict are likely shaped by the dynamic interactions of many sets of actors operating in the national security apparatus.

However, in many rational actor models of national security decision-making and diplomatic policy-making, the dynamic layering of bureaucratic decision-making and execution is not taken into account. Instead, scholars assume that the political push and pull within each state is of less significance to state policy than the overarching interest of the state writ large (Fearon 1995). In other words, in these models, the state is typically treated as if it were a single decision-maker – a "unitary actor" – with a single and invariant set of preferences.

This simplified conception of the state can be useful. For example, it can help establish how structural features of the international system constrain state behavior (see Waltz 2010), or how paradoxical bargaining incentives in negotiations can lead to less-than-ideal outcomes for states (e.g., Fearon 1995). However, many domestic political considerations, bureaucratic issues, organizational constraints, and group decision-making dynamics impact state policy formation and implementation in both domestic and foreign policy-making. Most importantly, the variation in these features systematically affects outcomes, and so cannot be ignored. As a result, after the heyday of structural theories of international relations such as a realism, many RCT models of politics began to disaggregate the state, incorporating domestic political factors into models of political choice. People who study institutional or bureaucratic dynamics within states generally label this class of challenges *principal-agent problems* – the difference between what one authority commands and what actually gets done by someone else. A principal – the president or another executive, for example – might demand that an agent – the federal bureaucracy – implement some policy. The choices bureaucrats make, however, dramatically influence the effect of the policy, often moving it away from the president's intention or "ideal point." In fact, a wide variety of institutional and individual factors influence the way states enact policies, and these produce consequences different than the ones leaders might prefer. For example, during the devastating COVID-19 pandemic of 2020, the president requested several times that the bureaucracy implement policies to relax social distancing rules, open schools, and end mandatory mask wearing in public spaces, despite medical experts' warning of the potentially dire public health consequences. Many medical appointees, though not all, in the administration resisted these demands.[1]

Importantly, this approach for disaggregating state behavior is still firmly in the rational choice tradition. According to RCT, the principal-agent problem of policy-making means that *individually rational* choices often lead to policies or outcomes that are nonetheless suboptimal *for the state*. Principal-agent problems are problematic, in part, because of the issue of *moral hazard*. Moral hazards exist when an agent has an incentive to engage in riskier or costlier decision-making because the principal, not the agent, bears the costs of those risks. For example, in foreign policy, the United States may unintentionally encourage bad behavior on the part of their allies by protecting these states from the consequences of poor decision-making, bailing them out of trouble. On the one hand, the United States does this because it is important to keep the regimes of its allies and client states stable in order to advance US interests: The relative insulation US aid provides to foreign leaders from the consequences of their actions can unfortunately, on occasion, create the instability which the aid was meant to prevent.

BPS approaches to state policy-making, however, go further in challenging the assumptions underlying the rational, unitary actor model of state action. These ideas, which we will discuss presently, demonstrate how psychological processes involved in group decision-making can make policy outcomes suboptimal for both the state *and* the individuals involved in the policy-making process. In this chapter, we thus present various disaggregated models of governmental decision-making that challenge the early unitary actor model of state behavior – beginning with rational choice approaches and moving toward BPS – to show how these models can augment unitary actor explanations and predictions of state policy.

First, *domestic politics* models of policy-making challenge the unitary state actor assumption, but retains the idea that leaders try to maximize their individual influence. Domestic politics models often begin by recognizing that a leader's preferences for political survival and/or popularity do not always mirror that of their constituents. This can sometimes produce policy outcomes that are suboptimal for the state as a whole, even if they are the best outcome for the leader. Importantly, these models still assume leaders are rational actors – they just hold preferences that do not necessarily align with the interests of the state writ large.

Organizational politics models of policy-making diverge slightly further from rational choice assumptions. In these models, policies follow standard operating procedures (SOP), and are reduced to *outputs*. Institutional constraints permit only a restricted set of policy options to emerge, and thus the state cannot always adapt optimally to developments on the ground. In other words, assumptions of procedural rationality do not necessarily hold, resulting in policies that are potentially suboptimal both for the state and the individual policy-makers. Though suboptimal, these policies are nonetheless stable equilibria, because they represent *the best each individual can do*, given the political, bureaucratic, and organizational constraints under which they operate.

A third class of models of policy-making fits more squarely in the realm of behavioral approaches, moving even further from standard rational choice assumptions about complete information processing. These approaches argue that elites – both individually and in group decision-making settings – suffer from the same cognitive, emotional, and motivational biases as average citizens. Moreover, the group decision-making process that unfolds in most policy formulation may *exacerbate* these biases rather than attenuate them. As a result, policy outcomes are typically not only suboptimal, but they are also "off the equilibrium path," meaning that individuals could have and should have made different choices that would have resulted in a higher overall utility. In this chapter, we will review these various models, examining the consequences of discarding the traditional unitary actor assumption for understanding state policy-making.

DOMESTIC POLITICS AND POLICY-MAKING

The policies of most states, democratic or not, are determined by an executive and implemented by a bureaucracy. In a democracy, elected officials are considered direct agents of the people – presumably offering policies that are in the best interest of the public's will. But elected officials and appointed bureaucrats have their own interests, and these can affect both which policies they work on and how those policies are implemented. This is the central claim underlying the *domestic politics* approach to politics (see, e.g., Milner 1997; Russett & Graham 1989) which adds nuance to realist theories of government policy-making without directly undermining the basic assumptions of rationality: individuals have consistent, ordered preferences and act in ways they believe will best achieve their goals. In other words, the individuals in government are still rational actors able to process information in ways that maximize their preferences, but their preferences include things like personal gain, staying in office, popularity, power, or even getting home from work early. However, these individual preferences may not necessarily be optimal from the perspective of *the state* or a majority of its citizens.

The problems introduced by the delegation of the authority to implement policies from elected leaders to policy experts in the bureaucracy is an example of a principal-agent problem (Jensen & Meckling 1976). The agent's interests can sometimes be at odds with those of the principal. For example, when selling a home, many people hire a real estate broker. The broker is the "agent," supposedly acting on behalf of the owner, the "principal." Real estate brokers work on commission – each typically makes a profit of about 3 percent of the sale price of the home. While both the seller and the broker would like to sell the home for the highest possible price, the seller's interest in maximizing the sale price is much greater than the broker's. This is because the seller makes 97 percent of the additional profit garnered by a higher sale price, while the broker makes only 3 percent of that additional profit. Increasing the sale price increases a specific cost to the broker: the time and effort that could be used selling other homes. This cost can be much larger than the benefit to the agent of a marginally higher closing price. Therefore, the broker often attempts to convince their client to accept a lower price sooner, rather than wait for a higher-priced offer in the future.

Many rational choice models of politics incorporate domestic political considerations into theories of state foreign policy-making. A common class of formal models, often labeled *accountability models*, explore this exact dynamic (see Ashworth 2012 for an overview). In accountability models, an elected official formulates policy while anticipating reactions from the electorate in a future round of the game. At risk to the elected official, of course, is that voters will withdraw the "benefit" of political power inherent in holding office. Voters are then a second player in the game, observing leaders' actions (or the outcome of those actions) and choosing whether or not to replace them. Accountability embodies the early idea of a "two-level" game (Putnam 1988), whereby political elites aim to formulate foreign policy that will allow them to "win" both internationally and domestically. This work has provided important insight into the relationship between domestic and international processes, clarifying how and when officials are most likely to formulate policy in line with the preferences and desires of voters (see, e.g., Canes-Wrone, Herron & Shotts 2001).

Most accountability models adopt all the basic assumptions of RCT. While they disaggregate the state and move away from a unitary actor assumption of state behavior, state policy is still largely viewed as the product of a strategic interaction between two (or more) maximizing actors – the leader and the electorate. Recent BPS models of domestic politics relax even these assumptions, and incorporate aspects of information processing that deviate from standard procedural rationality (see e.g., Bendor, Kumar & Siegel 2010; Little 2019; Woon 2012). This research is a welcome step in the formal study of domestic politics and policy-making.

Poliheuristic Theory and the Role of Non-Compensatory Dimensions

Poliheuristic theory (Mintz 1993, 2004) is a significant example of an approach stressing the importance of a two-level game in which policies cannot ignore *either* the interests of the leader or the will of the public. Indeed, understanding the importance of domestic-audience costs in elite decision-making (Downs & Rocke 1994) and principal-agent problems between the elected and the governed is at the core of poliheuristic theory

(Mintz 1993, 2004; Mintz et al. 1997). In particular, poliheuristic theory focuses on principal-agent problems in foreign policy-making, environmental policy-making, and foreign economic behavior, when elected officials have different preferences than those who elected them. The theory argues that, when formulating policies, leaders engage in a two-stage decision process (see Payne, Bettman & Johnson 1993). First, they use heuristics to reject any decision that would result in a major loss on a key dimension (the *non-compensatory principle*), typically one that would damage them politically. Second, once they are confident that "surviving alternatives" meet this criterion, leaders maximize the utility of the state by choosing among the remaining alternatives (Mintz et al,1997).

Poliheuristic theory integrates cognitive and rational elements, since the first stage involves the use of heuristics and the second relies on analytic, cost-benefit calculations (Mintz 2004; Geva and Mintz 1997). The non-compensatory principle means that any alternative that appears negative on the first dimension will be rejected outright. Leaders may thus reject even policies that are best for the country if they threaten their hold on power.

Poliheuristic theory has been used to help explain many historical and contemporary foreign policy decisions that seem inconsistent with a unitary actor, rational choice model of the state: Eisenhower's decision not to attack at Dien Bien Phu in Vietnam (DeRouen 2003), Jimmy Carter's decision to attempt a rescue of the Iran hostages (Brulé 2005), George H. W. Bush's choice to attack Iraq in the Gulf War (Mintz 1993), Bill Clinton's humanitarian intervention in Kosovo (Redd 2005), terrorist leaders' decisions (Chatagnier, Mintz & Samban 2012), and other war-and-peace decisions by leaders from Gorbachev to Saddam Hussein (see, e.g., Kinne 2005). In many of these cases, the non-compensatory nature of the political dimension influenced the policy outcome.

The non-compensatory principle of poliheuristic theory can also help explain individual voting decisions. Some voters may care primarily about one policy dimension (a voter might choose not to vote for candidates based solely on their support for banning abortion, or restricting the sale of firearms, or reducing taxes, etc.). For these "single (non-compensatory) issue" voters, candidates who do not come close to their preference will be disqualified immediately, regardless of how close they are on other issues. For example, for many National Rifle Association members, the right to bear arms is non-compensatory. They believe the Second Amendment gives citizens the right to keep and bear a wide variety of weapons and ammunition without government interference. The issue is so important relative to others that any candidate who disagrees on that one issue is disqualified from further consideration. Therefore, even if a different candidate is preferred substantially by the voter on other policy dimensions, s/he will choose the pro-gun rights candidate.

Poliheuristic theory can also be applied to strategic decisions involving multiple actors, making it suitable for incorporation into game theoretic models. In strategic settings, the Poliheuristic decision-maker eliminates, in the first stage, not only his or her non-compensatory alternatives, but also alternatives judged to be infeasible for an opponent on such dimensions (see Astorino-Courtois & Trusty 2003), as the decision-maker would anticipate that their rival would not select those options. The reduced-choice sets can then be subjected to a standard game-theoretic analysis in the second stage of the decision (Mintz & DeRouen 2010, p. 80). In a sequential interactive setting (e.g., when players make decisions at multiple times), each decision is part of a *sequence* of decisions by both players in a strategic interaction, each employing Poliheuristic calculations at each decision node in a strategic setting (Eisenband 2003). Because poliheuristic theory simplifies decision-making by emphasizing the role of shortcuts and rules of thumb, it can be useful for explaining complicated decisions, including those that involve multiple players, alternatives, and dimensions (Mintz & DeRouen 2010, p. 80).

In contrast to some standard rational choice approaches, however, poliheuristic theory is not only non-compensatory, but dimension-based (in the first stage), non-holistic, order-sensitive, and satisficing.[2] With its emphasis on the political dimension as non-compensatory for political leaders, it adds to our understanding of how leaders make decisions in democratic and non-democratic societies and can also be applied to domestic politics and electoral behavior.

Sofrin (2019) and Mintz and Sofrin (2017) introduced the two-group decision-making model. According to this model, foreign policy and national security decisions are made by two groups: a decision design group and a decision approval group. Intragroup and intergroup interactions, as well as choices made within each group, produce the final decision. In the following, we explore one example of how Poliheuristic theory can explain decision-making in conflict contexts.

Decision-Making in Terrorist Organizations: A Poliheuristic Perspective

For obvious reasons, it is crucial to understand why an individual or group chooses to engage in political violence.[3] Rational Choice models have been helpful – allowing the researcher to explore the strategic interactions between terrorists, governments, and civilian populations (Bueno de Mesquita 2005; Kydd & Walter 2006). However, these models begin with the assumption that terrorist organizations are unitary actors attempting to maximize fairly narrowly defined individual utilities (Mintz, Chatagnier & Samban 2020). Yet terrorism seldom seems to work to change policy. According to these models, choices that appear suboptimal are often the result of difficult strategic dilemmas, such as incomplete information and uncertainty. BPS has discovered richer explanations for these suboptimal outcomes. For example, the necessary information may have been available, but the *interpretation* of that information might have been biased. In other words, behavioral approaches contend that traditional rational choice assumptions of information processing and actor motivation may not hold. Scholars employing BPS explanations of terrorism are thus interested in understanding not just whether a group will engage in terrorism or not, but how they think and make decisions.

By knowing more about the way a decision-maker processes information and arrives at a choice, an analyst can reproduce the decision-maker's decision method and decision rule. This allows the analysis to trace back the path of decision-making. This technique, called Applied Decision Analysis (ADA), substantially improves predictive power, while simultaneously bridging the schism between rational choice and cognitive approaches. Poliheuristic theory has had considerable success in explaining the decisions of terrorist leaders, including Hezbollah's Hassan Nasrallah (Mintz & Chatagnier 2020) and al-Qaeda's Osama bin Laden (Mintz et al. 2006), as well as decisions by the Hamas group (Eisenband 2003).

For instance, Al-Qaeda's goals include the expulsion of non-Muslims from the Middle East and the re-establishment of a worldwide caliphate (Gunaratna 2002; Shay 2017); Hamas, meanwhile, seeks to eradicate Israel and replace it with an independent Palestinian state (Mishal and Sela 2006). These goals remain as elusive as ever, despite lengthy terrorist campaigns. It is this lack of success that has led researchers to question the effectiveness of terrorism as a credible means to a political end (Abrahms 2006; Crenshaw 1992; Fortna 2015). These studies suggest that terrorism seldom accomplishes the ultimate, stated goals of the organizations, implying that terrorists may have a second, unstated goal toward which they have been working: namely, the political empowerment and continuation of the terrorist organization and its leadership as political entities. Poliheuristic theory's emphasis on the importance of political survival might help explain this paradox. Ultimately, this theory can provide a convenient means for bringing together multiple schools of thought and be a highly useful tool for terrorism decision analysis.

One finding consistent with poliheuristic theory is that leaders of terrorist organizations will only make detailed evaluation of policy options that do not threaten the power or the standing of the terrorist leader. For instance, following the Second War in Lebanon of July–August 2006, Hezbollah's leader Hassan Nasrallah did not even consider either extreme policy option available to him: disarming Hezbollah or total war against Israel. He was in the domain of political gain and did not want to risk diminishing his accomplishments. This approach recognizes that Hamas and Hezbollah are primarily political organizations that use terrorism to advance their agendas, vision, ideology, and politics. Often, the purpose of terrorism is to build "market share" vis-à-vis competing organizations (Bloom 2004), as was the case when Hezbollah fought Israel in Lebanon until 2000. While political power is a non-compensatory dimension of critical importance for all these organizations, there are clear differences in how it is constructed. For Hamas, the intra-group competition between Hamas leaders in Gaza and Hamas leaders abroad, and between the military wing and political wing of the group, are the most important factors predicting the group's decisions (Chatagnier, Mintz & Samban 2012; Mintz, Chatagnier & Samban 2020). For Hezbollah, intergroup influence of external sponsors (i.e., Iran and Syria) is the most critical non-compensatory dimension (Chatagnier, Mintz & Samban 2012). For al-Qaeda, the political, non-compensatory dimension was also very different. Preventing one leader from upstaging another (Al Zarkawi versus Bin-Laden) powerfully structured the group's decisions (Chatagnier, Mintz & Samban 2012). However, despite these differences in the composition of the political dimension, this single consideration profoundly influenced outcomes. Understanding the politics of a terror organization's intra- and intergroup relations can thus help predict their behavior in subsequent decisions and conflicts.

BUREAUCRATIC POLITICS MODELS

The principal-agent problem identified in domestic politics models of policy-making thus extends to the government bureaucracy as well. According to a *bureaucratic politics* model of government policy-making, "the 'decision-maker' of national policy is obviously not one calculating individual, but is rather a conglomerate of large organizations and political actors" (Allison & Zelikow 1999, p. 3). In other words, even once a leader has decided on his preferred policy, he must rely on a host of other government officials to both (1) support and (2) carry out that policy. These other officials have some interests in common with the leader (e.g., the good of the state) but have other interests that do not necessarily align with the leader (such as their own ideological preferences, the success of their own agency or advancement of their career). In the Trump administration, for example, news stories frequently highlighted disagreements and discord within decision-making units that may have hindered the president's ability to carry out his policies. In September 2018, an anonymous White House staffer published an editorial outlining the various ways in which many high ranking officials were working "diligently from within to frustrate parts of (Trump's) agenda."[4] Needless to say, this is a clear example of a principal-agent problem, where the members of the president's staff tasked with implementing policies ("agents") instead actively undermined the president (the "principal").

The bureaucratic politics approach received a strong boost in the early 1970s as scholars such as Graham Allison began to theorize on the role of governmental bureaucracies and organizational factors in determining leaders' policy choices. An analysis of bureaucratic politics can help us understand the biases bureaucrats from different branches and organizations have when interpreting decision problems and solutions. This is the proverbial "where you stand depends on where you sit" (Allison & Zelikow 1999; Miles 1978): your position within the government (where you "sit") determines your worldview, preferences, and behavior (where you "stand"). For example, military leaders have international security mandates; diplomats representing the Foreign Ministry have distinct strategies for resolving conflicts; officers representing the intelligence community pursue particular sorts of information; and cabinet members have their own narrow constituencies.

How does one reach a policy decision in this context? Former Secretary of State Henry Kissinger describes the dilemma for political leaders concisely: "The conclusions of both the Joint Chiefs of Staff and the National Security Council reflect *the attainable consensus* among sovereign departments rather than a sense of direction" (Kissinger 1984, p. 227–228). In this view, policies are the outcome of internal bargaining, a negotiated settlement between sets of actors with often distinct goals and interests. They are the results of "compromise, conflict and confusion of officials with diverse interests and unequal influence" (Gvosdev, Blankshain & Cooper 2019, p. 175).

The role of organizational interests in policy-making contains both rational and behavioral components. On the one hand, agencies have distinct preferences – the State Department, for example, is likely to prefer a larger share of the budget than it currently gets vis-à-vis the Department of Defense (DoD), and the DoD likely feels the opposite. The RCT framework can easily accommodate these preferences by incorporating organizational interests (in addition to state interests) into an actor's utility function. However, there are also perceptual components to this dynamic, whereby someone's position in government affects how they *process* information, which then also affects their preferences on the issue. For example, an official from the State Department working on post-invasion Iraq in 2003 is more likely to focus on the reconstruction challenges there, and so focus on diplomatic solutions. In contrast, an official from the DoD is likely to focus on the acute security issues in Iraq, leading to an emphasis on military policies. As we have shown in Chapter 4, these perceptual frames can be very powerful in shaping preferences and behavior. As such, "where individuals sit in the process determines in large part the faces of the issues that they see and helps to determine the stakes that they see involved and hence the stand they take" (Halperin & Clapp 2007, p. 15–16, cited by Gvosdev, Blankshain & Cooper 2019).

Bureaucratic politics models may also help explain why Trump's former Attorney General, Jeff Sessions, almost immediately took positions that were at odds with President Trump's preferences. For example, Sessions recused himself and appointed Special Counsel Robert Mueller, a man known for his independence, to investigate Russian interference in the 2016 election. Of course, President Trump would have preferred for Sessions – a long-time ally – to head the probe in order to avoid the spectacle of an independent special counsel investigation.[5] However, acting as the head of the Department of Justice (DoJ), Sessions had individual and organizational interests to maximize, including the preservation of his reputation and that of the department. He recognized it would be inappropriate to maintain direct DoJ control of the investigation, given his own past involvement in Trump's presidential campaign.[6] Trump's next Attorney General, William Barr, supported this move by Sessions to recuse himself from the investigation, suggesting that Barr had similar organizational interests once he became the face of the DoJ.[7]

MUDDLING THROUGH: THE COGNITIVE CONSTRAINTS OF LEADERS

We have outlined how the domestic politics, poliheuristic calculations, and bureaucratic politics models of policy-making challenge the common assumption that policies are chosen solely to maximize the interests of the state. Rather, in these models, individuals – either leaders or bureaucrats – make decisions that maximize their personal or institutional interests. Of course, these models do not fundamentally challenge the assumption that each actor is attempting to maximize their utility in any given situation. They simply demonstrate that what is in an *individual's* interest can cause perverse outcomes for the state. These models still assume that choice processes are marked by "clarity of objective, explicitness of evaluation, a high degree of comprehensiveness of overview, and, wherever possible, quantification of values for mathematical analysis" (Lindblom 1959, p. 80). After all, government leaders are usually highly educated, experienced at policy-making, and motivated to produce the proper outcome. While citizens may fail to live up to the rational ideal because they either don't possess enough information or don't care enough to seek it out, political elites should get closer. BPS findings increasingly challenge this latter assumption.

Indeed, numerous BPS studies of policy-making have found that political elites often employ the same cognitive shortcuts and satisficing strategies as lay citizens do in order to make time-sensitive decisions under pressure (Simon 1956). Lindblom's (1959) famous paper "The Science of Muddling Through" contrasted a "rational comprehensive model" of governmental decision-making with the method of "successive limited comparisons" in which leaders choose among policy options that offer different combinations of values. He argues that it is only through this process of policy choice that the relative "value" an individual has assigned to each dimension is truly established. In other words, means are chosen *at the same time* as ends: decision-makers choose policies, and only through these choices do they gain a full understanding of the utility they have assigned to each dimension. This is inconsistent with assumptions underlying rational choice models of decision-making, whereby preferences (the ends) are chosen *first*, and then actions are designed to achieve them.

An example can help illustrate the challenge facing elites. Assume individuals have distinct ideas about the relative importance of *freedom* versus *security* in society. Both values are important to everyone, but they are often in conflict in the real world. Should we prevent the government from monitoring the personal communications of citizens, even if that mean we could miss the chance of uncovering and stopping a terrorist plot before it is carried out? However, the *exact* utility individuals assign to each value is difficult to discern and can often be divined only *after* various policy options are implemented. Should the United States remove due process for terrorism suspects? Should they do so only under very specific circumstances, such as in ticking-bomb situations? What exactly is a ticking-bomb situation? Are certain components of due process more important to maintain than others? Answering these questions helps the decision-maker to ascertain his or her true preferences on this multifaceted issue.[8] But recall that each of these individual policy features are often arrived at using a satisficing process, rather than one that begins with abstract preference orderings and then maximizes utility based on those preferences. If this is so, in the aggregate at least, the typical information processing and decision-making strategies humans use can compound individual deviations from traditional rational choice models, rather than reduce them.

AN ORGANIZATIONAL APPROACH TO POLICY DECISION-MAKING

One important RCT response to the discovery of bounded rationality at the individual level is that, in many cases, leaders do not make policy in isolation. They often have access to a range of experts who can provide them with the information and manpower needed to choose policies that maximize the interests of the state. Thus, while an individual may be irrational, the decisions of the "state" will not be. However, an important assumption baked into this argument is that aggregating decision-making reduces the pathologies we have mentioned previously. Unfortunately, work on *organizational politics* and *group processes* suggests that this may not always be so. Let's begin with the organizational politics approach as an example.

While bureaucratic politics models theorize government policy as "resultant" of individually rational negotiations between bureaucratic actors and agencies with different preferences, *organizational* models of policy-making go one step further – theorizing policies as "outputs" generated by a series of constraints and compromises inherent in the institutional structure, rather than as strictly conscious choices (Allison & Zelikow 1999). In other words, most bureaucratic politics models assume that individual decision-makers and their bureaucracies aim to *maximize* their utility (even if that utility diverges from that of the state writ large). Organizational approaches instead assume typically that decisions are the result of *satisficing* decision-making. According to the BPS school of thought, organizational constraints may prevent bureaucrats from considering the full range of potential policy options, resulting in even larger deviations from an optimal policy than a consideration solely of divergent interests. The use of SOPs is by itself a common and important heuristic.

March and Olsen's seminal (1983) paper "The New Institutionalism: Organizational Factors in Political Life" addressed these organizational constraints on decision-making, launching the field of *new institutionalism* with their argument that political institutions were neither a mirror of society nor strictly the realization of individual preferences: rather, institutions were autonomous factors that provide meaning and context to interactions. As such, institutions could be thought of as political actors themselves that structured the scope of "appropriate" actions through their norms and formal rules, fundamentally constraining the freedom of choice of individuals. In other words, when addressing new problems or situations, individuals in organizations would be likely to pull from a previously developed toolkit of "standard operating procedures" (Cyert & March 1963). Given this tendency, past decisions will weigh very heavily on current ones even if they lead decision-makers away from the strictly best alternative, a phenomenon known as *path dependence* (Pierson 2000). In other words, to fulfill their missions, different organizations develop a set of routines or SOPs that govern their day-to-day workflow. These are developed to facilitate the optimal completion of the limited set of tasks that fall within the organization's mandate. However, these same SOPs can become problematic when they (1) interact with the *different* SOPs of other organizations, and (2) are used for actions *outside* the original organizational scope. Because organizations consist of multiple individuals with agency at various levels, they cannot adapt as quickly or easily as any individual might (Gvosdev, Blankshain & Cooper 2019). Essentially, the Bayesian updating process RCT describes as critical to learning for an *individual* may be slower or stickier at the level of the *organization*. And this can lead to decisions or behaviors that may be suboptimal at the level of state policy.

The habitual behavior of numerous organizational actors means that policy outcomes are not necessarily the result solely of a top-down directive. Rather, a "bottom-up process" (Gvosdev, Blankshain & Cooper 2019) often occurs in which each actor within each organization seeks to fulfill his or her narrow objective. This may not, collectively, produce the best outcome for the state or the organization. For example, when planning a state visit, the organizational goal of the Secret Service – to keep the president safe – may be at odds with the organizational goal of the State Department – to improve the diplomatic relationship with an ally. Thus, while organizations solve some problems in policy-making – generating additional information with which to make decisions, leveraging comparative expertise, providing labor and manpower – they do not uniformly improve or optimize the policy-making process. Moreover, *just like individuals*, organizations may satisfice, rather than optimize, when making decisions. This means that organizational decisions, like individual ones, will be strikingly different based on (1) how they choose to search for alternatives, and (2) what their benchmark is for defining an "acceptable" option (Gvosdev, Blankshain & Cooper 2019).

SMALL GROUP DECISION-MAKING: ADVISORY GROUP STRUCTURE AND POLICY-MAKING

The organizational approach describes how organizations – which are helpful in many ways for policy-makers – may nonetheless be subject to the same types of satisficing, path-dependent processes that govern individual decisions. However, for the most part, this approach does not see organizational processes as making individual biases *worse* – they simply do not completely eliminate them. As such, given typical cognitive constraints faced by human beings, perhaps policy-making might be improved by insisting that people work in groups? While each individual may suffer from cognitive biases that make comprehensive information processing impossible, groups of advisors working together may help attenuate these problems because each person could bring distinct skills and abilities that do not overlap exactly with their colleagues, and so the group as a whole might behave more closely to the rational ideal of a complete information processer. Moreover, since this advisory group would work within a single organization the problems highlighted by bureaucratic and organizational models of decision-making may also be attenuated. For example, experimental evidence of group decision-making in crisis bargaining games suggests that groups may reduce the likelihood of bargaining failure (LeVeck & Narang 2017). This may be one reason for the oft-cited "democratic peace" – the idea that democracies are less likely to fight each other than other regimes. Democracies are more likely to make crucial foreign policy decisions in group settings and this may attenuate biases that escalate conflicts. However, many studies have shown that group decisions carry different biases and, at times, can make individual biases *worse*.

Group processes models of policy-making examine these challenges and illustrate various pathologies that can affect decision-making in group contexts, potentially exacerbating the cognitive and emotional processes affecting individual decision-making. For example, research investigating the role of presidential cabinet structure in government decision-making asks how presidents build advisory groups, and how these choices impact policy. Hermann (1980), for instance, explores the role of three types of decision units in affecting state action: (1) the powerful leader, (2) the single group, and (3) the coalition of autonomous actors. She finds that the process–outcome relationships shaped by these group structures impact policy in a variety of ways, changing how many resources are committed, the willingness to take initiative, and the instruments of statecraft used (Hermann 1980).

Richard Tanner Johnson's (1974) seminal book *Managing the White House: An Intimate Study of the Presidency* also focused on this central question of the building of advisory teams, pointing out three distinct types of advisory systems – formal, collegial, or competitive – that impact policy-making. The formal organization is "designed to reduce the effects of human error through a well-designed management system that is hierarchical, focused on issues rather than personalities, non-confrontational, and oriented toward evaluating rather than generating options and making the 'best' decision" (Hermann and Preston 1994, p. 78). The collegial style, in contrast, emphasizes the importance of "working as a team, sharing responsibility, and consensus-building with an interest in generating options, openness to information, and reaching a doable as well as the best decision" (78). In the competitive advisory system, advisors vigorously debate and argue perspectives, while the president stays above the fray until late in the decision-making process, effectively playing "the neutral or honest broker" role (Burke 2005). These distinct styles may impact the quality of content of policy decisions. For example, leaders who have more independent versus participatory leadership styles tend to adopt different postures vis-à-vis foreign allies and adversaries (Hermann 1980).

All these discussions suggest there are problems with the assumption of procedural rationality in group settings. In particular, the *composition and structure* of the leader's decision unit can fundamentally impact both the decision-making process and the outcome, potentially exacerbating individual cognitive biases that diminish the utility to the leader and the state as a whole. The phenomenon of "risky shift," where individuals working in groups actually each end up adopting riskier preferences than they would have when making decisions individually, is one such example (Maoz 1990; Stoner 1968). Several hypotheses are offered for this phenomenon: perhaps group settings diffuse responsibility, such that each individual feels less personally responsible for the weight of a potentially risk choice (Wallach, Kogan & Bem 1964), or perhaps risk-takers appear more confident and thus are better at persuading others to take risks (Collins & Guetzkow 1964). Regardless, this well-documented tendency demonstrates that group decision-making does not always reduce individual cognitive biases. Experimental findings on "hawkish biases" in group settings further caution against treating groups as a panacea for reducing biases. Recent studies have found that group settings are as likely as individuals to exhibit biases such as risk-taking to avoid a loss, the intentionality bias, and reactive devaluation (Kertzer, Holmes, LeVeck & Wayne 2021).

If group processes can exacerbate individual biases, government decision-making might fall even further from the rational choice ideal than the aforementioned domestic politics, bureaucratic, and organizational models. Suboptimal government policies would, therefore, not spring from domestic political interests, rational compromise among actors with divergent preferences, or sticky SOPs. Instead, psychological biases stemming from the social dynamics of group decision-making could lead to policy fiascos that *no* individual prefers (Janis 1982). Next, we explore in depth two theories of group dynamics – groupthink and polythink – that have influenced the way we think about how elites make foreign policy decisions in group settings.[9]

Groupthink

Irving Janis's acclaimed (1982) book, *Groupthink: Psychological Studies of Foreign-Policy Decisions and Fiascoes*, exemplifies the group dynamics approach to decision-making, emphasizing the importance of advisory group structure on foreign policy decision-making. In particular, the book highlights the importance of the psychology of group dynamics in altering policy outcomes. Reacting to national security fiascoes such as the Bay of Pigs incident during the Cold War, Janis challenged the standard unitary foreign policy actor model and instead unpacked the group processes that seemed to precede the invasion of Cuba by anti-Castro insurgents supported by the US military. Unlike the rational actor model of politics, Janis did not adopt a simple assumption of individual utility maximization. Instead, he posited groupthink: "a mode of thinking that people engage in when they are deeply involved in a cohesive in-group, when the members' strivings for unanimity override their motivation to realistically appraise alternative courses of action" (Janis 1982, p. 9). The implications of this phenomenon for national security decision-making are clear and deeply problematic. In a groupthink scenario, the overarching tendency to strive for consensus and uniformity supersedes the motivation to carefully review a set of diverse policy options, and this can lead to suboptimal decision-making and, with it, policy fiascoes with which we are all too familiar, such as the attack on Pearl Harbor (Janis 1982, Mintz & Wayne 2016).

In the years since *Groupthink*, many political scientists have investigated the role of group dynamics in foreign policy decision-making and tested the groupthink hypothesis. In *Beyond Groupthink*, 't Hart, Stern, and Sundelius (1997) review the functioning of small groups in policy-making processes. Many of these functions can trigger groupthink. For example, policy groups often try to serve as a "think tank," helping brainstorm ideas in order to make sound policy recommendations. Unfortunately, this task may be inhibited by the policy groups' more problematic roles, such as serving as a "smokescreen" which gives *illusion* of deliberation to already-decided policies, as an "ideologue" designed to help decision-makers *reinforce* their own entrenched ideologies, or as a "sanctuary" for group members to rehabilitate positive in-group *self-esteem* in the face of outside criticism ('t Hart, Stern & Sundelius 1997). These myriad, competing functions can lead to suboptimal decision-making processes that exacerbate the effects of groupthink and group polarization (Stoner 1961).

Polythink

While Groupthink is concerned with the biases that *cohesive* groups create, decision units and advisory groups are often fragmented and divisive.[10] As a result, group dynamics can be seen as a continuum, running from the most cohesive (groupthink) to completely fragmented (polythink) (Mintz & Wayne 2016, p. 5). Groups at either extreme risk making suboptimal policy decisions, albeit for very different reasons (see Figure 5.1). In *The Polythink Syndrome*, Mintz and Wayne (2016) introduce the polythink concept, a group decision-making dynamic in which members in a decision-making unit espouse a *plurality* of opinions and offer divergent policy prescriptions.

In a series of case studies, Mintz and Wayne (2016) demonstrate that groups in a polythink dynamic will exhibit several key symptoms in their decision-making process, all of which may contribute to suboptimal policy outcomes. For example, the failure to converge on a single understanding of the problem at hand may lead to excessive intragroup conflict, confusion, competitive framing, and, eventually, decision paralysis or inaction. Essentially, the high level of disagreement among group members may cause the leader to adopt lowest-common-denominator policies for which he or she can obtain at least tepid support from each important group member. The polythink group dynamic can be triggered by other characteristics of the government bureaucracy or political leader and thus has both rational and behavioral origins.

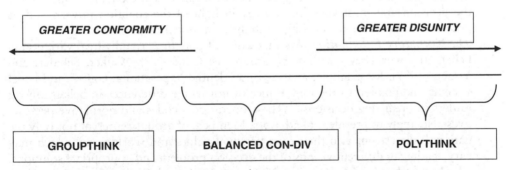

FIGURE 5.1 Continuum of group decision-making

The figure describes the psychological biases likely to take place in groups characterized by conformity versus disunity or fragmentation. More cohesive, homogeneous groups like those on the left side of the continuum are more likely to suffer from groupthink, where each member is so driven by the motivation to conform that they ignore important information in their deliberations that might challenge the consensus view. On the other end of the spectrum, fragmentation and disunity within the group can lead to a spiraling of alternative proposals that trigger polythink, that can likewise potentially result in decision paralysis or inaction.

Source: Mintz & Wayne (2016).

These include institutional dynamics, political concerns, normative processes, expert–novice divides, and leader–follower interactions (Mintz, Mishal & Morag 2005; Mintz & Wayne 2016):

1. *The Institutional, "Turf Wars" Explanation*: The phrase "where you stand depends on where you sit," (Allison & Zelikow 1999), described at length previously, adeptly summarizes the type of institutional thinking that can contribute to polythink. Under this explanation, the primary goal of any group member is to represent their bureaucracy or organization. Thus, presidential advisors, members of the military, intelligence officials, and cabinet members all have their own institutional perspectives and views and interpret and advance plans and proposals from these particular "lenses" and calculations (e.g., political, coalitionary, institutional, etc.). Due to intragroup and intergroup institutional competition over resources, attention, time, credit, and promotion, turf battles arise that hamper information sharing. Moreover, multiple gatekeepers at various organizations may emerge, holding information at control or choke points (Sullivan & Muetze 2007), and keeping the information close to their chests instead of sharing it.

2. *The Political Explanation*: Political decision-makers who engage in negotiation account for international considerations as well as domestic political considerations, such as political audience costs (Schultz & Weingast 2003). This is the two-level game (Putnam 1988). These various audiences play an important part in shaping the behavior of elected officials (Rubin & Brown 2013). In parliamentary democracies for example, where governments typically consist of representatives of different parties with different platforms, agendas, constituencies, and interests, a two-level game can contribute to polythink, as each member of the group represents not only the national interest but also his party and constituency's interests. Each member of the decision unit must view his strategy in light of the coalition process and its potential effect on the relationship with different potential partners.

3. *The Normative Explanation*: Another cause of polythink is individual variation in beliefs and worldviews within the group (see Chapter 7). Walker, Schafer, and Young (1999), for example, analyzed presidential "operational codes" and belief systems and pointed to the importance of normative differences in beliefs among leaders in predicting decisions.[11] These operational codes and normative perspectives also apply to presidential advisors. Members of groups represent not only the national interest but also their own personal values and worldviews, which may vary, leading to different visions of the decision problem and appropriate solutions.

4. *The Expert-Novice Explanation*: Novices process and recall information differently than experts. Whereas experts often focus on disconfirming evidence, novices typically focus on confirmatory information and strategies (Fiske, Kinder & Larter 1983). Naturally, these differences in information processing methods can have a drastic effect on the prevalence of polythink. Importantly, however, expertise does not always lead to better decision-making. Psychological and decision-science research has often demonstrated that, surprisingly, experts are frequently little better than chance at predicting or forecasting events (Tetlock 2005; Tversky and Kahneman 1974). Moreover, novices are able to make much more accurate and efficient decisions when the judgments required are novel or innovative (Jervis 1976). Thus, individual differences in experience or expertise can lead to different

approaches to problem-solving and a different view regarding optimal solutions (Horowitz, Stam & Ellis 2015).

5. *The Leader–Followers Explanation:* The management style of a group – the ability or inability of leaders to share goals or strategies with group members – may also contribute to polythink. For example, a "hands off" management style that gives subordinates a wide degree of autonomy, may contribute to polythink by exacerbating each group member's perceived independence and influence. Thus, the way in which a leader chooses to interact with his or her subordinates (Hermann 1980) can alter the decision-making style of the group in ways that reduce or increase the chances of a polythink dynamic developing.

These five causes of polythink are not mutually exclusive. There is a natural overlap between several. For example, the political positions of members of the coalition and their personal worldviews are related constructs that often interact. Likewise, institutional cleavages may be exacerbated by expert/novice dynamics in which advisors from the State Department know little about military options and advisors from the Department of Defense are unfamiliar with diplomatic possibilities. Thus, the rational and strategic components of group settings interact with behavioral dynamics to affect overall group cohesiveness and, as a result, the decision-making process and outcome.

Polythink can thus augment and add to rational choice explanations of state decision-making in two ways: (1) by moving from a unitary actor assumption of policy-making to a diverse group assumption, and (2) by shedding light on how the pull-and-push processes within a decision unit shape decision outcomes. Most importantly, unlike rational choice models that presume decision-makers will maximize utility, polythink demonstrates how decision-makers operating in group settings often arrive at suboptimal decisions.

As this discussion demonstrates, group dynamics – whether they produce the cohesiveness of groupthink or the discord of polythink – influence choices. Without understanding such dynamics, it is difficult to explain many important policy decisions, challenging the unitary actor assumption *and* the assumption that elites (or groups of elites) are less susceptible to the cognitive and emotional biases that impact the political decisions of the mass public.

Trump's National Security Team and Groupthink

Where did the Trump administration fall on this continuum of group decision-making? Did we see a unified, insular group of individuals who parroted each other's experiences, worldviews, and political attitudes? Or was his administration wracked by disunity and divisiveness as Trump struggled to bridge the divide between traditional Republicans and his campaign pledge to shake up Washington and "drain the swamp"? Alternatively, is there a way that President Trump threaded the needle – putting together a diverse decision unit that could nonetheless work together to accomplish crucial foreign policy goals? His original cabinet picks tell us a lot about the administration's early period in office.

At the beginning of his term, members of President Trump's national security team shared many foreign policy and national security positions and views that were susceptible to a groupthink dynamic. Consider the backgrounds of members of Trump's original national security team. Of the crucial national security positions Trump filled early in his term, four went to former military men (General Michael Flynn and then General H. R. McMaster for National Security Adviser, General James Mattis for Secretary of

Defense, General John Kelly for Secretary of Homeland Security, and Congressman Mike Pompeo for CIA Director). A fifth, the Director of National Intelligence position, went to a more establishment figure in former Senator Dan Coats. As such, the key players on this team, for the most part, all had extensive military backgrounds. They also shared the same views on deterrence, terrorism, threats to the United States, global hotspots, and with a few exceptions, potential solutions. In most cases, they even used the same terminology to describe such threats and solutions. Similar background and viewpoints, led by a charismatic leader, typically result in a groupthink mentality and behavior.

On the face of it, therefore, Trump's original national security team may have been susceptible to some key groupthink symptoms, having similar viewpoints on key issues, sharing the same background and led by a charismatic leader who has shown little patience for disagreements with his own views. Indeed, Trump's national security picks demonstrated his predilection for relying on a core of generals whom he entrusted to carry out his wishes and share similar views on most key national security issues (interestingly – the second Obama administration was structured similarly, after Obama's first-term "team of rivals").

However, Trump's leadership style also influenced the potential for groupthink stemming from an otherwise cohesive group. On the one hand, his alleged tendency to punish disloyalty and reward those who toed the line may have simply led his advisors to tell him what he wanted to hear – thereby increasing groupthink. This tendency also may have caused him to isolate or replace those appointees with whom he disagreed. And indeed, Trump showed both in business and in government that he did not hesitate to fire subordinates for disloyalty (e.g., James Comey), lying (e.g., Michael Flynn), or simply disagreeing on policy (e.g., Jim Mattis). Thus, frequent replacement of advisors, cabinet members, and others marked the tenure of the administration.

Trump's lack of national security knowledge and his reliance on the generals may have also caused him to be swayed by his decision unit's advice early on, leading his advisers to argue forcefully for different policy directions they believed the administration should take. The strong personalities of these officials likely contributed to a more contentious atmosphere among Trump's advisors and the ultimate decision unit. Unlike Trump's domestic cabinet picks, his national security advisers were largely veteran, senior military professionals with strong ties to Washington and the political-military apparatus. Though there was little outreach to independents or Democrats for key national security appointments, these more traditional foreign policy advisers may have sought to collectively direct US national and international security policy in a different direction than the president's by resisting radical foreign policy proposals. This is particularly likely given that many of Trump's policy positions were at odds with traditional conservative orthodoxy, such as the US relationship with Russia, and the US role within NATO and vis-à-vis European allies. An anonymous 2018 editorial by a staffer or advisor within Trump's national security team acknowledged that he or she was part of a "resistance" within the Trump administration, which was clear evidence of dissent on core issues.[12] Thus, while groupthink characterized much of the group's decision-making dynamic, fights and disagreements still broke out regularly, leading to a dynamic that oscillated quite dramatically across the decision-making spectrum.

CASE STUDY: THE ISLAMIC STATE CRISIS: ANALYZING US POLICY THROUGH DIFFERENT DECISION-MAKING MODELS

In the following pages, we apply the decision models discussed in this and the previous chapters to an important policy decision taken by the Obama administration vis-à-vis the ISIS organization. We then apply the different models of institutional decision-making described in this chapter (domestic, bureaucratic, organizational, and group) to some of President Trump's decisions on ISIS.

Background

Since the 2003 US invasion of Iraq and the overthrow of Saddam Hussein – and particularly since the withdrawal of US forces in 2011 – Iraq experienced a power vacuum. Into that vacuum flowed a variety of extremist groups intending to prosper and expand their reach. Thriving on the underlying sectarian tensions between Sunnis, Shi'ites, and Kurds, groups such as al-Qaeda in Iraq and more recently, the Islamic State (sometimes referred to as IS, ISIS, or ISIL) dominated large swaths of Iraqi territory. These groups subjected the country to another wave of violence as they implemented their extremist version of Islam and killed those they labeled infidels – 17,049 Iraqi citizens in 2014 alone.[13]

Officially created in 2006 as an offshoot of al-Qaeda in Iraq, the Islamic State's reach next expanded to Syria. The civil conflict there had also stoked sectarian violence and created another power vacuum that the Islamic State proved more than happy to fill, merging with extremist Sunni rebel groups there in late 2013. By the summer of 2014, the Islamic State had taken over major cities across Iraq, such as Mosul and Tikrit, and had attacked key oil fields and taken over strategic border town such as Al-Qaim on the Iraqi-Syrian border.[14] Moreover, as the Islamic State expanded their control to large swathes of Iraqi Kurdistan, Iraq's Christian and Yazidi populations were facing imminent genocide.

After months of advances by the Islamic State, the United States was forced to make a crucial foreign policy decision – should it attack ISIS to stop their expansion in the Levant? If so, what strategy would be most effective in degrading or destroying ISIS? This important foreign policy decision can be analyzed using several decision models to understand why the United States ultimately chose to engage in military action in a region it had just recently extricated itself from after eight long years of war. Did Obama's decision conform to traditional *rational choice* models, or was it more characteristic of *bounded rationality*? How did the use of heuristics, such as those described in *prospect theory* and *poliheuristic theory* affect his choice? Finally, what effect did *bureaucratic politics* and *group decision-making* have on this decision?

The US administration had several policy alternatives vis-à-vis the Islamic State, including:

1. Do Nothing: Maintain the status quo
2. Training: Train the moderate opposition forces in Syria and government forces in Iraq and supply them with military equipment
3. Limited Airstrikes: Limited air campaign against ISIS targets in Iraq
4. Airstrikes Only: Extensive air campaign that would include ISIS targets in Syria as well as Iraq
5. Airstrikes and Limited Boots on the Ground: Extensive air campaign, supplemented by troops on the ground in Iraq
6. Boots on the Ground: Extensive air and ground campaign that could potentially include intervention in the ongoing Syrian Civil War

These options were evaluated by the Obama administration based on the following criteria: domestic popularity, international diplomatic relations, humanitarian impacts, international security (i.e., from terrorism or instability in the Middle East), and, finally, the potential cost in American lives and material. We next describe how each decision-theoretic approach would have differentially explained the strategy to be pursued.

The Decision to Attack ISIS: A Rational Actor Explanation

When President Obama and his national security advisors evaluated their policy options vis-à-vis ISIS in summer 2014 in terms of these different policy options, there was a clear advantage to "Air Strikes Only" compared to all other options. Militarily, the expectation was that it would help the local population and potentially prevent genocide, saving the Yazidis and others in the region from certain death. Air Strikes Only also had the potential to tip the balance of power in favor of the anti-ISIS forces, perhaps even helping to eradicate the group entirely. It was also important that these airstrikes included ISIS havens in Syria, eliminating their home base. In terms of domestic politics, the declining popularity of President Obama and low approval of his policies, especially in the foreign arena, also may have led to the decision to launch airstrikes as a way to demonstrate strength and resolve. But perhaps the most important factor in favor of airstrikes versus boots on the ground was the relatively low risk to US and coalition lives. Boots on the ground would have led to coffins of dead soldiers arriving stateside – something presidents want to avoid, given the high domestic audience costs associated with military casualties.

The relatively low risk to US and coalition forces, the expectation that such a campaign could bring moderately positive results (at least preventing ISIS from opening the Euphrates Dam), and the political, domestic calculations in favor of airstrikes compared with doing nothing or committing massive numbers of ground troops presented the president with the highest net gain. This would be the optimal choice, according to the RCT model.

The Decision to Attack ISIS: A Prospect Theory Explanation

In a bounded rationality explanation, however, the administration could be seen as selecting a *satisficing* alternative of Air Strikes Only against ISIS, potentially forgoing higher utility that other options offered. On the military dimension, for example, airstrikes were unlikely to lead to the optimal outcome, as an air campaign *plus* a ground force campaign would have been more effective in defeating ISIS. On the other hand, it may have been seen as a better option than Doing Nothing. Based on the bounded-rational, satisficing model, not all dimensions of the alternatives and not all options would have been considered. Rather, Air Strikes Only was selected after it was deemed "good enough" in reducing ISIS's strength compared to Doing Nothing.

Prospect theory may be particularly useful in analyzing this decision. Even after Assad's forces used chemical weapons against their own population, the Obama administration refrained from using ground forces against Syria. The United States withheld the use of force against ISIS in Iraq even given the very rapid advance of ISIS forces in the power and governability vacuum created in Iraq and Syria. These consecutive failures placed the United States in the *domain of loss* in the Middle East and on the international scene. Furthermore, public opinion polls in the United States gave President Obama very low approval of his foreign policy performance, and the president's overall approval rate was also very low. The president was thus in the domain of loss both politically and internationally, as his foreign policy was perceived as weak and ineffective in the Middle East, Ukraine, and other places. The president had to "Do Something." In line with the prospect theory prediction of risk acceptance in the domain of loss, the president ordered air strikes on ISIS in Iraq and Syria.

The Decision to Attack ISIS: A Poliheuristic Perspective

With the growing public pressure on the administration to do something to save the Yazidis in Iraq, and in response to the atrocities committed by ISIS soldiers, a Poliheuristic perspective would argue that the administration had no choice but to reject the Do Nothing alternative. This policy alternative was non-compensatory for the administration on the political dimension, and perhaps also on the humanitarian dimension. The daily video demonstrations of ISIS barbarism – gruesome public executions of citizens and captured enemy combatants alike – cried out for a response. Similarly, supplying the opposition with weapons and/or training for their forces would have been too little, too late. On the other end of the scale, the horrific experience of US forces in Afghanistan and Iraq, where thousands of troop casualties had deepened the US public's war fatigue, eliminated Obama's appetite for committing ground troops. A ground invasion was thus also non-compensatory on the political dimension, and so was discarded.

As predicted by Poliheuristic model, the administration then evaluated the remaining policy alternatives based on rational calculations. In other words, once the Do Nothing, Train the Opposition, and massive commitment of Ground Troops options were eliminated, the decision boiled down to different types of air campaigns – a limited air campaign in Iraq, a more extensive air campaign in Iraq and Syria, or an extensive air campaign that supplemented by a small number of troops on the ground (mainly in "advisory" roles). Among these remaining options, the president chose in this crisis, the limited air campaign in Iraq, believing it offered the best utility on the remaining options.

The Decision to Attack ISIS: The Role of Bureaucratic Politics

In analyzing the ISIS decision, a bureaucratic politics approach would contend that it is crucial to take account of the many different actors and bureaucracies that were involved. Most importantly, there were of course, President Obama, Vice President Joe Biden, and the core advisory team at the White House. Other important advisors in this process included Chief of Staff Denis McDonough, Senior Advisors Valerie Jarrett and Dan Pfeiffer, and National Security Advisor Susan Rice.

Still other key actors came from the Cabinet (and Cabinet-ranked officials) – Secretary of State John Kerry and United States UN Ambassador Samantha Power. A third important constituency in the decision was the military, led by Secretary of Defense Chuck Hagel and frequently represented by the Joint Chiefs of Staff and its Chairman, General Martin Dempsey, the Chief of Staff of the Army, General Ray Odierno, or US CENTCOM Commander Lloyd James Austin III. Another important actor in this decision was the US Congress, who, in a rare show of support for the president's policies, seemed to back Obama's decision to launch an attack against ISIS. Finally, many components of the ISIS decision were international and multilateral; thus, many key actors were outside the United States, including NATO and other key US allies in Europe and the Middle East.

Based on the bureaucratic politics model, negotiation – pushing and pulling between various groups and bureaucracies – may have been what led to the decision to use airstrikes. Thus, whereas the Pentagon advocated a more aggressive approach, others in the administration were more hesitant to get involved. As such, the president, vice president, and Secretary of State, advocated the middle-ground airstrike option.

The Decision to Attack ISIS: Small Group Elite Decision-Making Models

The US decision to attack ISIS is also a good example of elite group decision-making models, as it highlights different group processes operating at the strategic level and one at the tactical level (Mintz & Wayne 2016). At the strategic level, the decision on what to do about ISIS was taken more or less in consensus, with little challenge to the dominant strategic view that "ISIS must be stopped," and thus exhibited characteristics of the groupthink syndrome and symptoms. However, the tactical decision on whether to train Iraqi and Syrian troops, attack ISIS from the air, or to put boots on the ground, followed more of a polythink syndrome and symptoms.

Specifically, following the atrocities committed by ISIS militants in areas they occupied in Iraq and Syria and the beheading of American journalists captured by ISIS, there was an overwhelming consensus that ISIS must be attacked in some way. The public, which just a few months earlier had opposed attacking the brutal regime of President Assad of Syria now overwhelmingly supported attacking ISIS. Similarly, there was strong bipartisan support in Congress for an attack. Furthermore, as in most groupthink situations, there was little to no opposition voiced within the group decision-making unit (in the White House, Pentagon, etc.). One, or in this case, a couple, pictures of US journalists beheaded by ISIS were stronger than any words, and there was virtually no challenge to this decision to counter ISIS in the administration.

In contrast, however, the decision about *how* exactly to attack ISIS, at the tactical level, was characterized by a polythink debate, with President Obama promising the American people that there will be "no boots on the ground" in Iraq and Syria, while Chairman of the Joint Chiefs, General Martin Dempsey hedging this statement, saying that if the air campaign proves insufficient, there would be a need to send troops to fight ISIS. This plurality of opinions at the tactical level extended to other actors as well. In short, it is safe to say that the US decision on attacking ISIS exhibited symptoms of groupthink at the strategic level and polythink at the tactical level (Mintz & Wayne 2016).[15]

In sum, even when these different models predict the same outcome, which is of course not always the case, they reveal a very different *process* of decision-making. The rational actor compares the net gains across the alternative courses of action and selects the "best" alternative. According to the bounded rational model, the president does not necessarily assess the various alternatives on all dimensions. Instead, he selects a good enough outcome, such as airstrikes on ISIS instead of a ground invasion. In prospect theory, the domain in which the president operated – whether it was loss or gain – influenced his decision-making process, whereas the Poliheuristic approach would begin with the *elimination* of several non-compensatory alternatives, such as Do Nothing and Ground Invasion, primarily on the political dimension, followed by a comparison across surviving alternatives on other dimensions (e.g., US and coalition forces casualties). In contrast, the bureaucratic politics model showed that the decision was the outcome of the push and pull bargaining among various agencies, bureaucracies, and constituencies.

Finally, small group elite decision-making models such as groupthink and polythink showed that different elements of the same overall policy exhibited different group-level biases: the strategic decision on what to do vis-à-vis ISIS exhibited symptoms of groupthink whereas key tactical decisions followed a polythink syndrome.

PRESIDENT TRUMP'S DECISION TO WITHDRAW FROM SYRIA AND THE POLYTHINK SYNDROME

These same models can be applied to President Trump's decision-making in the 2018 decisions vis-a-vis ISIS. On December 19, 2018, President Trump unilaterally declared that the fight against ISIS was finished in Syria. The president declared that "we have won against ISIS," and that "historic victories" over ISIS meant it was time for American troops to come home. The president announced the withdrawal of US troops from Syria, and that "they're coming back now."[16] However, the president's announcement was at odds with the advice of his senior advisors, clearly demonstrating a polythink syndrome in the administration. For example, Secretary of Defense Jim Mattis stepped down just one day after President Trump's announcement in protest of the move. A few days later, the special presidential envoy to the coalition fighting ISIS, Brett McGurk, also resigned, claiming that Trump's decision to withdraw was a complete reversal of policy. The president appeared to have rejected the counsel of many of his own top advisors and generals. Shortly after the president's announcement, for example, Trump's advisors came out with contradictory statements on the policy. On the one hand, John Bolton, the president's National Security Advisor, said that the United States would only leave when "it had assurances" that Turkey would not assault the Syrian Democratic Forces (SDF), the Kurdish-led group which provided the ground troops to fight ISIS. On the other hand, Secretary of State, Mike Pompeo, declared that the US withdrawal from Syria was "incredibly clear."[17]

As predicted by polythink, the presence of the syndrome delayed the implementation of the proposed policy to fully withdraw from Syria: after meeting the top US commander in Iraq and Syria, President Trump extended the drawdown from thirty days to four months. Indeed, for close to a year, the president's appointed staff essentially ignored this policy directive, "craft[ing] a Syria policy that was dependent on the United States maintaining an open-ended presence to continue the fight again the Islamic State and use American control over Syria's northeast as leverage to try and force the Assad regime to decapitate itself and pressure the Iranian government" (Stein 2019). According to Stein (2019), the National Security Council and senior members of the US government refused to accept the reality that President Trump "was planning on withdrawing combat forces from Syria."[18] As such, Polythink was an important dynamic that characterized the withdrawal decision and affected its implementation.

CONCLUSION

In this chapter, we discussed how the unitary actor assumption common to rational choice models of states' policy-making can be augmented by an understanding of the complexities of the policy-making process. These complexities include not only the competing interests highlighted by RCT domestic and bureaucratic politics models, but also by a BPS approach emphasizing the cognitive decision processes, organizational satisficing, and intragroup dynamics of policy-making teams. Various constraints – from domestic political concerns to bureaucratic deadlock to organizational standard procedures and norms, to group-based pathologies – can lead decision-makers to operate in a suboptimal way.

Specifically, the decision-making models discussed here (poliheuristic theory, bureaucratic politics, organizational politics, and group decision-making) make several assumptions that are distinct from unitary actor explanations of political behavior and leaders' decision-making. As discussed in Chapter 3, whereas rational decision makers strive for a maximizing choice, most BPS models are only *satisficing*. In addition, while rational choice models assume a holistic information search, behavioral models are non-holistic. Third, and relatedly, rational choice models assume comprehensive information processing, but BPS models emphasize the role of heuristics, rules-of-thumb, or standard operating procedures. Finally, rational choice models are compensatory, and at least some behavioral models are non-compensatory: choices with negative utility on certain dimensions, such as the political dimension, may be automatically eliminated from consideration. Incorporating these assumptions into models of foreign and domestic policy formation and implementation can help provide a richer, more nuanced understanding of international relations and domestic public policy and insight into decisions and policies that, on the surface appear suboptimal for the state.

6

Feeling Politics

How Emotions Impact Attitudes and Behavior

The 2020 US presidential election campaign may have been one of the most emotionally intense elections in a century, with turnout breaking records in many states and nationwide. In the end, over 81 million citizens cast their support to Joe Biden, the most ever cast for a president. Trump's tally was over 74 million, the second largest haul in American history. The level of vitriol in politics seemed unprecedented, and both before and after the election, Trump's rhetoric about electoral fraud appealed to millions.

During the 2016 campaign, Trump's team opened with the claim that illegal immigration was the nation's most serious problem, and that many Mexicans coming to the United States were rapists and criminals. Clinton claimed that half of Trump's supporters were "deplorable", especially for their hostile attitudes toward minorities. These and many other comments infuriated citizens on both sides of the aisle. Turnout on the right was high, with many voters who normally don't participate in politics – non-college-educated whites and rural residents – showing up for the first time and putting Trump over the top. In the 2018 congressional election, the pendulum seemed to swing back, with a "blue wave" of support driven by intense anger among Democrats, feminists, and non-whites about Trump's policies and personal behavior. This enabled the Democratic Party to take control of the House of Representatives.

While high emotions during campaigns are nothing new, both the 2016 and 2020 cycles displayed a high-water mark for the use of charged political rhetoric in the United States. But were the emotions experienced by the average voter in this election an independent causal force in the outcome? Or were they merely a consequence of the struggle over individual material interests that fundamentally drove participation and vote choices? The BPS paradigm argues that emotions are a critical driver of individual political cognition, behavior, and decision-making, independent of the real material stakes involved in a choice. This chapter will review several examples of the ways BPS research has explored the impact of emotion in politics.

One of the more common claims in the 2016 and 2020 political blogospheres involved the use of fear messages. According to the conventional wisdom, the surprisingly successful campaign of non-establishment candidate Donald Trump in 2016 was due to, in part, to the campaign's ability to capitalize on ethnocentric concerns about "others": immigrants, Muslims, Latinos, Black Lives Matter protesters, and so on. But where did such strong emotions about these groups come from? Perhaps they were rooted in economic insecurity and the shifting demographic and social structure in America. Populists, therefore, may simply have capitalized on the economic insecurity of many working and lower-middle-class white voters (Hetherington & Weiler 2009; Stenner 2005). By scapegoating minorities, then, *fear* could drive up support for these leaders. According to this view, support for candidates capitalizing on populist fears (e.g., the far right in Europe, leftist populists in countries like Venezuela, and to a certain extent the 2016 and 2020 Trump campaigns) is grounded mostly in anxiety about out-groups, and will therefore be maximized when fear is triggered among those with the most negative out-group attitudes.

However, two related arguments about the role of emotion in politics lead us to suggest fear may *not* have been such a powerful driver of support for Trump or candidates on the far right in Europe. First, according to *cognitive appraisal theories* of emotion, which we will discuss at length, fear occurs when threats are appraised as powerful and uncontrollable (Frijda 1986; Lazarus 1991; Roseman 1984; Scherer 1999). Fear should then lead people to withdraw from the situation and carefully consider how they might cope with that challenging threat. Affective intelligence theory (Marcus, Neuman & McKuen 2000), makes a similar prediction about anxiety, an emotion closely related to fear: It orients the brain to new information regarding the threat and away from habitual views, such as predispositions toward out-groups. Second, some evidence suggests that specific emotions and particular group attitudes can become linked as a result of socialization processes, and in the United States the strongest emotional substrate for racial attitudes is *anger*, not fear (Banks & Valentino 2012; Banks 2014). Similarly, Valentino, Wayne and Oceno (2018) posit that anger, but not fear, powerfully catalyzed support for Trump in the 2016 election, particularly among those high in sexism or ethnocentrism.

Of course, determining the causal effect of emotions on political behavior is challenging: in the real world, different emotions may occur simultaneously, and they are tied up with a host of other psychological factors (beliefs, predispositions, etc.). This makes it hard to disentangle the independent effects of emotions. An experiment that directly and randomly manipulates emotions – but nothing else – is one way to isolate the impact of the emotion on political attitudes while holding other forces constant. This is exactly what Valentino, Wayne, and Oceno (2018) did, randomly assigning respondents to one of three conditions. Respondents viewed an image of a woman making either a scared or angry face and then were asked to recall a time in their life when they personally had felt that way (either scared or angry). A third group, the control or baseline group, was asked to recall a time when they felt relaxed. This manipulation is called an *emotion induction* task – by recounting a time when they felt scared, fear is primed; thinking about being angry in the past primes anger. After triggering these emotions, the researchers asked individuals how much they supported Donald Trump using the same scale as in the previous study. They found that anger was associated with significantly higher support for Trump as compared to fear among those with strongly sexist and ethnocentric attitudes. In fact, fear actually *depressed* support for Trump among these same citizens relative to the control group in which emotions were not triggered.

These emotional dynamics also help us to understand the rise in popularity of the far right in Europe. For example, immediately after the deadly 2015 attacks on the Charlie Hebdo newspaper headquarters in January and various Paris locations in November, support for the far right *Front National* party in France became positively correlated with public anger but negatively correlated with fear about those events (Vasilopoulos, Marcus & Foucault 2018; Marcus et al. 2019).

This all points to a counterintuitive but important pattern in contemporary politics around the world. First, emotions can have significant, *independent* effects on political attitudes and impact citizens' vote choices. Second, popular debates about the role of negative emotions like anger and fear in politics often blur the conceptual distinction between them. These emotions have very different causes and consequences. While fear appeals are common, anger is often more likely to emerge when citizens feel threatened by newcomers, minorities, and religious outsiders. Further, anger is mobilizing, and may help to explain the rise in turnout, protest, and even political violence in the United States and around the world (Aytac & Stokes 2019). In the pages that follow, we discuss the role of emotions in politics – and how they undergird reason, to *both facilitate and undermine* individuals' ability to maximize their political interests and enhance their well-being. The study of emotions – their role in politics, their effect on voting, and on decisions about going to war or negotiating for peace – is one of the key schools within BPS.

RATIONAL MAN

Early theories of human nature relied heavily on the assumption that most people are simultaneously selfish and blindly driven by their passions. The ancient Greek philosopher Epicurus insisted that human nature is guided by *rational egoism*: we try to do what is in our immediate self-interest by making choices that maximize pleasure and reduce pain. If true, it seems like it would be very difficult to build enduring democratic institutions that served the public's interest over time. For an institution to last, especially one that would allow citizens to deliberate together, share information and arguments, and ultimately produce compromise solutions to problems that maximize the *public's* interest as a whole, we would need to set aside short-term individual insecurities, fear, anger, and even selfish hopes. The ancients, in other words, held that emotion should have no place in politics. However, the more we learn about how the human brain works, the more we realize that this imperative to "keep emotions out" of politics is both impossible and misguided (Marcus 2002).

In this chapter, we will first review in some detail this ancient idea that emotions systematically undermine our ability to reason effectively and efficiently about politics. We will then discuss new insights and evidence from the BPS tradition to suggest these intuitions are oversimplified. Emotions are, in many ways, a double-edged sword. While they can sometimes degrade our reasoning, they can also play a powerful and normatively positive role in our politics. Indeed, these new understandings about the psychology of emotion suggests that, without them, political reasoning would be deeply flawed. In a sense, rationality *demands* healthy and robust emotional reactions to threats and opportunities in the world around us. This topic, therefore, is one of the clearest examples of how BPS can help us understand when standard RCT assumptions are likely to hold, and when they will not.

ANCIENT NOTIONS ABOUT THE CONFLICT BETWEEN REASON AND EMOTION

Early political thinkers didn't think much of the mass public's ability to understand politics. Philosophers posited that some citizens were simply more gifted, more interested, and better positioned to help the rest of us figure out what was in our own best interests. Plato's *Philosopher King* embodies this idea: Society requires a benevolent ruler who does not simply *represent* the public's interests but can *divine what those interests are in the first place.* Only the Philosopher King was capable of choosing policies that achieved the common good. But how did the ruler accomplish all this amazing work? The answer came from Plato's tripartite theory of the human soul, and the particular and rare reasoning powers that a few citizens would possess.

In Plato's *Republic*, the human soul consists of three parts: *Appetite* (desire), *Logos* (reason) and *Spirit* (emotion). Appetites are short-term needs that drive us to maximize pleasure and avoid pain – an observation later picked up by Epicurus, as discussed previously. Reason is calm, forward-thinking, logical, and strategic. Spirit is passion triggered by injustice but can lead us to behave in ways that are foolish and harmful. Plato and his contemporaries argued that the ruling classes, and the Philosopher King in particular, are people who prioritized reason above emotion and desire. Governors are those rare citizens whose highly developed Logos allowed them to master the influence of emotion and appetite.

Unchecked emotion was often cited as a major obstacle standing between people and their goals. Ancient philosophers thought hard about how that obstacle could be overcome. Emotions were considered especially dangerous for elites in government. In *Politics*, Aristotle insisted "The law is reason, free from passion." Passion, ungoverned by reason, would distract rulers from pursuing the state's true interests. It would undermine their ability to build a system of laws that represented the preferences of the majority without violating the rights of the minority. In fact, the famous *Socratic method* is rooted in the belief that we can only get closer to the truth via open debate and deliberation about how things really are, free from emotion that might obscure the best way forward. Plato's chariot allegory in the dialogue *Phaedrus* describes the human soul as a charioteer driving two horses: "First the charioteer of the human soul drives a pair, and secondly one of the horses is noble and of noble breed, but the other quite the opposite in breed and character. Therefore, in our case the driving is necessarily difficult and troublesome" (Yunis 2011). The horse of "noble breed" represents rationality and moral impulses, while the other represents irrational passions and hedonistic needs. Needless to say, the horses do not always work well together in pulling the charioteer toward truth, and so many souls falter. This presumed tension between emotion and rationality lasted thousands of years, influencing psychological theories of human cognition, personality, and behavior into the twentieth century. Freud's psychoanalytic theory carried the same premise – that our minds are pulled in different directions by the passionate, irrational id and the cool, dispassionate superego. Even today, the presumption that reason and emotion are incompatible is common, in no small part because strong negative emotions naturally arise whenever terrible tragedies occur.

Consider, for example, the public's reaction to the horrific attacks of September 2001 in New York, Washington, DC, and Pennsylvania. Al-Qaeda operatives executed a coordinated set of airplane hijackings and intentionally crashed them into the Twin Towers of the World Trade Center, as well as into the Pentagon. A fourth plane, believed to be headed for the US Capital Building, crashed into a field in Pennsylvania when passengers on board confronted the hijackers. In total, more than 3,000 innocent civilians perished and another 6,000 were injured that morning. These terrifying events led many Americans to worry about the safety of airplane travel, and airlines recorded steep declines in revenue over the next several months. However, rather than flying or staying at home, people chose other forms of transportation to get where they needed to go. Chief among the alternatives was automobile driving. Unfortunately, automobile travel is much riskier than getting there in an airplane, *even granting* that prior estimates of the likelihood of terrorist hijackings had been too low. Several studies confirmed the bad news: At least hundreds and perhaps up to one thousand Americans died in traffic related fatalities after 9/11 that would not have occurred if the number of flyers had remained constant (Sivak & Flannagan 2004). We might speculate, then, that the powerful emotions experienced in the aftermath of 9/11 may have caused citizens to miscalculate the relative risks of driving over flying, and some literally paid with their lives.

Until very recently, most social science theories of human behavior adopted the wisdom of the ancients and presumed that emotional systems in the brain interfered with the rational pursuit of material and other goals. Contemporary approaches, however, have recognized that emotions can both hinder *and* help people to make decisions. For example, one of the great contributions of BPS has been to improve our understanding of the way the human brain deals with the overload of information pouring into our senses every waking moment. As you will recall, the first reformulation was Simon's notion of *bounded rationality*, which suggested people use stereotypes and heuristics in order simplify this large computational problem. But how, exactly, does the brain decide which situations warrant more or less effort? It turns out that our emotions regulate the systems in the brain that allocate attention to threats and opportunities.

So, our emotions, in fact, represent a crucial orienting mechanism in the brain, guiding the conscious mind to pay more attention to some things and less, or none at all, to others. Evidence that emotions are indeed a *necessary* part of rationality (sometimes called the *somatic marker hypothesis* in biology) – has accumulated at a high rate in the last twenty years. For example, a neurological study found that individuals who suffered brain trauma to the part of the prefrontal cortex which helps in the processing of somatic (e.g., emotional) signals exhibited compromised decision-making abilities in their daily lives (Bechara 2004).

The basic setup for the study was as follows. Subjects were given a gambling task, whereby they had to choose between using one of two decks of cards: one which yielded high immediate gain but large losses over time, and a deck that yielded lower immediate gain but larger wins over time. There were three groups of subjects: those with no brain damage, those with damage to a different part of their brain, and those with damage to the region thought to interfere with somatic signaling. The researchers found that the two groups without damage to the emotion management parts of the brain tended to avoid the "bad" decks – the ones that would have returned large losses in the longer term even though they could not explain why they were doing it. By contrast, patients with damage in the orbitofrontal region did not avoid the bad decks and, in fact, *preferred* them. These individuals were unable to make optimizing decisions that involved trading off immediate versus delayed reward and punishment. They were, essentially, unable to look very far into the future. These results suggest that emotional signals are actually "generated in anticipation of future events" and help us maximize our decisions (Bechara 2004, 32).

Examples like this show that the BPS tradition identifies emotion as a tool that sometimes dramatically improves decision-making, rendering both a process and an outcome similar to ones predicted by RCT. Those same emotional systems, however, can also explain why humans often eschew careful deliberation and rely so heavily on cognitive shortcuts, stereotypes, and habits of mind. Emotions can then lead to suboptimal decisions. We turn to a discussion of these insights next.

EMOTION AND COGNITION

Hot Cognition

Hot Cognition theory recognizes that reason and emotion are not distinct or inconsistent forces in human decision-making. In fact, the idea central to the hot cognition hypothesis is that we reason *from* our emotions. How so? The hypothesis suggests that emotions themselves can be used as information that helps us make better decisions.

Behavioral social scientists noticed that cognition can be "hot" – thoughts about a given object are often accompanied by strong feelings that arise as a person is exposed to new information. Political thinking, then, is guided by the *affective heuristic*. Immediate, even preconscious affective impressions rather than more detailed information about a given candidate, policy, or event get recorded in memory (Lodge, McGraw & Stroh 1989). These affective impressions cumulate into what we might consider our "gut feeling," a summary of the positive and negative feelings we have experienced when thinking about a given political object.

The hot cognition idea is therefore quite simple. Each time one encounters a candidate, party, or issue, one will log the simple affective tag that has occurred at that moment: "That candidate said something that made me feel good/bad." Later, we may be unable to remember any concrete semantic details of the speech – all that is kept is the affective tag. Over time, these tags produce an emotional "running tally." Eventually many political topics – voting, groups, parties, candidates, and policies – become affect-laden (Erisen, Lodge & Taber 2014). When asked to make a political decision, people retrieve from memory only the balance of positive and negative feelings generated by these individual encounters with the object. Afterward, if asked why they like a candidate, people will generate "facts" consistent with their preference, but those are often constructed on the spot, not stored in memory. This is what it means to say we reason *from* our emotions. We start with our affective summary and then generate substantive beliefs to justify that feeling. This is an important observation that provides a critical foundation for the larger theory of *motivated reasoning*, which we will discuss thoroughly in Chapter 8.

According to hot cognition theory, political decisions like the ones we make on Election Day are mostly driven by the emotional tallies of the alternatives being compared. This idea obviously stands in stark opposition to the basic assumptions about how democratic citizens might hold elected officials accountable to their substantive interests across a range of issues. According to this story, voters do not carefully weigh the strengths and weaknesses of each policy a candidate proposes or compare and contrast every character trait in order to decide whom to support. Instead, they quickly and automatically compare the affective tallies for each candidate and pick the one that gives them the most positive (or least negative) feeling.

The hot cognition approach explains a wide range of public reactions to policies that diverge from rational choice predictions. Take social welfare policy opinion, for example. Hot cognition suggests citizens hold a tally of positive and negative reactions to a variety of policies under this general umbrella concept. If one has been exposed to years of news and campaign rhetoric insisting welfare rolls are made up of lazy and unmotivated citizens who expect handouts from government, one might hold a very negative view of social welfare policy in general. Further, this might be true regardless of the benefits these programs provide for oneself or one's family. When exposed to a single piece of new information that contradicts this emotional tally – a news story for example highlighting the fact that the vast majority of welfare recipients are hardworking and have just fallen on tough times – such an individual would adjust their overall attitude only slightly, even if the new information should cause a large change in attitudes.

The hot cognition approach contradicts many of the strict assumptions underlying RCT. For example, citizens need not even remember specific information about how a policy will affect their pocketbook in the next election. They simply need to know whether one candidate made them feel more positive than another over a range of interactions and experiences during the campaign. On the other hand, the hot cognition approach is quite compatible with *bounded* rationality and with the use of heuristics in politics: Affective running tallies serve as heuristics individuals use to make more-optimal decisions while minimizing their investment of time and effort. They use their emotional response to information as a shortcut for deeply evaluating that information. Essentially, the balance of positive versus negative emotions toward a political figure or policy serves as a rough "affective" heuristic regarding the costs or benefits of supporting or opposing the policy or individual. Therefore, affect can either support or hinder rational decision-making. It can help individuals by providing an easy-to-access heuristic regarding complex stimuli, but it also may lead people astray because the simple affective tally might not validly weigh each dimension of the object under consideration.

Valence Theory

The theory of hot cognition relies on an assumption about emotional valence – the idea that the relative *strength* and *positive-negative* dimensions of emotions are the central attributes that impact cognition, decision-making, attitudes, and behavior. The positive-negative aspect of an emotion is called its valence and the relative strength of the emotion is its arousal. These two dimensions create an *affective circumplex* as illustrated in Figure 6.1 (Posner, Russell & Peterson 2005). Some emotions are highly arousing like anxiety, anger and elation, while others are less stimulating such as sadness and contentment. Emotions can be positively valenced, such as happiness or contentment, while others like sadness, anger and fear are negative.

The presumed benefit of this framework is that it mimics the way emotions are actually experienced. Most of us would have a hard time differentiating between emotions like nervousness and stress that are close to each other on the valence-arousal model. However, we can easily distinguish between emotions like happiness and sadness, which are on opposite sides of the circumplex. Thus, according to valence approaches, discrete emotions are less important than is the relative combination of valence and arousal. The key question is simply, how good or bad does an event, object, or person make you feel? Events that make us feel bad will generally lead to avoidance behavior while events that make us feel good will draw us closer (Tooby & Cosmides 1990).

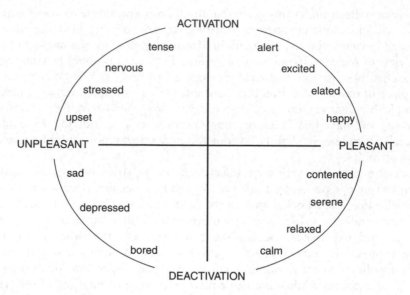

FIGURE 6.1 **The circumplex model of affect**
The circumplex model attempts to map all emotional states onto two dimensions roughly thought
to represent differences in overall arousal and valence. Note on the right side of the figure are
placed positive emotions that differ only in terms of intensity: elated is more intense than
contented. At the bottom of the figure, note that "calm" is only slightly more positive in valence
than "bored." The circumplex model was an attempt to reduce the complexity of emotional
experience to their most essential and important factors.
Source: Posner, Russell, and Peterson (2005).

Thus, in the valence conception of emotion, affect is seen as information that is easily
accessible and readily understood by the average citizen, who may not possess the time or
interest to consume multiple other sources of information on the issue or decision they are
facing. In other words, emotions serve as the primary tool by which individuals make
avoidance (negative) or approach (positive) associations with concepts, actions, and people.

The American National Election Study has found that answers to questions about
emotions toward politics frequently load onto one overall positive or negative
dimension (Marcus 1988) and instances of anger and fear are often highly correlated
in participants' responses, suggesting that people may have a hard time distinguishing
between these words. In their study of immigration attitudes, Brader, Valentino, and
Suhay (2008) found that anger and anxiety were part of a common factor and generated
similar survey responses from participants when analyzed separately and together. Using
these assumptions of valence theories of emotions, other studies have used similarly
valenced emotions as proxies for emotions of interest, measuring "afraid," "uneasy,"
and "disgust" as a proxy for anxiety and "proud," "hope," and "sympathy" as a proxy
for enthusiasm (Marcus, Neumann & MacKuen 2000). These and other studies
demonstrate the primary importance of "good" or "bad" affect toward an event or
object in determining subsequent attitudes and behaviors. Indeed, it appears that
emotions, used in this way, are a key tool for interpreting and manipulating novel
events or contexts.

Cognitive Appraisal Theories

Unlike the valence approach, cognitive appraisal theories posit that specific emotions like fear, anger, pride, disgust, and others reflect the individual's impressions about what caused an event to occur, who is to blame, and how one might react most effectively. In the political sphere, for example, we might assume emotional reactions to a candidate's speech require at least a sense for whether a policy proposal might help or harm the nation's economy, group interests, the environment, etc. This approach posits that cognition and affect are inextricably linked – beginning with the idea that emotions are the consequence of individuals' understanding of a triggering event as either consistent or inconsistent with their goals (Frijda 1986; Lazarus 1991; Roseman 1984; Scherer 1999).

Scholars working in the cognitive appraisal tradition have also refined the categorization of emotions, creating more discrete categories than the simple positive-negative, good-bad label used by affective intelligence and valence theorists. Namely, each emotion springs from a distinct pattern of cognitive appraisals triggered by the event. First the individual determines whether a political stimulus is negative or positive, a threat or an opportunity. Do immigrants help or hurt the US economy, crime rates, and culture? This is the primary appraisal process, and can occur very automatically and without much conscious effort at all. But subsequently, the individual carries out secondary appraisals that determine specific emotional reactions. Who is to blame for a political problem? Did they cause the problem on purpose? Could they have avoided that action and prevented the problem from occurring? These are the types of appraisals that determine which distinct emotional reaction the individual will have. Distinct emotions then produce very different political reactions. Figure 6.2 helps summarize the relationship between cognitive appraisals and emotional reactions. Here, we see a more complicated but comprehensive model about how emotions are triggered by the features of the situation and the individual.

An example is helpful to demonstrate the central difference between cognitive appraisal and simpler valence-based approaches. While a valence approach would postulate little difference between anger and fear (both are high arousal and negative), appraisal theorists categorize these two emotions as the product of very different circumstances, with different political consequences. Anger is triggered when individuals sense that they have been (1) unjustly treated (2) by an identified individual or group and (3) they have the power to do something about it – the power to right the perceived wrong. Fear, on the other hand, occurs when an individual (1) is threatened (2) by circumstances out of their control and (3) they do *not* have much power to address the negative circumstance head on. In politics, therefore, anger emerges when individuals feel empowered to address unfair treatment from a perceived enemy, whereas fear results when threatened individuals feel they do *not* have the strength to respond.

This difference in cognitive appraisals of intentionality and personal control is what leads the two emotions to have very distinct consequences for political behavior. While anger tends to lead an individual to be willing to take risks and expend resources in an attempt to right the wrong, fear may trigger avoidance. Anxious individuals may attempt to reduce this intensely negative emotion by distancing themselves from the threatening object or event. In other words, you are likely to be fearful of an approaching tornado, but angry at a neighbor who selfishly refuses to offer you shelter from the

	Positive Emotions (motive consistent)		Negative Emotions (motive inconsistent)		
	Appetitive	*Aversive*	*Appetitive*	*Aversive*	
Circumstance Caused					
Unexpected	SURPRISE				
Uncertain	HOPE		FEAR		Low Control Potential
Certain	JOY	RELIEF	SADNESS	DISTRESS	
Uncertain	HOPE		FRUSTRATION	DISGUST	High Control Potential
Certain	JOY	RELIEF			
Other Caused					
Uncertain	LIKING		DISLIKE		Low Control Potential
Certain					
Uncertain			ANGER	CONTEMPT	High Control Potential
Certain					
Self Caused					
Uncertain	PRIDE		REGRET		Low Control Potential
Certain					
Uncertain			GUILT	SHAME	High Control Potential
Certain					
			Non-Characterological	*Characterological*	

FIGURE 6.2 **Appraisal determinants of emotions**
A more complicated but comprehensive model of emotion springs from appraisal theories of emotion, like the one presented in the figure. Here, emotions are categorized in terms of the type of cause (natural circumstances, others, or the self), whether the result was positive or negative for the individual, and how much control the individual possessed in that situation.
Adapted from: Roseman (1996).

storm. Fleeing the tornado, a form of avoidance behavior, but actively criticizing the neighbor (an approach or attack behavior) are very distinct reactions. In both cases, the individual is guided by his emotions in order to deal optimally with an external threat.

These two emotions also impact information processing in distinct ways. While anger has been shown to activate simple heuristic modes of information processing (Bodenhausen, Sheppard & Kramer 1994), fear is more likely to encourage *systematic* information processing characterized by detailed and careful analysis of options (Renshon & Lerner 2012). Anger makes individuals more optimistic about future risk (Lerner & Keltner 2000) and, as a result, more risk-seeking (Lerner & Keltner 2001), whereas fear often triggers pessimistic risk assessments and a desire to seek risk-averse policy options (Lerner & Keltner 2001; Lerner et al. 2003). This is because fear – unlike anger – is an emotion is strongly connected to perceptions of uncertainty.

These different effects on information processing and action have important implications for political attitudes, decisions, and behavior. For example, researchers have found that anxiety about terrorism amongst American citizens *reduced* support for the war in Iraq, while anger increased it (Huddy, Feldman & Cassese 2007). Likewise, highly anxious Americans are more likely to support isolationism and were less supportive of aggressive action against terrorists than were those less anxious (Cheung-Blunden & Blunden 2008; Huddy et al. 2005; Lerner et al. 2003). Other studies have found anxiety reduces, while anger boosts, support for risky fiscal policies (Druckman & McDermott 2008). Anger may also be a more dominant emotion underlying support for aggressive counterterror policies than is fear (Wayne 2019; Fisk, Merolla & Ramos 2019). Again, these similar patterns emerge because anger *reduces* perceptions of risk, resulting in optimistic judgments of the future, while fear seems to *increase* risk perception and generate more pessimism about the future (Lerner & Keltner 2001).

Thus, cognitive appraisal theories emphasize the role that different interpretations of events play in shaping resultant emotions. These approaches do not insist that people think deeply about an event before experiencing an emotion, but they must extract key pieces of information from a situation: Is the event positive or negative? Was it caused by a person, or just an act of nature? Was it intentional or accidental? These appraisals can happen very quickly, even prior to conscious awareness, but they are still a critically important first step. Essentially, while other approaches tend to assume that emotions are entirely separate from "cognition," cognitive appraisal approaches insist these details trigger specific emotional responses. Our first evaluations of an event shape subsequent emotional responses, and these emotions profoundly influence opinion formation and behavior.

Affective Intelligence

Building on both the valence approach and cognitive appraisal theories, a further refinement of theories about the role of emotion in political decision-making also rejects the notion that strong emotions inevitably produce suboptimal results. Affective intelligence theory (AIT) argues that the traditional conception of emotions – as an evolutionarily antiquated cognitive "defect" that impedes rational decision-making – is deeply misguided. Without emotion, this approach insists, we could not possibly behave in ways RCT predicts (Marcus, Neuman & MacKuen 2000).

AIT draws on ideas from evolutionary and neuropsychology, arguing that emotions are *adaptive* ways of processing large amounts of information quickly and accurately. All this leads to the conclusion that, rather than seeking to eliminate emotions from political life in order to "protect against the danger of human passion," (p. 2), we must accept that strong emotions can be integral for helping individuals to understand and react to important stimuli events and trends (Marcus, Neuman & MacKuen 2000). Notably, this literature challenges ideas from international relations, which often assume leaders' emotions would lead to suboptimal "irrational decisions."

One of the key arguments of affective intelligence theory builds on some cognitive appraisal approaches we mentioned previously: emotions are *immediate* and preconscious reactions to stimuli that profoundly influence subsequent cognitions and prepare the person to act in the political domain.[1] Emotional reactions, in other words, are triggered by the scantest of information delivered by our senses, and occur before our conscious mind becomes aware of a given stimulus in our environment. The theory draws on insights about the brain's information processing abilities introduced by neuroscientists such as Antonio Damasio (1994), Joseph LeDoux (2003), and Jeffrey Gray (1990). The human brain, these researchers discovered, has evolved a fascinating ability to process a great deal of perceptual information *prior to and/or outside of conscious awareness*. Much of our behavior, then, is guided by these automatic and preconscious emotional processes that are carefully tuned to identifying threats and opportunities in our environment.

Affective Intelligence uses these insights from neuroscience to posit a *dual systems* approach to understanding political decision-making given these cognitive constraints. Under favorable circumstances, when we sense things are going well and we do not detect any threats, the brain employs the *dispositional system*. In these situations, people rely on their habits of mind, their standing assumptions about how the world works, their stereotypes, and the ways in which their friends and fellow group members would presumably behave. This is the "if it ain't broke, don't fix it" system, and it works quite well for most people most of the time. Of course, choices in such circumstances are not always beneficial to the decider or the target of that decision. For example, if someone holds a negative standing assumption about an out-group – that members of a group are violent, or undeserving of society's help – then that individual will continue to discriminate against the group even when that behavior is deeply unfair. We will continue to support policies that worked for us in the past, including those that undermine our own material interests in the present.

For example, Donald Trump consistently vilified immigrants, Muslims, and Mexican-Americans during his 2016 campaign and throughout his time in office. Many pundits and opponents accused him of using "fearmongering" toward these groups. The work we have reviewed would instead insist that Trump was probably strategically fomenting righteous anger against outsiders, an emotion that could trigger risk-taking behavior and political mobilization in his base. This tactic seemed to work: anger as measured by the American National Election Studies (ANES) was the highest it had ever been in 2016, and that level of intensity was maintained through 2020. Not surprisingly, turnout broke records again.

However, when we detect a novel or surprising stimulus – an event that might represent something new and especially harmful or beneficial to us – a different set of brain circuits is engaged. This *surveillance system* helps us evaluate any novel stimulus. It first prompts us to figure out if the object is likely a threat or an opportunity, and then to gather information about how we might react, to maximize benefits and minimize harm. These processes occur almost immediately after exposure, before "conscious thought" begins. In other words, the surveillance system orients the mind to learn, and readies the body to act.

There are many everyday examples of how the two systems operate. Imagine you are hiking in a pretty desert landscape in the spring, admiring the flowers, smelling the sagebrush after a rainfall, and appreciating the expanse of blue sky above. Your brain is relying on the dispositional system, rewarded by familiar sights and sounds, allowing your conscious mind to wander to thoughts and ideas perhaps involving similarly rewarding but distant experiences, people, and times. Many writers and artists seek out such situations because they seem to maximize creativity and imagination. In that moment, you are on autopilot, relying on previously acquired mental and physical habits to carry you forward through the landscape. Only something like the sharp sound of a rattle in the brush could bring your mind crashing back to earth and to the present.

The snake's rattle automatically triggers an alarm system in the brain even before you are consciously aware of it – between a third and a half a second after the soundwave enters your ear. The *surveillance system* focuses your attention and heightens your senses toward the source. Adrenaline is released into your bloodstream, causing your heart to race and readying your body to flee or fight. Many other physical systems are also engaged, and you enter an intense information gathering mode. You will stay in that frame of mind until the threat is resolved or until you are physically exhausted. A similar process can occur in the social world, in politics, and it has profound consequences for political behavior and decision-making.

Contrary to the conventional wisdom, this theory predicts that people learn *more* (not less) when politics make them anxious. And, indeed, evidence is mounting to suggest that this is exactly what happens. After the attacks of September 11, for example, conventional wisdom was that George W. Bush convinced an anxious American public to support going to war in Iraq. This was based partially on a set of claims about the link between then–Iraqi President Saddam Hussein and those who planned the attacks. One prominent study found this narrative to be incorrect. Feldman, Huddy, and Marcus (2015) found that many anxious Americans paid *closer* attention to mainstream newspapers that were running high-quality investigative stories on the lack of a link between Hussein and 9/11. These individuals came to oppose the invasion of Iraq in 2003 much more than those who were not feeling as anxious in the wake of the attacks.

A similar pattern emerged during the Coronavirus pandemic of 2020–2021. As a result of the Trump administration's framing of medical experts' advice about the disease,[2] Democrats and Republicans came to experience very different emotions and exhibited very different health behaviors as a result. Typically, Democrats were much more anxious and concerned about the disease, and were also much more likely to follow health guidelines like mask wearing and social distancing. Many Republicans around the country began, in contrast, to angrily deny the seriousness of the disease, and some even took much greater personal risks by violating public health orders.[3] By late 2020, over 200,000 Americans contracted the virus per day, and over 2,000 people died each day beginning in November and lasting into the winter.[4] By March 2021, the United States had surpassed 500,000 deaths. Many public health experts believe that this death toll could have been reduced if leaders from both parties had sent a consistent message about the importance of social distancing, mask use, and vaccination.

The orienting effects of anxiety on the brain – to make some features of one's surroundings relevant and others not – produces specific patterns of learning and attitude change. Thus, while anxiety may increase learning, it can also trigger biased patterns of information processing. Anxious people are more receptive to specific *types* of information than others. For example, when the surveillance system is activated, we are much more attentive to negative as opposed to positive information (Gadarian & Albertson 2014). When we hear about a terrorist attack, we pay more attention to various stories about the severity, the level of threat posed by the perpetrators in the future, and the likelihood that our own communities are at risk. We pay less attention to more positive stories about how well the city responded, how fewer people were injured than could have been, or how people helped each other in the moment. Why the attention to the negative? Perhaps the most negative information will give us the worst-case scenario that we can then attempt to avoid. This bias toward negative information in situations of threat may help explain why so much of the news tips toward the negative: It is the unconscious preference of newspaper readers who feel threatened in some way. The tendency for people to orient themselves toward negative rather than positive news is also important for understanding the ways political communication can influence the public (Soroka 2006), and is also in line with prospect theory's predictions regarding loss aversion.

One of the most important advances in the study of emotion in politics builds on AIT to describe the unique political impact of emotions of the same valence and intensity. For example, anger and fear have played strong and distinct roles in the processing of political information. Anger springs from the dispositional system, activating simple heuristic modes of information processing, leading individuals to resort to stereotyping (Bodenhausen, Sheppard & Kramer 1994). Angry individuals are also more likely to rely on superficial cues (Tiedens & Linton 2001) in decision-making. In contrast, as we have discussed, fear boosts information gathering and careful deliberation. One might say anger is a "certainty" emotion, while fear is an "uncertainty" emotion leading individuals to engage in more information search and systematic information processing. This enhanced information search process has been demonstrated in political campaigns, where anxious individuals were more likely to pay attention to a campaign and decrease their reliance on habitual voting cues when choosing candidates (Marcus & MacKuen 1993). This led to increased learning but not necessarily to increased participation. Anger, in contrast, mobilizes people into politics, leading them to take risks and expend scarce resources on policies and candidates they might otherwise oppose (Valentino et al. 2011). Therefore, the emotions we feel can actually change the way in which we seek out and filter information, altering the decision-making process in ways that deviate from standard RCT assumptions regarding holistic information search and integration into our utility calculations.

While AIT's relatively simple model of political emotion has had a major impact on the way political psychologists understand the causes and consequences of emotions in politics, a few of its core assumptions remain contested. In particular, the idea that emotions come *before* conscious evaluation of the implications of an event seems implausible, especially for complicated stimuli like the evaluations of candidates, policies, and campaigns. This is the main distinction between AI and the cognitive appraisal theories discussed previously: The latter places heavier weight on the role of conscious processes in the generation of politically consequential emotions.

BIOLOGICAL APPROACHES TO EMOTION AND POLITICS

Work at the intersection of biology and political science aims to shed light on this interaction between emotion and cognition, tapping directly into what is happening in the brain during times of stress, deliberation, and even political action (see, e.g., the Special Issue of *Political Psychology* 2012)[5]. These advances are made possible by newly available and affordable measurement techniques that have paved the way for new exploration into the potential biological explanations of political behavior. These include tools such as fMRIs to investigate brain activity; DNA analysis of genetic markers; blood, saliva, or hair tests to measure hormone levels (such as the stress hormone, cortisol); optical tracking of eye movements to examine attention and interest; or skin conductance to measure relative arousal and stimulation. In the words of Aristotle, "Man is, by nature, a political animal" – and now researchers possess the tools to observe the physiological bases for reactions to important events.[6]

Biological approaches to politics offer researchers the chance to gain additional insight into some of the many factors that, taken collectively, may have a strong impact on the political and social behavior of people. These approaches can be grouped in four broad categories: (1) evolutionary, (2) genetic, (3) physiological, and

(4) neurological. Though these approaches can be used to study a broad array of phenomena in addition to emotions, they can be particularly valuable for the study of emotions in politics, as we detail here.

Evolutionary Approaches

The study of intergroup relations is one key area in which evolutionary approaches may shed light on human behavior. According to this approach, humankind would have been predisposed to view in-group members with trust and empathy and out-group members with suspicion and misgiving. When humans were separated into small, often violent tribes competing over scarce natural resources, this natural aversion to outsiders would have been evolutionarily beneficial: those early humans that either hid from or preemptively attacked members of another group would be more likely to survive than naïve, trusting humans – better safe than sorry, as the old adage goes. This natural tendency may deeply inform modern political behavior; for example, why "the same person can be deeply cooperative, even loving, to an in-group member, while retaining murderous intent toward out-group members" (Hatemi & McDermott 2011, p. 14). In other words, though "large-scale political behavior is an extremely recent phenomenon in the span of human evolution, the initial evidence suggests that it relies on genetic and neural mechanisms that evolved to solve basic social problems" (Fowler & Schreiber 2008, p. 912). This evolutionary theory of intergroup relations and conflict has been explored by a host of research (Axelrod & Hamilton 1981; Kruger 2003; Thayer 2004; Trivers 1971).

Researchers have also hypothesized that information seeking and learning may be guided by evolutionarily adaptive, energy-preservation principles. For example, earlier in this book we discussed how citizens and leaders often fail to update their attitudes when presented with new information in ways consistent with Bayesian logic. This may stem from an evolutionary imperative to conserve cognitive energy: once a task is learned, it is more energy efficient to ignore information that might suggest a need to relearn, because the need to relearn may simply be comparatively rare. In this sense, the general strategy that leads someone to avoid attitudinal updating may be rational, even if it leads to significant errors in individual cases. Applied to emotions, evolutionary theory may help explain, for example, the dominance of fear in structuring political attitudes and behavior. Individuals and groups of early humans that were more predisposed to fear may have fared better than their less-fearful counterparts – being warier that the rustling in the bush was a rattlesnake, for instance, or running for cover faster when the winds indicated a storm coming. Over thousands of years then, these reactions would have been evolutionary selected, as fear helped individuals live longer and increased their chances of reproducing.

These types of evolutionary approaches to politics thus take the long view of rationality – and the role emotions play in shaping it. Namely, a strategy or trait that is "evolutionarily rational" may be suboptimal (and irrational) for an individual in a specific moment or even over their entire lifespan. Recall that RCT tends to view utility maximization in a more temporally narrow way. It is harder to predict specific decisions when people are willing to sacrifice their life for the benefit of future generations than when actors behave according to more immediate, individual payoffs. In other words, while evolutionary approaches are intuitively appealing, they are almost impossible to falsify: for example, someone could always argue that strategies that appear irrational are only so because not enough time has passed to judge the outcome. As a result, evolutionary rationality at times risks becoming a tautology: "if you observe many humans doing X, it must be rational in the long run."

Genetics and Politics

A related stream of research has looked at the genetic components of emotions and politics. In other words, why do people often respond differently to the same political stimuli? Is it entirely due to socialization or is there indeed a genetic component to the experience of emotion? How do these differential tendencies affect social and political behavior? Twin studies have been the primary method used to help understand the heritability of political attitudes and political behavior (Alford, Funk & Hibbing 2005; Carmen 2007; Jost & Amodio 2012).

For example, one study showed that physiological sensitivity to threat triggered by greater activity in a brain region called the amygdala was correlated with conservative political orientations (Oxley et al. 2008). So could people be born conservative or liberal? Probably not, but studies *have* shown that genetic variation is correlated with the positions people take on issues involving criminal justice and personal and national security threats. These differences can obviously have important consequences when people enter the political sphere (Alford, Funk & Hibbing 2005). Genes may also influence the strength of party identification (Hatemi et al. 2009), or the likelihood of experiencing "social fear" which manifests in political attitudes toward immigration and segregation. Other studies have found a significant genetic component to political participation and voting (Fowler, Baker & Dawes 2008), to predispositions toward trust and cooperation (Cesarini et al. 2008), to altruism and risk-taking (Cesarini et al. 2009). One study even demonstrated that physical strength (among men in particular, as measured by the circumference of their biceps) is positively associated with using force to resolve disagreements, being more likely to exhibit anger, and being more likely to prevail in bargaining contexts (Sell, Tooby & Cosmides 2009). These genetic components of our political attitudes suggest that automatic emotional processes occurring outside of our awareness may indeed be a primary step in the causal process of attitude formation and decision-making. To the extent that these processes are heritable, they may also be one source of the variation in preferences across individuals.

Physiological Approaches

Using new measurement technologies, scholars have also attempted to resolve the debate regarding the place of emotion in the causal chain from perception to behavior with physiological approaches, focusing on the chemical and physical responses of individuals to stimuli. For example, Renshon, Lee, and Tingley (2015) found that incidental anxiety (anxiety unrelated to the subject at hand) increased physiological arousal and, in turn, boosted anti-immigration attitudes. Likewise, Oxley and colleagues (2008) discovered that individuals with lower physical sensitivity to sudden noises or threatening visual images were more likely to support a host of traditionally liberal political policies such as foreign aid, liberal immigration policies, pacifism, and gun control. In contrast, those with high physical sensitivity held more conservative attitudes on issues such as defense spending, capital punishment, the value of patriotism, and support for the 2003 Iraq War. Similarly, other researchers have explored the hormones that may affect aggression and support for war (Johnson et al. 2006; McDermott et al. 2009) and the neural and chemical basis of emotional responses to threats (Cahill et al. 1999; Ledoux 2003; Waismel-Manor, Ifergane & Cohen 2011). Smith and colleagues (2011) found that physiological disgust reactions were correlated with attitudes toward homosexuality. Physiology even appears to impact participation in politics writ large. Gruszczynski and colleagues (2013) found that individuals who are more easily aroused – measured by how easily the skin releases sweat in reaction to a given stimulus – were more likely to be active participants in political life.

This physiological research helps address the core question of whether emotions are immediate, unconscious processes or calculated responses to cognitive interpretations of events and is based on the core assumption that "human thought, emotion and action are physiologically embodied phenomena … that the mind has a literal physical substrate that can be validly and reliably measured" (Smith & Hibbing 2011, p. 226). As such, this area of research serves as a bridge between genetic and psychological theories of political behavior. For example, physiological responsiveness may be the mechanism through which genetic differences between individuals become manifest in distinct social and political attitudes.

Neurological Basis of Emotions and Politics

Finally, advances in brain imaging technology such as fMRI, PET, and EEG have enabled researchers to explore the neural basis of emotions, getting inside the human brain to look at the ways our brains process and respond to emotional stimuli. This type of research has also proven helpful in untangling the causal chain of emotions (Landau-Wells & Saxe 2020). fMRI studies in particular have been able to point to activity in the brain as a sign of cognitive effort. The way fMRI technology works is that the MRI machine can track neural activity in the brain, with increased neural activity suggesting an increased amount of cognitive effort in that area. To the extent that we know which parts of the brain are most active during different tasks, we can untangle the neural basis of complex social and political phenomena.

Neurological methods have uncovered brain centers that seem to be associated with attitude formation and political behavior. A study by Spezio and colleagues (2008) used neural imaging to assess how the physical appearance of candidates affected neural responses and subsequent attitude expression. They found that losing candidates elicited greater activation in the insula and ventral anterior cingulate than images of winning candidates, suggesting that negative attributions from appearance exerted a stronger influence on voting than positive attributions. This result may be particularly important when voters do not have access to specific information about a candidate's issue positions or background, instead being forced to use only thin-slice visual information to make their electoral decisions. Westen et al. (2006) similarly found a strong neural basis of political choice – specifically in processes of motivated reasoning – when individuals aim not necessarily for accuracy in their judgments, but hope to reach a specific conclusion that comports with their preexisting views.[7] They found that, among partisans exposed to threatening information about their chosen candidate, motivated reasoning was associated with activations of the ventromedial prefrontal cortex, anterior cingulate cortex, posterior cingulate cortex, insular cortex, and lateral orbital cortex. Interestingly, there was no increased neural activity in regions previously linked to cold reasoning tasks and conscious (explicit) emotion regulation, suggesting that indeed subjects were engaging in a process of hot cognition designed to maintain their preexisting positive beliefs about their chosen candidate (Westen et al. 2006). fMRI studies are particularly useful for studying the places where threats get processed in the brain (Landau-Wells & Saxe 2020).

Importantly, this burgeoning line of research does not suggest that brain processes *predetermine* political and social choices, only that biological processes (which can themselves be changed and trained) may play some role in undergirding human political and social behavior. Thus, to the extent that emotions both cause and are caused by strong biological factors, we must consider these individual differences in our theories about political behavior, political decision-making, and opinion formation. Do these findings prove that the rational choice approach is completely misguided? Not at all, but we must remember that different people will react very differently to the same threats and opportunities, challenging simple understandings of social dynamics based on utility maximization. Let's now review a few examples of the ways that emotions affect real-world political behavior – potentially impacting both the decision-making process and the very goals individuals seek to achieve.

EMOTIONS IN PARTICIPATION AND MOBILIZATION

Integrating emotion into the study of politics can be used to understand one of the most important questions in democratic politics: What drives some people, but not others to participate in politics? Why would people engage in costly or risky acts that help the collective, even when they would have received that same benefit had they stayed home? The discussion of voter turnout earlier in this book introduced one example of this in the Paradox of Voting. Why do people turn out to vote when they have so little chance of altering the outcome of the election, and when the relative payoff from electing one candidate rather than the other is often so small? Scholars of rational choice have attacked this problem from different angles, for instance, by introducing various psychological incentives such as the commitment to civic duty (Riker & Ordeshook 1968) or group identification (Morton 1991) that transcend typical material interests. Political psychologists have pursued additional explanations, in particular by exploring the emotional processes that facilitate risk-taking and costly behavior.

The puzzle is simple: Given that payoffs for participating in elections are usually small, why do some people low in resources participate at all? And why do some folks very high in resources sometimes stay home? Since socioeconomic resources like education, income, residential stability, and the like are quite constant for most people over long stretches of their lives, how can we explain why people turn out in one election but not the next? The findings about the role of emotion in politics that we reviewed previously can help us advance better explanations.

First, we know the average voter is low in information about policy details and often does not know where candidates stand on those same policies; is unable to put issues together in a coherent and reliable way; and is not motivated to devote time and energy to becoming politically knowledgeable. How does that citizen both choose which political candidate to support and then overcome any material obstacles to voting on Election Day? The answer might lie in emotional processes.

Studies have shown that emotions like enthusiasm, fear, and anger, when elicited by campaign communication, have quite distinct effects on political participation (Valentino et al. 2011). Since various forms of political action can be costly, even physically risky in some places, understanding when people are feeling angry or enthusiastic will help us predict when participation will rise or fall. Anxiety focuses our attention on information about candidates' policy positions and helps us distinguish between them. This is critically important for making vote choices that maximize our representation in government. Exposure to political threats, for example, can trigger emotional processes that enhance rather than undermine the ability of citizens to meet the basic standards of democratic theory. Fear and anxiety, long impugned as harmful for democratic politics, might in fact play a crucial role in the development of responsible citizens who can at least occasionally learn what they need to know.

Different emotions may serve different functional purposes for individuals; while fear or anxiety is designed to focus attention on an anxiety-inducing object or event and inhibit action, enthusiasm boosts "psychic involvement," and encourages participation in the arena of the triggering object or event (Valentino et al. 2011). For example, Brader (2005) found that political ads that evoke enthusiasm motivate voter participation and activate existing loyalty to candidates, whereas ads that induce fear or anxiety often lead voters to engage in information search and, as such, can be very persuasive. Thus, enthusiasm can be used to strengthen existing partisan ties, while fear can be used to move potential swing voters from one party to another (Brader 2005). Thus, in elections, different emotions serve distinct functional purposes for individuals trying to make sense of new stimuli (i.e., new candidates). This has important implications for political marketing and campaigns.

In another study, researchers asked one group of respondents to write about something that made them feel angry about the presidential campaign of 2008, while another group wrote about something that made them feel afraid (Valentino et al. 2011). The key advantage of this manipulation is that respondents are not asked to focus on a specific event that the researchers think causes fear or anger, since of course each person might react with different emotions toward the same event. Instead, they generate the emotion internally, by calling up events in memory that made them feel strong anger or fear. The results of this study were fairly clear: After thinking about things that made them angry, regardless of the specifics, respondents were more likely to claim they would participate in the 2008 presidential election in some way. Fear, on the other hand, did not have this effect. Only when the act was very inexpensive, or mostly involved expressing opinions rather than taking risks, did fear show a positive effect. This basic pattern has been replicated in several other studies. Thus, though anger and fear are both negatively valenced, high-arousal emotions, they had vastly different effects on political behavior. Anger was mobilizing, while fear was not.

Differential levels of anger among various segments of the population then may be one critical factor explaining turnout gaps in the electorate. For example, white Americans are consistently more likely to vote than non-white Americans. This racial turnout gap has ranged between 13 and 25 percent: that is, the self-reported turnout rates among minority group members was between 13 and 25 percent *lower* than for white Americans (Fraga 2018). Fraga offers a variety of explanations for this gap, ranging from differences in income and education to active voter suppression campaigns against minority communities. However, one underexplored possibility is the emotional undercurrents of turnout. Phoenix (2019) demonstrates that African Americans, who have experienced discrimination, prejudice, and overt violence for centuries in the United States, feel a strong sense of *resignation* regarding the state of politics. This, in turn, contributes to a persistent "anger gap" – with African-Americans reporting significantly lower levels of anger than whites about political issues and candidates – which helps explain their lower levels of mobilization, above and beyond other material factors (Phoenix 2019).

Differential levels of anger across political parties may have been an important factor in the 2016 and 2020 US presidential elections as well. For example, throughout the 2016 campaign, Hillary Clinton's messages were dominated by anxiety cues: causing fear in her supporters about what might happen to them under a Trump presidency. Trump, on the other hand, ran a campaign based on anger and outrage toward "politics as usual" and those in power. While Clinton did surpass Trump by millions of votes countrywide, she lost important Midwestern swing states including Wisconsin, Michigan, and Pennsylvania. One speculation drawn from BPS work on the role of emotions in political decision-making is that Trump may have simply been more effective at generating anger among his base, increasing turnout among Republicans in the 2016 election in these key battleground states.

In 2018, the left may have been more effective at this same strategy, mobilizing their base with the rhetoric of moral outrage about Trump's policies and personal behavior. Then in 2020, we witnessed very high levels of emotional intensity, especially anger, in partisans on *both* sides of the aisle. According to the *Washington Post*, the result was the highest level of turnout as a proportion of voting eligible citizens in the United States since 1900, when women, Asian Americans and Native Americans were disenfranchised by law and African Americans were disenfranchised in practice.[8] Over 66 percent of those eligible to vote cast a ballot on November 3rd, 2020. And again, these increases in voting were broad based: Turnout records were shattered in almost every state. Of course, the simple fact that turnout was high and people were angry is not evidence of a causal connection between the two. The COVID-19 pandemic led many states to make voting by mail much easier as well, and more ballots were cast in that way than in any other election in American history. Still, the pandemic also surely provided additional obstacles to many who would have liked to vote in person but worried about the health risks. Overall, the pattern of emotional intensity and turnout in 2020 is consistent with the general theory of emotional mobilization laid out by BPS theories.

RISKY POLITICS: PROTEST BEHAVIOR AND THE ARAB SPRING

Another obvious place to look for the impact of emotions in politics is when political action gets risky. One instance where this is obviously true is in an average citizen's decision to protest against the state: Protesting in an autocracy, risking bodily injury, prison, and death, is exponentially more so. So why do people do it? During late fall of 2010 and the winter of 2011, a large number of Egyptians took to the streets to express their frustration about the economic deprivation they were experiencing. Public anger toward their leader, then–President Hosni Mubarak, ran high, presumably for failing to improve their living conditions, including poverty, growing youth unemployment, etc. The massive street protests that followed were largely peaceful, but anti-insurgent security forces regularly attacked the protestors in an attempt to disperse them and end the threat to the regime. Hundreds of thousands of Egyptians risked arrest, injury, and even death in these protests. The BBC reported that 846 Egyptians were killed and thousands more injured in clashes with military, police, and irregular security forces during the three weeks of intense protests beginning in January of 2011 in Cairo.[9] Eventually, however, Hosni Mubarak was overthrown and then convicted of corruption and negligence in the deaths of many peaceful protestors during the uprising.[10]

Why would any individual take such risks, especially since his or her contribution to regime change in a large country like Egypt is likely to be infinitesimal? This collective action problem is exactly the same as the one described for voting, but with much higher potential risks and costs. As a result, standard rational actor models have a hard time explaining this type of behavior. One possibility is that only an irrational person, debilitated by his or her emotions, would engage in such behavior. Indeed, this type of argument lay at the core of Lasswell's argument in his seminal 1930 book entitled *Psychopathology and Politics*. Adopting Freud's psychoanalytic approach, Lasswell suggested that those willing to take the greatest individual risks to attack existing institutions of government were out of touch with reality in very important ways. They were those who were likely to "exaggerate the difference between one rather desirable social policy and another, much as the lover ... is one who grossly exaggerates the difference between one woman and another." Emotions, therefore, might lead people to do less rational or even irrational things, to take unreasonable risks, and to act in ways that contradict their individual interests. Indeed, as we described previously, there is ample evidence that anger affects risk calculations, leading individuals to assess risk substantially lower than they otherwise might (Lerner & Keltner 2001). Anger also leads individuals to increase their probability assessments of the likelihood of future anger-inducing events (DeSteno et al. 2000), increase reliance on "chronically accessible scripts" (Tiedens 2001) and superficial cues (Tiedens & Linton 2001) in decision-making (see Lerner & Tiedens 2006 for a review), and activate simple heuristic modes of information processing such as stereotyping (Bodenhausen, Sheppard & Kramer 1994). As a result, emotional, angry citizens may, in part at least, be more likely to underestimate their risk of harm from protesting. However, emotion's role in altering political behavior is not solely due to fogging individuals' ability to think clearly about their interests. In fact, even in the realm of risky participation, there are ways in which emotions can sometimes help people make good decisions.

The notion that emotions peak before and during political protests, both large and small, is not contested. Most theorists, even those who would posit explanations based on individual material gains from engaging in protest behavior, would accept that protestors experience high levels of anger, fear, hope, etc. The key question, of course, is whether such emotions play any independent causal role in the generation and maintenance of protest movements, or whether these are simply *incidental*. Is the experience of strong emotions really necessary for engaging in protests, and if so, how? We think the answer is that, indeed, emotions play a critical independent causal role in these behavioral patterns. Furthermore, they help to explain why people will take risks under some conditions but not others.

So how do emotions help motivate risky behavior like political protesting (which is particularly risky in authoritarian regimes) in ways that still might be considered "rational" or utility maximizing? The key insight may be in recognizing that goals may be short- or long-term, and that they may be individual or group-based. Powerful emotions can help individuals break the shackles of individual utility maximization and undertake actions that maximize longer-term outcomes for their group. Emotions bind members of a social movement together and may therefore help groups to organize effective protests (Collins 1990). BPS argues, therefore, that bringing emotions into the causal explanation for protest behavior is not necessarily to abandon the notion that individuals are purposive or driven to maximize the welfare of their families, neighborhood, ethnic group, or even nation (Jasper 1998). Instead, emotions are the critical causal mechanisms lying *between* interests and political action.

One way to understand the events of the Arab Spring is that widespread public anger led Egyptians to act even when they knew it was personally very risky by altering their perceptions of self-interest and helping to foment group consciousness. Moreover, anger may have shifted individuals' utility calculation from an "instrumental" approach to a "values-based" calculation that made protest an optimal action, despite the risks of personal harm (Pearlman 2013). Significant anger about regime corruption, growing unemployment, and a deteriorating economy, therefore, may have enabled individuals to overcome the collective action problem that plagues most puzzles in political participation in general. Anger might help individuals to act on behalf of their group, tightening the bonds of identity and increasing their sense of empowerment. In other words, anger may be particularly helpful in identifying threats to the group and motivating collective action to protect those interests rather than simply one's individual safety. As such, automatic emotional regulation processes may help us understand how people regularly overcome collective action problems.

EMOTIONS AND THE POWER OF PARTISAN IDENTIFICATION

Of course, partisanship (and its strong emotional components) is another primary motivator for political action. Strong partisans often resist important new information in ways that seem to violate basic assumptions of RCT, a phenomenon we discuss at greater length in Chapter 8, but partisans are also much more likely to participate in politics (Rosenstone, Rosenstone & Hansen 1993). Why is this?

As you will recall from our discussion in Chapter 2, a puzzle that rational choice models have long struggled with is that simple models of the individual vote calculus predict that virtually no one should turn out on Election Day. Yet millions do vote. One hunch Downs (1957) had was that the stronger one's partisan identity, the larger the benefit from voting might be. This is simply because party identity in the rational choice approach is itself a consequence of the distance between the party platforms and the overlap of an individual's ideology and material interests with one or the other of them. But even if the parties presented quite distinct platforms, it is still not obvious why any individual would choose to vote in countries such as the United States, because the chance that they could affect the outcome of an election in a large electorate is so remote. So, the collective action problem remains. Why not just stay home and let others do the work of politics?

The answer may be that we are wired to react emotionally to group competition, even when the stakes are low. Strong partisans are more likely to vote not because they receive substantially larger material benefits than independents from doing so (Groenendyk and Banks 2014). Instead, they participate because they react specifically with anger or enthusiasm, not fear or anxiety, to the game of politics. When they see a candidate from their own party attacked in an advertisement they get *mad*. Further, they get mad not because they have carefully considered the arguments the opponent is making and determined them to be objectively false, but simply because a member of *their team* has been attacked. Weaker partisans, or those who label themselves Independents, do not react to politics with these mobilizing emotions. Instead, they are more likely to experience anxiety or even fear at the thought of the political game. They may react this way even though they have the same material stakes on the line.

As we have discussed, fear and anxiety generally do not have the same effects on participation as anger does (Valentino et al. 2011). Automatic emotional reactions to the competition of politics, the game of it all, powerfully influences the desire to join the fray and see our own side win. All of this leads us to the conclusion that in any complex social system there will be some who feel motivated to join partisan teams and cheer on their side whenever the game is on. Others, even if they share many of the same material incentives, will be less likely to care about the sport of politics, and will stay home. But context matters too, because some events will trigger emotions in some individuals but not others, depending on their relevance to specific identity groups. It is similar to sport fans who get angry about verbal attacks on their team and subsequently attend games even when their team performs poorly.

There were plenty of examples during the 2020 election of this pattern. Turnout went way up among African Americans in Georgia. Stacy Abrams, a candidate for governor in 2018, had worked tirelessly across the state to register and mobilize the group after her narrow loss, one which she and others attributed directly to voter suppression efforts by her opponent, then Georgia's Secretary of State, Brian Kemp.[11] Kemp denied these charges, arguing that his efforts were simply designed to "assure the identity and eligibility of voters and to prevent fraudulent or erroneous registrations."[12] After her loss by a mere 50,000 votes, Abrams crisscrossed the state, informing African American voters of the threat of disenfranchisement they faced. The effort seemed to pay off, with an increase of nearly 800,000 new voters in Georgia by November of 2020.[13] The state narrowly chose a Democrat, Joe Biden, for president for the first time since Bill Clinton's landslide victory in 1992. Kemp's alleged efforts to undermine the voting rights of African Americans led to a powerful mobilizing anger, but only when Abrams was able to reach individuals face-to-face to explain the challenge and how to respond to it. These results show how efforts to demobilize voters can backfire, when the target group becomes aware of the threat and reacts with anger (Valentino & Neuner 2017). Obviously, this discussion continues as many conservative state legislatures take up laws to make voting more difficult after Trump's defeat in 2020.

The relationship between partisan attachments, emotions, and political participation is a good example of how BPS has advanced our understanding beyond what could be learned from previous models based on rational cost-benefit assumptions. From the rational choice perspective, strongly identified citizens might participate more because they get targeted by organized groups – including parties themselves – for mobilization during elections, thereby reducing the costs of getting involved. So strong partisans should be more likely than the disaffected to participate in general, but that cannot explain why some highly identified partisans would participate in one election but not the next. The strength of partisanship is a highly stable attribute, so it should make a fairly constant contribution to models of participation. Therefore, one of the important contributions BPS makes to our understanding of the real world of politics is by revealing the causal mechanisms underlying decisions to participate under some circumstances but not others.

Emotions and Leadership

We also now recognize the importance of emotional processes in the decision-making of not only the mass public, but our leaders as well, exploring the ways in which political elites are guided by their emotional reactions in certain situations. This concept of *emotional leadership* stands in stark contrast to the image of the cool-headed decision-maker often postulated by the rational choice tradition. RCT models have mostly avoided incorporating emotion in foreign policy decision, but they may be a key *implicit* component of a foundational international relations theory: realism (Goldgeier & Tetlock 2001). In fact, fear, revenge, and uncertainty in affecting the war-and-peace decisions of states are central to this theory. Uncertainty, realists posit, is an inevitable consequence of an anarchic global order in which no state can ever be truly certain of other states' intentions (Mearsheimer 2001; Waltz 2010). Therefore, states must take certain precautions to ensure their own security, such as arming themselves. However, armament even in self-defense makes other states more uncertain and fearful, causing a security dilemma that triggers a parallel increase in arms by other states– triggering a classic arms race (Jervis 1978). Crawford (2000, p. 116), for example, has argued that "deterrence theory may be fundamentally flawed because its assumptions and policy prescriptions do not fully acknowledge and take into account reasonable human responses to threat and fear." We would not equate threat and fear, as Crawford's argument does. Fear is, in fact, only one possible emotional response to threat. Still, the bottom line is that human information processing is influenced by emotional processes largely outside of and even preceding conscious awareness according to some neuroscience theories (see Marcus 2002 for a review).

Thus, fear, revenge, anger, and risk-assessment are key factors even in RCT models of world politics and international relations. It is perhaps an ironic feature of the theory that "deterrence policies can intensify adversarial feelings of insecurity and thereby elicit the very behavior they seek to prevent" (Jervis, Lebow & Stein 1989, p. ix). However, the effect of fear on information processing, decision-making, and political action, particularly in the realm of international relations, remains understudied. This omission is important, because the research that has been done in this area has shown that specific emotions can affect both the *content* and *process* of elite decision-making. For example, Druckman and McDermott (2008) find that risk-assessments can be fundamentally altered by the emotional states of the decision-makers: anger leads to more positive risk assessments than fear or anxiety. Anger can also impact international politics, as elites use angry rhetoric to construct an issue as particularly sensitive and volatile (Hall 2011). This performative anger can, in turn, influence the intrinsic emotional reactions elites have to a given policy dispute (Hall 2011). That is, while anger might be intended to signal the importance of an issue to an adversary, expressing anger can actually increase the commitment of the state in subsequent international negotiations (Hall 2011). Thus, the dominant emotion a decision-maker feels in response to world events may highly impact their decision-making process and ultimate policy choice. While rational choice scholars often treat emotions as self-evident, less relevant than other cost-benefit considerations, idiosyncratic, or simply too difficult to measure at the elite level (Crawford 2000), BPS suggests they are an important independent force in many political domains.

The recurrent violence between Israel and Hamas in the Gaza Strip is a striking example of the power of emotional factors influencing foreign policy, both at the leadership level and among the citizenry. In 2014, the discovery of Hamas tunnels underneath the border with Israel drove Israel to launch a ground operation to destroy them in Gaza. Prior to this discovery, most commentators assumed the Israeli operation against Hamas in Gaza would be restricted to airstrikes designed to deter Hamas from launching rockets into Israeli territory (a tactic largely neutralized by the success of Israel's Iron Dome Defense System). However, the discovery of these tunnels – "terror tunnels" as the Israeli government deemed them – forced the government to act to protect citizens in border communities near Gaza. This is despite the fact that tunnels are rarely a strategic game changer in tactical war strategies, although they can be very dangerous to citizens who live nearby. According to historian Gerard DeGroot, "In more than 2,000 years of warfare, tunnels may have mattered more for their impact on the psychology of the combatants – both aggressors and defenders – than for their battlefield results."[14] This may hold true in the Israeli case as well. The tunnels facilitate attacks against IDF units and the kidnapping of civilians and soldiers in border communities. Both of these possibilities are incredibly frightening to the Israeli public and dangerous; yet it is the citizens' fear associated with one's enemies surreptitiously popping out from under the ground that makes these tunnels an especially effective terror mechanism. "An enemy that is underground and invisible carries a multiplier effect that corrodes morale … In this case, the horror of what might lurk beneath inspires a reaction out of proportion to the actual threat."[15] Thus, Israel's leaders, driven by the need to protect fearful citizens in this area from Hamas combatants' aggressive infiltration from these tunnels into Israeli territory, chose to launch an internationally unpopular military engagement in Gaza. Similarly, at the end of 2018, the IDF launched a campaign to destroy several large tunnels constructed by Hezbollah at the Israeli border with Lebanon.

Indeed, the prevalence of anger and fear in war-and-peace decisions, and in generating domestic pressure from citizens, may explain the tendency of political leaders to "do something." This often results in a "hawkish bias" in decision-making. As we discussed in Chapter 3, Kahneman and Renshon catalogued a list of cognitive biases discovered in forty years of psychological research and found that nearly all of them would be likely to favor a more hawkish perspective "than an objective observer would deem appropriate" on issues of war and peace (Kahneman & Renshon 2007, p. 79). It is a clear example, then, of the basic architecture of human emotional systems biasing decision-making in very high-level policy debates about matters of war and peace, and therefore the importance of incorporating BPS insights in this domain.

Bush Sr. and Bush Jr. Decisions on Invading Iraq

Another example of the power of emotions to impact the foreign policy behavior of elites is the decision by US leaders – in both 1991 and 2003 – about the use of military force in Iraq. How can we understand why Bush Sr. decided not to launch a ground invasion in Iraq in 1991 even though there were strong military and perhaps economic incentives to do so, whereas President Bush Jr. did so in 2003? The RCT explanation for these decisions emphasizes different strategic environments, but we believe BPS, and, in particular, the emotional foundations underlying decision-making, can significantly augment our understanding of these events.

Near the end of Operation Defensive Storm in February 1991, US and coalition forces were able to kick Saddam Hussein's forces out of Kuwait and to considerably weaken him and his armed forces. Militarily speaking, many analysts suspected that the US and coalition forces could have successfully reached the Iraqi capital, Baghdad, removed Saddam from power, and utterly destroyed his loyal forces. However, President Bush Sr. and his advisers decided *not* to do so. Instead, the US and its coalition partners decided to impose a no-fly zone and economic sanctions on Iraq. In contrast, following 9/11, and after providing information to the American public and the world at the UN regarding Iraq's weapons of mass destruction (WMD) program, the Bush Jr. administration reversed the decision of Bush Sr. and decided to invade Iraq. What explains these divergent choices? Let us consider these decisions through a rational choice versus a BPS lens.

An expected utility approach to the decision not to attack Baghdad in the first Gulf War in 1991 but to then do so in 2003 would emphasize the varying costs of war as compared to the status quo in both cases. For example, after the success of Operation Desert Storm, the United States and its allies were in a great position militarily to continue the march to Baghdad and the Iraqi military was no match for the allied forces. This meant that the probability of success was relatively high, with the large potential benefit of removing an adversarial dictator from power. However, continued military action did have some risks and potential downside costs. Any operation to remove Saddam Hussein from power would have necessitated sending ground forces deep into Iraq. This could have led to the deployment of large numbers of US and allied forces and would potentially also have meant a costly occupation of Iraq. Thus, though the operation was likely to be successful, it may have been costly. Moreover, President Bush was concerned that the UN mandate given to the coalition did not extend to regime change and any such attempt would have lost the support of the international community. The president may also have been concerned about losing domestic support, jeopardizing his reelection campaign.[16] Thus, according to a rational choice framework, President Bush assessed these potential costs as higher than the potential benefit of removing Saddam Hussein from power.

In turn, according to a rational actor explanation, the reversal of this decision occurred in 2003 largely because Iraq was linked by US (and other) intelligence agencies to 9/11. Hussein actually did not aid the 9/11 initiators and operatives, but at the time the decision to attack Iraq was made, this was uncertain. This meant that, while the costs of war were still high (due to long-term involvement and US troops losses) the perceived cost of leaving Hussein in power was higher. Moreover, since the United States and its allies were still much more powerful than Iraqi forces, and Iraq had repeatedly violated UN sanctions, President George W. Bush might have thought it was a mistake by his father not to invade Iraq in 1991 and decided to do so in 2003. However, behavioral political scientists contend that this explanation for Bush Jr.'s decision to topple Saddam is not sufficient: it is not that the cost of Saddam remaining in power had substantially shifted – what had changed was America's emotional willingness and risk acceptance to engage in military conflicts in the wake of the 9/11 tragedy.

A BPS approach would highlight additional factors that RCT would otherwise discount. For example, one BPS idea that can shed light on the president's decision not to invade Iraq in 1991 and the reversal of his decision by his son in 2003 is prospect theory, which we discussed in Chapter 4. A key tenet of prospect theory is that decisions are anchored by a reference point and that decision-makers are risk-acceptant in the domain of loss and risk-averse in the domain of gain. How does this theory apply to the US decisions on Iraq? President Bush Sr. enjoyed an unprecedented 89 percent job approval rating at the end of the war in the Gulf. He was, from the perspective of prospect theory, operating in the domain of gain and accordingly did not want to risk his popularity with a risky maneuver in Iraq. In contrast, after 9/11, the president may have perceived his nation to be in the domain of loss, as a consequence of suffering more than 3,000 casualties and experiencing an alarming attack on one of its iconic financial centers – the World Trade Center. As a result, he would have been willing to take much greater risks in invading Iraq before even being certain that Saddam Hussein was involved in the attack. Though the objective military facts were quite similar in both situations, the shift in the domain of perceived gains or losses may have contributed to these distinct policy choices.

Another BPS factor that may have impacted these policy choices, and the focus of this chapter, is emotional processes. The 1991 invasion of Iraq was driven by the United States' desire to protect the sovereignty of another country, Kuwait. In contrast, the 2003 invasion occurred in the aftermath of the 9/11 attacks, when the US homeland had itself been targeted. Thus, the emotional climate was quite different. While there was outrage toward Saddam in 1990 at the violation of state sovereignty, this outrage did not come close to the level of anger the US population felt in the wake of the September 11 attacks. As we have shown in this chapter, anger is a deeply powerful motivator of political attitudes and behavior, and the action it mobilizes is often aggressive (Berkowitz 1990), punitive (Johnson 2009), and militant (Cheung-Blunden and Blunden 2008). Thus, George W. Bush may have been in a better position to capitalize on desire for revenge and widespread public anger (Wayne 2019), satisfying his own emotional desire to seek revenge as well as to "correct" his father's mistake by launching the full-scale invasion of Iraq in 2003. As such, incorporating BPS approaches into the analysis of these crucial foreign policy decisions can provide a more holistic picture of the complex mixture of factors that led to divergent policy choices in these otherwise similar scenarios.

CONCLUSION

One of the most important takeaways from this chapter is that emotions can both alter the process of our decision-making and shape the goals we pursue. This is a key contribution of the BPS paradigm. Interestingly, how people and leaders actually process information – through their identities and with the help of their emotions – can sometimes lead them to decisions that are similar to those which would be produced by a procedurally rational *Homo economicus*, is another important finding. Rather than two opposing forces, like the black and white steeds in Plato's chariot allegory, we can indeed reason *with* rather than *against* our emotions. Of course, there are also circumstances when emotions seem to undermine our ability to think clearly about what is best for us, our cherished groups, and our nation. The key insight is that passion itself is not at odds with reason, since all reasoning takes place on the foundation of our emotional experience. Our negative emotions are not things to always avoid, and not all positive emotions are beneficial in all circumstances either. These systems have evolved over the millennia to help us make decisions that work on average, most of the time. It is helpful to remember, however, that politics often happens *outside* those moments when systems are working well at the individual or institutional level. Thus, emotional processes that help us in our everyday lives could serve us poorly in moments of upheaval and uncertainty – the precise moments in which political decisions carry such important weight.

Understanding the role of emotion in political deliberation and in the cognitive processes of political decision-making can help rational choice theorists build more realistic assumptions and therefore improve our explanatory theories. To date, many RCT models simplify all negative political circumstances into the conceptually uniform notion of "threat." Accordingly, threats lead to problem solving and utility maximization unless highly negative emotions derail our ability to deliberate the best way forward. To the contrary, we now know that threats often cause powerful negative emotions, but not always the same one (e.g., anger is at least as important a response to threat as fear) and the consequences of these different negative emotions are themselves quite distinct. However, understanding the nature and intensity of emotional responses to threats is key to explaining political behavior in threatening environments. This is, then, another powerful way in which BPS can improve rather than replace RCT models.

In conclusion, these breakthroughs in the study of emotion in politics have contributed to entirely new approaches to the way we think about politics. Some of the conclusions from this chapter help inform further theories we will discuss later. In Chapter 7, for example, we will discuss the role of values in political decision-making and in Chapter 8 we will discuss motivated reasoning theory. Both of these approaches rely to some degree on the importance of emotions in decision-making. BPS also helps us understand why people are often so resistant to new and valid arguments that, if heeded, might significantly improve their lives. Why do people ignore new information that contradicts their previous beliefs? In fact, we have all experienced situations where our conversation partners resist new information so powerfully that they adhere even more strongly to their preexisting beliefs and views. What is even most startling is that this phenomenon is pronounced among the people who know the *most* – those who are highly involved and interested in the issue at hand, and therefore might also have the most at stake (Federico & Deason 2012; Lodge & Taber 2005). Before we get to that, we must review another important source of reasoning about politics that BPS has revealed: the norms, values, and personality traits that can function in consistent ways across a variety of political contexts to shape individual differences in preferences.

7

The Origins of Political Preferences

Material Self-Interest or Personality, Moral Values, and Group Attitudes?

A standard assumption invoked in the rational choice tradition is that short-term, material self-interest often drives political behavior. However, the expected utility approach used by many rational choice theorists is capable of accommodating various nonmaterial preferences that behavioral political scientists have identified as important in political decision-making.[1] For example, pioneering early work in BPS has found that individuals derive value from a variety of "symbolic" attachments that are often quite independent of short-term, tangible, and private material gains (Sears et al. 1980). These symbolic values spring from a wide variety of sources, such as our personality, social norms, identities, and intergroup animosities, and they can be quite unrelated to an individual's short-run, material bottom line (see, e.g., Sidanius 1993). Incorporating these symbolic or value-based motivations – which vary broadly across individuals, groups, and societies – into our understanding of the preferences people seek to maximize can thus greatly improve our understanding of political decisions and outcomes.

This chapter explores how BPS helps us understand the *origins* of political preferences, a process that is "black boxed" in most RCT models. Such models begin with assumptions about what people prefer and then draw out precise logical predictions for behavior derived from those preferences. RCT can therefore make specific, falsifiable predictions about politics in a wide variety of domains, from citizen policy opinion formation to leadership decision-making in war. However, these predictions depend on correct assumptions about preferences, while *how* people form preferences in the first place receives less attention. Of course, if assumptions about preferences are wrong, predictions about behavior will be wrong as well. BPS approaches delve into preference formation in more detail and have made significant improvements in predicting behavior as a result.

For example, as we have discussed, standard rational choice models of voter turnout in the United States assume that citizens prefer election outcomes that appreciably improve their personal wealth and prosperity – their wages, tax burden, or government benefits. Since an individual's chances of affecting the outcome of an election is infinitesimal, we would assume such material preferences would lead almost no one to vote, let alone donate substantial amounts of time or money to politics. However, two distinct facts persist: (1) Large numbers of people do vote; (2)

Voters often prefer candidates and policies that do not maximize their individual, short-term material interests. Therefore, one might suspect that voters attempt to maximize nonmaterial preferences.

As we discussed in Chapter 2, one simple approach to this problem is to assume that people attach nonmaterial value to the act voting – a "D" term in the utility calculation that captures the psychological benefit of performing a civic duty (Riker & Ordeshook 1968) – that helps outweigh the cost of going to the polls. In this model, voters receive some satisfaction or sense of purpose from voting. This satisfaction could be driven by societal norms, personal values, attachments to or animosities about social groups, or concern for national collectives. Adding nonmaterial motives to the utility calculation renders the act of voting more cost effective. Thus, this model adopts a broader definition of self-interest beyond direct wealth maximization (Morton 1991; Weeden & Kurzban 2014).

Nonmaterial interests not only affect whether individuals vote but which candidates they choose. For instance, there are many circumstances in which voters do not seem to evaluate candidates based on their personal financial situation, either prospectively or retrospectively (Kinder & Kiewiet 1979). Instead, they reward or punish candidates based on national-level economic trends that might have little or nothing to do with their own pocketbooks. Evidence from the United States suggests personal economic concerns can be a significant influence, but only when they are especially salient. For example, when a survey interviewer asks about one's vote choice immediately after discussing personal circumstances, the effects of personal economic concerns is enhanced (Sears & Lau 1983). The real world can make self-interest salient enough to influence political decisions as well, as Sears and Citrin (1985) found. Homeowners in their study were much more likely than renters to favor 1978 California's Prop 13, which drastically cut and capped the property tax rate throughout the state. Finally, some personal interests are held so intensely that they will affect narrow policy views, as when gun owners are far less likely than non-gun owners to support gun bans or waiting periods for gun purchases (Wolpert & Gimpel 1998). So, narrow material self-interests can and do matter, as these examples demonstrate. However, they have often proven to be weak and inconsistent predictors of political behavior and attitudes, especially compared to abstract values and identities. These nonmaterial forces are frequently gathered under the label *symbolic politics*, which we consider to be a substantial branch of BPS (Sears & Funk 1990; Sears et al. 1980; Sears, Hensler & Speer 1979).

The importance of nonmaterial interests or group-based self-interest is not limited to voting. For example, work as far back as the 1970s showed that individuals with children, who would be impacted by a policy of busing to achieve school desegregation in the early 1970s, were no more likely than those without children in public schools to oppose busing. Instead, it was negative attitudes about African Americans that powerfully boosted opposition, regardless of the personal benefit and impact of the policy (Sears, Hensler & Speer 1979). A similar debate exists today with immigration attitudes: while some work has suggested that proximity to immigrants increases hostile immigration attitudes (Enos 2014), most work finds no such effect (Hainmueller & Hiscox 2010; Hainmueller & Hopkins 2014).

In response to these findings, newer models proposed by RCT scholars have begun to consider symbolic values or group-based considerations in the utility functions of citizens and elites. These would be the more subjective benefits that individuals derive from group membership, acceptance, and fellowship. These newer approaches do not give up on the notion that people are self-interested, only that the things they care about are not always short-term, tangible, material, or financial. For example, maintaining group memberships might not benefit our interests directly or in the short run, but they might do so in the longer term (Weeden & Kurzban 2014, 2017). Studies showed that one might prefer a policy that discriminates against a disliked out-group, even if it costs real material wealth in the short run, because it maintains the dominant social status of one's group over time (Sidanius 1993). We could, therefore, broaden the concept of self-interest if group success provides tangible benefits at the individual level. For example, if our individual fates are tied closely to that of an ethnic group, then we could use what was good for the group as a shortcut for maximizing our material interests. Dawson's conception of the "Black Utility Heuristic" explains why middle-class African American voters often align their preferences with working class or poor members of their racial group, due to the idea that, what is good for their broader racial group is likely good for them as well (Dawson 1995). But this pattern still reveals a puzzle: Even when the group's interests are perceived to *directly* contradict ours as individuals, we still often prefer what is best for the group instead (Conover 1985). This suggests that some nonmaterial, symbolic, group identity-based forces are also important to voters' decision-making.

While utility functions can be stretched to accommodate a host of motivations underlying individual preferences, most RCT theories still generally assume that the distinction between "symbolic values" and simple material self-interest is conceptually trivial or empirically inconsequential. Indeed, the broadest interpretations of rationality in decision-making assume almost nothing about what people want, simply stating that rationality is taking actions that an individual believes are best suited to maximize their goals, whether those goals are material or symbolic. BPS scholars do not dispute this broad interpretation but often find it unsatisfying: any action can be justified as rational if we can retroactively identify a preference that motivated that action. For example, a voter who disapproved of a candidate from a different ethnic group might simply believe that candidate would pursue policies that would be bad for them personally, or bad for their group. However, these two values do not always push in the same direction – individuals can prefer a policy from a symbolic or normative standpoint, even if it does not maximize their personal material interest.

For example, many wealthy Democrats support redistributive economic policies, even though they would pay a higher share of their income in taxes. Yet, even when material self-interest and "symbolic" attachments *do* push in the same direction, we still might want to know which one is causally central. A candidate might win because he promises to cut taxes and to halt immigration. Someone with conservative racial views might vote for such a candidate on the second issue, regardless of the costs or benefits of the first. Of course, some symbolic preferences are very difficult to quantify: losing one's health insurance might actually not be considered as costly as preserving cultural heritage or traditions. How can we assign a value to a unit of "cultural tradition" so that we might make a prediction about what decision a given person would make when it is threatened?

In short, BPS scholars by and large accept a broader understanding of rationality that incorporates nonmaterial motives in political decision-making. However, where BPS differs is in seeking to examine *why* these symbolic or nonmaterial preferences exist and empirically establishing the relative weight these factors play in politics under a variety of different contextual scenarios.

For example, in the 2016 presidential election, many voters who had previously voted for Barack Obama did not vote for Hillary Clinton. Why would voters who had preferred Obama to Romney in 2012 subsequently support Trump over Clinton in 2016, even though Clinton's policy views were much closer to Obama's than were Trump's? Perhaps it was because voters disliked Clinton, not because of her policy views but because of other perceived character traits that simply *weighed more* in their decision calculus. In this sense, their choice to vote both for Obama and Trump is "rational" but might be based on nonmaterial considerations (emotions, values, etc.), rather than the standard material considerations we think about in politics (e.g., economic prosperity, security, discrete policy preferences).

BPS approaches can help us understand when these nonmaterial preferences are more or less central to structuring individual decision-making. This is because BPS opens up the black box of preference formation, asking why specific preferences are formed, when different sets of preferences will take precedence over others, and how these preferences vary across individuals, groups, and societies. Thus, for example, factors such as personality, commitment to abstract values, and the role of beliefs and norms in constraining behavior are the focus of many BPS theories. All of these forces could be, and many have been, formally incorporated into the expected utility framework commonly employed by rational choice theorists. In other words, the formal methods underlying much of RCT can be used regardless of the specific assumptions we make about the preferences people hold.

We therefore hold to the same conclusion as a prominent contributor to the BPS tradition, Dennis Chong (2000), who wrote: "I think not only that rational choice can be sustained but also that proper recognition of the significance of the work of symbolic theorists ought to result in a more realistic and robust rational choice model" (p. 26). By improving our assumptions about what makes up people's utility functions, we will strengthen our ability to explain and predict politics using the rigor of the RCT approach. This chapter considers the importance of these various factors in turn, reviewing the unique ways in which each informs the utility function of individuals and affects political attitudes and behavior.

In the end, we think one of the most important insights to emerge from the long debate on the impact of self-interest in politics is that the material stakes are sometimes weighted so lightly in individuals' priorities that standard RCT predictions fail (Aldrich 1993; Chong 2013). In such situations, the psychological effects of personality factors, group identities, short-term emotional reactions to threats, and abstract moral values or societal norms may loom much larger. The measurement of these forces is difficult and imprecise, but that does not mean we should give up on those efforts. We turn next to some of the various nonmaterial factors that are part of the BPS exploration of preferences, highlighting the systematic ways in which each may impact political decision-making.

THE ROLE OF PERSONALITY IN MASS POLITICS

Most rational choice theories of politics assume that the *context* in which an individual operates, and subsequently makes decisions, comprises the primary determinant of political attitudes and policy preferences. Personality traits – stable psychological orientations that guide behavior and are resistant to variation in real-world circumstances – should play only a small role. This reasoning is often explained using the analogy of the burning house – if your house is on fire, you will run from it regardless of your personality, values, or predispositions (Wolfers 1965). However, this analogy falls into the same trap as the previous debate: the implications of immediate self-interest in most political decisions are not as clear as whether or not it would be best to leave a burning building. The political world is ambiguous. The "correct" course of action for most citizens, most of the time, is not always obvious. Indeed, we often find people in very similar material conditions exhibiting great *variation* in their political attitudes and behavior. For example, why would some citizens at the bottom rungs of the economic ladder in society identify as highly conservative while others see themselves as liberal? Why do some wealthy people support a progressive tax system that raises their taxes while others do not? Why do some citizens who can overcome all the material barriers to participation still decide to stay home instead of voting, while others for whom the costs are much higher nonetheless turn out? There seems to be a great deal of explanatory power for individual differences in political life beyond the material constraints of a given context. Considered in an expected-utility framework, these *individual differences* would form the basis of distinct preferences that, in turn, may account for differences in behavior we observe across otherwise similarly situated individuals.

The basic idea that people are born with tendencies to react to the world around them in consistent ways across a variety of situations is the core of what some refer to as trait theory (Allport 1937; Matthews, Deary & Whiteman 2009; Mondak 2010). Typically, the discussion about how personality traits influence politics adopts a so-called Big Five dimensional view (Costa & McCrae 1992; Goldberg 1990; McCrae & Costa 1987). These five dimensions are: (1) openness to experience, (2) conscientiousness, (3) extraversion, (4) agreeableness, and (5) emotional stability. This five-factor approach to personality has been influential for several decades and has been validated numerous times. According to this approach to personality, individuals possess a set of internal traits that are observable, fixed, and enduring, and that influence their behavior across contexts. This is in stark contrast to situation-focused theories (Ross 1977; Zimbardo 1971), which we will discuss at more length in the following sections, that argue internal traits do not exert predictable, patterned behavioral responses from individuals.

One particularly vibrant issue area in which the Big Five has been examined is the study of political ideology – why do some individuals seem drawn to conservative ideology while others take a more liberal stance? Work in this area has suggested that relative openness to experience is strongly correlated with ideological identification, such that more open individuals tend to be left-wing, while high conscientiousness, on the other hand, appears to be strongly associated with conservatism (Carney et al. 2008). Other individual differences have also been found to highly correlate with ideological preferences, including relative need for closure, dogmatism, intolerance of ambiguity, and integrative complexity (Jost et al. 2003).

The Big Five approach is, however, only the most recent in a long string of theories about individual personality differences and their impact on politics. Research on the so-called authoritarian personality is an early example of influential research in this general tradition. The study of authoritarian personality traits in politics received a boost following World War II and, specifically, the Holocaust. The horrors of the Nazi regime during the era of the Holocaust – in which 12 million people, more than

6 million of whom were Jews, were systematically slaughtered – catalyzed research about the roots of fascism and anti-Semitism in Europe. How could this catastrophe happen? What types of people were more likely to support the Nazi party and either tacitly support or perpetrate such crimes? Led by Theodor Adorno, these scholars developed a scale (an "F-Scale") that purported to measure individual differences in *authoritarian personality*, a cluster of stable traits that predicted support for fascist leaders and policies (Adorno et al. 1950). The F-Scale was based on nine key traits: conventionalism, authoritarian submission, aggression, anti-intellectualism, anti-intraception (against the use of feeling or emotion in processing), superstitiousness, proneness to stereotypes, sensitivity to levels of power, and toughness (Adorno et al. 1950).

Though Adorno and his colleagues made an important start in understanding the role played by early childhood experiences and personality on political attitudes and behavior, the work was also plagued by poor measurement and flawed methodology: the questions on the scale did not specifically tap authoritarian impulses and may simply have tapped differences in political ideology. For example, one item used to measure "conventionalism" asked for agreement with the statement: "The businessman and the manufacturer are much more important to society than the artist and the professor." If the typical respondent believed the first two categories were ideologically conservative and the latter two were liberal, then the item would be tapping political ideology rather than an authoritarian personality tendency to value strong government and rigid social norms regardless of ideological leaning.

Research on the authoritarian personality – and personality, more generally – also took a large hit in the 1960s and 1970s, as studies discovered context mattered a great deal when it came to political behavior. For example, in 1963 and 1971, two influential experiments in social psychology seemed to demonstrate the powerful role of the situation in determining action, thereby casting doubt on the role of innate personality differences in explaining distinct behaviors. These studies (see Milgram 1963; Zimbardo 1971; see also Mischel 1973) demonstrated large in-person variations in behavioral responses to events depending on specific circumstances (e.g., a person who scored high on extroversion could in fact appear very introverted in certain contexts; individuals who did not originally appear to manifest characteristics of sadism and brutality could in fact be made to do sadistic and brutal things very easily, etc.). Importantly, these studies suffered from important ethical issues regarding the use of human subjects, as they caused immense distress to participants. They could not, and should not, be replicated today. However, because of their centrality in shaping the field of social psychology, we describe both at length.

The first study was the Milgram Experiment (Milgram 1963). Stanley Milgram set out to investigate the so-called "banality of evil" (Arendt 1963) exposed during the trial of Nazi war criminal Adolf Eichmann in Jerusalem. In the trial, most observers were shocked and outraged at Eichmann's apparent "normalcy" as well as his insistence that he had been "following orders." However, how could a "normal" individual commit such terrible, evil acts for the sake of following orders? It seemed very difficult to imagine. Milgram set out to test this idea – to what extent would "normal" people follow immoral orders from an authority figure? Was evil truly banal? Or were there specific types of people or societies more likely to perpetrate physical violence against innocents? The results of his study were shocking.

Milgram set up an experiment where participants were told they were participating in a study on education. They were to administer ever-increasing levels of shocks to a student (unbeknownst to them, a confederate of the experimenters) if the student gave incorrect answers on an administered quiz. The "student" was in another room and could be heard but not seen. As the participants administered higher and higher voltage shocks (or so they thought – the shocks were not actually administered), the "student" in the other room would cry out in pain, bang on the wall, complain about his heart condition, and even beg them to stop. The experimenter would respond four times to complaints from the participants (who became extremely distressed upon hearing the cries of the "student"), asking them to continue with the experiment. After the fourth complaint from a respondent, the experimenter would end the experiment. In the absence of four complaints, the experiment would only terminate once the participant had administered a lethal shock of 450 volts three times. The researchers reported that all the participants exhibited extreme distress as they went through this protocol, often questioning the experimenter and asking to stop. Still, 65 percent of participants fully completed the experiment, administering the final, lethal 450-volt shock. Milgram (1973) summarized the results as follows:

The legal and philosophic aspects of obedience are of enormous importance, but they say very little about how most people behave in concrete situations. I set up a simple experiment at Yale University to test how much pain an ordinary citizen would inflict on another person simply because he was ordered to by an experimental scientist. Stark authority was pitted against the subjects' strongest moral imperatives against hurting others, and, with the subjects' ears ringing with the screams of the victims, authority won more often than not. The extreme willingness of adults to go to almost any lengths on the command of an authority constitutes the chief finding of the study and the fact most urgently demanding explanation.

Milgram ultimately concluded that there was nothing innately *authoritarian* about these particular individuals (indeed all of them at some point expressed extreme discomfort with the task), but instead that most people could inflict extreme harm on others if ordered to do so by a trusted authority. Subsequent variations on the experiment seemed to reinforce the point that authority was necessary – if the experimenter gave orders over the phone rather than in person, compliance dropped; if another confederate of the experimenter publicly disagreed with the continuation of the experiment, participation dropped; if, on the other hand, the participant was distanced from the administration of the shocks (he or she asked the questions, but someone else administered the shock), participation immensely increased to over 90 percent compliance. Milgram concluded that, ultimately, the diffusion of responsibility that comes from "following orders" – rather than any particular personality pathologies – was the central explanatory variable in understanding how and why ordinary people could commit extraordinarily terrible acts. Of course, this finding does not absolve or justify in any way those who commit heinous crimes of responsibility for their terrible acts. It demonstrates that the impetus for cruel behavior may be largely social and less trait-based. It does not justify such acts. The implications of the study were profound and, of course, extremely troubling: some "normal" people may commit extraordinary evil in the presence of a trusted authority.

Situational constraints exhibited enormous power over individual behavior in another famous study, conducted some seven years after Milgram's. The Stanford Prison Experiment (1971), led by Philip Zimbardo, was designed to test the effect of role assignment on behavior. Two dozen Stanford University students were randomly assigned to the role of jailor or prisoner in a fake prison constructed in the basement of Stanford's psychology building. The hypothesis was that taking on the role of a jailor would quickly lead an individual to become crueler and more punishing, compared to taking on the role of a prisoner. Because the participants were randomly assigned to these two roles, the effect of innate personality differences that might otherwise guide selection into these positions was eliminated. While people with cruel streaks might be more likely to choose careers as prison guards in the real world, the design, in theory, allowed Zimbardo to attribute differences in behavior solely to the *situation*, not the personality of the individuals.

Once again, the results were shocking. Within a day of the start of the experiment, students fully embodied their roles – the prisoners protested their treatment at the hands of the guards and the guards retaliated severely. Prisoners were soon forced to stand in a line for roll-call multiple times a day, bathroom breaks were cancelled and prisoners were forced to go in a bucket placed in their cell instead, mattresses were removed, and so on. The environment became so depraved that the experiment was terminated early, after only six days. Strikingly, the only reason for this was that a graduate student was brought in to conduct interviews for the project and voiced ethical objections to the maltreatment of the students. Indeed, it appeared that even the experimenters had internalized their role as "wardens" to a certain extent. Only once outside observers came in and witnessed the experiment, were the experimenters able to see how damaging the environment had become. Today, the results of this study have been called into question by researchers who have criticized both the ethics and scientific nature of the experiment[2] or failed to replicate the findings (Reicher & Haslam 2006); however, its impact on the field of psychology is hard to overstate.

These studies remain two of the most influential – and controversial – studies in psychology today. Numerous researchers have critiqued the projects on methodological and ethical grounds. However, these results, even if overstated by the researchers, do demonstrate the immense power of context to determine individual behavior. As a result of these and other studies, the exploration of personality and individual differences tapered off after the 1950s. However, beginning in the 1980s there was a resurgence of work in this area, spurred on by Bob Altemeyer's acclaimed book, *Right Wing Authoritarianism*.

Altemeyer took the original Adorno authoritarian measures and refined them, addressing the multiple methodological critiques that had been levied at this scale over the years. Using only three of the original nine components of the scale (submission, aggression, and conventionalism), he sought to streamline the concept of the authoritarian personality down to its core elements. Concerned with the methodological shortcomings of previous work (e.g., that the factors did not seem to "hang together"), Altemeyer spent a great deal of time validating his new scale – making sure that the items were all interrelated and varied together. His final scale included items such as "our country desperately needs a mighty leader who will do what has to be done to destroy the radical new ways and sinfulness that are ruining us" (Altemeyer 1981).

However, this work was also subsequently critiqued on measurement grounds by Feldman and Stenner (1997) and further developed by Stenner (2005). Feldman and Stenner argued that Altemeyer's scale was essentially tautological, since the outcomes the scale was meant to explain (support for authoritarian political systems) were embedded in the scale itself, which asked questions directly about political views about the role of the state.[3] They developed a scale that was better able to get at the underlying personality dimensions that lent themselves to the subsequent development of authoritarian *political* attitudes. Namely, they simply asked respondents what lessons were more important to impart to children. For example, was respect for authority and obedience to one's parents the most critical value? Or, on the other hand, was it freedom of expression and creativity? For Feldman and Stenner, authoritarianism thus essentially boiled down to a tolerance of difference – should children be taught to be individuals who explore and restructure their world, or should they be taught obedience and deference to an existing system? They found that these child-rearing values were correlated with Altemeyer's original RWA scale, as would be expected if RWA was an outcome, not a personality factor. Feldman and Stenner's authoritarianism scale is widely used today and various studies have found strong correlations between this scale and a variety of political attitudes. Authoritarianism is correlated with support for more aggressive counterterror policies (Hetherington & Suhay 2011), prejudice and attitudes toward out-groups (Kalkan, Layman & Uslaner 2009; Sibley & Duckitt 2008), and support for Donald Trump over other GOP candidates during the 2016 Republican primary elections (MacWilliams 2016) and throughout his administration.[4]

Today, the so-called person-situation debate over the role of stable internal traits versus changing external contexts in structuring behaviors (see Lucas & Donnellan 2009) has receded as scholars have coalesced around a more flexible model of personality and trait theory. Now, most scholars accept Mischel and Shoda's (1995) if-then conception of traits, whereby stable personality differences emerge in distinct ways depending on the contexts. So, for example, a person may, in general, be agreeable with authority figures but disagreeable with underlings; or an individual may be introverted in large groups and with strangers but extroverted among close friends and family; or individuals may possess authoritarian predispositions that are only activated under situations of perceived societal threat, and so on. Indeed, research on the connection between authoritarianism and political attitudes has generally found that authoritarianism becomes "activated" in certain contextual settings, in response to threatening or fear-inducing events in the news cycle (Feldman & Stenner 1997; Hetherington & Suhay 2011; Lavine, Lodge & Freitas 2005). This stream of research is also an excellent example of how various behavioral factors – including personality predispositions, emotions, and cognition – all interact to affect political preferences. Today, observational studies in American politics almost always include these types of dispositional variables in their analyses.

PERSONALITY IN POLITICS: LEADERSHIP STYLE & BELIEFS

Though the individual-differences approach has become very active in the study of *mass* political behavior, studies exploring the role of personality in political elites' behavior have remained rare. This is most likely due to both practical and theoretical reasons. First, practically, it is difficult to convince elites to take surveys – getting a president, government official, or sitting congressperson to complete an academic questionnaire is no easy feat. Second, the rational choice paradigm assumes that individual differences in personality matter less than stable structural characteristics of the system or strategic constraints of an interaction and takes preferences as exogenous and given. Because of the dominance of RCT in the study of elites, exploring personality differences between leaders has been seen, mistakenly in our view, as less central to understanding the policy-making process. In other words, the origin of different preferences among leaders is not often questioned because scholars assume that political leaders, in general, want to achieve the same goals (e.g., staying in office, the prosperity and security of their country) regardless of their personal traits and characteristics. Moreover, because policy is ultimately the product of group decision-making processes (e.g., advisory groups, majority votes, etc.) and bureaucratic structures (see Chapter 5), the role of the predispositions of the individual leader has been seen as less central in these models. Because of these assumptions, most of the dominant schools of thought in international relations (realism, institutionalism, and others) assume that the *context* in which a leader was selected, and subsequently makes decisions is the fundamental determinant of their policies. In other words, the individual differences in personality and preferences among various leaders has often been treated as, at best, a minor influence that is overwhelmed by situational constraints.

This conclusion, however, runs against evidence about the ways in which leaders make decisions. A core assumption of democratic theory is that who we elect to lead *matters* and that different elected officials will make different policy choices. Particularly, when examining the role of society's leaders, we tend to think that it was their *individual personality or beliefs* that shaped the context, rather than the other way around. For example, would the Civil Rights Movement have occurred the way it did without Martin Luther King Jr.? Would the Cuban Missile Crisis have ended differently if Kennedy had not been the US president at the time? How could we explain "World War II or the Holocaust without Hitler? Soviet policy in the 1930s and 1940s without Stalin, Chinese foreign policy without Mao, or contemporary Russian policy without Putin" (Levy 2013)?

Thinking about more recent politics, it is hard to imagine that Joe Biden would have handled the COVID-19 crisis in the same way as President Trump did. Would Al Gore have invaded Iraq after the 9/11 attacks (Lieberfeld 2005)? Would Hillary Clinton have made similar policy choices to President Trump – enforcing a ban on immigration from seven Muslim-majority countries, withdrawing from the Iran nuclear deal, and moving away from free-trade economic policies? Would President Clinton have treated Black Lives Matter protestors the same way as President Trump did? It appears, intuitively, that leaders with different backgrounds, experiences, and personalities will likely pursue divergent policy agendas, respond to unfolding events in disparate ways and, ultimately, make different decisions on important political issues – beyond the dictates of the specific context. Exploring these heterogeneous preferences among leaders, and the impact these preferences have on politics, is a key goal of BPS.

The issue of leader personality – and its role in policy-making – has reemerged as a particularly crucial question for researchers since the election of Donald Trump. There has been no shortage of news articles and punditry attempting to analyze the personality of President Trump and how traits such as narcissism, grandiosity, and disagreeableness may manifest themselves as policy outputs in the Oval Office.[5] One key question was the extent to which Trump's personality and leadership style would upend traditional approaches to policy-making and foreign relations versus the extent to which the Washington bureaucracy would constrain Trump's ability to drastically alter US policy. This question echoes an early approach to the study of political leadership called the "great man" approach, advanced by Thomas Carlyle, who famously argued that "history is nothing but the biography of the great man" (Carlyle 1841, republished 1993). In other words, a state's policies were leader-driven, solely the result of their leaders' "great" personalities, rather than based on the institutional structure or situational constraints of the time.

Of course, this is a relatively simplistic view of history that provides no space for context to affect individual behavior. More modern work on the subject of leader personality has taken a more nuanced position, arguing that a leader's personality interacts with situational factors of the environment to impact policy. For example, Fred Greenstein's (1969) work suggests that a leader's personality will play a dominant role in the formation of state policy under a few key conditions: (1) when the actor occupies a strategic location in the decision-making process, (2) when the situation is ambiguous, (3) when there are no clear precedents for behavior, and (4) when effortful behavior is required. Stone and Schaffner's (1988) field model of political leadership is helpful in illustrating this nuanced view most modern personality theorists take of personality's impact on political outcomes (Figure 7.1). Personality matters, but only in the context of the larger situation.

The making of foreign policy is one such area in which these four conditions are often met and in which both the actor and his or her chosen action is "indispensable" to the outcome (Greenstein 1967). In fact, the "two presidencies" theory echoes this idea – that presidents have much more autonomy and freedom of action in the making of foreign policy than domestic policy (e.g., they essentially have two different presidencies) (Wildavsky 1998). This is perhaps why many career foreign policy bureaucrats in Washington (including some from the GOP) were so nervous about the nontraditional candidacy, and then presidency, of Donald Trump[6] – it is in foreign policy where presidents have the most independent leeway. Indeed, throughout Trump's presidency, he found his legislative agenda frequently stymied by Congress (on immigration reform and health care, for example) but has been able to issue several executive orders with huge ramifications for foreign policy, including his decision to withdraw the United States from the Trans-Pacific Partnership trade agreement with many Asian nations; his move to pull the United States from the Paris Climate Agreement, of which every other country in the world (aside from Syria and Nicaragua) are signatories; and his decision to withdraw from the 2015 Iranian nuclear deal. Trump also issued a plan to "defeat the Islamic State of Iraq and Syria" that may have involved softening the rules of engagement, accounting for a dramatic spike in civilian casualties from US airstrikes in 2017.[7]

However, researchers interested in exploring the role of personality in leadership are still left with a fundamental methodological challenge – how to determine whether personality caused a policy choice (above and beyond the situation), when researchers have little to no access to the actual leaders. One way researchers have attempted to get around this conundrum is to engage in psychological profiling of leaders. These psychological profiles can be done qualitatively, using principles of psychodynamic theory and publicly available biographical information on the leader; or quantitatively, using content analysis of leaders' speeches and private communication. Jerrold Post and Stanley Renshon's work are prime examples of the former. For example, in Post's (2005), *The Psychological Assessment of Political Leaders* (Post 2005), he and other researchers use psychodynamic theory to develop detailed psychological profiles of Saddam Hussein and Bill Clinton. There has been no shortage of "at-a-distance" profiles of Donald Trump as well. A paper by psychologist Aubrey Immelman, for example, has already attempted to profile Trump's leadership style, summarizing his leadership traits as follows: "an active-positive presidential character with mobilization – the ability to arouse, engage, and direct the public – as

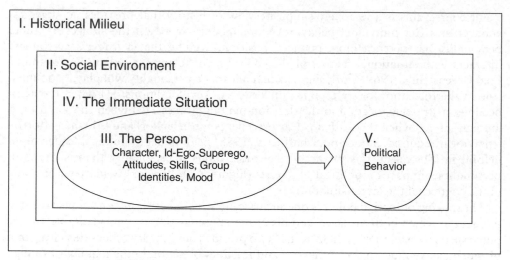

FIGURE 7.1 **Field model of political leadership**

Some researchers use the principles of psychodynamic theory to construct psychological profiles. These are used to evaluate whether a leader's personality traits affected their policy decision-making. The central point the figure makes is that personality traits and individual characteristics are important, but only in the context of forces external to the individual, in terms of their social environment and the historical moment. These larger forces interact with individual traits to produce policy outcomes.

Source: Post (2005). Adapted from: Stone & Schaffner (1988).

his key leadership asset; an overall leadership style that is distinctively charismatic and nondeliberative; and a high-dominance, extraverted, influential foreign policy orientation" (Immelman 2017, p. 1). This psycho-biographic and psychoanalytic approach aims to "understand shaping life events that influenced core attitudes, political personality, leadership, and political behavior" (Post 2005, 70). However, this approach is often criticized as reflecting the inherent bias of the profiler, as well as the bias of hindsight. In other words, it is potentially easier for researchers to look back at Abraham Lincoln's childhood and determine that he was an honest child, or that Richard Nixon was a conniving one, given their later infamous accomplishments and failures.

Given the limitations of these qualitative profiling strategies, other researchers have attempted to use quantitative analysis to reduce the level of potential researcher bias. Content analysis is one such way in which researchers attempt to turn qualitative evidence into a more systematic quantitative analysis. They do this by calculating the ratio of certain types of words (e.g., words indicating dominance versus collaborative intent) as compared to others and then statistically testing whether these differences are associated with distinct political outcomes. This tool can thus be applied to the study of leader personality at-a-distance (Winter 1993a). Peter Suedfeld's well-known work on integrative complexity is one example of a research program that utilizes this method of analysis. As described by Suedfeld, integrative complexity is essentially a personality trait whereby an individual integrates the recognition of multiple perspectives and possibilities into their thinking and reasoning process. Suedfeld's work suggests that changes in the level of integrative complexity in leaders' public speeches can be used to forecast the likelihood that international crises will end in negotiations or war (see, e.g., Suedfeld & Tetlock 1977; Suedfeld, Tetlock & Ramirez, 1977). David Winter's research on the role of different motives in impacting leaders' cognition is another primary example of this work. His work uses content analysis of leaders' speeches to determine the presence of various motives, such as need for power, achievement, or affiliation (Winter 1973). These motives have, in turn, been found to affect a host of political outcomes, such as a candidate's ideological position during elections (Winter 1982), Supreme Court justices' tendency to write majority opinions (Aliotta 1988), and leaders' tendency to end crises using violence (Winter 1993b).

Work on leaders' "operational code" (George 1969; Walker, Schafer & Young 1998) also utilizes content analysis as a primary tool. A leader's operational code is defined as his or her fundamental beliefs regarding the nature of political life and the best approaches to selecting and achieving political goals. So, for example, leaders may vary on the extent to which they believe politics is essentially competitive versus cooperative, whether they are fundamentally optimistic or pessimistic about achieving their political values, and how much control they have over history versus the role of chance (George 1969). They will also possess differing perspectives regarding how best to pursue their objectives – whether through force or diplomacy, risk-taking or risk-avoidance, and so on. Walker, Schafer and Young (1998) developed a scoring system for assessing these various beliefs using the content of leaders' public speeches. They found that there was indeed considerable consistency in a leader's operational code across issue areas, suggesting that there may be a single underlying belief system that structures a leader's political action. So, for example, leaders who believe the world is fundamentally competitive will be more likely to use force or the threat of force to achieve their aims than those who believe the political world is cooperative (Walker 1977; Walker, Schafer & Young 1999).

While each of these schools have focused on *one aspect* of a leader's personality in influencing their policy preferences, other researchers have sought to quantitatively test the impact of *personality as a whole* on leadership style. Margaret Hermann's (1980) work on personality characteristics of political leaders is an important example. She examines six personality characteristics for forty-five different political leaders – nationalism, sense of personal efficacy (internal locus of control), need for power, need for affiliation, conceptual complexity in decision-making, and suspiciousness of others. These traits are also coded using content analysis, this time from leaders' "meet the press" sessions. They are then analyzed collectively in the form of a general "independent" versus "participatory" orientation. Using a database of foreign policy events from 1959–1968, she finds that an independent personality orientation had the most significant impact on foreign policy behavior, leading to less cooperative or multilateral diplomatic initiatives.

However, though these various research programs point to the potential importance of personality as a factor that influences leaders' preferences and, therefore their policy choices, this method of content analysis of speeches has been challenged in two critical ways: performance and independence. Namely, leaders' speeches are by nature *performative* and therefore may not be an accurate measure of the leader's true personality – often the leader does not even write speeches. Moreover, attempting to explain leaders' behavior while in office by using their behavior is essentially a circular process with no clear separation between the independent and dependent variables of interest – if a leader's personality is judged by his actions in office, are the personality traits driving the behavior, or are these personality traits simply assumed because researchers have witnessed the behavior and policy choices we associate with that trait? Future studies in this area should find a way to assess leader personality as *distinct* from their behavior while in office and as a genuine reflection of a leader's underlying interests and motivations. One way of accomplishing this would be to examine leaders' *private* communications from *before* their time in office. One might also collect and analyze confidential documents that leaders never intended to be public, performative statements. For example, one of the most famously studied incidents of leader decision-making in history is President John F. Kennedy's discussions and debates with his national security team during the Cuban Missile Crisis. Alas, these types of conversations are rarely available for scholarly analysis in any country, even the United States.

MORAL VALUES

Just like personality and other predispositions, morals and values can also play a large role in structuring preferences and, therefore, decisions. These BPS dimensions could, likewise, be formalized and brought into expected utility models of political behavior. For example, a common question in the study of voting behavior in the United States is why do so many poor people vote Republican? If voters only maximize short-term economic self-interest, the poor might be expected to prefer the Democratic Party, which typically supports redistributive economic policies and the provision of social services. However, a significant plurality of poor Americans votes for Republican candidates in election after election. This question could, of course, be flipped as well, as we discussed previously – why do some rich Americans vote for the Democratic Party, when their immediate economic self-interest would appear to be better served by the policies of the Republican Party? There are at least two possible answers. First, citizens simply *may not know* the differences between the parties in terms of redistribution and are then tricked into voting for the "wrong" party by charismatic candidates. If this explanation were true, we would expect efforts to inform voters of the political platforms of each party would change voting behavior. Second, short-term, individual economic self-interest may not be the primary dimension that voters are trying to maximize. Many voters may simply have other concerns that are far more important to them, such as their commitment to individualism (Feldman 1982) or other social values, like those concerning the role of religion in the state, abortion, or gay rights. In this case, information would do little to change voting behavior, as the relative economic benefit a candidate offers a voter is typically rarely decisive. However, more abstract values are difficult to quantify, which makes it more challenging to incorporate them into expected utility frameworks.

What precisely is a value? Values have five crucial attributes that distinguish them from attitudes: they are (1) concepts or beliefs, (2) that pertain to desirable end-states or behaviors, (3) transcend specific situations, (4) guide selection or evaluation of behavior and events, and (5) are ordered by relative importance (Schwartz & Bilsky 1987, 1990). In other words, a main difference between attitudes and values is that values are enduring and transcend specific issue domains. One can have a political attitude concerning welfare policy, but this attitude may be rooted in a deeper value that one holds regarding fairness or reciprocity. Interestingly, it appears that these values may have their root in evolutionary psychology and the benefits they may have provided to our early ancestors. For example, the pioneering Rokeach Value Survey (1973) found that individuals *across the globe appeared* to base their values around *the same* eight motivational components (Schwartz 1992): prosocial, restrictive conformity, enjoyment, achievement, maturity, self-direction, security, and power. These striking similarities in value foundations around the world suggest that the inculcation of certain types of values in a social group may have been crucial to survival for early man. These values would constrain and shape individual behavior in such a way that would be beneficial for the group in the long term.

Using these evolutionary principles, work on moral foundations theory (Graham, Haidt & Nosek 2009) has suggested that there may be as few as five key dimensions on which values are grounded in all human groups: harm/care, fairness/reciprocity, in-group/loyalty, authority/respect, and purity/sanctity. Again, each of these values would have been very important to optimal group functioning for our ancient ancestors. For example, the value of caring would have been crucial for bringing up helpless infants in the safety of the group; reciprocity was important for survival as well (e.g., some members of the group would "gather" while others would "hunt" and they would then share these spoils collectively); in-group loyalty and respect for authority would help in maintaining group structure and strengthening the group against hostile enemies encroaching on their territory; and rules regarding purity may have kept early humans safe from disease. However, in modern society some of these values have become less important, or at least for a significant segment of the population. This may explain why differences in political attitudes between liberals and conservatives seem so difficult to bridge – these attitudes rest on distinct *moral foundations*. This is the fundamental argument of moral foundations theory – that those who ascribe importance to all five moral dimensions are much more likely to express conservative belief systems, while those who have deemphasized the need for the last three (in-group loyalty, respect for authority, and purity) are much more likely to be liberal. The degree to which these moral foundations are heritable versus socialized has been a subject of important debate (Smith et al. 2016). However, either way, these moral foundations might explain why debates surrounding value-laden issues appear to go nowhere – the parties are unable to comprehend the moral perspective of the other side because they are simply using different sets of moral foundations to make their political judgments. Figure 7.2 illustrates the divergence between self-described liberals and conservatives in the United States regarding which values they find relevant to their own moral judgments (Graham, Haidt & Nosek 2009).

Why does the distinction between values and attitudes matter? One key difference is that values are thought to be much more rigid and less malleable than attitudes. In other words, values do not lend themselves to compromise. Those who hold political attitudes rooted in core values are (1) much less likely to change their opinions, and (2) much less willing to compromise. This is because value-laden attitudes are likely to be more deeply held (Seul 1999), difficult to divide (Svensson 2007), and less easily subject to trade-offs (Atran, Axelrod & Davis 2007). In other words, political attitudes based on values are subject to core problems of issue indivisibility (Svensson 2007) and "taboo trade-offs" (Fiske & Tetlock 1997; Tetlock et al. 2000) or "cognitive incommensurability" (Durkheim 1973). *Issue indivisibility* is when a contested issue cannot be shared or split – for example, when there is a debate over who should be king (Fearon 1995), only one person can be king and so the kingship is not divisible. Taboo trade-offs are essentially when an individual must compare the worth of two competing values (for

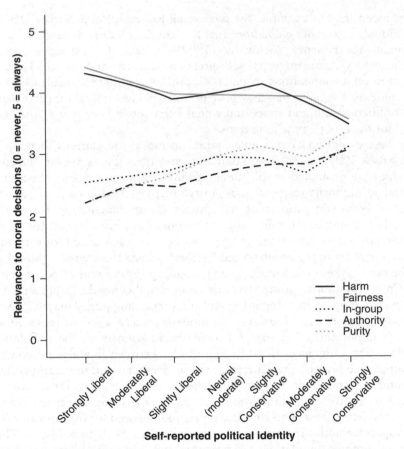

FIGURE 7.2 **The relationship between moral foundations and political ideology**
The figure displays the relationship between self-reported political ideology, from "liberal" to
"conservative," and the reported importance of five distinct moral values for making decisions.
Liberals emphasize the avoidance of harm (or maximizing care) for others and the fairness of
outcomes when making political judgments. Conservatives value those things too, on average, but
are also drawn to solutions that maximize in-group benefits, respect for authority, and
maintaining bodily purity. The theory suggests that these basic differences in commitments to
different moral values undergird policy preferences around the world.
Source: Graham, Haidt & Nosek (2009).

example, love and money) that feel wholly incomparable – for example, how much
money would one need to be offered before selling one's children? The absurdity and
incomprehensibility of this question for most demonstrates how taboo these trade-offs
are. For most, "merely making explicit the possibility of certain trade-offs weakens,
corrupts and degrades one's moral standing" (Fiske & Tetlock 1997, p. 256). The two
values are simply not commensurable – you cannot (and do not want to) compare their
worth. For example, while one may expect that an individual's attitude toward global
climate change may be affected by evidence regarding the extent of the problem, we do
not (or should not) expect the same for an individual's attitude toward abortion.
A person's perception about abortion, and whether or not it should be legal, is laden

with value judgments about its morality, and this makes compromise on this issue very difficult.

It is this characteristic of so-called "protected" values that makes them more difficult to incorporate into traditional expected utility frameworks: they cannot be easily substituted for material concerns as individuals often express the value as "infinitely" more valuable (Baron & Spranca 1997). Individuals who are asked to compromise on protected values will, as a result, tend to exhibit several responses that are at odds with traditional rational choice assumptions about decision-making (Baron & Spranca 1997): First, they will display *quantity insensitivity* – the quantitative scale of the consequences of an action do not matter. For those morally opposed to the death penalty, it does not matter whether the law would lead to the execution of 10 or 10,000 people. Second, individuals will express *agent relativity* – participation in the act is more important than the consequences. For example, even if anti-abortion activists recognized that women denied legal abortions would simply get less safe, illegal ones, they would still oppose legal abortion because the act of *allowing* even a single abortion is deemed morally wrong. Third, people will feel a sense of *moral responsibility* – all individuals are required to behave in a certain way, regardless of their personal situation. Values will also interact with other behavioral factors in decision-making, such as emotions and cognitive biases. When asked to consider trade-offs to protected values, individuals will likely react with intense anger. Because individuals seek to avoid trade-offs at all costs, they will also be more likely to express *wishful thinking* – denying the need to make trade-offs at all. Essentially, moral values make compromise extremely difficult.

Work by Tim Ryan sheds light on this issue. He finds that when political attitudes become "moralized," those who hold them oppose compromises, punish politicians who do compromise and are actually willing to forsake material gains to avoid compromising (Ryan 2017). Thus, for example, the 2013 shutdown of the US federal government due to deadlock in the American Congress over the budget (something that both Republicans and Democrats presumably wanted to pass) may have been caused by an inherent value conflict. Newly minted "tea-party" delegates had come to Washington after the 2012 election diametrically opposed to "big government," and these attitudes against government interventionism were rooted in values of freedom and self-determination that (as they saw it) the government had trampled on. As such, these new members of Congress were willing to achieve a suboptimal outcome (from an economic standpoint) – the shutdown of the entire US government – for the sake of defending their core values.[8]

Atran and colleagues (2007) explore this dynamic in the context of international relations in their work on sacred barriers to conflict resolution. Studying the Israeli-Palestinian conflict, they find that the use of *material* incentives by third party mediators to promote the peaceful resolution of political and cultural conflicts will backfire when the adversaries treat these contested issues as sacred values (Atran, Axelrod & Davis 2007). In other words, offering money to the Palestinian Authority to give up perceived right to their land, or security guarantees to the Israelis in exchange for giving up parts of the holy city of Jerusalem have not worked thus far, according to these researchers, and can even provoke a backlash effect (Atran, Axelrod & Davis 2007). The parties are offended at the insinuation that they would be willing to trade off goals they view as sacred in exchange for material benefit. Instead, symbolic gestures (such as an apology or recognition of the other's claims) may be more likely to lead to a compromise. Some

Palestinians have emphasized the importance to them of Israel recognizing, in principle, the right of return of Palestinians (even if this poses a danger to Israel and cannot be practically accomplished), while the Israelis often reference the need for Palestinians to recognize Israel as the Jewish homeland. The importance of such demands cannot be understood by models of political behavior that do not incorporate values into the utility calculations of the actors. Though utility functions have included "value" considerations, it is typically more difficult to put an explicit, numeric cost and benefit on these types of symbolic issues and, as such, they are often excluded.

Similar results have also been demonstrated in how the public responds to terrorist violence. Wayne (2019) argues that, though the prevalence of fear and cognitive biases in risk perception are often hypothesized as the mechanism underlying support for militant responses to terrorism, there are many puzzles in the terrorism literature that suggest this risk mechanism may not, in fact, be the dominant cognitive response of publics to terrorist violence. For example, national rather than personal threat is a larger driver of policy preferences in many countries (Huddy et al. 2005). Moreover, though citizens express higher levels of perceived threat in the wake of terrorist attacks, only a minority actually feel high levels of fear or anxiety as a result (Huddy et al. 2002). In fact, civilians who report high levels of fear in response to terrorism are less supportive of aggressive counterterror policies (Huddy et al. 2002; Skitka et al. 2006), even though publics as a whole are generally more militant following exposure to terrorism (Gadarian 2010; Getmansky & Zeitzoff 2014).

Together, Wayne argues, these patterns indicate the dominant response of civilian populations to terrorism may not be overestimation of personal risk and fear, but, rather, anger and a desire for vengeance. In a series of experimental studies in the United States (Wayne 2019), she finds substantial support for the centrality of this "moral outrage" pathway in shaping citizens' political attitudes. While citizens in the United States do believe future attacks on the country are more likely following exposure to threatened and actualized militant violence, they are no more likely to believe these attacks will personally threaten them. On the other hand, citizens are very likely to view terrorism as immoral and the goals of its perpetrators, illegitimate. After exposure to an attack, citizens – particularly those who feel less personal threat and more moral outrage over terrorist violence in the United States – become substantially more supportive of retaliation against the attackers, *even if this does little to prevent the future risk of terrorism*. What's more, citizens primed to feel anger unrelated to terrorism are significantly more supportive of retributive violence against terrorists than those who were not.

These results are important because, while we might expect fearful publics to seek deterrence, avoid a conflict, or even concede policy goals, publics morally outraged by terrorist violence would not support concessions and would be much more predisposed to punitive action (Wayne 2019). A deeper understanding of the role that values play in shaping public opinion around terrorism can thus help reconcile competing findings in the public opinion literature, including why exposure to terrorist violence generally triggers a conservative or right-ward shift, but occasionally leads to a dovish or left-wing shift (Bali 2007; Gould & Klor 2010; Thomas 2014).

This willingness to trade off immediate, individual material benefits for more abstract, psychological, and value-laden ones is also shown when individuals who *violate* societal values are "moralistically punished" by other members of the society, even when it costs those who do the punishing (Kurzban, DeScioli & O'Brien 2007).

A person who was focused on maximizing individual, material gain would not be willing to pay such high costs to punish those who do not directly affect their well-being. Again, a broader understanding of self-interest is required to understand this behavior. Those who choose to engage in costly punishment against moral transgressors may view the transgressions as endangering the health of the society as a whole, indirectly affecting their well-being. In any case, moral values at least lead to a more expansive conception of self-interest and utility than is normally specified in rational choice models.

This demonstrated willingness of individuals to trade off economic benefits for value-laden ones, time and time again, shows why incorporating value functions into individual preferences is crucial for rational choice models that seek to predict equilibrium outcomes. If *values* are what individuals are attempting to maximize, rather than economic self-interest, as many BPS studies suggest, then outcomes that at first may have appeared wholly suboptimal suddenly make sense.

SOCIAL NORMS

But where do these values come from in the first place? Work on social norms explores the way these values are socialized into societies. Some work has suggested that norms, like values, have an evolutionary basis. The central puzzle of the evolutionary approach to norms is that norms (and the enforcement of these norms) are collectively beneficial but often individually suboptimal. So, for example, a norm against cheating benefits the party that might be cheated but harms the party that might have the incentive to cheat. Likewise, if someone does cheat or otherwise violate a norm, punishing these norm violators is individually costly, even if it is collectively beneficial. So how do these norms develop and sustain themselves when each individual has a rational incentive to defect? Work by Robert Axelrod (1986) seeks to address this question using computer simulations to demonstrate how norms for punishing rule-breakers develop over time as a mechanism by which to regulate conflict in groups, even in the absence of a central authority. Once one takes a broader understanding of self-interest, there are indeed "rational" or adaptive reasons for enforcing norms. For example, individuals who cheat or violate norms will suffer reputation costs that impede their ability to get the best outcome down the road (e.g., once you cheat, people no longer trust you and are less willing to do business with you).

On the other hand, it is not always this sort of cold forward-thinking rationalization that leads individuals to follow norms. One helpful example is to think about the case of murder – most individuals choose not to murder other people, *not* because we believe we will be punished for this act (and therefore it will not be in our rational self-interest), but because we believe that murder is inherently wrong. Murder is simply not an option for us when we consider potential courses of action vis-à-vis other people. Why is this? It is because norms become *internalized* over time.

From a BPS point of view, there is ample evidence that norms surrounding certain core political values have changed dramatically over time. For example, norms regarding human rights have been one of the major changes in the international system since World War II. The spread of human rights norms has accelerated in the aftermath of the two World Wars and the founding of the United Nations. These norms against certain forms of human rights abuses have then been codified into international law by the Geneva Conventions (among others). Of course, many times they are not followed, but it is difficult to argue that these strong norms do not act to constrain

behavior in important ways. For example, it is difficult to imagine democratic states such
as Germany would today engage in the widespread use of poisonous mustard gas that
was commonplace during World War I.[9] These human rights norms also affect domestic
policies – no US politician today would argue slavery could be morally justified, whereas
such arguments were commonplace in the 1800s. While widespread discrimination and
prejudice doubtless remain a huge problem in American politics, there is, fortunately, no
serious political leader advocating a return to slavery or forced legal racial separation.
Our beliefs regarding these things have changed drastically, though of course it is always
worth attending to the erosion of such norms.

From a rational choice framework, these internalized norms may be thought of using
the game-theoretic terminology of *common conjectures* – shared understanding between
all "players" in the game about which strategies every other player will use (Morrow
2002). But how does this happen? Thus far, RCT has not interrogated the origins of
these common conjectures or how they evolve over time. How does a course of action
that was once deemed completely appropriate become simply off limits? This is the
process of normative change or "norm cascades" (Sunstein 1997) as they are often
referred to in the social sciences.

The "ultimatum game" is a powerful way to illustrate the way in which internalized
norms govern individual behavior. The ultimatum game is played as follows: there are
two players, Player 1 and Player 2. Player 1 makes a take-it-or-leave-it offer to Player 2
of some sum of money between 0 and 100 dollars. If Player 2 accepts Player 1's offer,
Player 2 receives the money offered and Player 1 receives what remains of the 100
dollars. So, for example, if Player 1 offers $10 and Player 2 accepts, Player 2 gets $10
and Player 1 gets $90. If Player 2 does not accept, then neither player gets any money.
From a strictly rationalist viewpoint, where individuals seek to maximize their economic
well-being, what will the equilibrium outcome be? It is simple. Player 1 will offer the
lowest possible dollar amount greater than zero to Player 1 (in this case, one penny) and
Player 1 will accept it, because they are economically better off with 1 cent than with
nothing. However, when researchers ask people to actually play this game, this was not
the most common outcome. Often, Player 1 would offer Player 2 much larger sums of
money, between 30 and 50 dollars. Moreover, if Player 1 offered substantially less than
half (less than $20), Player 2 often declined the offer (see Sunstein 1996 for a detailed
overview of this and other examples of normative behavior). In other words, Player 2
was willing to take an economic loss, because they felt that the offer was *unfair*. This is
how norms work. Player 2 values the norm of fairness *higher* than the value of Player 1's
offer and so rejects low offers. What's more, Player 1 *knows* that Player 2 will value
fairness (and, perhaps, Player 1 values fairness as well) and so makes higher offers than
the equilibrium suggests they should, to ensure that Player 2 accepts their offer. Again, to
say that either player is acting *irrationally* would be to mischaracterize the heart of what
is going on here. Both players are acting in their rational self-interest – they simply have
a broader conception of what that self-interest is, beyond economic benefit. They also
value abstract ideas like fairness.

How do these social norms translate into political behavior? Work on the
democratic peace theory in international relations is one of the most prominent
examples of the ways researchers have sought to understand the role norms
(specifically, norms of non-violent resolution of disputes) play in political
phenomena. The democratic peace theory arose as a way to explain the apparent
empirical reality that democracies don't fight wars against each other. This is the crux

of the *liberal school* of international relations – that a country's internal domestic character will fundamentally impact its external relations with other actors in the international system. Doyle (1986) typifies this strain of liberalism in his paper, "Liberalism in World Politics," one of the first to examine the empirical regularity that democracies do not seem to fight wars against each other (also see Russett 1993a, 1993b). In seeking to explain this empirical phenomenon, Doyle relies on Kant's *Perpetual Peace* theory (Kant 2015), arguing that democratic states attempt to externalize their norms of solving conflict nonviolently; however, at the same time, liberal ideology has also created new reasons to fight wars (e.g., new norms focused on countering illiberalism that have led to humanitarian interventions, pushes for regime change in autocratic countries, etc.), so democratic states will still fight autocracies. This explains why democracies are not more peaceful with everyone, but only more peaceful *with each other*. Maoz and Russet's (1993) empirical examination of the democratic peace are consistent with Doyle's hypothesis – that normative explanations have stronger explanatory power than institutional ones in explaining this empirical regularity.[10] From a decision theoretic point of view, this explanation of the democratic peace is based on a single (non-compensatory) dimension (regime type of the adversary) in a bounded rational environment, instead of a comprehensive evaluation of multiple, competing alternatives in a more holistic way as expected by the rational choice school.

The democratic peace phenomenon could also be understood by combining work on norms with the poliheuristic theory of decision-making (see Chapter 5). Leaders of democratic states may refrain from attacking other democracies because such an act would be perceived by the *public* as a failure of their foreign policy. For example, a US president would not consider using military force against Australia, Great Britain, New Zealand, or Israel because such an act would be perceived by the public as demonstrating his or her diplomatic and political incompetence (Mintz & Geva 1993; Geva, DeRouen & Mintz 1993). This policy option is therefore non-compensatory from the point of view of the leader. It would be a violation of norms cherished by the public and so would result in a significant loss of electoral support. If a president is primarily concerned with a decision's impact on the political dimension (e.g., public support or opposition to the use of force against the target), the president may eliminate the use of force option when the target is a democracy. However, this calculus would not, according to these authors, affect presidential decisions to use force against nondemocratic regimes.

The democratic peace is not the only area in which international relations scholars have investigated the impact of norms, however. International law, and human rights in particular, is another core issue on which the power of norms appears to constrain political behavior. The central puzzle for rational choice theorists is: why do states uphold human rights when they could conceivably gain more power and security through the violation of said rights? In some areas, violations of human rights may cause a mutual violation on the other side (the principle of *reciprocity*), such as in the treatment of enemy soldiers during wartime. In these scenarios, states may be upholding human rights to avoid harm befalling their own citizens (Morrow 2007). Thus, in these kinds of cases, human rights may be respected because of mutual self-interest, explainable under a rational choice paradigm. Similarly, the norm against the use of nuclear weapons may also have developed during the Cold War because of these same concerns about "mutual assured destruction" should either the USSR or the United States choose to launch their nukes (von Neumann 1953).

However, in the case of *domestic* human rights abuses, this principle of reciprocity and mutual self-interest does not work as well – there is no reciprocal action one state can take to punish a state for hurting its own citizens. So why do many states nonetheless respect human rights domestically? Scholars in the normative tradition argue that states follow international law and/or respect human rights *not* because of self-interest and fear of reciprocity, and *not* because of institutional constraints on their behavior, but largely because certain norms have been *internalized* to the point that following the norm is no longer a conscious choice – norms are followed due to "habitual obedience" (Koh 1997). This habitual obedience comes as human rights norms become "socialized" into the international system over time (Efrat 2016; Risse & Sikkink 1999).

These examples offer just a taste of the large body of work that has been conducted on the role of norms in affecting political preferences and, as a result, behavior. Indeed, much of the work on norms – how they emerge, cascade, and become internalized – has been conducted in the *constructivist* school of political science. One of the core differences between the constructivist approach to political science and the BPS approach is that constructivist scholars are less concerned with the psychology of decision-making and political behavior, focusing instead on the social construction of beliefs and behavior.[11] They also emphasize less quantitative and explicit empirical hypothesis-testing than behavioral political scientists.

Work on the role norms play in individual and societal behavior has huge implications for political science and public policy and is a prime example of how BPS can contribute to our understanding of such intangible factors as attitude formation and decision-making in politics. If *norms* are indeed an important driver of behavior, as some have suggested, and on par or even more important than traditional conceptions of economic self-interest, then the most effective way of changing political behavior may be to change the norms surrounding the behavior, rather than the economic utility an individual would receive for adopting the behavior. Take, for example, the prevalence of hybrid vehicles in the state of California: these cars are still more expensive than comparable gas vehicles, but they have become ubiquitous there. This is likely because of social norms that have arisen surrounding green living and sustainability in that part of the country, more than the cost-savings individuals receive by driving a hybrid vehicle. In other words, preferences may not be static and unchanging – evolving norms can actually alter citizens' preferences in such a way that they will voluntarily change their behavior to match.

CONCLUSION

This chapter explored a few of the many factors that can lead individuals to have *varying preferences* that change their political behavior. We have demonstrated how behavioral political scientists seek to augment RCT's "black box" of preference formation, understanding the dynamic process by which preferences are formed, changed and adapted over time. The work we reviewed helps understand how and why individuals weigh different and sometimes conflicting preferences, and the ways in which these preferences might vary across individuals and entire cultures over time.

One of the key insights in this chapter is that certain values are worth incorporating into a cost-benefit utility maximization, yet doing so is not as straightforward as adding a "value" quantity to an expected utility function. Research suggests that factors such as personality traits and stable commitments to abstract values and norms can constrain behavior in significant ways – often as much, if not more, than economic self-interest. However, these values are often viewed as non-compensatory and so need to be modelled differently than compensatory material considerations to accurately reflect the ways in which these considerations shape individual judgment and choice. BPS can therefore enrich rational choice models by improving assumptions about which preferences are being maximized in the first place, moving the discussion of preferences beyond the "rational versus irrational" dichotomy.

Admitting that values and norms might influence our decisions is the easy part. It is harder to demonstrate these causal relationships empirically. These are among the most challenging phenomena to study for social scientists, for two reasons. First, factors like values and norms are difficult to measure. They usually require us to ask citizens questions in surveys in the hope they will search their memory and report their position to the interviewer truthfully. But when asked how strongly one agrees that "everyone should be treated equally," it might be very hard to disagree. Second, it is very difficult to know whether the answer to that question is stable over time and across contexts, so that it might causally precede a specific decision the citizen will need to make in a given election. More work needs to be done in the field of political socialization in order to understand whether these values and norms are, indeed, fundamental and causally prior to the decisions people make in adulthood.

8

Better to Be Right or to Belong?

Motivated Reasoning in Politics

THE CONNECTION BETWEEN REASONING & BEHAVIOR

Most theories of democracy require citizens to be responsive to the world around them and for the public to have some shared perception of reality. To effectively self-govern, democratic citizens must update their beliefs as new and credible information is encountered. For example, when a citizen is exposed to information suggesting that their representative has failed to deliver on an important promise, they would log the disappointment on that dimension and update their general evaluation of the politician negatively. Citizens must monitor the political environment closely enough to keep track of the important dimensions that could reasonably alter their candidate preferences. On Election Day, they could call upon a wealth of information stored in memory, compare their judgments of each candidate on various dimensions, and finally choose the one that is closest to them on average. Likewise, elites, who are elected by the public to serve the interests of the state, should be able to process new information about allies and adversaries. They use this information about the threats and opportunities facing their country that help them choose optimal policies. The motivated reasoning school of thought challenges these foundational assumptions.

As we have shown in previous chapters, most citizens in the United States and many other countries don't monitor the political information environment very closely (Prior 2007). They cannot remember much about the performance of elected officials on the issues that matter most to them (Delli Carpini & Keeter 1996), they are extremely myopic when it comes to how far back in time they reach in order to evaluate candidate performance (Achen & Bartels 2017), and they hold elected officials accountable even for natural events out of any human's control (Achen & Bartels 2017). In other words, not only is it a challenge for most citizens to hold democratically elected officials accountable for their choices in office, many citizens also seem motivated to hold elected officials responsible for things in hypothetical worlds. The proliferation of public acceptance of *fake news,* conspiracy theories like *Pizzagate* discussed in Chapter 1, suggest that under some circumstances, people are willing to believe almost *any claim* about politicians they dislike, no matter how outrageous, unlikely, and baseless.

Vivid recent examples of this come in the public's reaction to public health officials' guidance about how to address the devastating COVID-19 pandemic, and in the events

160

following the 2020 presidential election leading up to the insurrection at the Capitol Building on January 6, 2021. In the first case, elected officials politicized basic public health measures like mask wearing and social distancing, leading citizens from different parties to engage in dramatically different health and safety behavior. Many Republican voters were far less likely to accept the seriousness of the disease and were therefore less likely to protect themselves and their loved ones from the virus. In the second case, millions of Republicans were led to believe that electoral fraud was rampant in the 2020 election, despite the nearly complete absence of evidence in support of such claims. It seems obvious from these examples that partisanship leads citizens, at least under some circumstances, to believe they are living in completely separate realities.

A good deal of attention has been paid in political science to the role that partisanship plays in the process of opinion formation. In the 1960s, the discovery of "party identification" revolutionized theories of voting behavior in the United States (Campbell et al. 1980). Originally conceived of as a psychological attachment to the party label, early empirical research noticed that it seemed to have a vastly larger impact on voter preferences than contemporary information about the performance of the candidates on issues. In fact, these scholars found that partisanship seemed to act as a "perceptual filter" through which campaign communication passed before it would affect a citizen's judgments. Contrary to classical conceptions of the rational democratic citizen, these party identifiers seemed instead to be guided first by their allegiance to their party, even to the point where they substantially changed their preferences on issues in alignment with what party elites advocated during campaigns. Rather than holding elected officials accountable for their issue preferences, then, voters seemed to choose candidates first and foremost based on party.

The precise origins and role of partisan identification and its role in information processing and decision-making has been hotly debated for decades. Still, the consensus remains that the average citizen cannot, or at least under normal conditions does not, hold their representatives to some set of strongly held and stable issue preferences. Converse (1964) demonstrated that the public's positions on issues, even those of significant national import, were quite unstable over time and mostly unstructured by even a simply left-right ideological framework. This finding, and ones that followed (see, e.g., Lewis-Beck 2008), represented a serious shot across the bow for the "rational actor" model. How could elected officials be held accountable for their performance on issues if citizens didn't even hold the same preferences from month to month? How could they choose a party to support if they did not organize issues on the same dimension that separated the parties? Needless to say, the first generation of public opinion scholars created quite a stir in debates about what citizens were capable of, and whether they could come even begin to approximate the ideal of the Economic Man.

Subsequent theories of political persuasion and attitude change (Zaller 1992) were guided by the finding that issue positions themselves were, at least under the right circumstances, the result of elite rhetoric as opposed to voters' own interests: citizens seemed to understand little about the issues and how specific policies would affect their material well-being, and instead appeared willing to adopt the issue positions of the trusted party leaders. For example, beliefs about the existence of global warming itself, let alone the most desirable policy solutions to launch at the problem, seem driven more by one's partisanship than the ability to understand climate science (Kahan 2012). In some ways, this reliance on elite cues could be thought of as rational, or at least boundedly rational: the world is too complicated for most citizens to track all the relevant information. Relying on the media and opinions of those elites whose views one trusts can be a handy shortcut. But clearly this strategy can often fail.

This top-down understanding of political opinion formation also echoes the *Elaboration Likelihood Model of Decision-Making* (Cacioppo & Petty 1986), which postulates that attitude changes can be the result of two distinct processes: a central route and a peripheral route. The peripheral route – the one we likely use most often – relies on heuristics, with attitude change being the result of the positive or negative cues a stimulus or source provides us regarding the merits of an argument. In other words, if the source of information is a political elite in my party, I will be more likely to trust that information and change my attitude than if the source is an out-party. On the other hand, the central route of attitude change is much more cognitively intensive, resulting from a person's careful thought and consideration of the validity of different arguments.

However, another explanation for this willingness to rely on elite cues, even when these messages contradict previously held issue positions, has potential behavioral roots. Perhaps, the power of group identity (in this case, partisanship) *motivates* our reasoning, leading us to reach conclusions that make us feel good. This recent recognition of the power of identity to shape reasoning has led to the very pessimistic conclusion that people may not hold real issue preferences at all. Instead, as we have discussed, people's policy views are guided entirely by "feelings" they have in reaction to elite messages or highly salient news events (Achen & Bartels 2017; Bartels 2002). It can be difficult to reconcile this assessment of citizen capacities with that of rational actors cast by democratic theories both ancient and contemporary.[1] Furthermore, if these deficiencies are widespread, it is hard to imagine how citizens can be represented at all. If there are no real issue preferences, then there are no real constraints on what elected officials can and cannot do in office. According to this approach, most of politics, then, is about elites constructing and then policing the identity boundaries of the party: who is in and who is out becomes more important than what should be done to solve the real and pressing social problems of the day.

While this phenomenon of biased partisan beliefs regarding political figures is by no means new, the 2020 US election campaign and the presidency of Donald Trump seem to have raised the issue to new heights. Both Democrats and Republicans have expressed dismay at the new "post-truth" era which the United States and several other countries have appeared to enter. For example, in a commencement address on to the Virginia Military Institute, former Trump Secretary of State Rex Tillerson bemoaned what he perceived to be a growing crisis in ethics and integrity in government, stating:

If our leaders seek to conceal the truth, or we as people become accepting of alternative realities that are no longer grounded in facts, then we as American citizens are on a pathway to relinquishing our freedom ... A responsibility of every American citizen to each other is to preserve and protect our freedom by recognizing what truth is and is not, what a fact is and is not, and begin by holding ourselves accountable to truthfulness, and demand our pursuit of America's future be fact-based.[2]

These warnings from someone who had just served at the very highest levels of government suggest the problem may be large and widespread.

When facts appear to threaten a closely held group identity, citizens sometimes simply refuse to believe them, even if the evidence is clear, persistent, and undeniable. For example, following the 2016 election in the United States, and even though Hillary Clinton's official, government-certified popular vote margin was 3 million votes, only 52 percent of Republicans believed she had received the most votes.[3] The holding of patently false beliefs is not, however, a problem reserved for the ideological right. Prominent Democrats such as Robert Reich (former Secretary of Labor under Bill Clinton) claimed that violent, left-wing protests at universities in the wake of Trump's election were organized by Trump ally Steve Bannon, and many liberals seem to believe it, despite evidence that the protests arose organically via local activists.[4] Moreover, these motivated misperceptions do not apply only to the Trump era. For example, in 2012, liberals were much less likely to blame President Obama for high gas prices than they were to blame President George W. Bush.[5] It may be that the news environment on either side of the partisan aisle may be warping the citizenry's basic perceptions of reality. Partisanship is not the only source of these warped perceptions, of course. Indeed, conspiracy theories and misperceptions are widespread, even when there exists broad scientific consensus on an issue (Flynn, Nyhan & Reifler 2017). For example, large numbers of Americans continue to believe that vaccines cause autism (Freed et al. 2010), that genetically modified foods are not safe to consume (Entine & Randall 2015), and that widespread evidence demonstrating mankind's role in global warming is fake (McCright & Dunlap 2011). The denial of the seriousness of the COVID-19 pandemic among many, and the subsequent refusal to follow basic health guidelines such as mask wearing and social distancing that according to experts could save hundreds of thousands of lives, is yet another example. It is important to understand why people believe such claims in the wake of overwhelming evidence to the contrary.

The answer seems to lie in a set of biases related to *motivated reasoning*. A growing body of research suggests that, when people watch the news, they often *hear what they want to believe*. This violates the common RCT assumption that people update their beliefs appropriately when new and credible information challenging what they thought was true arrives. Prior to the development of the motivated reasoning school of thought, behavioral researchers tended to assume that individuals held somewhat stable issue preferences, even if these preferences were not as fixed as assumed in RCT models.[6] Essentially, memory-based models of decision-making argue that people's opinions about politics are based on information they have been previously exposed to, which they have stored in memory, and that they can call upon whenever they are faced with a relevant decision. This is not limited to citizens who are uninterested in or less knowledgeable about politics. In fact, the most partisan, passionate, and politically sophisticated citizens are often *most* willing to accept messages that conform to previous beliefs, even when those messages contain information that is patently false (Taber & Lodge 2006).

An excellent example of this approach comes from Zaller's (1992) *Receive-Accept-Sample* (RAS) model of public opinion formation and change. In this model, an individual's expressed opinions are first a function of those received from political elites. You cannot have an opinion about a policy you have never heard of, and you usually hear about policies from journalists, candidates, and other experts in the news. Second, only those substantive considerations a person has previously accepted and stored in memory will be available as a tool for evaluating a candidate. In other words, you might not have only one real opinion about a given policy domain as complicated as immigration, the environment, abortion, or crime. Instead, you might have several opinions about each of these policies and those opinions might cover a significant range. Third, from those opinions you do hold, those at the "top of one's head" at the moment of the decision will have the largest influence. But the more information you have to back up your current opinions, and the more passionate you are about the issue or party, the better able you will be to refute and defend against any new information that might contradict your beliefs.

The RAS model accepts the premise of *bounded rationality* discussed in Chapter 3: While citizens are not capable of recalling and carefully weighing *every* piece of information to which they have been exposed when making a political decision, they do rely on *some* substantive information stored in memory, made salient in the moment. The model also accepts the idea that elites have considerable influence in mass opinion formation, because they help convey the set of available arguments to which most citizens will be exposed. Therefore, the RAS model incorporates behavioral ideas about bounded rationality and elite cues, but without fundamentally undermining the idea that citizens have substantive issue preferences. However, a more recent set of BPS ideas has begun to replace memory-based explanations of opinion formation and change. These new models describe a process of *motivated reasoning* at odds with all three central assumptions in the RAS model (Lavine, Johnston & Steenbergen 2012; Lodge & Taber 2013), and also pose a more significant challenge to RCT explanations of politics.

First, as we learned in Chapter 6, democratic citizens around the world often have quite incomplete information about policies and candidates that they encounter in the media or anywhere else. Political awareness is higher in some countries than others on average, and the United States often lags behind other democracies in terms of political knowledge, but the claim holds in general. Instead, people seem to retain only basic *feelings* about those arguments: positive or negative in the case of the hot cognition argument, or perhaps more complicated emotional tags according to appraisal theories of emotion. These emotions build up to a strong impression over time, a tally which then gets activated automatically as the individual makes decisions that are relevant to the candidate or policy being considered.

Second, people do not seem to consider every message in their environment in a fair and balanced way. Instead, we are motivated reasoners: we process new information only if we have some preexisting reason to do so, and our motivations also influence whether we accept or reject the message once it is considered. In the United States, political conservatives may not visit news websites and channels other than Fox News, and, if they do, they may immediately discount news accounts that challenge their views on the performance of Republican elected officials. Likewise, political liberals are less likely to consume and accept news from conservative sources, perhaps relying on liberal sources such as MSNBC instead. Understanding the complex motivations that underlie our information search patterns and reasoning processes is critically important for predicting how people make sense of new information. It appears that the motivation to be accurate is, in fact, only one of many reasons citizens hold the beliefs they do.

So, in this chapter, we will first review the basic logic underlying the idea of motivated reasoning. In particular, we focus on the psychological mechanism – the strong social group identities linked to politics – that underlie the effect. Then, we discuss the widespread and potentially dangerous effects of motivated reasoning for democratic accountability and regime stability. Next, we discuss the limits of motivated reasoning, since knowing what constraints exist on these biases will be vital if we ever hope to design institutions resistant to their often-unfortunate consequences. Finally, we conclude the chapter by discussing some of the responses to these claims that have been made by those in the RCT tradition, and highlight recent efforts to bridge the gap between RCT and BPS in this regard.

Accuracy vs. Directional Motives

One of the central organizing principles in the motivated reasoning literature was first provided by Kunda (1990), who argued that two powerful but competing motives determine what people will do when they are confronted with new information that contradicts their current beliefs. First, and perhaps obviously, people are motivated to be *accurate*. If a person finds out something that may render their previous belief untrue, they will be motivated to change their belief. The accuracy goal is simply the desire in any decision situation to get the right answer, and that often is key to maximizing all sorts of interests. If a stockbroker believes a company is profitable and healthy, but then finds out it has been cooking the books and is actually close to bankruptcy, she will be motivated to change her view and presumably to change her investing behavior as well. This is essentially the dominant assumption about information processing in RCT – that people overwhelming want to get to the "right," truthful answer so they can make choices that maximize their personal utility. When we are motivated to be accurate, we work hard to weigh new information against what we already know, even if it challenges our beliefs and subsequent behavior.

Without any motivation to hold accurate beliefs about the world around us, it is hard to understand how our ancient ancestors would have survived, especially in small groups living in dangerous environments and competing with others for scarce resources. It is obvious that, to avoid threats and take advantage of opportunities, we need to accurately perceive the world around us. There may be diminishing marginal returns on this ability, perhaps accounting for our reliance on shortcuts and other heuristics in decision-making. However, it seems likely that the better one is at this, the more successful one will be in most situations. Our ancestors, for example, had to identify safe food and water and avoid predators on a near-daily basis to survive. Holding inaccurate beliefs about the existence of a pack of large predators prowling just outside the light of one's campfire could prove fatal for anyone needing some time alone.

If this were our only motivation, standard RCT assumptions about preferences would be sufficient to explain much of human behavior and decision-making. What then accounts for the deviations we have discussed in this book from the RCT model? Motivated reasoning theory suggest we also hold *directional* motivations, which sometimes push us away from accurate beliefs and back toward our preexisting notions. When this happens, people begin to violate the simple assumptions of most rational choice models, which rely on the idea that individuals' ability to maximize utility would be invariably harmed by inaccurately perceiving the world around them. But why would people *prefer* to be wrong about objective facts? It is because holding on to preexisting notions about how the world really works, even if wrong, sometimes helps individuals reach other, nonmaterial personal goals. In the next section, we will suggest why. The answer has a lot to do with the fact that, sometimes, being correct is not as helpful as a positive self-image and being welcomed and protected by one's identity groups. It is this motivation that can lead to massive departures from "rational" behavior defined by the utility maximization models that emphasize only material motivations.

Incorporating identity considerations into models of decision-making often, though not always, yields different predictions than those based on standard economic preferences. For example, if the payoffs of the same action are *different* for members of different groups (e.g., male vs. female), due to internal dissonance or external sanction, identity could then explain behaviors that otherwise seem suboptimal or even detrimental (Akerlof & Kranton 2000). If one's identity is proscribed by others, as is often the case with groups associated with physical appearance (gender, race etc.), then identity may be the central factor determining political behavior. Social identities also help us understand how policy preferences can change over time – as the social construction of a group changes, the payoffs associated with certain policies will also change (Akerlof & Kranton 2000).

So, to repeat, people are not only motivated to reach accurate conclusions about how the world works, they are also motivated to reach *particular* conclusions, regardless of the evidence before them. There are lots of reasons we might do this. One is that we simply have sunk costs in our previous beliefs. After spending a great deal of extra money for years buying "organic" fruit, we might be quite resistant to new studies that demonstrate the organic label to perhaps be assigned quite arbitrarily and to have little to do with the actual quality of the food we eat. If we believe these new studies, then we would feel bad about our past behavior and all the money we wasted on organic produce. As such, motivated reasoning may indeed be, in part, a result of the sensitivity to sunk costs bias we discussed in Chapter 3. Another explanation is that we might derive some benefits from being perceived by others as a consistent person who does not change course every time a new piece of information appears on our favorite internet news site. An even larger source of directional motivations, however, may be the social commitments to important group identities that we have built up over the course of our lives. This will be the focus of most of our thinking about motivated reasoning in this chapter.

SOCIALLY MOTIVATED REASONING

Most of us can remember playing games as kids and witnessing the arguments two teams get in over close calls. Was that baseball foul or fair? Is it just a coincidence that the defense all agreed it was foul, while the team at bat was absolutely sure it landed inside the line? It seems odd that something so cut and dried as the place a ball bounced could produce perceptions so perfectly in line with the fortune of one's own team. These sorts of arguments can get heated enough to become violent. What is going on here? Is one side just willfully rejecting reality in a bald-faced attempt to win the game by any means necessary? Motivated reasoning theory suggests not. Instead, a great deal of evidence suggests that each player, on both sides, *truly perceived* the ball to have fallen where it would help their team most. The motivation to defend one's group can be so powerful at times that it actually alters our conscious perception in fundamental ways. We see the world differently when an outcome valuable to a cherished group is "on the line." In the language of the theory, people often reason *from their beliefs to their perceptions*, rather than the other way around (Lodge & Taber 2013). This is called top-down, rather than bottom-up, information processing. Put plainly, we filter information based on our prior beliefs, rather than using information to potentially change these beliefs. Note how problematic this is for standard RCT, which assumes people will seek out new information in an unbiased way, even if employing heuristics in the process, to see if it confirms or disconfirms what they thought was true. In other words, a rational choice approach assumes that *perceptions inform beliefs more than beliefs inform perceptions*. However, the motivated reasoning approach contends that this straightforward perception-to-belief process will only take place when people are highly motivated to be accurate, a condition that turns out to be quite rare.

The basic cognitive process at the heart of motivated reasoning is depicted in Figure 8.1, from Lodge and Taber (2013). Note the key elements of the figure are the inclusion of prior attitudes and incidental emotional reaction well prior, temporally, to conscious evaluation and deliberation. Even the recognition of basic considerations – thoughts about the features of the object itself such as a candidate's appearance or issue stands – come slightly after, not before, the formation of attitudes about the object. The second important point is the feedback loop between deliberation and evaluation on the right side of the figure, which is where people are performing effortful and engaged thinking about decisions in politics. The path from evaluation to deliberation represents rationalization: thinking hard about things that help the individual justify their previous evaluations, pro or con, about a candidate. In general, the point is that

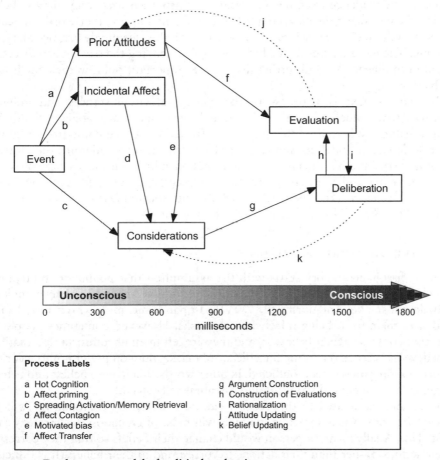

FIGURE 8.1 **Dual process model of political evaluation**
The dual process model integrates a host of psychological processes that cognitive and social psychologists have discovered over the last 50 years. On the left hand side of the figure, we see processes that occur in the first 500 milliseconds after exposure to a stimulus, before conscious awareness is possible. Those processes drive what we think of as conscious awareness, which occurs after at least 1,200 milliseconds have passed. The point is that many factors we think of as the consequences of conscious decisions are actually their causes.
Source: Lodge & Taber (2013).

deliberation – what many textbooks claim is critical for making good decisions and strengthening democracy – comes at the very end of the process rather than the beginning.

Finally, one of the most important, and potentially problematic predictions of motivated reasoning theory is that solutions often proposed for eliminating biases related to our *ability* to process information accurately – education, scientific literacy, and the like – may not work very well at all when the biases are *motivational* in nature. In other words, if people have an intrinsic preference for reaching certain conclusions, interventions designed to address *capacity* will be ineffective. In fact, it seems motivated reasoning may be even *stronger* among the highly sophisticated, educated, and informed (Lodge & Taber 2013; Taber & Lodge 2006). Why would this be the case? The more sophisticated a person becomes about a particular topic, the better they are at generating arguments and evidence from memory that comports with what they already believe, allowing them to reject the new, contradictory information. In other words, we cannot de-bias – "educate" – ourselves or others out of this seemingly irrational type of reasoning. The more we know, the better we are at denying the truth when directional goals are prominent. We will further discuss this important point in the conclusion of this chapter.

What comes next is a review of the contextual circumstances and individual differences that influence whether directional versus accuracy goals will dominate decision-making. Where does this socially motivated reasoning come from, and when does it dominate political decisions? Two older ideas help to undergird the motivated reasoning theory and have led us to a better understanding of exactly where directional goals come from and when they are most influential for political decision-making: *cognitive dissonance* (Festinger 1956, 1962) and *social identity theory* (Tajfel & Turner 1986). We will briefly review each idea in turn.

COGNITIVE DISSONANCE THEORY

Cognitive dissonance theory starts with the assumption that people are motivated to hold beliefs that correspond to their behavior. For example, most who believe smoking is deadly do not smoke. And during the COVID-19 pandemic, most who believed a mask would save them from being infected wore masks. However, sometimes people hold beliefs that contradict their behavior, and they are left in an uncomfortable situation. If you believe the science regarding the efficacy of masks, but you prefer not to wear them for some reason, you will feel conflicted. In other words, when one's beliefs and behavior diverge, it causes mental discomfort and threatens self-esteem.

The dissonance related to this conflict can be resolved by changing one's beliefs, behavior, or both. It is assumed individuals will most often choose the strategy that is easiest. This usually means a person would change their beliefs so that they correspond to their actions, rather than their actions to correspond to their beliefs. It is difficult to quit the addictive habit of smoking. Therefore, a smoker may simply reason that smoking is not *as bad* as people make it out to be (McMaster & Lee 1991).

Turning to a political example, you might care deeply about the environment and believe that climate change is a threat to humankind and many other species on Earth. However, the average citizen in most advanced industrial democracies produces far more carbon dioxide than other people on the planet because of their daily lifestyle choices. When first exposed to a message detailing this fact about their likely impact on the environment, they would experience dissonance, and the dissonance should be highest among those folks most strongly attached to their group identity as a "liberal environmentalist." To reduce such dissonance, there are only two choices: drastically change one's lifestyle to bring one's behavior into line with the norms of the group, or somehow reinterpret or counterargue the new information. Not surprisingly, people are much more likely to do the latter because it involves far less effort, sacrifice, and expense (Gifford 2011). So, for example, a person in that situation might argue that the new information was unreliable or exaggerated (Whitmarsh 2011). These identity motivations have important implications for how we think about public engagement with science. If individuals are *motivated* to disbelieve climate change, increasing the frequency of exposure to scientific evidence via the media or schooling is unlikely to be persuasive (Hart & Nisbet 2012).

Likewise, this same dissonance makes it difficult for individuals to hold competing beliefs, given a political preference. Views about ongoing political conflicts are a prime example. For instance, in Israel, views on the Israel-Palestinian conflict can be split into two main camps: the "dovish" camp that believes in the principle of exchanging land for peace and eventually pursuing a two-state solution, and the "hawkish" camp that believes the idea of land for peace is misguided. What is interesting about these two camps, however, is that their arguments for and against a two-state solution are typically made on two different, orthogonal dimensions – the moral one and the security one. So, for instance, a hawkish Israeli might argue that a one-state solution is best because, *morally* speaking, Jews have a stronger historical or religious claim to the land than Palestinians and therefore settlements in pursuit of a "Greater Israel" are justified. Or they might argue that the status quo is best because Israel's *security* would be threatened by an armed Palestinian state on its borders, should a two-state deal be implemented. On the other hand, a dovish Israeli might argue that controlling the West Bank is *immoral* and so Israel should withdraw from areas past the 1967 borders, in order to allow a Palestinian state to form there.

There is no rational reason that these two arguments – morality and security – should always be related. However, it is unlikely that many Israeli citizens hold these conflicting views – dovish Israelis will tend to believe that a two-state solution is better on *both* moral and security dimensions, while hawkish Israelis will believe the opposite. This so-called parallel reasoning is a fundamental by-product of cognitive dissonance and motivated reasoning. In other words, if one believes that Israel's control of the West Bank is bad on one dimension, but good on another, one of these beliefs is likely to be changed to reduce the dissonance between them and one's pre-existing preferences (e.g., support for or opposition to the two-state solution). This, of course, can then result in more polarized attitudes toward the conflict. A two-state solution becomes desired (or abhorred) for *all* reasons, rather than just one.

It is easy to see how this parallel reasoning process could occur in other contexts as well. For example, prior to Donald Trump's 2016 election to the presidency, many Republicans spoke out against his candidacy during the Republican primary, arguing that, though he spoke to a large segment of disaffected primary voters, his lack of conservative credentials and inflammatory statements were marks against his suitability for the Republican nomination. However, once he was elected president, these concerns seemed to disappear, and these GOP critics of Trump became stalwart allies lauding his values and performance on many dimensions.[7]

SOCIAL IDENTITY THEORY: THE NEED TO BELONG, RATIONAL EGOISM
& GROUP INTERESTS

Another powerful motivation undergirding directional goals in reasoning is social identity and the importance of group membership to individual identity and self-worth. For example, some of the earliest research by social psychologists into the causes of political conflict and violence in the early 1960s discovered that group memberships and sentiments often seem to obscure individual material interests in structuring people's preferences and behavior. Donald Campbell, who proposed *realistic group conflict theory* (RGCT), was one of the first to speculate that previous behavioral theories based on individual hedonistic factors missed a large part of what makes humans tick (Campbell 1965). Campbell speculated that conflicting group-level goals and competition for scarce resources were more likely to cause prejudice and intergroup hostility than unmet individual needs and wants. Even if an individual was well off, RCGT suggested he might feel strong hostility toward an out-group that threatened less wealthy members of his own group.

Campbell's claim that zero-sum competition over rights and resources at the level of groups, not individuals, caused prejudice and conflict was revolutionary for two reasons. First, it greatly expanded the scope of behavioral explanations beyond individual calculations of utility. It helped to explain decisions that previous theories would have considered highly irrational: the choice to engage in highly risky and potentially costly political protests even when a person could get very little in return either individually or in terms of changing the policy with which they disagreed.

A second truly groundbreaking prediction of RGCT was that prejudice and hostility were caused by *situations* and were therefore not stable factors within the individual. If true, prejudice and hostility should rise and fall with competition rather than remain stable over time. For example, changes in economic conditions should greatly affect the level of group hostility we observe at the aggregate level over time. Of course, in many ways, this theory preserved much of the basic architecture of RCT models of decision-making. It posited that people would react rationally to incentives – real conflict over actual material interests – but that we must simply pay attention to such incentives at the level of the *group*, not primarily the individual. It also produced the hope that individuals could change their prejudicial attitudes and behavior toward out-groups as long as material group competition could be reduced.

This theory of human behavior is in line with research by evolutionary psychologists. These researchers argue that behaviors that tend to favor in-group members and respond forcefully to potential threats from external sources were evolutionary beneficial for ancient humans, who were, more often than not, likely to be killed or driven out by outside groups encroaching on their territory. However, in the modern world, these once-adaptive social processes may play a major role in many of the negative social and political interactions we witness today – racism, discrimination, violent conflict, and so on (Bowles 2009; Fiske 2002). For example, it has been found that the evolutionary predisposition to favor in-groups can be triggered even by the most arbitrary social categorizations, and even if this behavior is individually costly (Hammond & Axelrod 2006). This prejudice is often triggered subconsciously, even amongst individuals who do not express overt racial bias or prejudicial attitudes (Fiske 1998; Macrae & Bodenhausen 2000).

Indeed, as reviewed in Chapter 6, there is a connection between biological responses, emotion, and political attitudes toward out-groups. For example, researchers have looked at the role of testosterone in aggression in war games (McDermott et al. 2007), the stress hormone cortisol and exposure to violence or terrorism (Canetti et al. 2017), how oxytocin fosters trust (Kosfeld et al. 2005), and the role of Monoamine Oxidase A (the so-called warrior gene) in aggression (McDermott et al. 2009), to name a few (see Chapter 6 for a more detailed discussion on these biological approaches).

In reaction to RGCT, social psychologists began to examine the role of group competition in provoking violent political conflict. In a famous demonstration of the power of group attachments over individual interests, Sherif and his colleagues (1961) randomly assigned boys at a summer camp into two teams that would compete for valued prizes. In this "Robbers Cave Experiment," the researchers found that very quickly, the boys developed strong positive in-group associations and negative attitudes toward the other group, demonstrating the power of group competition to foment prejudice and conflict. Taking the formation and consequences of social identity seriously has been central in BPS explanations of group conflict and prejudice.

However, the theory's focus on group competition for scarce material resources was still rooted in basic principles of RCT. Individual needs and wants were simply supplanted with the interests of the group. This theory, relying on real material competition fomenting prejudice, would explain, for example, why whites who lived in political districts with large percentages of African American voters were most supportive of highly racially conservative candidates in the Jim Crow South (Key 1949). Of course, this logically implied that, *in the absence of material competition*, prejudice would lose much of its force. On this score, unfortunately, the theory failed. Thus, for example, whites who lived in areas with fewer minorities competing for jobs should be less supportive of prejudicial candidates or policies. However, this prediction is often contradicted. Several studies in the United States have demonstrated that opposition to immigration seems to have little to do with economic threats, either real or perceived (Hainmueller & Hopkins 2014).

The prevalence of prejudice seemingly in the *absence* of competition over real material interests cannot be explained by RGCT. Thus, in the 1970s, social psychologists sought to understand the origin of intergroup conflict. These researchers postulated that identity itself could be a motivation for conflict. Building on work by Sherif and others on the origins of group prejudice, Tajfel and colleagues (1979) ran a serious of experiments to investigate exactly *how much* actual competition was needed to produce prejudice, conflict, and hostility between groups. The surprising answer was "almost none at all." So little, in fact, that the investigations that were used to demonstrate them became known as *"minimal group experiments."*

A typical experiment in this paradigm went as follows: Individuals were asked to estimate the number of dots on a page. They were then randomly assigned to one of two groups. One group was told that they were overestimators: They had counted more dots than there actually were on the page. These subjects were not actually any more likely to overestimate than those in the other group, they were simply randomly assigned to the group that was told this. The other group was told they were underestimators: They had counted too few dots. Both groups were also informed about the existence of the other group, though they never actually interacted with any other experimental participant. They were then asked to divide resources between members of their "group" and those from the other group, none of whom they had ever met.

Payoffs in the experiment were set up so subjects gained no material benefit from punishing the out-group, and sometimes even incurred a cost to do so. Therefore, *there was no competition or scarcity of resources.* Nonetheless, subjects consistently exhibited strong in-group favoritism and out-group discrimination in the distribution of resources. Individuals did not simply try to maximize the material gains of the in-group - they tried to maximize the relative advantage of their group over the other, *even if that meant their group got much less.* Essentially, individuals were willing to forego utility if it meant the in-group got relatively more than another group did, even though there was no real competition over resources. These results formed the foundation of social identity theory (SIT) – that social identities provide positive self-esteem such that discriminatory or prejudicial behavior emerges spontaneously as soon as social categories are made salient. One's self-esteem comes, at least in part, not only from belonging to a group that is materially well off, but one that is *better off* than other groups (Tajfel et al. 1979).

These two theories therefore postulate different explanations for conflict between social groups. RGCT is material and rational at its core if we focus on group, rather than individual level interest. SIT identifies social psychological motivations – the esteem that comes from belonging to the "best" group – that can lead to outcomes which undermine material welfare. As we discussed in Chapter 7, some RCT models have begun to include nonmaterial benefits such as self-esteem. However, they usually assume that self-esteem benefits are interchangeable with material well-being – that achieving material goals would also help individuals achieve esteem goals and vice versa. BPS contends that these two goals can in fact be orthogonal and identity goals may not be calculated the same way as material goals. The prevalence of identity goals, and the complex way in which they factor into preference formation, may help explain cases where RCT models fail.

There are many good examples of the subtle distinction between behavioral, psychological, and economic approaches to human decision-making, and we will review several of them. However, while we can expand what is "rational" beyond what maximizes our individual well-being, we must do so carefully. We are on a slippery slope to say that individuals will act in ways that make them feel good about themselves because it can render predictions tautological. Still, if in fact humans think and act this way, if they depend substantially on psychological benefits like self-esteem derived in large part from the sense of belonging to valued social groups, then we need to take such ideas into account in order to make good predictions about when conflicts will arise and how they might be addressed. SIT explains why individuals react with hostility to members of out-groups *even when they are not in competition over material resources,* and so it is a significant scientific breakthrough in the study of human behavior.

These ideas about the power of simple group-belonging to cause prejudice and discrimination might also be linked to basic information processing strategies that we were concerned about at the beginning of the chapter. Recall that motivated reasoning suggests people are often quite automatically motivated to reject new arguments and information and defend their preexisting views, even when they would benefit materially by giving up those incorrect beliefs. SIT provides one explanation for this phenomenon.

The group attachments that help maintain positive self-esteem also structure beliefs about the world in important ways. One simple example of this is the link between membership in religious organizations and beliefs about the origins of our world and the human race. In many churches and across most world religions, membership depends on the individual pledging that they believe in the truth of part or all of the ancient scriptures in their tradition. For example, believing that the Earth, and not the Sun, was at the center of the physical universe was part of the belief system of some religions. Based on motivated reasoning one would predict, therefore, that someone who strongly identified with some of these religions in 1633 might resist, counterargue, or otherwise disregard any scientific evidence suggesting that in fact the Earth and all the other planets in our solar system instead revolved around the sun, as Nicolas Copernicus had proposed about a century prior. Of course, that is exactly what Galileo discovered with his telescope, and he was condemned for it. He paid a very high personal price for insisting that his observations and measurements were correct, dying under house arrest nine years later, in 1642.

There are often powerful tensions between our group memberships and what careful scientific observation tells us is true. It is this very real tension caused by the connection between identity and belief that can sometimes lead to dramatic departures from predictions based on assumptions about materialistic incentives in human nature. So, when are people able to overcome such motivational biases and come to accept new information that challenges long held and sacred beliefs?

THE EFFECTS OF MOTIVATED REASONING

Now that we have defined motivated reasoning and discussed one of its major sources – social group identities – we briefly summarize some of its consequences for political decision-making and behavior. Many papers are published each month in journals across fields as diverse as psychology, political science, communication studies, marketing, and business on this subject. To date, scholars have discovered major consequences of this bias in at least three domains: belief persistence, counterarguing, and attitude polarization.

Belief persistence, as the phrase implies, is simply the tendency for one to hold tight to a belief about the world even when it has been shown to be demonstrably false. A simple example of this would be the stubborn clinging to a conspiracy theory even when seemingly incontrovertible proof arrives to the contrary. History is replete with groups who believe the world will end on a given date, only for that day to pass without incident. The reaction of nearly all group members is not to abandon their faith but more often to set another date for Earth's demise sometime in the future. In the political realm, there are many perhaps more consequential examples. The refusal of large proportions of the American public to accept the overwhelming scientific consensus about the rise of global temperatures has been well documented, despite scientific evidence and communication on this issue. Endorsing positions on climate change that are at odds with overwhelming scientific consensus seems irrational but can be conceived of as "expressively rational" if the goal is to solidify one's identity or membership in an ideological or cultural group (Kahan 2012). The consequences of belief persistence in this domain, however, may be catastrophic, especially if the largest producers of greenhouse gasses are unwilling to even accept that there is a problem in the first place.

One particularly interesting study on belief persistence by Redlawsk (2002) demonstrates the power of motivated reasoning perceptions about political candidates. The study first found that it takes significantly longer for someone to process negative information about a candidate they like compared to when they process positive information about the same candidate. Study participants also sought nearly 50% more information about the candidate they preferred compared to what would be expected by chance (Redlawsk 2002, p. 1033). Thus, voters generally did not access information about candidates they disliked, only ones they originally preferred. Even more strikingly, voters who *did* encounter negative information about their preferred candidates exhibited *stronger support* for them. This demonstrates the power of motivated reasoning: negative information about liked candidates not only failed to get voters to revise their ratings of those candidates downwards, but also triggered a backlash effect in which participants claimed they liked the candidates even more. One reason for this effect may be that motivated reasoning is likely to increase individuals' efforts to *counterargue* when presented with facts that do not fit their preferred narrative, coming up with a host of reasons, some of which might be quite thin, for why they should not change their mind in the face of new information. In study after study, researchers have found that citizens are much more scrutinizing of evidence and arguments that contradict their existing beliefs compared to information that confirms them. For example, in one careful set of studies (Taber & Lodge 2006), respondents were shown a set of arguments that were likely to challenge versus confirm their preexisting views on affirmative action and gun control. When confronted with attitudinally challenging information, even of high quality and credibility, respondents spent much more time considering, counterarguing, and denigrating such points of view.

This tendency to counterargue is often thought of as a means for maintaining stable beliefs rather than a political consequence per se, but counterarguing can have significant impacts on the climate of political discourse in our country. Rather than carefully listening to one's opponent in a given debate and considering the strengths and weaknesses of a given argument, counterarguing mandates the manufacture of a contradictory statement of some kind. The rise of *fake news* makes this tendency even more dangerous.

Finally, beliefs that are affected by a motivated reasoning process are likely to become *polarized,* when belief persistence and counterarguing produce a widening gulf between groups on either side of an issue until they begin to dislike each other. It can occur when those who are invested in one side of an argument react to contradictory information not just by counterarguing or rejecting the message, but by taking an even more extreme position than they previously held. This is often called a backlash or contrast effect. In one study, for example, attempts to correct candidate's misleading claims not only failed to reduce misperceptions among supporters, but also increased them (Nyhan & Reifler 2010). Backlash effects, and the polarization between groups that can result, can have serious and harmful effects in a democracy.

Emotions are hypothesized to be a central component of motivated reasoning. In particular, negative emotions about out-groups may powerfully shape information processing and contribute to polarization. This process becomes cyclical – the more polarized a population is, the more they will engage in motivated reasoning, which will further polarize them. Recall that, according to SIT, negative emotions are powerful because they are experienced automatically, simply because of the *existence* of an out-group, even when objective competition for rights and resources is absent. These automatic emotional reactions in modern societies make conflict much more common than RCT would predict, because disagreement about real-world policies or issues is unnecessary. As a result, elites can generate mass support for policies framed as a defense of the in-group – a nation, a religious tradition, or an ethnic faction – even when there is very little at stake materially. The challenge of producing efficient, egalitarian, and effective public policies in such an environment is obvious.

Indeed, identification with a group creates positive feelings toward others within the in-group (empathy, trust, compassion, etc.), while simultaneously engendering negative feelings toward out-group members (fear, distrust, anxiety, or even disgust, anger, and hatred). These powerful emotions can in turn spur potentially violent attitudes and behaviors toward out-group members. For example, *affective polarization* has dramatically increased in recent years in the United States (Iyengar, Sood & Lelkes 2012). In 2015, Democrats and Republicans disliked each other far more than they did in 1980. The dislike is so intense, in fact, that one study showed that the average citizen is now far more likely to oppose a family member marrying someone from the opposing party than they are to oppose marriage to someone from a different racial background (Iyengar & Westwood 2015). During and since the presidency of Donald Trump, such polarization has been even more pronounced.[8]

Exploring the roots of this partisan polarization has only just begun, but work on the topic seems to indicate that social identities which underlie partisanship are to blame (Mason 2015). Note that this pattern is entirely consistent with the basic tenets of motivated reasoning in politics that we have discussed. Groups do not only have rational disagreements about issues that they can then deliberate about and compromise on; instead, group identities can become aligned with partisan cleavages such that individuals in each party come to dislike, distrust, and reject members of the opposing party *even when they do not fundamentally disagree about policies or national goals*. Negative affect, then, leads them to take different positions on issues, to justify their feelings. Finally, elites in each party witness their constituents expressing such negative views about the out-groups, and then begin to capitalize on powerful negative emotions like anger in order to mobilize them. This process stands in direct opposition to what we would hope would drive democratic decision-making.

While partisan polarization has become a prominent BPS topic of study in the realm of mass politics, research exploring the behavior of political elites, such as members of the US congress, has relied largely on RCT assumptions. However, if most citizens are subject to significant constraints on information processing and display powerful motivations to maintain and defend existing beliefs rather than update and learn, can we reasonably expect legislators and other elites to do behave differently?

The reason most Congress scholars either implicitly or explicitly assume some version of Economic Man operates in these areas is that members of Congress are typically highly educated, wealthy, and therefore motivated to become informed so that they can best maximize their own (and presumably their constituency's) interests. Because they are motivated to stay in office, they should maximize the interests of the citizens they represent.

On their face, the features of the Rational Actor – a completely informed, utility-maximizing, reliable decision-maker – do seem reasonable for this group. However, many of the biases in human decision-making, group decision-making, and information seeking that we have discussed in this book should operate among elites and masses alike. This is particularly true with motivated reasoning, which involves preconscious and automatic processes that are not easily controllable and may operate *even more* powerfully among the most sophisticated members of society, presumably including Congress.

Take, for example, the topic of party polarization. The mass public's strong defense of group boundaries at the expense of many other gains, explained by motivated reasoning, seems potentially inconsistent with the rational actor approach. But what about among party elites? Why would elites from either party be so motivated by dislike for the opposition that they would even propose policies that are often likely to fail?

The rational actor model has struggled to explain elite partisan behavior in the area of candidate selection for major elections in the era of polarization. In 2010, conservative Tea Party candidate Christine O'Donnell defeated a more experienced and moderate Republican, Michael Castle, for the Delaware Senate seat vacated by Vice President Joe Biden in 2008. Winning the seat would have been vital for the party in their bid to take over the majority. At the time of her upset victory, Democratic and Republican pundits alike felt Castle had a far better chance to defeat the Democratic candidate, Chris Coons. In the end, Coons easily won the election by a margin of 57 percent to 40 percent.

The same puzzling pattern played out in 2012 with Senator Richard Lugar in Indiana. After his landslide victory against a Democratic incumbent in 1977, Luger served his state for six consecutive terms – thirty-six years. During most of his career, Luger was seen as a moderate Republican, often working together with Democrats to propose and shepherd legislation that would find bipartisan support on the floor of the Senate. While he opposed President Obama's landmark health care reform bill, the Affordable Care Act of 2009, he was also one of the party's strongest supporters of gun control legislation, receiving an "F" from the National Rifle Association in 2012. Lugar, who passed away in 2019, was the longest-serving senator in Indiana's history, and was the most senior Republican senator in 2012. In that year, he was attacked from the right by a little-known Tea Party conservative – Indiana State Treasurer Richard Mourdock. Mourdock claimed that Lugar was too willing to compromise, and that he was much more moderate than the Republican voters in the state. He argued that bipartisanship and collegiality was the source of many of the country's problems, and that confrontation with Democrats and Obama in particular was the only to achieve the goals of the party and help the citizens of the state. Outside Tea Party groups poured nearly $2 million into Mourdock's campaign, much of that going to air caustic advertising attack ads, significantly outspending the incumbent. On primary election day, Mourdock won by a whopping 61 percent to 39 percent, a nearly unprecedented margin against a long-term incumbent not suffering from a personal scandal. Mourdock was then beaten soundly by the Democratic candidate in the general election. In supporting a relatively inexperienced candidate from the right wing of their party, Republicans not only lost a reliable seat, they further handicapped themselves in their fight to take back the majority of the Senate. Why would party elites nominate candidates in primaries who had no chance to win a general election, and would cause the party to lose a critical seat in a year when they had been poised to take over the majority in the Senate?

It seems plausible that the emotional processes underlying motivated reasoning at the level of the mass public as well as intraparty, suboptimal political considerations, might also help us explain these significant departures from the rational actor model. While these examples might simply be dismissed as "out of equilibrium," rare events, BPS has a way to understand them more comprehensively. Elites, like mass citizens, are sometimes able to make strategic, forward-looking choices that maximize their own interests. But only sometimes! BPS gives us a set of tools for identifying the conditions under which decision-makers will depart from the ideal of standard RCT models.

We think, therefore, there is a large opportunity to conduct more research on motivated reasoning in elite strategic interactions within democratic institutions in order to see if explanations of legislative productivity, institutional design, and intragovernmental interaction can be better understood with the same insights that have helped us improve our understanding of mass politics.

Motivated reasoning also helps us to understand why groups would be willing to support costly and risky policy actions even when they individually stood to gain very little. Intergroup emotions theory posits that, when individuals begin to identify as members of a social group, that group becomes an integral extension of the individuals' self-identity (Mackie, Devos & Smith 2000). Thus, as we discussed in Chapter 6, the group acquires strong emotional significance, triggering emotional reactions when events affect the group writ large, due to group identification and perceived membership in a group (Mackie, Devos & Smith 2000). In other words, "wars, terrorist attacks, or natural disasters that affect a country as a whole generate feelings of sadness, anger, and fear among those who identify with the country even if they themselves or their families and friends are not directly affected" (Smith, Seger & Mackie 2007, p. 431). These group emotions can be distinct from emotion at the individual level; an individual can feel happy and satisfied with their own life but angry and dissatisfied over the life of their social, economic, religious, or ethnic group. An individual can feel guilty as an American for collateral damage in Iraq but feel personally moral and upright; fear as a Jewish person in response to anti-Semitic attacks in foreign countries but personally secure in their locale. Likewise, women or men might be angry about gender gaps in education and income, despite being individually educated or wealthy. However, the potency of these group emotions may depend on the relative strength of identification with the group. Thus, intergroup emotions and strong identification with an in-group are often highly correlated (Yzerbyt et al. 2003).

We now think that motivated reasoning, and the group-based emotions that trigger it, can powerfully influence citizens' attitudes about violent national and international conflicts. In times of war, the social identity of individuals as the collective "community" of a particular nation can be enhanced (Anderson 1983), leading to strong in-group identification and even more powerful emotional responses to events affecting the in-group. In the words of sociologist Mabel Berezin (2001), "modern nation-states serve as vehicles of political emotion ... nation-states move the epistemological – citizenship as category – toward the ontological – citizen as felt identity." As social identities magnify emotional reactions to events that may have little to do with the real interests at stake, mass publics may come to support costly and highly risky military strategies that may, in expectation, reduce national security and prosperity.

Intergroup threat theory (Stephan & Stephan 2000; Stephan, Ybarra & Morrison 2009) represents one key application of these ideas. An intergroup threat is experienced when "members of one group perceive that another group is in a position to cause them harm," either physically (realistic threat) or to the group's meaning (symbolic threat) (Stephan, Ybarra & Morrison 2009). In the interstate context, these threats would typically be to the nation from an external actor. These perceived threats can trigger fear or anxiety, emotions with strong action tendencies and implications for political attitudes and behavior. Consider, for example, President Trump's hardline immigration rhetoric characterizing immigrants as criminals who threaten our national security.

The exact circumstances under which motivated reasoning is likely to be more or less prominent have been explored across a variety of issue domains. For example, Levendusky (2013) found that partisan media contributes to polarization not only because it presents arguments in unbalanced ways (e.g., without persuasive counterarguments to the preferred ideological issue position), but because it presents all issues and facts as partisan in the first place. This effectively primes partisan identity prior to and during exposure to this information, heightening the directional group identity goals at the heart of motivated reasoning (Levendusky 2013). However, the prevalence of the backlash effect in motivated reasoning may be overstated. Guess and Coppock (2020) find that respondents presented with pro or anti arguments on a variety of policy issues from gun control to welfare readily change their attitudes in the direction of the information given, rather than in support of their pre-existing attitudes (Guess & Coppock 2020). More recent evidence suggests that persuasion is most effective when the message aligns with an individual's motivation – whether that be accuracy, the affirmation of group identity, or the affirmation of motives and values (Bayes et al. 2020). Thus, motivated reasoning often prevents persuasion, but effective messages can still be designed, provided they are tailored to fit the target's motivations. This has huge implications for political marketing and campaign strategy, as evident by personalized messages sent to millions of voters during the campaigns of 2012, 2016, and 2020.

Thus, the likelihood and severity of motivated reasoning can vary across contexts and issue domains. However, the problematic consequence of motivated reasoning – wherever it occurs – is that it can lead people to hold stubbornly inaccurate beliefs about the world around them. In short, misperceptions will be widespread. Misperceptions are different (and potentially more problematic) than ignorance in that they are held with a high degree of certainty, and the people who hold them *believe* they are actually well-informed (Flynn, Nyhan & Reifler 2017). They are not uninformed; they are confidently misinformed (Kuklinski et al. 2000). Misperceptions have been documented by researchers in a host of policy areas, including the economy (Bartels 2002), the Iraq War (Kull, Ramsay & Lewis 2003), gun policy (Aronow & Miller 2016), immigration (Sides & Citrin 2007), the COVID-19 pandemic of 2020,[9] and more.

CONTROLLING MOTIVATED REASONING

Motivated reasoning, and the misperceptions it creates, clearly present normative challenges for politics. If beliefs about the world are not based in objective fact, but rather are tied to individuals' unique social identities, the ability of politicians to compromise in order to produce sound public policy will be severely hindered. So how do we reduce the impact of motivated reasoning on political attitudes? In many circumstances where cognitive biases are concerned, the first solution most would propose involves more information, education, or learning processes. In the case of stereotyping or some other automatic cognitive biases that we have discussed in other parts of the book, this really seems to work. Letting people know that subconscious biases may influence the choices they hold toward particular groups seems to reduce the impact of such biases, while taking away the time or cognitive resources required to combat stereotypic thinking makes the problem worse (Devine 1989).

But what about motivated reasoning? One might assume the same solution would work. Just get folks to think harder about a given topic and they will set aside their directional motivations, at least for a moment, and consider the new information in a way that leads them to hold more accurate beliefs in the future. This should subsequently produce better behaviors, which should then reinforce the decision to think carefully. A virtuous feedback loop will be set in motion and eventually the bias toward maintaining one's prior, but incorrect, beliefs will disappear. Unfortunately, it seems that this is not what happens.

As we pointed out, highly sophisticated, informed citizens are much *more* likely to be motivated reasoners than are less informed citizens, and are therefore more likely to reject new and credible information. Lodge and Taber (2013), for example, ran several experiments in which the researchers first recorded individuals' issue positions and attitude strength (how confident they are in their opinion) on a variety of topics such as gun control and affirmative action. Respondents were then assigned to look at an information board on a computer which allowed them to look for pro- versus counter-attitudinal information about these same issues. They found that the people who knew the *most* and felt the strongest about these issues to begin with were most likely to seek out confirming evidence and avoid information that they suspected might contradict what they already believed. Sophisticates were also more likely than others to rate pro-attitudinal arguments as stronger, and contra-attitudinal arguments as weaker, even when the strength of the arguments was balanced. Those who knew more about a topic in these experiments scrutinized counter-attitudinal information more carefully than if the argument was consistent with their priors, and wrote more thoughts contradicting arguments with which they disagreed. In fact, those with weaker attitudes or less sophisticated understandings of politics were much *less* likely to make these mistakes. This motivated reasoning bias among sophisticated citizens exists for both Democrats and Republicans, men and women, whites and non-whites. The conclusion is that getting people to think harder and more carefully about why they hold the opinions they do may not fix the problem and instead could, in fact, make things much worse.

This means that political elites may be just as – if not more – susceptible to motivated reasoning as the mass public, despite their political sophistication and strategic incentives for accuracy. Though this chapter has focused on the mass public, there are ample examples of political elites appearing to express motivated biases as well. For example, the pivot by President Donald Trump on North Korea could be seen in this light. Early in his term, President Trump regularly attacked North Korean President Kim Jung Un as a "tyrant" and North Korea as a "prison state" and "a hell that no one deserves."[10] Less than six months later, after a symbolic summit with the North Korean leader, President Trump was much more positive in his assessment of the leader, calling him a "tough guy," "very talented," "smart," and a "good negotiator."[11] This change of heart is difficult to explain without incorporating potential esteem motives Trump may have in making these different assessments. When Trump was considering war with North Korea, he perceived Kim Jung Un as a tyrannical dictator. Once diplomacy was back on the table – less than six months later – Kim Jung became a smart, tough world leader with whom he could negotiate.

Of course, motivated reasoning is not the *only* explanation when two people reach different conclusions after viewing the same information. For example, the idea that exposure to new information might not reduce, and will sometimes exacerbate, disagreement between partisans can be consistent with Bayesian logic. As Bullock (2009) demonstrates, there are a wide variety of circumstances in which Democrats and Republicans will diverge when exposed to new information even when they agree on its credibility. As such, divergent interpretations of the same event or information is likely often driven by a combination of people holding different prior beliefs (and therefore weighting new evidence differently) and the directional goals of motivated reasoning theory (Jefferson, Neuner & Pasek 2020).

Some research has shown that instead of fixing motivated reasoning by providing more information, an emotional route might work better. Given the centrality of affect (emotion) in causing motivated reasoning in the first place, it makes sense that this emotional route may be more effective. One strategy that has proven promising is that of emotion regulation and cognitive reappraisal (Gross 2014), which can occur by changing the emotional cues accompanying a conflict event. The idea is that by attaching emotions to a political object, you can affect policy views. In the context of the Israeli-Palestinian conflict, for example, subjects taught to reappraise conflict events were more supportive of conciliatory policies toward the Palestinian Authority in the aftermath of their UN bid for statehood, even five months following the experimental treatment (Halperin et al. 2013). A reappraisal process may be the result of a shift in information processing that we discussed in Chapter 6 while discussing the theory of affective intelligence (Marcus, Neuman & MacKuen 2000). In order to overcome motivated reasoning, the goal is to get the mind to abandon the "dispositional" system, heavily reliant on habits of mind and bound by inflexible predispositions – in favor of the "surveillance system," where more careful deliberation and consideration of new alternatives is possible. This experimental evidence on the importance of emotions in shaping motivated reasoning and political attitudes may call into question more traditional rational choice models of war onset and termination. Acknowledging that our conscious awareness represents such a sliver of what our brains are doing to affect our decisions is the first step in understanding how to modify standard assumptions of rationality.

DISTINGUISHING MOTIVATED REASONING FROM A RATIONAL CHOICE APPROACH

In response to the mounting evidence regarding the prevalence of motivated misperceptions in politics, there has been a renewed focus on the extent of motivated reasoning and the degree to which its central tenets can be incorporated (or not) into RCT models of decision-making and political behavior. For example, one central challenge for motivated reasoning theory is disentangling the mechanisms underlying differences in beliefs. Essentially, differences in political attitudes among individuals belonging to different identity groups (e.g., political parties, ethnicities, religion, etc.) is not, on its own, enough evidence to assume that the reasons for these differences are directional motives associated with respondents' social identity. Indeed, there are several other mechanisms that could lead to these same results, many of which are easier to integrate into a rationalist framework, including expressive responses, source credibility, and non-common priors. Teasing out the relative importance of these various mechanisms is a central avenue of research in work on motivated reasoning today.

Most evidence for motivated reasoning comes from survey research, in which respondents are asked to answer questions about their political attitudes. However, some scholars have questioned whether respondents actually *believe* the answers they provide on surveys regarding the performance of their preferred candidate or political party on a given issue. In other words, are survey respondents simply using their responses to express their identity or engaging in "insincere cheerleading" (Peterson & Iyengar 2021) without actually believing their answer to accurately reflect the world? Would respondents actually behave in ways consistent with these expressed beliefs if doing so was costly? There is at least some evidence that they may not. For example, in one study, when researchers presented subjects with tangible motives to be accurate in their response (a financial incentive), partisan differences in assessments of the economy were significantly reduced (Prior, Sood & Khanna 2015). However, is this due to a reduction in cheerleading or has increasing the accuracy motive actually changed processing in such a way that underlying beliefs change? It is difficult to disentangle the two (Bullock & Lenz 2019), but the distinction has important implications for our understanding of politics. If stated beliefs are simply expressive (cheerleading) and do not actually shape or change behavior, motivated reasoning does not pose an inherent challenge to RCT models of politics – people may *claim* to believe, for example, that their candidate is doing well in office, but privately understand that they are not, and so place their vote accordingly. However, if partisan identity is actually shaping beliefs, leading to "congenial inference" (e.g., inferences in line with our partisan identities), motivated reasoning presents a deeper challenge to RCT models and a normative problem for democracy (Bullock & Lenz 2019). Though such studies show that the effects of motivated reasoning on behavior can be reduced in certain contexts by increasing accuracy motives, most evidence still points to the internalization and stubborn persistence of motivated misperceptions above and beyond cheerleading (Peterson & Iyengar 2021), even when individuals are presented with information that proves these beliefs to be false (Nyhan & Reifler 2010).

If individuals indeed truly hold divergent beliefs, as motivated reasoning theory claims, what else might explain this phenomenon, apart from the identity-motivated directional goals central to motivated reasoning theory? One explanation lays in "source credibility" – the degree of trust different individuals place in various institutions and leaders. This could explain why corrective information is more persuasive when presented by ideologically sympathetic sources (Berinsky 2017). For example, the well-known findings whereby more informed partisans are *less* receptive to new information that contradicts their beliefs than are less informed partisans could be, in part, a result of source credibility. Bolsen and Druckman (2018) find that some well-informed Republicans are not receptive to messages reporting the scientific consensus surrounding climate change. Is this because they are the most motivated to reject these messages? Or is it because they distrust the source (the scientific community) and so discount the veracity of messages this source sends (Druckman & McGrath 2019)?

However, while source credibility no doubt plays a role in shaping responses to information, other studies have found that motivated reasoning can persist above and beyond this issue. For example, Republicans and Democrats have been shown to assess the credibility of polls based on whether the poll shows their party leading or trailing in an election, regardless of the ideological alignment of the source (Kuru, Pasek & Traugott 2017). President Trump, fearing a loss in the 2020 election, preempted by repeatedly claiming that mail-in voting would produce false results. Moreover, recent work has suggested that source credibility can *itself* be a product of motivated reasoning processes. In an important example of how BPS assumptions can be studied using the tools of formal theory, Little (2019) demonstrates the directional motives underlying the distortion of so-called related beliefs. He formally demonstrates that if, for example, a newspaper reports a story unfavorable to one's preferred candidate, beliefs about the quality of the candidate and the quality of the newspaper will become linked. If voters are motivated to preserve their positive views of the candidate, they must change their views about the credibility of the source – the newspaper. As such, auxiliary beliefs that are intrinsically important to an individual (e.g., the quality of a "source"), nonetheless, become distorted because these distorted beliefs are central for propping up the core (distorted) beliefs over which we possess directional motives. Thus, assessments of source credibility are in fact inextricably linked to motivated reasoning and cannot be considered a completely separate explanation for divergent responses to the same information.

Another explanation for divergent beliefs among members of different identity groups is the idea of *non-common priors*. In Chapter 2, we reviewed the canonical RCT model of belief formation, Bayes Rule, in which new information (e.g., a positive test result) would shape our beliefs about the likelihood of an event (e.g., the probability of having a disease). These updated beliefs, however, are not only based on the new information (the positive test result) but are also heavily weighted by our prior beliefs regarding the likelihood of this event (e.g., the base rate of illness in the population). But what happens when two people hold different prior beliefs about the likelihood of an event? What if one person believes 1 percent of the population has an illness and another person believes 50 percent of the population has that same illness? Even if they both process and incorporate the new information (the positive test result) into their updated beliefs in the same way, they would *still* arrive at different likelihoods regarding the probability of an event occurring because of these different prior beliefs. In short, two people can see the exact same evidence, take that evidence into account in the same way, and still possess different beliefs. This often looks observationally equivalent to the biased information processing patterns we expect to see with motivated reasoning and can be difficult to tease apart. Indeed, evidence for directional motivated reasoning requires proof of two factors: (1) an individual possesses a directional goal, and (2) information processing is tailored to achieve that goal (Druckman & McGrath 2019, p. 114). Verifying these two components of motivated reasoning can be quite challenging.

Non-common prior beliefs thus represent a potential alternative explanation to directional motives in explaining individuals' distinct responses to the same stimuli. For example, one study Jefferson, Neuner, and Pasek (2020) examines the responses of white and African American respondents to news of an officer-involved shooting, manipulating the race of the officer and the victim. They find that African American respondents are much more likely than whites to blame a white officer for using force unnecessarily against an African American suspect. The authors find some evidence for motivated reasoning – respondents who more strongly identified as African American or as white exhibited more divergent information search patterns. However, they also observe the impact of non-common priors: differences in the evaluations of who was at fault for the encounter strongly tracked with ex ante beliefs about the typical behaviors of African Americans or of the police. Thus, for example, African American respondents, who have had qualitatively different interactions with the police over the course of their lifetime, were more likely to *expect* the officer to have done something wrong and, so, when presented with an ambiguous circumstance, used their priors to inform their new belief about this event, that the officer was at fault (and vice versa for white respondents). However, as with source credibility, the question remains: why do individuals possess different ex ante beliefs in the first place? In part, the origins of these different beliefs may themselves be a product of motivated reasoning. Thus, even non-common priors cannot wholly explain away the importance of directional goals in shaping reasoning, and the implications this poses for political attitudes and behavior. A recent example of this can be found in the widely varying reactions to the Black Lives Matter protests that swept the nation in the spring and summer of 2020. Sparked by a series of killings of unarmed African Americans by police, these events were immediately politicized by elites on either side of the aisle. Many conservatives characterized the protests as riots and protestors as criminals coming from outside the community, bent on looting and the destruction of private property. Liberals described the same events as mostly peaceful interventions by local residents who were trying to bring change to their local law enforcement policies and procedures in interactions in their communities. Anyone familiar with the images of these protests shown in the media will understand how prior beliefs about the identity and motivations of the protestors could dramatically alter what one "saw" on the news. Conservatives and liberals were essentially viewing different events, even while watching the same footage.

CONCLUSION

In this chapter, we presented work that demonstrates how good most people are at defending their existing beliefs, even in the presence of strong contradictory evidence. Even more surprising is the well-replicated finding that the more sophisticated a person becomes – as they get more education and experience deliberating about the issues – the better able they are to reject new, credible information. When citizens reject new information that would help them make more accurate decisions – ones that lead them to be more successful at getting the kind of representatives in government who will defend their interests – how can democracy really work the way the Founders promised it would? If educating citizens is not only ineffective at solving the problem of motivated reasoning for basic democratic accountability, but actually makes the problem *worse*, what can we do? These questions are among the most exciting and important ones in the field of political science. Political psychologists, scholars of voting behavior and participation, and political theorists are thinking hard about all of them.

While BPS has discovered no simple solutions, there are some hints. One candidate is for persuasive communicators to be well versed in the psychological research and its findings you are reading about in this book. For example, the first step toward reducing motivated reasoning biases is for public officials to try and avoid litigating every detail of a policy in the court of public opinion. This can be particularly important in the domain of public health, where politicizing issues on which there is broad scientific consensus, such as vaccines, GMOs, and climate change can have highly undesirable health-relevant and economic consequences for the entire population. However, this prescription is difficult to implement, as there remains a significant incentive for elected officials to politicize issues to gain an electoral advantage. That problem poses perhaps a larger hurdle, since the solution would entail a norm that both parties would agree to avoid rhetorical strategies that would undermine the broad public good but advantage some important part of their electoral coalition.

If the above advice works – imploring elites to avoid unnecessarily politicizing issues where a clear public health benefit is at stake – perhaps journalists could employ the same solution? If the salience of group identities is positively linked to motivated reasoning biases, then one might imagine that at least two sorts of communication strategies could help undermine these biases at the individual level. First, news organizations could work harder to avoid framing stories about policies in terms of partisan or group conflict at all. Despite the powerful incentives to focus on winners and losers in a given policy debate – much of which is contrived and motivated by the actors themselves rather than grounded in real differences of utility – journalists could work to avoid politicizing issues and framing debates in highly partisan terms. Of course, the politicizing of issues may be inevitable, given the strategic incentives of elites on either side of the aisle in a highly partisan environment.

Second, news frames about public health issues, should avoid pitting social or political groups against each other. Instead, an issue like vaccinations could be framed as protective of some superordinate identity, such as that of the nation as a whole. During the vice-presidential debate of 2020, Senator Kamala Harris contended that if the scientific community recommends a vaccine against COVID-19, she would take it. But if President Trump advocated a particular vaccine, she would not. This rhetoric risked politicizing the vaccine, leading Democrats to potentially avoid taking medicine that might actually protect them, and further pushing Republicans to adopt Trump's claims about COVID-19. Emphasizing a superordinate identity, such as patriotism toward America as a country, could lead more people to follow health guidelines.

Of course, these suggestions presume political actors on both sides will agree to avoid rhetorical strategies designed to trigger motivated reasoning, to potentially sacrifice short term electoral goals in order to protect the public good. If the provision of high-quality news information is a collective action problem, as many have argued, the only way out of a very harmful societal equilibrium is to convince both sides that we would all be better off in the long run by cooperating on these basic principles. This is the challenge of the current historical moment.

The number of questions far outweighs the number of answers in this corner of BPS. We predict the problem of motivated reasoning as an obstacle to democratic representation, sound policy-making, and resolution of violent conflicts between groups will be central for generations to come. Exploring the conditions under which people can accept the possibility that they are wrong and consider new information that might lead them to change their minds, their policy preferences, and maybe even their partisanship, is an ongoing call that BPS can and should address.

What is needed is a bridge between the simple, elegant, and logically rigorous models of RCT, and the more empirically realistic but sometimes theoretically messy patterns of human cognition and behavior from psychology. Some scholars from the RCT tradition have begun to build such bridges by incorporating some of the political psychological insights discussed previously into their formal models. Acharya, Blackwell, and Sen (2018), for example, incorporate cognitive dissonance and motivated reasoning biases into a model to explain, among other things, why strong partisanship develops in a two-party system despite the fact that the policy space surrounding each individual is multidimensional. Recall that, according to cognitive dissonance theory, the discomfort people experience when their behavior contradicts their preferences often leads them to adjust the latter rather than the former. Acharya, Blackwell, and Sen (2018) present a model that predicts voters with such motivations might begin with a diverse set of specific issue preferences at odds with the official platform of their party but would over time bring those issue positions into line with their preferred party rather than changing their preferred party to match some weighted average of their policy preferences. Other researchers (Little, Schnakenberg & Turner 2020) have sought to use formal models to untangle the specific mechanisms through which motivated reasoning may be so pernicious to democratic accountability. They find that it is not necessarily because *partisans* get more polarized, but because *all* voters become less sensitive to changes in incumbent performance, which has important implications for how best to address the negative consequences of directional motives on democratic accountability.

Another pioneering approach is adopted by Bendor et al. (2011) in the book *A Behavioral Theory of Elections*. They attack one of the largest paradoxes in RCT, the fact that many voters participate in elections despite the fact that decision-theoretic utility maximization theories predict they should not. The theory acknowledges and builds on the basic human cognitive limitations posited by Simon (1955) in his theory of bounded rationality that we discussed in Chapter 3. Finally, they strengthen the predictive power of previous models based on Simon's notion of "satisficing" by specifying when people will decide an alternative is "good enough" to be chosen over the status quo. The basic innovation they provide is to show that individuals will compare payoffs for alternatives based on some reference point, rather than an objective good-enough standard like the one proposed by Simon. People will then be more likely to use strategies in the future that returned positive payoffs relative to their reference point, and less likely to pursue those that would return negative payoffs. It is a simple advance over Simon's theory, because it specifies more precisely where the reference point people use comes from. The process of building a coherent reference point is inherently dynamic and based on psychological processes that are well understood such as relative deprivation, cognitive dissonance, and other biases. This is exactly where we think the field should continue to move, and scholars from both economic and psychologically oriented traditions can learn a lot from the intellectual bridging represented by efforts like these.

9

Looking Forward
How Behavioral Political Science Can Help Policy-Makers

How do individuals make decisions about politics? As we discussed throughout the book, research in academic disciplines such as economics, sociology, communication, political science, and many others long assumed that people's political beliefs and actions were rooted in individualistic, materialistic preferences. Scholars often further assumed, quite explicitly in many cases, that people were *capable* of reliably and consistently calculating which choices among those in this great "blooming buzzing confusion" – to use William James' description of the social world – would do the trick. This theory of "Economic Man" reigned for thousands of years, from Aristotle until the twentieth century, and modern rational choice theory (RCT) was built on these central assumptions.

In the 1950s, contemporaneous revolutions in the study of human psychology and political behavior began to shake the assumptions at the heart of Economic Man. Scholars began to examine the empirical correspondence between how people *actually decided and acted* with what rational actor models had long assumed. What they found was shocking. People around the world seemed to hold very little information about their leaders and could not even put issue positions together consistently in the ways that party elites did. The way a political message was framed, rather than simply its information content, dramatically altered the way citizens responded. Rather than accepting new, credible information and updating their beliefs accordingly, citizens sometimes ardently resisted and counterargued in order to defend their group identities. Political elites, surprisingly, often seemed to fare just as poorly in processing complex political information and making optimal decisions.

THE SIX SCHOOLS OF BEHAVIORAL POLITICAL SCIENCE

Behavioral political science (BPS) explores these issues, asking questions about a wide range of political phenomena – from turning out to vote to organizing or participating in a demonstration, to the conduct of foreign policy, national security policy, and war initiation and termination. Behavioral political scientists thus examine political behavior at multiple levels of analysis: from the attitudes and behavior of individuals, to group processes, to the decisions of entire nations. BPS also crosses traditional subfield divides in political science, addressing core questions in American politics, comparative politics, public policy, and international relations. To cover such a broad array of topics, behavioral political scientists have used a variety of methods and approaches. Though known most for experimental and survey research, BPS studies have increasingly employed case studies, observational designs, Large-N statistical analyses, and formal modeling as well.

By and large, the BPS paradigm consists of six major schools of thought, which we have reviewed in turn throughout this book. The first is the "cognitive school," focused on understanding how the limits of human cognition, the idea of bounded rationality, and the prevalence of various cognitive biases and heuristics shape people's ability to process information. The second is research that focuses explicitly on a prominent category of biases – framing effects and nudging – and the pervasive role they play in shaping information processing and decision-making. The third school, rather than focusing on individual decision-making, turns its focus to the roles that *group* biases, processes, and institutional structures play in shaping decision-making. This school explores the way that cognitive biases "aggregate" to the group contexts in which most government policy is often made.

The fourth school moves away from the emphasis on cognitive constraints to explore the roots of human motivation. It targets how *emotions* both shape individual preferences and affect individuals' ability to process information. Research in this tradition also often uses biological approaches to understand the role of genetics, physiology, and neurological changes in shaping individual responses to stimuli. Like the emotions school, the fifth BPS school also emphasizes the importance of nonmaterial goals in shaping decision-making, exploring preference heterogeneity often stemming from nonmaterial sources, including personality differences, values, morals, and societal norms. Finally, the sixth BPS school examines how information processing can be distorted by the powerful pull of social identity and group-esteem based motivations rather than accuracy goals. Each school fosters several ongoing and comprehensive research programs.

The Appendix lists various examples of important studies that have been conducted in each of these schools. This list is, of course, by no means exhaustive. Interested readers should explore further any of these schools of thought as a way to improve the rigor of their own theories and extend knowledge of BPS more broadly. In the following, we review the contributions of each school, summarizing the ways in which they force us to reconsider core assumptions of RCT. We then discuss how policy makers in the United States, the United Kingdom, and Israel, to name a few countries, have benefited by utilizing behavioral insights in formulating policies.

The first BPS school focuses on limitations in the capacity or *ability* of individuals to process information rationally (Chapter 3). It began in the late 1950s with Herbert Simon's famous paper, "A Behavioral Model of Rational Choice," (1955) which made the case for the boundedness of human rationality. Simon's early work suggested that we must greatly reduce our expectations about the computing power humans possess on average. At the same time, it offered hope that such infinite processing abilities are unnecessary for making satisfactory decisions in the political arena. With the aid of heuristics or "cognitive shortcuts," people often can arrive at decisions that are good enough to reach their goals, but not as costly as strategies that require perfect information and unlimited computational ability.

These paired ideas of *bounded rationality* and *cognitive satisficing* led to tremendous conceptual breakthroughs in the explanatory and predictive power of behavior decision theories. However, we still do not know enough about where this tendency to satisfice comes from, and when it might actually improve the quality of decisions. Moreover, the use of heuristics can often lead people to make mistakes when processing information and to reach suboptimal or even mistaken decisions. In other words, satisficing can lead to incorrect decisions and can introduce a host of harmful *biases* into the decision-making process. Optimistic overconfidence and sensitivity to sunk costs are just two examples of the errors in judgment individuals can make when relying on heuristic processes. The cognitive approach to decision-making challenges a core assumption of RCT: that individuals are able to systematically process information in their environments in ways that lead them to make consistent, optimal choices. Work in the cognitive school of BPS suggests that, instead, individuals routinely take cognitive shortcuts that can lead to inconsistent choices or actions that do not maximize utility.

A related BPS school highlighting the importance of *framing effects and nudging* in decision-making, demonstrates the limitation of the invariance assumption of rational choice, and reiterates some of the problems that stem from our sensitivity to the way information is presented (Chapter 4). Prospect theory, one of the more famous theories of this school, demonstrates this quite clearly. Individuals are sensitive to "anchors" and will reach different conclusions depending on whether they are in a domain of gain versus loss. Currently, work in this area of cognition and on bounded rationality continues with research on, for example, "nudging" (see Chapter 4), which explores how simple changes in the way choices are presented can impact behavior and shape policy outcomes (Thaler & Sunstein 2008).

The third school moves up a level of analysis, focusing not on individuals but on *group* and *organizational* decision-making (Chapter 5). Work in this area emphasizes the importance of bureaucratic politics, institutional or electoral constraints, organizational processes, and group dynamics on decision-making. Importantly, these research programs break down the unitary actor assumption common to many rational choice models of government and explore how organizational features of the state can *exacerbate or reduce* the influence of behavioral preferences on policy-making. These biases in group decision-making affect leaders' decisions in foreign policy, national security policy, domestic policy, and internal matters. This school of research is particularly important for BPS research in the fields of international relations and domestic policy-making processes, since the actors involved in these decisions in democratic states are often not necessarily *individuals*, but aggregate actors reasoning and making decisions in group settings (Powell 2017). This research likewise challenges RCT assumptions about procedural rationality, but extends this challenge to elite and group decision-making settings, settings in which RCT scholars have argued that cognitive biases may play a less deleterious role (see discussion in Chapter 5).

The fourth BPS school has produced insights about the foundational role of *emotional* reactions to threats and opportunities in conditioning political attitudes and behavior (Chapter 6). These emotional reactions have cognitive, social, and biological components. Thus, work in this area includes evolutionary, physiological, and neurological approaches and greatly contributes to our understanding of political phenomena. Research on emotions challenges two different assumptions from the RCT tradition. First, emotions can alter the *process* of decision-making. Emotional reactions to events can serve as "affective heuristics" guiding decision-making. As with many shortcuts, these heuristics can sometimes help individuals reach an optimal choice, but can also lead people astray. Emotions can also increase individuals' susceptibility to cognitive biases; thus, emotion and cognition are fundamentally linked, interacting to shape how individuals process information and make decisions. In addition, work on emotions demonstrates that the preferences that are often assumed in basic RCT models (e.g., regarding material utility) may not be the dominant drivers of behavior. People possess emotional preferences that include things like retribution for wrongdoing, pride in one's actions, and fear for other people in addition to oneself. Thus, the emotions school suggests augmenting RCT assumptions surrounding how individuals process information and the motivations guiding their choices in the first place.

Fifth, we discussed the individual differences school (Chapter 7), which explores preference heterogeneity and, in particular, the prevalence of other nonmaterial goals in politics in addition to emotions. This research encompasses work on personality, norms, and values and helps to open up the black box of preferences that RCT usually takes as given. It helps us to understand why two individuals in similar situations may nonetheless form different political attitudes or engage in distinct political behavior. At the elite level, understanding leaders' personality and decision-making style can be critical to understanding and predicting foreign and domestic policy. Research in this school helps us understand how to incorporate diverse nonmaterial preferences into the utility calculations used in RCT models of politics. While some of these preferences may be easily added or substituted as a term in expected utility calculations, others may exhibit different properties, which are harder to reconcile with RCT models. For example, they may be *non-compensatory* (see Chapter 3) or resistant to trade-offs (see *taboo trade-offs* (Chapter 7), which can complicate traditional RCT assumptions surrounding individuals' utility calculations.

Finally, we reviewed the motivated reasoning school (Chapter 8), which emphasizes the importance of self-esteem, identity, and in-group attachment in preference formation and information processing. In particular, this school of thought examines the importance of social identity and directional goals in shaping information processing and decision-making. Without understanding the effect of these factors, it would be difficult to understand how leaders and citizen form preferences and make important decisions. The motivated reasoning school raises two main issues regarding RCT assumptions about preferences. First, as with the individual differences school, this school emphasizes the primacy of nonmaterial goals in shaping preferences. Second, it demonstrates that these nonmaterial goals can actually *themselves* shape information processing in biased ways. Thus, directional motives do not simply affect the output of a utility function, but shape individuals' perception of subsequent information. This research thus suggests that RCT assumptions about Bayesian updating based on new information are unlikely to hold on issues for which directional motives are strong.

These six schools of BPS each contribute to a more refined understanding of the motives that shape political attitudes as well as the process by which individuals (e.g., leaders, voters, demonstrators, and others) make decisions about politics. Our hope is that this collection of insights that represent the BPS paradigm will, incrementally and over time, lead to stronger theories that can help us both predict and explain why people do what they do in the real world of politics. Whether we are trying to understand why people vote, donate to political campaigns, engage in nonviolent protest, or take up arms, a better conversation between the psychological and economic traditions so vital to understanding political phenomena will be advantageous.

Systematic biases in information processing and decision-making challenge the rational actor approach to revisit the conditions under which citizens can or will maximize personal utility of any kind, let alone narrow material goals. When, if at all, will people systematically take in new information about issues, candidates, and parties, add that new information to what they already know, and then calculate the choice at the voting booth that would maximize their goals after the election? Not very often, according to the breakthroughs of the last half-century of BPS.

But, one might respond, perhaps people strive for the ideal captured by Economic Man, but fall short in ways that still led them to behave, on average, "as if" they were dispassionate utility maximizing machines (Friedman 1953). In some cases, they may. This is the advance provided by Simon's insights about limited information processing capability and heuristic decision-making and the five other schools represented by BPS. Based on our reading of work in this tradition, we would say yes. Sometimes, humans seem to be able to approximate this ideal by using shortcuts and thin-slices of information. However, the evidence discussed in this book also suggests that the political world is so complicated, and human computational powers so meager and ridden with biases, that elites maintain substantial influence to set agendas, engage in international conflict or cooperation, and even to drive mass preferences over policy priorities.

These discoveries have profound implications for all of politics. They threaten the very heart of democratic theory, because they imply citizens are rarely capable of forming the kind of stable and rich policy opinions that could hold elected officials accountable to the public's will. Can a real democracy exist with citizens limited in their knowledge, so uninformed about the positions of their elected officials, and so often motivated to resist new information that challenges their existing beliefs? Some might disagree, arguing that thanks to the Internet, information on political matters has never been as plentiful. Misinformation can be addressed with the truth. Journalists can fact-check. Still, understanding what citizens are actually capable of and willing to process with help guide our decisions about how government institutions are designed. Could we structure campaign finance laws or voting rules to maximize the amount and quality of information the average citizen has access to or is motivated to seek? Shouldn't we make voting easier and simpler, so more eligible citizens can participate? Can we design international agreements, for example, through nudging, so that they avoid the obstacles posed by limited information, risk perceptions, and other sources of bias in information processing identified by BPS? These are all big normative questions, and this book is only meant to pose them rather offer confident answers. The first step toward politics that improves the human condition is incorporating what we know about how humans actually think, make decisions, and act in the political arena.

So, what does all this do for our understanding of how actual politics works? Can we really apply psychological advances in our understanding of human decision-making to understand phenomena as diverse as voting behavior, policy opinion formation, civil war, international conflicts, and peace agreements? We think the answer to this question is a resounding yes, as the many examples about President Trump and others in this book illustrate.

We realize that the integration of new BPS insights into rigorous formal theoretical models will be difficult, but some work in this area has already begun. Thus, we reiterate the early call for a "modeling dialogue" (Myerson 1992) in which behavioral assumptions discovered through empirical work can not only stand alone to explain political behavior, but can also be incorporated into the structure of formal models of political behavior and rational choice, in order to "capture and clarify the important aspects of real situations" (Myerson 1992, p. 64). Of course, as our assumptions get more complicated and nuanced, so too do the mathematical models needed in order to derive specific predictions.

SYNTHESIZING RATIONAL AND BEHAVIORAL APPROACHES TO POLITICS

This book organizes existing scholarly work into an overarching paradigm, *Behavioral Political Science*, so that students and scholars can think more systematically about how their own research contributes to a broader tradition. It is based on the six distinct schools that, together, explain a wide variety of important political phenomena, across the various subfields of political science. By incorporating psychological theories of political decision-making and political behavior into the rational choice model, BPS focuses not only on outcome validity but also on *process* validity.

Throughout the book, we show how individual human motivations and cognitive abilities matter for all these questions, and our understanding of both the process and the outcomes in the political sphere can be improved by bringing Behavioral Political Science insights into the study and understanding of politics. Political Science questions are about how people make individual and collective decisions, so understanding the regularities and biases of human psychology is a mandatory element for theory building and testing. To illustrate the usefulness of BPS insights and explanations, we applied them to many contemporary political examples, including elite and public decision-making since the 2016 election of Donald Trump as president of the United States. Integrating behavioral or so-called nonstandard assumptions into models of politics is not always easy, but can provide important insights into political phenomena. Below, we discuss the primary criticisms of BPS approaches and the BPS response.

Scholars in the RCT tradition often level three central critiques at behavioral researchers. The first is that the BPS deviations from standard RCT expectations about utility maximization may not be large enough to matter in the aggregate. For example, it may be that these deviations are random, thereby cancelling out in the aggregate; that "irrational" actors either learn from or get driven out by more rational actors; or that irrational actors can nonetheless arrive at approximately rational choices, rendering the distinction between bounded and procedural rationality observationally moot. These are important claims; however, as our discussion has hopefully made plain, in many cases, aggregating individual choices to the level of society does *not* "wash out" the effects of behavioral tendencies on macro-level outcomes. This is because behavioral factors such as cognitive biases, emotions, and values are not randomly distributed, but rather vary in ways that are *systematically* different from some of the core assumptions of RCT. Moreover, while bounded rational thinkers can approximate strategic rationality in some circumstances, in others – including scenarios that are particularly novel or complex – the heuristics individuals rely on can lead them astray.

A second critique from RCT scholars of behavioral approaches, and this is particularly true with BPS approaches to the study of political *elites*, is a two-fold argument: (1) that political leaders are an informed, strategic subset of the general population who are less susceptible to "irrational" decision-making, and/or (2) political leaders make policy decisions within group or institutional structures that help mitigate the effects of individuals biases or psychological motivations on decision outcomes (Hafner-Burton 2017; Powell 2017). These critiques are both important considerations for BPS scholars seeking to analyze topics outside of public opinion and voting behavior. Studies that explicitly draw on elite samples to test susceptibility to, for example, cognitive biases in decision-making, have largely found that elites are just as likely to experience these biases as the masses (see, e.g., Baekgaard et al. 2019; Brooks, Cunha & Mosley 2015; Kertzer 2020; Kertzer, Rathbun & Rathbun 2020; LeVeck et al. 2014; Poulsen & Aisbett 2013; Sheffer et al. 2018; but see Mintz et al. 2006). Meanwhile, a promising behavioral agenda explicitly examining the "aggregation question" (Levy 1997) has likewise found evidence that groups have a variety of effects on decision-making, depending on both the composition of the group and the decision-making context. For instance, one study (Kertzer et al. n.d.) testing the efficacy of groups to reduce the impact of "hawkish biases" (Kahnemen & Renshon 2007) on decision-making using three online group experiments, found that group discussion did little to reduce prominent cognitive biases such as sensitivity to gain/loss frames, reactive devaluation, or the intentionality bias.

Finally, RCT researchers argue that – even if we acknowledge that individual decisions are often "irrational" – the choice to focus on the structure of the strategic environment will nonetheless still yield more useful and fruitful insights in politics than focusing on the attributes of individual actors and their psychology (see, e.g., Lake & Powell 1999; Morrow 1999). That is, RCT is making a "research bet" that more insights will come from a focus on the strategic environment than from the focus on individual attributes and decision-making pathologies. Models are simplifications of the real world and, as such, always miss some detail. The question then becomes which model is most *useful* in helping us understand and predict political behavior? This is an important point to acknowledge – all models, *including* BPS models, are abstractions from the real world. However, the focus on RCT versus BPS "research bets" creates a false dichotomy between the two approaches that can impede fruitful collaboration between these approaches.

We hope this book will continue the growing dialogue between RCT and BPS about how to better understand politics as it is today. Many of the studies highlighted in this book demonstrate the very powerful way in which the psychological study of cognition, information processing, emotions, and reasoning can improve the assumptions driving RCT models and their predictions, more accurately reflecting how people think and act under a variety of real-world contexts.[1] Next, we take one last opportunity to show how insights from BPS research have already begun to guide and potentially improve public policy in several democracies.

THE CONTRIBUTION OF BPS TO POLICY-MAKING

Throughout this book, we have described the ways in which BPS can improve our understanding of political processes and outcomes. But can policy-makers actually utilize BPS's insights to directly improve public policy, increase voter turnout, launch effective campaigns, and enhance the quality of strategic and tactical decisions? If so, how?

Evidence from the United States, the United Kingdom, Israel, and other countries shows promise. Although the concepts, models, and insights often differ from country to country, many studies have shown that BPS's recommendations and interventions can make a positive difference across countries and cultures. Potential uses of BPS insights in the political domain include: increasing voter engagement and participation; designing more effective political campaigns; persuading nations not to use force; deterring countries from launching war; marketing peace and war policies to domestic constituencies; improving governmental programs and proposals at the federal, state, and local levels; and more. While many of these advances seem on their face to be normatively desirable, they could also lead to increased conflict and human suffering. While this is true for most breakthroughs in knowledge about human systems, the potential hazards of policy interventions deserve special attention.

The US Experience

On September 15, 2015, President Obama issued a Presidential Directive calling upon US governmental agencies to utilize insights from behavioral science to "better serve the American people." Examples included the way the government could present or frame governmental services, reform programs, and increase the likelihood that such reforms would actually be implemented. President Obama explained:[2]

Where Federal policies have been designed to reflect behavioral science insights, they have substantially improved outcomes for the individuals, families, communities, and businesses those policies serve. For example, automatic enrollment and automatic escalation in retirement savings plans have made it easier to save for the future and have helped Americans accumulate billions of dollars in additional retirement savings. Similarly, streamlining the application process for Federal financial aid has made college more financially accessible for millions of students.

Of course, different governance orientations lead some to question the effectiveness of some of these programs; however, others argue that these proposals represent an important example of how behavioral science can help to design government programs that benefit the public. To realize the benefits of behavioral insights more fully and deliver better results at a lower cost for the American people, President Obama also argued:[3]

The Federal Government should design its policies and programs to reflect our best understanding of how people engage with, participate in, use, and respond to those policies and programs. By improving the effectiveness and efficiency of Government, behavioral science insights can support a range of national priorities, including helping workers to find better jobs; enabling Americans to lead longer, healthier lives; improving access to educational opportunities and support for success in school; and accelerating the transition to a low-carbon economy.

So just how can leaders accomplish this goal and use BPS insights to improve decisions to benefit the public? How can governmental proposals and reforms be structured to improve service, streamline operations and lead to better decisions? At Harvard University, the Behavioral Insights Group (BIG) focuses on these issues. It aims to improve "how decisions are made, both by leaders, and by individuals" and is "driven by the belief that improving the quality of . . . leaders' decisions are a core lever we possess to improve the world."[4] BIG aims to improve leader decision-making across a variety of policy areas, from educational systems, to healthcare, to environment protection, financial management, discrimination reduction, and more.

BOX 9.1: **President Obama's presidential executive order: Using behavioral science insights to better serve the American people**

The White House. Office of the Press Secretary, September 15, 2015

Executive Order – Using Behavioral Science Insights to Better Serve the American People

A growing body of evidence demonstrates that behavioral science insights – research findings from fields such as Behavioral Economics and psychology about how people make decisions and act on them – can be used to design government policies to better serve the American people.

Where Federal policies have been designed to reflect behavioral science insights, they have substantially improved outcomes for the individuals, families, communities, and businesses those policies serve. For example, automatic enrollment and automatic escalation in retirement savings plans have made it easier to save for the future and have helped Americans accumulate billions of dollars in additional retirement savings. Similarly, streamlining the application process for Federal financial aid has made college more financially accessible for millions of students.

To more fully realize the benefits of behavioral insights and deliver better results at a lower cost for the American people, the Federal Government should design its policies and programs to reflect our best understanding of how people engage with, participate in, use, and respond to those policies and programs. By improving the effectiveness and efficiency of Government, behavioral science insights can support a range of national priorities, including helping workers to find better jobs; enabling Americans to lead longer, healthier lives; improving access to educational opportunities and support for success in school; and accelerating the transition to a low-carbon economy.

NOW, THEREFORE, by the authority vested in me as President by the Constitution and the laws of the United States, I hereby direct the following:

Section 1. Behavioral Science Insights Policy Directive.

(a) Executive departments and agencies (agencies) are encouraged to:
   (i) identify policies, programs, and operations where applying behavioral science insights may yield substantial improvements in public welfare, program outcomes, and program cost effectiveness;
   (ii) develop strategies for applying behavioral science insights to programs and, where possible, rigorously test and evaluate the impact of these insights;
   (iii) recruit behavioral science experts to join the Federal Government as necessary to achieve the goals of this directive; and
   (iv) strengthen agency relationships with the research community to better use empirical findings from the behavioral sciences.
(b) In implementing the policy directives in section (a), agencies shall:
   (i) identify opportunities to help qualifying individuals, families, communities, and businesses access public programs and benefits by, as appropriate, streamlining processes that may otherwise limit or delay participation – for example, removing administrative hurdles, shortening wait times, and simplifying forms;

(ii) improve how information is presented to consumers, borrowers, program beneficiaries, and other individuals, whether as directly conveyed by the agency, or in setting standards for the presentation of information, by considering how the content, format, timing, and medium by which information is conveyed affects comprehension and action by individuals, as appropriate;

(iii) identify programs that offer choices and carefully consider how the presentation and structure of those choices, including the order, number, and arrangement of options, can most effectively promote public welfare, as appropriate, giving particular consideration to the selection and setting of default options; and

(iv) review elements of their policies and programs that are designed to encourage or make it easier for Americans to take specific actions, such as saving for retirement or completing education programs. In doing so, agencies shall consider how the timing, frequency, presentation, and labeling of benefits, taxes, subsidies, and other incentives can more effectively and efficiently promote those actions, as appropriate. Particular attention should be paid to opportunities to use nonfinancial incentives.

(c) For policies with a regulatory component, agencies are encouraged to combine this behavioral science insights policy directive with their ongoing review of existing significant regulations to identify and reduce regulatory burdens, as appropriate and consistent with Executive Order 13563 of January 18, 2011 (Improving Regulation and Regulatory Review), and Executive Order 13610 of May 10, 2012 (Identifying and Reducing Regulatory Burdens).

Sec. 2. Implementation of the Behavioral Science Insights Policy Directive.

(a) The Social and Behavioral Sciences Team (SBST), under the National Science and Technology Council (NSTC) and chaired by the Assistant to the President for Science and Technology, shall provide agencies with advice and policy guidance to help them execute the policy objectives outlined in section 1 of this order, as appropriate.

(b) The NSTC shall release a yearly report summarizing agency implementation of section 1 of this order each year until 2019. Member agencies of the SBST are expected to contribute to this report.

(c) To help execute the policy directive set forth in section 1 of this order, the Chair of the SBST shall, within 45 days of the date of this order and thereafter as necessary, issue guidance to assist agencies in implementing this order.

Sec. 3. General Provisions.

(a) Nothing in this order shall be construed to impair or otherwise affect:
   (i) the authority granted by law to a department or agency, or the head thereof; or

> (ii) the functions of the Director of the Office of Management and Budget relating to budgetary, administrative, or legislative proposals.
>
> (b) This order shall be implemented consistent with applicable law and subject to the availability of appropriations.
>
> (c) Independent agencies are strongly encouraged to comply with the requirements of this order.
>
> (d) This order is not intended to, and does not, create any right or benefit, substantive or procedural, enforceable at law or in equity by any party against the United States, its departments, agencies, or entities, its officers, employees, or agents, or any other person.
>
>
>   BARACK OBAMA
>   THE WHITE HOUSE,
>   September 15, 2015.

The United Kingdom

The UK government is also a global leader in the use and application of behavioral science insights. Almost every government department in the United Kingdom is using behavioral science to help improve the way public services are run, or policies are delivered (Behavioural Insights Team annual report 2015–16, p. 5).

The Behavioural Insights Team (BIT) in the United Kingdom is partly owned by the UK Government. BIT started at the Prime Minister's Office as the world's first government institution dedicated to the application of behavioral sciences. BIT's core objectives include: (1) making public services more cost-effective and easier to use; (2) improving outcomes by introducing more realistic models of human behavior to policy; and (3) enabling people to make better choices for themselves (BIT annual report 2015–16).

BIT does this "by redesigning public services and drawing on ideas from the behavioural science literature" (BIT annual report 2015–16). For example, BIT publishes policy memos on topics from improving economic outcomes using behavioral nudges and encouraging consumers to reduce their carbon footprint through "green nudges" that set default options, change the framing of choices, and harness the power of social influence to help the environment.[5] To accomplish its goals, BIT uses empirical techniques to rigorously test the implications of behavioral science ideas before they are scaled up to actual government programs. According to BIT's advisory board member, the well-known economist and Nobel laureate, Richard Thaler, this process helps BIT find out what works and, importantly, what doesn't work (in other words, where the impact of the intervention was no better than the control group): "BIT can help ensure that [policy] is designed correctly so that it has the greatest chance of achieving its desired ends" and is "a central part of how government goes about its business. So successful is it that its services are now purchased by other governments and organizations around the world" (BIT annual report 2015–16, p. 4). And indeed, behavioral science insights, recommendations and interventions in the UK government now abound in the areas of health policy, energy and sustainability, crime and fraud, education and skills policy, recruitment and selection processes, economic growth, and the rigorous use of policy evaluation research "to test what works" in [various] settings (ibid).

In the words of one prominent member of the UK government: "there is no doubt that Behavioral Science is becoming more mainstream across the UK Civil Service and increasingly, amongst governments around the world. Not only are we now seeing behavioural insights being applied in more areas, but we are also seeing the development of more complex interventions and evaluations."[6] Perhaps one of the more unique aspects of BIT research is the evaluation of the effects of behavioral science insights as interventions in policy-making.

In 2020, during the COVID-19 pandemic, the UK government of Boris Johnson applied nudge theory and other insights from behavioral science to encourage "herd immunity." Instead of quarantine measures, it advocated: wash hands, don't shake hands with others, don't touch your face, stay at home if you feel ill, etc. It remains to be seen if these measures will be successful in tackling the pandemic, but their application on a massive scale by the UK government is an important sign of the acceptance of behavioral insights by policy-makers.[7]

Israel

Israel has also been using behavioral science insights to inform its policy-making. As early as 2012, the Ministry of Environmental Protection in Israel, for example, advocated the use of principles and methods of behavioral social science, broadly defined, in designing governmental policies. The idea is to use these new insights to "optimize citizens' decisions on health-related issues, environmental decisions, pensions, safety decisions, consumer choice and other policy domains" (Tzachor, personal communication 2016).

The Ministry of Environmental Protection is working to establish ties between academics and government officials in order to facilitate communication and knowledge transfer from the world of academia to government (Tzachor, personal communication 2016). The aim of the Ministry is to demonstrate how Behavioral Economics and BPS can contribute to the policy process, including policy design, implementation, and evaluation (Tzachor, personal communication 2016). For example, the Behavioral Political Science Lab at the IDC in Israel has worked with the office of the president of Israel, Reuven Rivlin, to formulate policies that would reduce intergroup cleavages and hostility among the "four tribes" of Israeli societies: secular, orthodox, religious-national, and Israeli-Arab citizens of Israel.

The Israeli Ministry of Finance has also organized a workshop entitled "Nudgeton: How Behavioral Economics Tools Can Assist Policy Makers," featuring the Director of the Budget and the Chief Economist of the Ministry as well as leading academicians. In addition, in 2017, Israel became the first country to develop a universal children's savings account program that provides monthly deposits from the government in the child's name that will be available for them when they reach the age of twenty-one. This policy was built on the entitlement grant to create long-term savings and investment for children and reduce intergenerational poverty (Grinstein-Weiss et al. 2017b). The design features of this policy heavily build on lessons from Behavioral Economics and incorporate techniques such as automatic enrolment, defaults. This universal, automatic enrolment design provides options for active enrolment in the program or allows children to be enrolled in a default selection. The program also includes a default investment selection of a low yield investment fund. This default selection promotes greater asset accumulation for people who do not actively enroll in the program, relative to the most conservative deposit options of bank accounts.

A choice architecture makes depositing additional savings the most salient option. The choice to deposit an additional 50 NIS monthly is both preselected for parents during online enrollment and is the first listed option. The choice architecture of the savings decision also lists saving into higher-yield investment accounts above bank accounts (Grinstein-Weiss et al. 2017c). This component has been very effective, as two-thirds of households who made an active choice to enroll in the program chose to make an additional 50 NIS deposit into the account (Grinstein-Weiss 2017c). This is an initiative that heavily relies on Behavioral Economics techniques to increase savings among low-income households, Refund-to-Savings (R2S), and uses tax-time as a moment to increase savings. R2S builds on the online tax-filing platform. When citizens finish filing their taxes, they reach a screen asking them how they would like to receive their refund. The first option is to deposit their entire refund into a savings account. This choice architecture manipulation increased average savings (Davison et al. 2018; Grinstein-Weiss et al. 2017c).

Tax filers were also encouraged to pledge that they would save their refunds before they got to the screen asking them to select how they wished to receive the money. This intervention reflects prior research that shows that people are more likely to engage in a behavior if they make a commitment ahead of time ("pre-commitment"). In yet another R2S experiment, tax filers were given messages about why it is important to save their refunds, such as to be prepared for emergencies, reflecting the concept of framing – presenting choices in ways that highlight positive aspects of the choice (Davison et al. 2018; Grinstein-Weiss et al. 2017b; Grinstein-Weiss et al. 2017c).

In 2021, during the COVID-19 pandemic, there were scientists who advocated the use of nudging to influence those who were reluctant to take the vaccine. An article in *Nature* (2021) encouraged scientists to test behavioral nudges to boost COVID immunization. Patel (2021) has argued that studies that promote uptake are essential to have the population vaccinated on a massive scale.

As these examples, and examples from Australia, the Netherlands and other countries demonstrate, insights from BPS have begun to influence policy-makers and politicians alike and shape public policy. In addition, BPS has important implications for political campaigns and political marketing: who to vote for, who not to vote for, how to encourage/discourage political participation, market peace processes, frame and draft referenda, refrain from trade, engage in wars, make foreign policy and national security decisions (such as deterrence, threats, negotiations, compromises, etc.), establish governing coalitions, win elections, and more. For example, leaders frequently market and frame their preferred policy to the public in order to get widespread public support to ratify peace initiatives. They use different framing tactics to market their policies to the public and to counter-frame policies and acts of their opponents. Such "purposeful framing" is well documented in the literature on peace and war marketing in the United States and elsewhere (see Mintz & Redd 2003). Thematic and evaluative framing, spinning, highlighting potential gains instead of losses as well as the positive versus negative consequences of a peace agreement affect public perceptions of the situation and consequently influence public support or opposition to the peace agreement. In this respect, it is not so different from behavioral marketing approaches to promote corporate decisions or policies.

Figure 9.1 lays out the many public policy areas in which BPS insights can be helpful for policy-makers and elected officials.

FINAL THOUGHTS

Distinct theories of human decision-making, each with broad implications for politics, have been proposed in a diverse set of academic fields including psychology, economics,

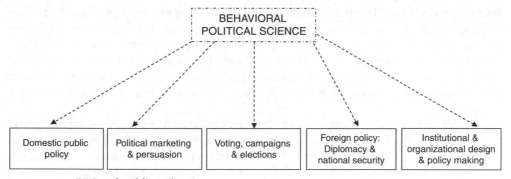

FIGURE 9.1 **BPS and public policy issue areas**
As we have shown throughout the book, BPS is a broad umbrella paradigm that has been applied to a broad set of domains of inquiry within political science, crossing traditional subfields' boundaries with numerous important policy applications.

political science, sociology, communication, and many others. But while theories in each field may be marked by their own unique academic nomenclature, they all share basic features. Each posits a set of core human motivations and needs such as individual material wealth, family security, social group interests, moral values, and many others that structure individuals' preferences. Each approach also makes assumptions, either explicitly or implicitly, about the typical human constraints on cognitive capacity to hold and process information relevant to achieve these aims.

In this book, we have contrasted one of the most common, foundational approaches – Rational Choice Theory – with a paradigm we introduce and call Behavioral Political Science. The differences here, we hope the reader sees, are smaller than sometimes assumed but nonetheless very important. BPS highlights psychological aspects of the decision-making process, and points to heuristics and biases as factors leading individuals to deviate from the processing assumptions common in RCT. Furthermore, while RCT does not spend as much time debating where preferences come from, BPS does, finding that material motivations represent only a subset of the goals individuals prioritize when engaging in political decision-making.

We argue that one of the greatest contributions of RCT is its insistence on clear assumptions and strong logic in all theorizing about human political choices. These features increase the value of any research program for obvious reasons: we know when our theories are wrong, at least probabilistically. But the empirical breakthroughs in the study of human psychology – from severely limited capacity to store and process information to the centrality of motives related to group membership and identity rather than individual material wealth and security – have dramatically improved our understanding of some of the most important political phenomena of our time. The incorporation of these new findings into our models of politics has the potential to greatly improve our understanding of political behavior and outcomes. We are excited for the future of our field, as RCT models become more closely integrated with these empirical advances in our understanding of human psychology.

We also would like to encourage dialogue between researchers and the public policy community. Over the last few decades, it has become easier to communicate with each other and with strangers, in our families and communities, and across borders. Falling barriers to trade have led to a dramatic increase in the movement of products and labor, helping to lift vast numbers of people out of poverty in developing nations. All these advancements should help transform zero-sum competition between close neighbors into positive-sum agreements for people and institutions separated by great distances. And yet, as we write, many governments around the world seem to be moving away from the enlightenment ideals of policy informed by objective science and economic integration.

The rise of populist and anti-immigrant parties in many democracies seem to move in lockstep with polarization and political gridlock. Such trends, especially in interaction with the effects of the COVID-19 pandemic, are likely to broaden economic inequalities and increase poverty around the world. The very communication technologies that bring us so many benefits – increasing social connection, the mobilization of social movements, and increased access to news and information from around the world – also proliferate misinformation, fake news, and propaganda so subtle it is often impossible to identify and control. These trends may undermine the institutions of democracy itself – election systems and access to the ballot in the United States and around the world. Furthermore, using new communication technologies, the power of bad actors to inflame racial and ethnic tensions and even to cause lethal violence at the individual and state level seems to be on the rise. Conspiratorial thinking, anti-scientific sentiment, ethnic and racial animus, and extremist ideologies all seem to find it easier to operate in such an open political and economic environment.

As if all that weren't enough, these threats come at time when our trust and affection toward others has declined dramatically. The polarization of parties – and especially the expression of animus for those on opposite sides of the political spectrum – is on the rise in country after country. How can we find a path toward sound and majoritarian policy-making based on mutual respect and compromise in such a moment? The stakes could not be higher, as scientists discover, for example, that our inaction even for the next few decades on issues of climate change could have consequences that last centuries.

Understanding these momentous shifts, both positive and negative, is only possible via a broader and more inclusive view of the motivations and abilities that typical humans bring to each decision they make in the public sphere. The BPS paradigm, of which we have only reviewed a small slice, seems uniquely positioned for understanding and explaining these puzzles. This research might even help address how we got to this political moment and where we might go next. The great strength of BPS is its intellectual diversity: It draws on a broad and interdisciplinary set of research programs and scholars who have studied human cultures and contexts from every angle and perspective. We hope this book inspires others to continue this exciting journey.

APPENDIX

A Sampling of Works across Behavioral Political Science Schools

BOUNDED RATIONALITY

- Ariely, D., & Jones, S. (2008). *Predictably Irrational*. New York: Harper Audio.
- Bendor, J. (2010). *Bounded Rationality and Politics*. Oakland: University of California Press.
- Bendor, J., Diermeier, D., Siegel, D. A., & Ting, M. M. (2011). *A Behavioral Theory of Elections*. Princeton, NJ: Princeton University Press.
- Jones, B. D. (2001). *Politics and the Architecture of Choice: Bounded Rationality and Governance*. Chicago: University of Chicago Press.
- Mintz, A. (2007). Behavioral IR as a subfield of international relations. *International Studies Review*, 9(1), 157–172.
- Ostrom, C. W. Jr., & Marra, R. F. (1986). US spending and the Soviet estimate. *American Political Science Review*, 80(3), 819–842.
- Poulsen, L. N. S., & Aisbett, E. (2013). When the claim hits: Bilateral investment treaties and bounded rational learning. *World Politics*, 65(2), 273–313.
- Simon, H. (1957). *Models of Man*. Hoboken, NJ: Wiley and Sons.
- Steinbruner, J. D. (2002). *The Cybernetic Theory of Decision: New Dimensions of Political Analysis*. Princeton, NJ: Princeton University Press.

HEURISTICS

- Ballew, C. C., & Todorov, A. (2007). Predicting political elections from rapid and unreflective face judgments. *Proceedings of the National Academy of Sciences*, 104 (46), 17948–17953.
- Farnham, B.R. (2000). *Roosevelt and the Munich Crisis: A Study of Political Decision-Making*. Princeton, NJ: Princeton University Press.
- Gigerenzer, G. (2008). Why heuristics work. *Perspectives on Psychological Science*, 3 (1), 20–29.
- Kuklinski, J. H., Quirk, P. J., Jerit, J., Schwieder, D., & Rich, R. F. (2000). Misinformation and the currency of democratic citizenship. *Journal of Politics*, 62 (3), 790–816.
- Lau, R., & Redlawsk, D. (2001). Advantages and disadvantages of cognitive heuristics in political decision making. *American Journal of Political Science*, 45(4), 951–971.
- Lupia, A. (1994). Shortcuts versus encyclopedias: Information and voting behavior in California insurance reform elections. *American Political Science Review*, 88(1), 63–76.
- Sniderman, P. M., Brody, R. A., & Tetlock, P. E. (2010). *Reasoning and Choice: Explorations in Political Psychology*. Cambridge, UK: Cambridge University Press.

- Steenbergen, M. R., & Colombo, C. (2019). Heuristics in political behavior. In A. Mintz and L. Terris (eds.), *The Oxford Handbook of Behavioral Political Science*. Oxford, UK: Oxford University Press.
- Tversky, A., & Kahneman, D. (1973). Availability: A heuristic for judging frequency and probability. *Cognitive Psychology*, 5(2), 207–232.
- Tversky, A., & Kahneman, D. (1974). Judgment under uncertainty: Heuristics and biases. *Science*, 185(4157), 1124–1131.

COGNITIVE BIASES

- Bolsen, T., & Druckman, J. N. (2018). Do partisanship and politicization undermine the impact of a scientific consensus message about climate change? *Group Processes & Intergroup Relations*, 21(3), 389–402.
- Bullock, J. G., & Lenz, G. (2019). Partisan bias in surveys. *Annual Review of Political Science*, 22(10), 325–342.
- Feddersen, T., Gailmard, S., & Sandroni, A. (2009). Moral bias in large elections: Theory and experimental evidence. *American Political Science Review*, 103(2), 175–192.
- Holsti, O. R., & George, A. L. (1975). The effects of stress on the performance of foreign policy-makers. *Political Science Annual: An International Review*, 6, 255–319.
- Huber, G. A., Hill, S. J., & Lenz, G. S. (2012). Sources of bias in retrospective decision making: Experimental evidence on voters' limitations in controlling incumbents. *American Political Science Review*, 106(4), 720–741.
- Maoz, I., Ward, A., Katz, M., & Ross, L. (2002). Reactive devaluation of an "Israeli" vs. "Palestinian" peace proposal. *Journal of Conflict Resolution*, 46(4), 515–546.
- Payne, K. (2015). *The Psychology of Strategy: Exploring Rationality in the Vietnam War*. Oxford, UK: Oxford University Press.
- Redd, S. (2002). The influence of advisers on foreign policy decision making: An experimental study. *Journal of Conflict Resolution*, 46(3), 335–364.
- Snyder, G., & Diesing, P. (1977). Information processing. In G. Snyder & P. Diesing (eds.), *Conflict among Nations: Bargaining, Decision Making, and System Structure in International Crises* (pp. 282–339). Princeton, NJ: Princeton University Press.
- Sylvan, D., Goel, A., & Chandrasekaran, B. (1990). Analyzing political decision making from an information-processing perspective: JESSE. *American Journal of Political Science*, 34(1), 74–123.
- Weeden, J., & Kurzban, R. (2014). *The Hidden Agenda of the Political Mind: How Self-Interest Shapes Our Opinions and Why We Won't Admit It*. Princeton, NJ: Princeton University Press.
- Thaler, R. H. (2008). Mental accounting and consumer choice. *Marketing Science*, 27(1), 15–25.

DECISION RULES; POLIHEURISTIC THEORY

Decision Rules

- Brannick, M. T., & Brannick, J. P. (1989). Nonlinear and noncompensatory processes in performance evaluation. *Organizational Behavior and Human Decision Processes*, 44(1), 97–122.
- Bueno de Mesquita, B. (1981). *The War Trap*. New Haven: Yale University Press.

- Einhorn, H. J. (1970). The use of nonlinear, noncompensatory models in decision making. *Psychological Bulletin*, 73(3), 221–230.
- Einhorn, H. J. (1971). Use of nonlinear, noncompensatory models as a function of task and amount of information. *Organizational Behavior and Human Performance*, 6(1), 1–27.
- Johnson, E. J., & Meyer, R. J. (1984). Compensatory choice models of noncompensatory processes: The effect of varying context. *Journal of Consumer Research*, 11(1), 528–541.
- Mintz, A. (1993). The decision to attack Iraq: A noncompensatory theory of decision making. *Journal of Conflict Resolution*, 37(4), 595–618.
- Payne, J. W., Bettman, J. R., & Johnson, E. J. (1988). Adaptive strategy selection in decision making. *Journal of Experimental Psychology: Learning, Memory, and Cognition*, 14(3), 534–552.
- Tversky, A. (1972). Elimination by aspects: A theory of choice. *Psychological Review*, 79(4), 281–299.

Poliheuristic Theory

- Christensen, E. J., & Redd, S. B. (2004). Bureaucrats versus the ballot box in foreign policy decision making: An experimental analysis of the bureaucratic politics model and the poliheuristic theory. *Journal of Conflict Resolution*, 48(1), 69–90.
- James, P., & Zhang, E. (2005). Chinese choices: A poliheuristic analysis of foreign policy crises. *Foreign Policy Analysis*, 1(1), 31–35.
- Mintz, A., & Geva, N. (1997). The poliheuristic theory of foreign policy decision-making. In N. Geva & A. Mintz (eds.), *Decisionmaking on War and Peace: The Cognitive-Rational Debate* (pp. 81–202). Boulder, CO: Lynne Rienner.
- Mintz, A. (2004). How do leaders make decisions? A poliheuristic perspective. *Journal of Conflict Resolution*, 48(1), 3–13.
- Mintz, A., Geva, N., Redd, S. B., & Carnes, A. (1997). The effect of dynamic and static choice sets on political decision making: An analysis using the Decision Board platform. *American Political Science Review*, 91(3), 553–566.

PROSPECT THEORY, FRAMING, COUNTER-FRAMING, AND NUDGING

Prospect Theory

- Farnham, B. (1995). *Avoiding Losses/Taking Risks: Prospect Theory and International Conflict*. Ann Arbor: University of Michigan Press.
- Kahneman, D., & Tversky, A. (1979). Prospect theory: An analysis of decision under risk. *Econometrica*, 47(2), 263–292.
- Levy, J. S. (1997). Prospect theory, rational choice, and international relations. *International Studies Quarterly*, 41(1), 87–112.
- McDermott, R. (1998). *Risk-Taking in International Politics*. Ann Arbor: University of Michigan Press.
- Stein, J. G. (1992). International cooperation and loss avoidance: Framing the problem. In J. G. Stein & L. Pauly (eds.), *Choosing to Cooperate: How States Avoid Loss* (pp. 199–201). Baltimore, MD: Johns Hopkins University Press.

Media Framing

- Berinsky, A. J., & Kinder, D. R. (2006). Making sense of issues through media frames: Understanding the Kosovo crisis. *Journal of Politics*, 68(3), 640–656.
- Druckman, J. N. (2011). The implications of framing effects for citizen competence. *Political Behavior*, 23(3), 225–256.
- Druckman, J. N. (2004). Political preference formation: Competition, deliberation, and the (ir)relevance of framing effects. *American Political Science Review*, 98(4), 761–86.
- Iyengar, S. (1991). *Is Anyone Responsible?* Chicago: University of Chicago Press.
- Iyengar, S., & Simon, A. (1993). News coverage of the Gulf crisis and public opinion: A study of agenda-setting, priming, and framing. *Communication Research*, 20(3), 365–383.
- Nelson, T. E., Clawson, R. A., & Oxley, Z. (1997). Media framing of a civil liberties controversy and its effect on tolerance. *American Political Science Review*, 91(3), 567–84.
- Price, V., & Tewksbury, D. (1997). "News values and public opinion: A theoretical account of media priming and framing." In G. A. Barnett and F. J. Boster (eds.), *Progress in Communication Sciences* (Vol. 13, pp. 173–212). Greenwich, CT: Ablex.

Leader Framing

- Chong, D., & Druckman, J. N. (2007). A theory of framing and opinion formation in competitive elite environments. *Journal of Communication*, 57(1), 99–118.
- Garrison, J. A. (2001). Framing foreign policy alternatives in the inner circle: President Carter, his advisors, and the struggle for the arms control agenda. *Political Psychology*, 22(4), 775–807.
- Klar, S., Robinson, J., & Druckman, J.N. (2012). Political dynamics of framing. In T. N. Ridout (ed.), *New Directions in Media and Politics* (pp. 173–192). Abingdon, UK: Taylor and Francis.
- Maoz, Z. (1990). Framing the national interest: The manipulation of foreign policy decisions in group settings. *World Politics*, 43(1), 77–110.
- Mintz, A., & Redd, S. B. (2003). Framing effects in international relations. *Synthese*, 135(2), 193–213.
- Norris, P., Kern, M., & Just, M. (2003). *Framing Terrorism: The News Media, the Government, and the Public*. Abingdon, UK: Routledge.
- Sniderman, P. M., & Theriault, S. M. (2004). The structure of political argument and the logic of issue framing. In W. E. Saris & P. M. Sniderman (eds.), *Studies in Public Opinion: Attitudes, Nonattitudes, Measurement Error, and Change* (pp. 133–165). Princeton, NJ: Princeton University Press.

Nudging

- Grinstein-Weiss, M., Cryder, C., Despard, M., Perantie, D., Oliphant, J., & Ariely, D. (2017). The role of choice architecture in promoting saving at tax time: Evidence from a large-scale field experiment. *Behavioral Science & Policy*, 3(2), 21–38.
- Grinstein-Weiss, M., Russell, B. D., Gale, W. G., Key, C., & Ariely, D. (2017). Behavioral interventions to increase tax-time saving: Evidence from a national randomized trial. *Journal of Consumer Affairs*, 51(1), 3–26.

- Hausman, D. M., & Welch, B. (2010). Debate: To nudge or not to nudge. *Journal of Political Philosophy*, 18(1), 123–136.
- Patel, M. S., Volpp, K. G., & Asch, D. A. (2018). Nudge units to improve the delivery of health care. *The New England Journal of Medicine*, 378(3), 214.
- Selinger, E., & Whyte, K. (2011). Is there a right way to nudge? The practice and ethics of choice architecture. *Sociology Compass*, 5(10), 923–935.
- Thaler, R. H., & Sunstein, C. R. (2008). *Nudge: Improving Decisions about Health, Wealth, and Happiness*. New Haven, CT: Yale University Press.

THE LIMITS OF THE UNITARY ACTOR MODEL OF GOVERNMENT; GROUP DECISION-MAKING MODELS

- Barr, K. & Mintz, A. (2021). Did groupthink or polythink derail the 2016 Raqqa offensive? In A. Mintz and L. Terris (eds.), *The Oxford Handbook of Behavioral Political Science*. Oxford, UK: Oxford University Press.
- Barr, K., & Mintz, A. (2018). Public policy perspective on group decision-making dynamics in foreign policy. *Policy Studies Journal*, 46, S69–S90.
- Garrison, J. A. (2003). Foreign policymaking and group dynamics: Where we've been and where we're going. *International Studies Review*, 5(2), 177–202.
- Janis, I. L. (1972). *Victims of Groupthink: A Psychological Study of Foreign-Policy Decisions and Fiascoes*. Boston: Houghton Mifflin Company.
- Mintz, A. & Wayne, C. (2016). *The Polythink Syndrome: US Foreign Policy Decisions on 9/11, Afghanistan, Iraq, Syria, Iran and ISIS*. Stanford: Stanford University Press.
- Redd, S. B. (2002). The influence of advisers on foreign policy decision making: An experimental study. *Journal of Conflict Resolution*, 46(3), 335–364.
- Saunders, E. N. (2017). No substitute for experience: Presidents, advisers, and information in group decision making. *International Organization*, 71(1), 219–247.
- Schafer, M., & Crichlow, S. (2010). *Groupthink versus High-Quality Decision Making in International Relations*. New York: Columbia University Press.
- t'Hart, P. Stern, E. K., & Sundelius, B. (eds.). (1997). *Beyond Groupthink: Political Group Dynamics and Foreign Policy-Making*. Ann Arbor: University of Michigan Press.

EMOTIONS & POLITICAL ATTITUDES

Emotions & Information Processing

- Brader, T. (2006). *Campaigning for Hearts and Minds: How Emotional Appeals in Political Ads Work*. Chicago: University of Chicago Press.
- Druckman, J. N., & McDermott, R. (2008). Emotion and the framing of risky choice. *Political Behavior*, 30(3), 297–321.
- Erisen, C., Lodge, M., & Taber, C. S. (2014). Affective contagion in effortful political thinking. *Political Psychology*, 35(2), 187–206.
- Gadarian, S. K., & Albertson, B. (2014). Anxiety, immigration, and the search for information. *Political Psychology*, 35(2), 133–164.
- Isbell L.M., Ottati V.C., & Burns K.C. (2006). Affect and politics: Effects on judgment, processing, and information seeking. In D. P. Redlawsk (ed.), *Feeling Politics* (pp. 57–86). New York: Palgrave Macmillan.

- Keltner, D., Ellsworth, P. C., & Edwards, K. (1993). Beyond simple pessimism: Effects of sadness and anger on social perception. *Journal of Personality and Social Psychology, 64*(5), 740–752.
- Lerner, J. S., & Tiedens, L. Z. (2006). Portrait of the angry decision maker: How appraisal tendencies shape anger's influence on cognition. *Journal of Behavioral Decision Making, 19*(2), 115–137.
- Lerner, J. S., Gonzalez, R. M., Small, D. A., & Fischhoff, B. (2003). Effects of fear and anger on perceived risks of terrorism a national field experiment. *Psychological Science, 14*(2), 144–150.
- Marcus, G. E., Neuman, W. R., & MacKuen, M. (2000). *Affective Intelligence and Political Judgment.* Chicago, IL.: University of Chicago Press.
- Schwarz, N., & Clore, G. L. (1983). Mood, misattribution, and judgments of well-being: Informative and directive functions of affective states. *Journal of Personality and Social Psychology, 45*(3), 513–523.
- Tiedens, L. Z., & Linton, S. (2001). Judgment under emotional certainty and uncertainty: The effects of specific emotions on information processing. *Journal of Personality and Social Psychology, 81*(6), 973–988.
- Valentino, N. A., Hutchings, V. L., Banks, A. J., & Davis, A. K. (2008). Is a worried citizen a good citizen? Emotions, political information seeking, and learning via the internet. *Political Psychology, 29*(2), 247–273.

Emotions & Participation

- Brader, T. (2005). Striking a responsive chord: How political ads motivate and persuade voters by appealing to emotions. *American Journal of Political Science, 49* (2), 388–405.
- Getmansky, A., & Zeitzoff, T. (2014). Terrorism and voting: The effect of rocket threat on voting in Israeli elections. *American Political Science Review, 108*(3), 588–604.
- Jasper, J. M. (1998). The emotions of protest: Affective and reactive emotions in and around social movements. *Sociological Forum, 13*(3), 397–424.
- Marcus, G. E., & MacKuen, M. B. (1993). Anxiety, enthusiasm, and the vote: The emotional underpinnings of learning and involvement during presidential campaigns. *American Political Science Review, 87*(3), 672–685.
- Pearlman, W. (2013). Emotions and the microfoundations of the Arab uprisings. *Perspectives on Politics, 11*(2), 387–409.
- Phoenix, D. L. (2019). *The Anger Gap: How Race Shapes Emotion in Politics.* Cambridge, UK: Cambridge University Press.
- Valentino, N. A., Brader, T., Groenendyk, E. W., Gregorowicz, K., & Hutchings, V. L. (2011). Election night's alright for fighting: The role of emotions in political participation. *The Journal of Politics, 73*(1), 156–170.
- Valentino, N. A., Gregorowicz, K., & Groenendyk, E. (2009). Efficacy, emotions, and the habit of participation. *Political Behavior, 31*(3), 307–330.

Emotions & Partisanship

- Groenendyk, E. W., & Banks, A. J. (2014). Emotional rescue: How affect helps partisans overcome collective action problems. *Political Psychology, 35*(3), 359–378.
- Iyengar, S., & Westwood, S. J. (2015). Fear and loathing across party lines: New evidence on group polarization. *American Journal of Political Science, 59*(3), 690–707.

- Marcus, G. E., Valentino, N. A., Vasilopoulos, P., & Foucault, M. (2019). Applying the theory of Affective Intelligence to support for authoritarian policies and parties. *Political Psychology*, 40(S1), 109–139.
- Valentino, N. A., Wayne, C., & Oceno, M. (2018). Mobilizing sexism: The interaction of emotion and gender attitudes in the 2016 US presidential election. *Public Opinion Quarterly*, 82(S1), 213–235.

Emotions & Intergroup Attitudes

- Banks, A. J. (2014). *Anger and Racial Politics: The Emotional Foundation of Racial Attitudes in America*. Cambridge, UK: Cambridge University Press.
- Brader, T., Valentino, N. A., & Suhay, E. (2008). What triggers public opposition to immigration? Anxiety, group cues, and immigration threat. *American Journal of Political Science*, 52(4), 959–978.
- Huddy, L., Feldman, S., Taber, C., & Lahav, G. (2005). Threat, anxiety, and support of antiterrorism policies. *American Journal of Political Science*, 49(3), 593–608.
- Sirin, C. V., Valentino, N. A., & Villalobos, J. D. (2021). *Seeing Us in Them: Social Divisions and the Politics of Group Empathy*. Cambridge, UK: Cambridge University Press.
- Vasilopoulos, P., Marcus, G. E., & Foucault, M. (2018). Emotional responses to the Charlie Hebdo attacks: Addressing the authoritarianism puzzle. *Political Psychology*, 39(3), 557–575.
- Wayne, C. (2019). Risk or retribution: The micro-foundations of state responses to terror. Doctoral dissertation, University of Michigan.

Emotions & Political Elites

- Crawford, N. C. (2000). The passion of world politics: Propositions on emotion and emotional relationships. *International Security*, 24(4), 116–156.
- Goldgeier, J. M., & Tetlock, P. E. (2001). Psychology and international relations theory. *Annual Review of Political Science*, 4(1), 67–92.
- Hall, T. H. (2011). We will not swallow this bitter fruit: Theorizing a diplomacy of anger. *Security Studies*, 20(4), 521–555.
- Lupia, A., & Menning, J. O. (2009). When can politicians scare citizens into supporting bad policies? *American Journal of Political Science*, 53(1), 90–106.
- Mercer, J. (2010). Emotional beliefs. *International Organization*, 64(1), 1–31.
- Mercer, J. (2013). Emotion and strategy in the Korean War. *International Organization*, 67(2), 221–252.
- Sasley, B. E. (2011). Theorizing states' emotions. *International Studies Review*, 13(3), 452–476.

BIOLOGY OF POLITICS: EVOLUTION, NEUROSCIENCE, PHYSIOLOGY & GENETICS

- Alford, J. R., Funk, C. L., & Hibbing, J. R. (2005). Are political orientations genetically transmitted? *American Political Science Review*, 99(2), 153–167.
- Axelrod, R., & Hamilton, W. D. (1981). The naked emperor: Seeking a more plausible genetic basis for psychological altruism. *Science*, 211, 1390–1396.

- Fowler, J. H., Baker, L. A., & Dawes, C. T. (2008). Genetic variation in political participation. *American Political Science Review, 102*(2), 233–248.
- Hatemi, P. K., & McDermott, R. (eds.). (2011). *Man Is by Nature a Political Animal: Evolution, Biology, and Politics*. Chicago: University of Chicago Press.
- Hatemi, P. K., & McDermott, R. (2011). A neurobiological approach to foreign policy analysis: Identifying individual differences in political violence. *Foreign Policy Analysis, 8*(2), 111–129.
- McDermott, R., & Hatemi, P. K. (2016). The relationship between physical aggression, foreign policy and moral choices: Phenotypic and genetic findings. *Aggressive Behavior, 43*(1), 37–46.
- McDermott, R., Fowler, J. H., & Smirnov, O. (2008). On the evolutionary origin of prospect theoretic preferences. *Journal of Politics, 70*(2), 335–350.
- Smith, K. B., Oxley, D., Hibbing, M. V., Alford, J. R., & Hibbing, J. R. (2011). Disgust sensitivity and the neurophysiology of left-right political orientations. *PloS one, 6*(10), e25552
- Wright, N. D. (2015). The biology of cooperative decision-making: Neurobiology to international relations. In M. Galluccio (ed.), *Handbook of International Negotiation* (pp. 47–58). New York: Springer.

INDIVIDUAL DIFFERENCES AND THE ORIGINS OF POLITICAL PREFERENCES

Personality & Other Predispositions

- Adorno, T. W., Frenkel-Brunswik, E., Levinson, D. J., & Sanford, R. N. (1950). *The Authoritarian Personality*. London: Verso Books.
- Altemeyer, B. (1981). *Right-Wing Authoritarianism*. Winnipeg: University of Manitoba Press.
- Carney, D. R., Jost, J. T., Gosling, S. D., & Potter, J. (2008). The secret lives of liberals and conservatives: Personality profiles, interaction styles, and the things they leave behind. *Political Psychology, 29*(6), 807–840.
- Feldman, S. (2003). Enforcing social conformity: A theory of authoritarianism. *Political Psychology, 24*(1), 41–74.
- Feldman, S., & Stenner, K. (1997). Perceived threat and authoritarianism. *Political Psychology, 18*(4), 741–70.
- Hetherington, M., & Suhay, E. (2011). Authoritarianism, threat, and Americans' support for the war on terror. *American Journal of Political Science, 55*(3), 546–560.
- MacWilliams, M. C. (2016). Who decides when the party doesn't? Authoritarian voters and the rise of Donald Trump. *PS: Political Science & Politics, 49*(4), 716–721.
- McAdams, D. P., & Pals, J. L. (2006). A new Big Five: Fundamental principles for an integrative science of personality. *American Psychologist, 61*(3), 204–217.
- Mischel, W., & Shoda, Y. (1995). A cognitive-affective system theory of personality: Reconceptualizing situations, dispositions, dynamics, and invariance in personality structure. *Psychological Review, 102*(2), 246–268.
- Mondak, J. J. (2010). *Personality and the Foundations of Political Behavior*. Cambridge, UK: Cambridge University Press.
- Pratto, F., Sidanius, J., Stallworth, L. M., & Malle, B. F. (1994). Social dominance orientation: A personality variable predicting social and political attitudes. *Journal of Personality and Social Psychology, 67*(4), 741–763.

- Sibley, C. G., & Duckitt, J. (2008). Personality and prejudice: A meta-analysis and theoretical review. *Personality and Social Psychology Review*, 12(3), 248–279.

Leader Personality & Style

- Greenstein, F. I. (1967). The impact of personality on politics: An attempt to clear away underbrush. *American Political Science Review*, 61(03), 629–641.
- Greenstein, F. I. (1967). Personality and politics: Problems of evidence, inference, and conceptualization. *American Behavioral Scientist*, 11(2), 38–53.
- Hermann, M. G. (1980). Explaining foreign policy behavior using the personal characteristics of political leaders. *International Studies Quarterly*, 24(1), 7–46.
- Hermann, M. G. (1999). *Assessing Leadership Style: A Trait Analysis*. Columbus, OH: Social Science Automation.
- Hermann M. G., Preston, T., & Young, M. (1996). Who leads can matter in foreign policymaking: A framework for leadership analysis. Paper presented at the annual meeting of the International Studies Association, San Diego.
- Holsti, O.R. (1970). The 'operational code' approach to the study of political leaders: John Foster Dulles' philosophical and instrumental beliefs. *Canadian Journal of Political Science*, 3(1), 123–157.
- Post, J. M. (2005). *The Psychological Assessment of Political Leaders: With Profiles of Saddam Hussein and Bill Clinton*. Ann Arbor: The University of Michigan Press.
- Suedfeld, P., & Tetlock, P. (1977). Integrative complexity of communications in international crises. *Journal of Conflict Resolution*, 21(1), 169–184.
- Schafer, M., & Walker, S. (eds.). (2006). *Beliefs and Leadership in World Politics: Methods and Applications of Operational Code Analysis*. Basingstoke, UK: Palgrave Macmillan.
- Walker, S. (1977). The interface between beliefs and behavior: Henry Kissinger's operational code and the Vietnam War. *Journal of Conflict Resolution*, 21(1), 129–168.
- Winter, D. G. (1993). Power, affiliation, and war: Three tests of a motivational model. *Journal of Personality and Social Psychology*, 65(3), 532–545.

Leaders' Perceptions & Misperceptions

- Dyson, S. B., & Preston, T. (2006). Individual characteristics of political leaders and the use of analogy in foreign policy decision making. *Political Psychology*, 27(2), 265–288.
- Hermann, R. K. & Keller, J. W. (2004). Beliefs, values, and strategic choice: US leaders' decisions to engage, contain, and use force in an era of globalization. *Journal of Politics*, 66(2), 557–580.
- Holsti, O. R. (1967). Cognitive dynamics and images of the enemy. *Journal of International Affairs*, 21(1), 16–39.
- Jervis, R. (1976). *Perceptions and misperception in international politics*. Princeton, NJ: Princeton University Press.
- Kahneman, D., & Renshon, J. (2007). Why hawks win. *Foreign Policy*, No. 158, 34–38.
- Khong, Y. F. (1992). *Analogies at War: Korea, Munich, Dien Bien Phu, and the Vietnam Decisions of 1965*. Princeton, NJ: Princeton University Press.

- Kim, W., & Bueno de Mesquita, B. (1995). How perceptions influence the risk of war. *International Studies Quarterly*, 39(1), 51–65.
- Larson, D. W. (1994). The role of belief systems and schemas in foreign policy decision-making. *Political Psychology*, 15(1), 17–33.
- Levy, J. S. (1994). Learning and foreign policy: Sweeping a conceptual minefield. *International Organization*, 48(2), 279–312.
- Sheffer, L., Loewen, P. J., Soroka, S., Walgrave, S., & Sheafer, T. (2018). Nonrepresentative representatives: An experimental study of the decision making of elected politicians. *The American Political Science Review*, 112(2), 302–321.
- Stein, J. G. (1985). Calculation, miscalculation, and conventional deterrence. In R. Jervis, R. N. Lebow & J. G. Stein (eds.), *Psychology and Deterrence* (pp. 34–59). Baltimore, MD: Johns Hopkins University Press.
- Vertzberger, Y. (1986). Foreign policy decisionmakers as practical-intuitive historians: Applied history and its shortcomings. *International Studies Quarterly*, 30(2), 223–247.
- Vertzberger, Y. (1990). *The World in Their Minds: Information Processing, Cognition, and Perception in Foreign Policy Decisionmaking*. Palo Alto, CA: Stanford University Press.

Moral Values

- Atran, S., Axelrod, R., & Davis, R. (2007). Sacred barriers to conflict resolution. *Science*, 317(5841), 1039–1040.
- Fiske, A. P., & Tetlock, P. E. (1997). Taboo tradeoffs: Reactions to transactions that transgress the spheres of justice. *Political Psychology*, 18(2), 255–297.
- Graham, J., Haidt, J., & Nosek, B. A. (2009). Liberals and conservatives rely on different sets of moral foundations. *Journal of Personality and Social Psychology*, 96(5), 1029–1046.
- Haidt, J. (2012). *The Righteous Mind: Why Good People Are Divided by Politics and Religion*. New York: Pantheon.
- Ryan, T. J. (2017). No compromise: Political consequences of moralized attitudes. *American Journal of Political Science*, 61(2), 409–423.
- Schwartz, S. H., & Bilsky, W. (1987). Toward a universal psychological structure of human values. *Journal of Personality and Social Psychology*, 53(3), 550–562.
- Sears. D., Sidanius, J., and Bobo, L. (eds.). (2000). *Racialized Politics: Values, Ideology, and Prejudice in American Public Opinion*. Chicago: University of Chicago Press.
- Seul, J. R. (1999). "Ours is the way of god": Religion, identity, and intergroup conflict. *Journal of Peace Research*, 36(5), 553–569.
- Smith, K. B., Alford, J. R., Hibbing, J. R., Martin, N. G., & Hatemi, P. K. (2016). Intuitive ethics and political orientations: Testing moral foundations as a theory of political ideology. *American Journal of Political Science*, 61(2), 424–437.
- Tetlock, P. E., Kristel, O. V., Elson, S. B., Green, M. C., & Lerner, J. S. (2000). The psychology of the unthinkable: Taboo trade-offs, forbidden base rates, and heretical counterfactuals. *Journal of Personality and Social Psychology*, 78(5), 853–870.

Social Norms

- Axelrod, R. (1986). An evolutionary approach to norms. *American Political Science Review*, 80(4), 1095–1111.

- Baron, J., & Spranca, M. (1997). Protected values. *Organizational Behavior and Human Decision Processes, 70*(1), 1–16.
- Fiske, A. P., & Tetlock, P. E. (1997). Taboo tradeoffs: Reactions to transactions that transgress the spheres of justice. *Political Psychology, 18*(2), 255–297.

MOTIVATED REASONING IN POLITICS

Information Processing & Attitude Formation

- Aronow, P. M., & Miller, B. T. (2016). Policy misperceptions and support for gun control legislation. *The Lancet, 387*(10015), 223.
- Flynn, D. J., Nyhan, B., & Reifler, J. (2017). The nature and origins of misperceptions: Understanding false and unsupported beliefs about politics. *Political Psychology, 38*(S1), 127–150.
- Jones, B., & Baumgartner, F. (2005). *The Politics of Attention: How Government Prioritizes Problems.* Chicago: The University of Chicago Press.
- Kunda, Z. (1990). The case for motivated reasoning. *Psychological Bulletin, 108*(3), 480–498.
- Nyhan, B., & Reifler, J. (2010). When corrections fail: The persistence of political misperceptions. *Political Behavior, 32*(2), 303–330.
- Taber, C. (1991). The interpretation of foreign policy events: A cognitive process theory. In D. A. Sylvan & James E. Voss (eds.), *Problem Representation in Foreign Policy Decision Making* (pp. 29–52). Hillside, NJ: Lawrence Erlbaum.
- Voss, J. F., Wolfe, C. R., Lawrence, J. A., & Engle, R. A. (1991). From representation to decision: An analysis of problem solving in international relations. In R. J. Sternberg & P. A. Frensch (eds.), *Complex Problem Solving: Principles and Mechanisms* (pp. 119–158). Hillsdale, NJ: Lawrence Erlbaum Associates.

Social Identity Theory

- Brewer, M. B. (2001). The many faces of social identity: Implications for political psychology. *Political Psychology, 22*(1), 115–125.
- Enos, R. D. (2014). Causal effect of intergroup contact on exclusionary attitudes. *Proceedings of the National Academy of Sciences, 111*(10), 3699–3704.
- Evans, A. (2015). Ideological change under Vladimir Putin in the perspective of social identity theory. *Demokratizatsiya: The Journal of Post-Soviet Democratization, 23*(4), 401–426.
- Fowler, J. H., & Kam, C.D. (2007). Beyond the self: Social identity, altruism, and political participation. *Journal of Politics, 69*(3), 813–827.
- Hainmueller, J., and Hopkins, D. J. (2014). Public attitudes toward immigration. *Annual Review of Political Science, 17*, 225–214.
- Harshe, R. (2006). Culture, identity and international relations. *Economic and Political Weekly, 41*(37), 3945–3951.
- Iyengar, S., Sood, G., & Lelkes, Y. (2012). Affect, not ideology: A social identity perspective on polarization. *Public Opinion Quarterly, 76*(3), 405–431.
- Lebow, R. N. (2008). Identity and international relations. *International Relations, 22*(4), 473–492.

- Renshon, J. (2016). Status deficits and war. *International Organization*, 70(3), 513–550.
- Sides, J., & Citrin, J. (2007). European opinion about immigration: The role of identities, interests and information. *British Journal of Political Science*, 37(3), 477–504.
- Tajfel, H., & Turner, J. C. (1979). An integrative theory of intergroup conflict. In W. G. Austin, & S. Worchel (eds.), The Social Psychology of Intergroup Relations (pp. 33–47). Monterey, CA: Brooks/Cole.
- Tajfel, H., & Turner, J. C. (1986). The social identity theory of intergroup behavior. In S. Worchel & W.G. Austin (eds.), *Psychology of Intergroup Relation* (pp. 7–24). Chicago: Hall Publishers.
- Wong, C. J. (2007). "Little" and "big" pictures in our heads: Race, local context, and innumeracy about racial groups in the United States. *Public Opinion Quarterly*, 71 (3), 392–412.

Origins & Effects of Motivated Reasoning

- Baekgaard, M., Christensen, J., Dahlmann, C. M., Mathiasen, A., & Petersen, N. B. G. (2019). The role of evidence in politics: Motivated reasoning and persuasion among politicians. *British Journal of Political Science*, 49(3), 1117–1140.
- Bayes, R., Druckman, J. N., Goods, A., & Molden, D. C. (2020). When and how different motives can drive motivated political reasoning. *Political Psychology*, 41(5), 1031–1052
- Cottam, R. W. (1977). *Foreign Policy Motivation: A General Theory and Case Study*. Pittsburgh, PA: University of Pittsburgh Press.
- Druckman, J. N., & McGrath, M. C. (2019). The evidence for motivated reasoning in climate change preference formation. *Nature Climate Change*, 9(2), 111–119.
- Hart, P. S., & Nisbet, E. C. (2012). Boomerang effects in science communication: How motivated reasoning and identity cues amplify opinion polarization about climate mitigation policies. *Communication Research*, 39(6), 701–723.
- Kahan, D. M. (2012). Ideology, motivated reasoning, and cognitive reflection: An experimental study. *Judgment and Decision Making*, 8, 407–424.
- Kertzer, J. D., Rathbun, B. C., & Rathbun, N. S. (2020). The price of peace: Motivated reasoning and costly signaling in international relations. *International Organization*, 74(1), 95–118.
- Kuru, O., Pasek, J., & Traugott, M. W. (2017). Motivated reasoning in the perceived credibility of public opinion polls. *Public Opinion Quarterly*, 81(2), 422–446.
- Lodge, M. & Taber, C. S. (2005). The automaticity of affect for political leaders, groups, and issues: An experimental test of the hot cognition hypothesis. *Political Psychology*, 26(3), 455–482.
- Lodge, M. & Taber, C. S. (2013). *The Rationalizing Voter*. Cambridge, UK: Cambridge University Press.
- McCright, A. M., & Dunlap, R. E. (2011). Cool dudes: The denial of climate change among conservative white males in the United States. *Global Environmental Change*, 21(4), 1163–1172.
- Peterson, E., & Iyengar, S. (2020). Partisan gaps in political information and information-seeking behavior: Motivated reasoning or cheerleading? *American Journal of Political Science*, 65(1), 133–147.

- *Political Psychology* – Special Virtual Issue on Motivated Reasoning – August 2012.
- Redlawsk, D. P. (2002). Hot cognition or cool consideration? Testing the effects of motivated reasoning on political decision making. *Journal of Politics*, 64(4), 1021–1044.
- Taber, C. S., & Lodge, M. (2006). Motivated skepticism in the evaluation of political beliefs, *American Journal of Political Science*, 50(3), 755–769.

SUPPLEMENTARY ONLINE CHAPTER QUESTIONS

Beyond Rationality: Behavioral Political Science in the 21st Century

Chapter 1. Living in Interesting Times: How Can Behavioral Political Science Help Us Understand the Current Political Moment?

- What is meant by *Behavioral Political Science* (BPS), and how is it distinct from *Rational Choice Theory* (RCT)?
- What are the main schools of thought represented by BPS?
- What are the two crucial assumptions underlying most theories of how democracy works? Why can't democracy work without these assumptions?
- How does the concept of "fake news" threaten the full functioning of American democracy?
- What did Walter Lippmann mean by the "pseudo-environment"? How is the "pseudo-environment" created?
- What is a "Type II" error? Are these types of errors better, worse, or just different than "Type I" errors? Explain why, using examples.
- According to the authors, what are two key ways in which BPS augments and improves standard *rational choice* models?
- What are some of the ways in which BPS differs from RCT in terms of the abilities it assumes political actors possess?
- What are some of the ways in which BPS differs from RCT in terms of the motivations for human decision-making?
- What are the four main methodological approaches in the BPS tradition?
- Think of one example of a current governmental decision, by a candidate or a party, that you think might contradict the predictions of RCT and explain why.
- Think of an example of a current governmental decision that can be explained by BPS and not by RCT.

Chapter 2. The Rational Actor Model of Political Decision Making

- How might recent US presidential election outcomes challenge standard *rational choice* explanations for voter behavior?
- What is the *paradox of voting*, and how does BPS solve it?
- Discuss a few reasons that RCT approaches are so popular, and in many cases useful, in the study of politics.
- Which motivations do RCT models often assume about people when they make decisions in politics?
- What level of ability do RCT models often assume about people when they are making political decisions?

- How might RCT models explain *altruistic* behavior?
- What does it mean to say a decision is *procedurally rational*?
- What does it mean to assume preferences are *complete*?
- What are *transitive* preferences? Describe a political decision that would violate the transitivity assumption in RCT.
- What is *Bayes' rule*, in your own words? How does it help us understand why people sometimes do not collect the information they would need to make the best possible decision about politics?
- What are the main strengths of formal approaches to the study of politics?
- What are the main challenges of incorporating findings from BPS into formal models of politics? What is one example of how researchers might do so?
- According to RCT, will citizens be more or less likely to turn out to vote when candidates are further apart in terms of the policy views they endorse? Why is that?
- Do you think teaching Bayes' rule to young adults would help them become better democratic citizens? Why might that not work?

Chapter 3. The Limits of Human Processing: Bounded Rationality, Heuristics & Biases

- What is *bounded rationality*? What set of assumptions – those related to motivation or ability – in RCT does this idea challenge most directly?
- What did Herbert Simon mean by *cognitive satisficing*? How does that strategy affect decisions in ways different than ones assumed by RCT?
- Would you expect that cognitive biases like satisficing are weaker among leaders and other sophisticated elites than they are among lay citizens? Why or why not?
- What is a *heuristic*? Discuss one common heuristic voters use in making decisions about for whom to vote.
- In what ways does the heuristic school of thought challenge RCT?
- What are the advantages and disadvantages of using heuristics when making decisions?
- What is meant by the term *naïve realism*? What problems can this bias create in a public full of diverse viewpoints and perspectives?
- Name one example of a specific bias discussed in this chapter. What is the bias and why is it potentially problematic for politics?
- What is the *mental accounting bias*? Name one implication of this bias in the political realm
- What is the difference between a maximizing versus satisficing search pattern in decision-making?
- Voters may use various different voting rules when deciding whom to support. Describe one type of voting rule and explain its implications for candidate choice.

Chapter 4. What You Say May Matter Less Than How You Say It: The Role of Framing in Political Communication Effects

- What is Prospect Theory's definition of the concept of *framing*?
- Why do rational choice approaches often predict that framing an event in a particular way for the public will not have much effect on mass opinion?
- What does *Expected Utility Theory* mean by the assumption of the *independence of irrelevant alternatives*?

- What is *loss aversion*, and what are the dominant explanations for this phenomenon? Why is so important in politics?
- What is the *endowment effect*? How does this bias affect political decisions? Use an example.
- What is the definition of the *availability bias* in Prospect Theory? Give an example.
- What is *anchoring* in prospect theory?
- What is the distinction between *episodic* and *thematic* news frames? Give a specific example of how this distinction could affect public opinion on a given issue.
- What does *nudging* refer to? Give an example of a successful nudge in politics or in public policy making.
- How does elite competition alter the effect of framing on public opinion? What is *counter-framing*?
- In your opinion, which of the framing effects in Chapter 4 most seriously threaten the basic assumptions of *Expected Utility Theory*? Explain why.
- Who are *choice architects*? What do they do?
- What are *emphasis* frames, and how are they different than *equivalency* frames according to Druckman?

Chapter 5. The Limitations of the Unitary Actor Model of Government

- What is the *unitary actor model* of government?
- What are *principal-agent* problems? How do governments try to solve them?
- Explain how RCT can incorporate domestic political considerations into theories of foreign policy making.
- Summarize *Poliheuristic Theory*, and distinguish it from standard RCT approaches that came before. What are the main differences?
- What is a *poliheuristic bias*? Provide an example.
- What is a *rational comprehensive model* of policy making and how does it compare to the method of *successive limited comparisons*? Which do you think is a more realistic model of government policy making?
- What is *applied decision analysis* (ADA)? How does it uncover decision processes in a different way than RCT?
- What is the *bureaucratic politics* model of policymaking? How is it distinct from the *organizational politics* model?
- What is a *standard operating procedure*? How is it useful and when can it be problematic?
- What are three different types of advisory systems that can affect government decision-making processes and outcomes?
- How is decision making at the elite level affected by *groupthink*?
- How is *groupthink* distinct from the *polythink syndrome*?

Chapter 6. It Just Doesn't Feel Right: How Emotions Impact Political Attitudes

- How can emotional dynamics help us understand the rise in popularity of populist parties in Europe and the USA?
- Does the notion that emotions influence decision making undermine the assumption that people are rational? Can political rationality be reconciled with emotion?
- Discuss Plato's view about the role of emotion in politics.

- What is *Hot Cognition theory*? How does it incorporate the importance of affect in political judgment?
- How does the *circumplex model of affect* differ from more simple models like *hot cognition*?
- What are the differences between *cognitive appraisal* theories of emotion and *valence-based* approaches, including the *circumplex model*?
- What do you think comes first – emotion or cognition? Why does it matter for how we think about attitudes and behavior?
- Which emotions increase people's willingness to accept risk? Why is that?
- What is the main distinction between the effects of anger versus fear as drivers of political behavior?
- What is meant by the *surveillance system* in Affective Intelligence Theory?
- Which emotions are associated with the *disposition system*?
- Under what emotional states does *Affective Intelligence Theory* suggest people will learn the most about the political world around them?
- How can *evolutionary theories* help understand the role of emotion in modern day politics?
- What biological approaches can be used to study emotion?
- How do emotions help us understand why strong partisans participate intensely in some elections but not others, or choose to protest in some instance but not others?

Chapter 7. The Origins of Political Preferences: Material Self-Interest or Personality, Moral Values and Group Attitudes?

- What does it mean to discuss the "black box" of preference formation?
- What is the central claim of *Symbolic Politics* Theory, and how is that different than the basic assumptions of rational choice?
- What is the *Black utility heuristic*, and what does it explain?
- How does the "big five" conception of personality relate to liberal versus conservative political ideology?
- What are the main features of an *authoritarian* personality?
- Why did personality theory fall out of favor among scholars in the 1960's and 1970's?
- What is the person-situation debate and what are the implications for politics if innate personality versus situational constraints are more prominent drivers of behavior?
- Describe the main features of the *field model* of political leadership.
- When will a leader's personality exert a stronger influence on policy-making outcomes?
- What is the definition of a moral value? What is the main difference between attitudes and values?
- What is meant by a *taboo tradeoff*?
- What is *quantity insensitivity*?
- What happens to decision-making when political attitudes become *moralized*?
- How do monetary incentives often affect the likelihood of compromise over deeply held values?
- What is *Moral Foundations Theory* and how does it relate to political ideology?
- Where do social norms and values come from? Can they evolve and change dramatically over time, or are they very stable?
- What is the *democratic peace* phenomenon, and how is it related to social norms?

Chapter 8. Better to Be Right or to Belong? Motivated Reasoning in Politics

- What was Converse's surprising finding in 1964 about the stability of Americans' issue preferences over time, and their linkage to a liberal-conservative ideology?
- Discuss whether the public's reliance on elite cues to help determine their issue preferences is consistent or not with the basic assumptions of RCT.
- Define *motivated reasoning*. Provide an example on how it affects politics.
- How is motivated reasoning at odds with the central assumptions of RCT?
- Who is most susceptible to motivated reasoning, the least or the most politically sophisticated? Why is that?
- What are the basic assumptions of Zaller's *receive-accept-sample* model of public opinion formation?
- What is the difference between *accuracy* and *directional* motivations?
- What are some of the major effects of motivated reasoning in politics?
- When will accuracy motivations outweigh directional motivations?
- What is *cognitive dissonance*? What is one way in which people attempt to reduce dissonance?
- What is the central argument underlying *Social Identity Theory*? How is it different from *Realistic Group Conflict Theory*?
- To what does the *minimal group paradigm* refer?
- What is *affective polarization*, and why has it grown so substantially over the last 30 years?
- How might motivated reasoning be reduced?

Chapter 9. Looking Forward: How Behavioral Political Science Can Help Policy-Makers

- What are the six schools of BPS? In general, how do they contribute to our understanding of political phenomena.
- Are RCT and BPS fundamentally at odds or are they complementary approaches for understanding the way politics works in the real world? Explain your rationale.
- What are the main critiques leveled by rational choice theorists at BPS? How might BPS researchers respond to such concerns?
- Describe one example of how policy-makers are currently using BPS insights to improve policy-making.
- In what ways could BPS help policy makers in various countries (the US, the UK, Israel, or any other country) address other policy issues in the future?

Notes

I   LIVING IN INTERESTING TIMES

1. www.npr.org/2016/11/05/500782887/donald-trumps-road-to-election-day
2. www.nytimes.com/interactive/2016/12/10/business/media/pizzagate.html?_r=0
3. www.publicpolicypolling.com/pdf/2015/PPP_Release_National_120916.pdf
4. www.latimes.com/nation/la-na-sandy-hook-conspiracy-20170203-story.html
5. www.washingtonpost.com/lifestyle/style/how-alex-jones-conspiracy-theorist-extraordinaire-got-donald-trumps-ear/2016/11/17/583dc190-ab3e-11e6-8b45-f8e493f06fcd_story.html?utm_term=.d64462e467fb
6. See, for example, www.washingtonpost.com/news/monkey-cage/wp/2014/08/21/conspiracy-theories-arent-just-for-conservatives/
7. https://data.bls.gov/timeseries/LNS14000000
8. While these different preferences can easily be incorporated into RCT models, most RCT approaches tend to take these preferences as "given," rather than exploring where they come from in the first place.
9. www.theguardian.com/politics/2017/jan/19/crisis-of-statistics-big-data-democracy?utm_content=buffer62f0c&utm_medium=social&utm_source=facebook.com&utm_campaign=buffer
10. While most modern Rational Choice theorists accept this idea, they still contend that cognitively bounded processes result in decisions that are "as if" rational. In other words, individuals often reach the same decision they would have if they had considered every alternative in depth. However, BPS scholars have highlighted numerous examples where this is not the case. Heuristic processing often leads to different, and sometimes distinctly suboptimal, decisions.
11. www.whitehouse.gov/the-press-office/2015/09/15/executive-order-using-behavioral-science-insights-better-serve-american

2   THE RATIONAL ACTOR MODEL OF POLITICAL DECISION-MAKING

1. www.sciencedaily.com/releases/2015/10/151020120844.htm. Another explanation was that traditional Republican voters who disliked Trump, could nonetheless not bring themselves to vote for the Democratic candidate.
2. One rationalist explanation that has been put forward for this choice by Sanders's supporters is that they may have preferred Trump, believing his candidacy would bring a true revolution closer, a form of "Trotskyist voting." From a Trotskyist point of view, a win for the least appealing candidate (i.e., Trump) would help to move the country one step closer to meaningful change or even revolution.
3. www.npr.org/2020/11/19/936317341/why-were-the-polls-off-pollsters-have-some-early-theories

4. Positivism is an approach whereby every assertion is thought to be able to be scientifically verified. Today, social science that is "positivist" in nature is designed to explore what *is* rather than *what ought to be*. This is one of the key differences between the majority of political science research, which is positivist, and public policy, which is normative – focusing on what ought to be and how best to achieve it.

5. In other words, individuals might not have all the information, but if they do, they will be able to use it properly to make the best possible decision, given the available information and any other constraints they face (lack of money, power, etc.).

6. Of course, the costs associated with having cancer and failing to treat it are high, so risk-averse individuals may proceed as if they definitively have cancer. We discuss the idea of risk and loss aversion in subsequent chapters.

7. www.sciencedaily.com/releases/2015/10/151020120844.htm

8. Where P(A) and P(~A) are the prior probabilities of A and of ~A occurring. In our example, P(A) is the probability of an attack before getting intelligence (0.001). P(~A) is the probability that no attack is forthcoming (0.999). P(B|A) is the conditional probability of intelligence about an impending attack given that an attack is actually pending (0.60). P(B|~A) is the false positive rate of 0.01. P(A|B) is the quantity of interest: the probability that an attack is pending given intelligence that says it is. Using the formula, we can use simple arithmetic to produce the result: $\frac{(.001)*(.60)}{(.001)*(.60)+(.999)*(.01)} = \frac{.0006}{.01059} = 5.67\%$.

9. www.washingtonpost.com/world/national-security/black-budget-summary-details-us-spy-netw orks-successes-failures-and-objectives/2013/08/29/7e57bb78-10ab-11e3-8cdd-bcdc09410972_ story.html

10. www.btl.gov.il/About/newspapers/Pages/EivaNetunim.aspx.

11. www.cbs.gov.il/reader/shnaton/templ_shnaton_diag.html?num_tab=24_10&CYear=2015

12. However, behavioral researchers have found that even this simple task is susceptible to a range of biases, such as the tendency to overweight recent events (Huber, Hill & Lenz 2012).

13. www.independent.co.uk/news/world/americas/donald-trump-weekly-list-immigrant-undocum ented-crimes-dhs-thomas-homan-mexico-citizenship-a7640491.html

14. object.cato.org/sites/cato.org/files/pubs/pdf/immigration_brief-1.pdf

15. www.economist.com/news/united-states/21716055-least-it-didnt-when-america-tried-1960s-kicking-out-immigrants-doesnt-raise

16. www.brookings.edu/blog/the-avenue/2015/04/29/dont-blame-the-robots-for-lost-manufact uring-jobs/

17. And indeed, we see that when the costs do go up – it is raining or difficult to get off work – turnout declines.

18. This move is distinct from the "behavioral revolution" in IR that began in the early 1960s with J. David Singer and others who pioneered the use of large-N, quantitative, empirical analysis in international relations research (see e.g., Singer 1972). What was revolutionary about this earlier work was not the focus on psychological explanations, but rather, the use of cross-national, quantitative analysis.

19. Subsequent bargaining models explicitly incorporated the push-and-pull of domestic politics into international bargaining. These models will be covered at length in Chapter 5.

20. See the 2017 Special Issue of the journal *International Organization*, for example, and the 2007 *Forum of International Studies Review* on behavioral IR.

21. Another way to think of it is like poker – you can bluff in an attempt to secure a higher payoff (i.e., win), but this may or may not work; whether or not you should fold or bluff depends on what you think the other players in the game intend to do (would they believe you or call your bluff?). Researchers solve these games by assigning mathematical values to certain outcomes (i.e., 'war' or 'giving in to threat' or 'signing a trade agreement') that can be different for each player (so, if one player acquiesces to a threat by another, his value for that outcome could be –10 while the other player's value could be +10, because he would get his desired choice). More complicated games will add in beliefs players possess regarding other players' probable

actions. These beliefs are modeled as probabilities (i.e., there is a 90% chance that player A will resist my threat and a 10% chance that he will acquiesce).

22. Behavioral models of politics also make simplifications to increase tractability. An important example of this is the assumption that decision-making biases such as group animus scale-up to the level of the state. In other words, many behavioral models implicitly assume, as rational choice models do, that the state can be treated as a unitary actor, just one with "non-standard" preferences. Whether and how individual preferences interact with the organizational structure of the state is thus an important research question for behavioral political science moving forward. Indeed, whether the bureaucracy of the state attenuates or amplifies the impact of the individual-level biases we have discussed remains a subject of debate (see, e.g., Kertzer et al., n. d.). Much work in the behavioral tradition suggests that the organizational apparatus of the state may increase their impact (see Chapter 5 for our overview), but other work suggests organizations may mitigate them (see, e.g., Saunders 2017).

3   THE LIMITS OF HUMAN PROCESSING

1. In politics, these material interests can be broadly construed to mean not only money or economic security, but also safety, security, and other tangible interests, such as access to health care, education, and so on.
2. www.nytimes.com/politics/first-draft/2016/04/02/donald-trump-tells-crowd-hed-be-fine-if-nato-broke-up/
3. www.nbcnews.com/politics/white-house/trump-reverses-nato-it-no-longer-obsolete-n745601
4. In budgeting, "fair share" refers to allocating a fair proportion of additional resources or budgets to various units, whereas incremental spending refers to the practice of allocating additional amounts to existing programs/units, instead of demanding zero-based budgeting.
5. In contrast, the term "taste-based discrimination" is used to describe "real" prejudice, whereby individuals have an intrinsic animus against individuals of other racial backgrounds that structures their behavior toward these groups, regardless of the base likelihood the individual is going to commit a crime. In the first case, people are engaging in a boundedly rational decision-making process, using a coarse rule of thumb to make a judgment about someone. In the second case, people are expressing non-material, prejudicial preferences. Importantly, in either case, individuals are violating one standard assumption of traditional RCT – either the process is not fully rational or the underlying motivation is not material in nature.
6. Bayes' rule is discussed at length in Chapter 2.
7. www.ice.gov/voice
8. www.nytimes.com/2019/01/08/us/politics/trump-speech-transcript.html
9. www.pollingreport.com/immigration.htm
10. www.nytimes.com/2019/05/13/upshot/illegal-immigration-crime-rates-research.html
11. This bias may also be related to the endowment effect: individuals place higher value on things they already possess compared to things they do not.
12. www.pewresearch.org/fact-tank/2016/11/09/why-2016-election-polls-missed-their-mark/
13. https://fivethirtyeight.com/features/why-fivethirtyeight-gave-trump-a-better-chance-than-almost-anyone-else/
14. http://thewall-usa.com/summary.asp#year
15. www.economist.com/democracy-in-america/2018/06/05/why-people-vote-against-their-econo mic-interests
16. Closely related to the preference-over-preference bias is the *locking in on a preferred alternative* bias, whereby individuals decide early on regarding their choice and then stop processing information relevant to the decision that may indicate another choice is actually preferable.
17. The canonical example of deterrence theory relates to nuclear weapons and the idea of "mutually assured destruction." During the Cold War, scholars in the realist tradition

argued that nuclear weapons could, in fact, have a pacifying impact on international conflict, as long as the great adversarial powers (in this case, the United States and the USSR) each possessed a "second-strike" capability – the ability to retaliate against their enemy, should the other side ever try a nuclear strike first. Mutual second-strike capability would render attacking first suicidal, thus dramatically reducing the likelihood of nuclear war.

18. In the post-WWII era, there is the United Nations peacekeeping force; however, their strength and enforcement power are deeply constrained by those of the individual superpowers (e.g., Russia, China, the United States) and, as such, do not serve as a true superordinate force to maintain order.

19. Portions of this section are reported in Mintz & Redd 2009.

20. Fifty military officers participated in the experiment. The military commanders were recruited from a leadership course taught over two semesters at the National Defense University. The military officers who participated in this study included a Brigadier General, thirteen Colonels, thirty-one Lt. Colonels and five Captains. These officers represented all four branches of the US armed forces, and several branches of the Reserve and National Guard.

21. This function is as follows: Faced with a risky choice leading to gains, individuals will have a concave value function (e.g., individuals will be risk-averse, preferring solutions that lead to a lower expected utility but with a higher certainty). In contrast, faced with a risky choice leading to losses, individuals will have a convex value function: they will be risk-seeking, preferring solutions that lead to a lower expected utility as long as it has the potential to avoid losses.

22. This phenomenon is not limited to citizens; political leaders are also susceptible to the order in which choices are presented. For example, leaders are sensitive to negative political information and may discard alternatives that are damaging for them politically, even before considering the economic or diplomatic benefits of a policy (Mintz 2005). Thus, if a political advisor sets the meeting agenda, it might lead to a different decision by the leader than if, for example, a military advisor had presented the options (beginning with the military dimension associated with each alternative).

4 WHAT YOU SAY MAY MATTER LESS THAN HOW YOU SAY IT

1. Expected utility theory, as we discuss in Chapter 2, simply states that the value of a certain strategy is a combination of the potential value of the outcomes to which it may lead, multiplied by the probability of each of those outcomes. In short, if investing $100 in stock A means that I have a 90% chance of gaining $10, but a 10% chance of losing $100, then my expected utility of investing in stock A equals: $(0.9)(10) + (0.1)(-100) = 9 - 10 = -1$. If investing in stock B means that I have a 80% chance of gaining $10 and a 20% chance of losing $30, then my expected utility of investing in stock B equals: $(0.8)(10) + (0.2)(-30) = 8 - 6 = 2$. Thus, I have a higher expected utility from investing in stock B, so that is the stock I should choose.

2. www.cdc.gov/flu/weekly/index.htm

3. While the specific profile of the prisoners who were released differed (e.g., some high-value prisoners that had been on the 2011 list were not released), the fact that the overall number stayed so close to the original Hamas offer is striking.

4. www.ynetnews.com/articles/0,7340, L-4681905,00.html

5. http://edition.cnn.com/2015/09/17/politics/republican-debate-winners-losers-donald-trump

6. http://edition.cnn.com/2015/09/20/politics/carly-fiorina-donald-trump-republican-2016-poll/

7. www.nytimes.com/2015/08/22/world/europe/president-erdogan-of-turkey-to-call-for-new-election.html

8. www.gpo.gov/fdsys/pkg/FR-2015-09-18/pdf/2015-23630.pdf

9. www.nytimes.com/politics/first-draft/2015/09/26/bill-clinton-blames-g-o-p-news-media-for-wifes-email-woes/

10. Associated Press. 2015. Kerry: Rejecting nuke deal would be 'self-destructive'. *The Times of Israel*. www.timesofisrael.com/kerry-rejecting-nuke-deal-would-be-self-destructive/?fb_comment_id=1 258647924161440_1258733050819594#f23f3959e8ca8a
11. http://israelbehindthenews.com/white-house-and-israel-release-competing-descriptions-of-obama-netanyahu-phone-call-on-iran deal/12838/?utm_source=wysija&utm_medium=email &utm_campaign=ibn-today
12. Ibid.
13. http://iranmatters.belfercenter.org/blog/translation-iranian-factsheet-nuclear-negotiation
14. https://thehill.com/policy/international/250332-obama-links-republicans-to-iranians-chan ting-death-to-america
15. www.wsj.com/articles/cash-for-the-revolutionary-guards-1438814759
16. www.telegraph.co.uk/news/worldnews/northamerica/usa/11758986/Iran-nuclear-deal-Dont-waste-best-chance-at-peace-Kerry-tells-US-Congress.html
17. www.msnbc.com/rachel-maddow-show/obama-reminds-mccain-how-foreign-policy-works
18. www.wsj.com/articles/BL-WB-54460
19. www.timesofisrael.com/irgc-officer-we-laugh-at-obamas-ridiculous-military-threats/
20. www.timesofisrael.com/irgc-officer-we-laugh-at-obamas-ridiculous-military-threats/
21. www.timesofisrael.com/irgc-officer-we-laugh-at-obamas-ridiculous-military-threats/
22. obamawhitehouse.archives.gov/the-press-office/2015/04/11/remarks-president-press-conference-after-summit-americas
23. www.israelnationalnews.com/News/News.aspx/224465

5   THE LIMITATIONS OF THE UNITARY ACTOR MODEL OF GOVERNMENT

1. https://abcnews.go.com/Politics/trump-versus-doctors-president-experts-contradict/story?id =70330642
2. These shortcuts and decision rules are described in more depth in Chapter 3.
3. This section is adapted from Mintz, Chatagnier & Samban (2020).
4. www.nytimes.com/2018/09/05/opinion/trump-white-house-anonymous-resistance.html
5. www.cbsnews.com/news/trump-lambasted-jeff-sessions-after-special-counsel-appointment-mue ller-report-quote-president-trump-im-f-ked/
6. www.washingtonexaminer.com/jeff-sessions-fires-back-at-trump-i-will-continue-to-discharge-my-duties-with-integrity-and-honor
7. www.c-span.org/video/?c4773873/william-barr-jeff-sessions-recuse-russia-probe
8. This is similar to the notion of bounded awareness: "when cognitive blinders prevent a person from seeing, seeking, using, or sharing highly relevant, easily accessible, and readily perceivable information during the decision-making process" (Bazerman & Chugh 2006). This phenomenon is assumed away by most rational choice models.
9. Portions of this section are adapted from Mintz & Wayne 2016.
10. Portions of this section are adapted from Mintz & Wayne 2016.
11. A leader's operational code is defined as her or his "beliefs about the nature of politics and political conflict, his views regarding the extent to which historical developments can be shaped, and his notions of correct strategies and tactics" (George 1969). Operational codes are discussed in more detail in Chapter 7.
12. www.nytimes.com/2018/09/05/opinion/trump-white-house-anonymous-resistance.html
13. www.iraqbodycount.org/
14. www.cnn.com/2014/06/21/world/meast/iraq-crisis/index.html?iref=allsearch
15. These group dynamics were also important in subsequent decisions vis-à-vis the Islamic State. For example, the role of group processes in the Obama administration's decision to attack Raqqa, the capital of ISIS, in 2016, has also been analyzed in a series of papers (Barr 2019; Barr & Mintz 2021). Whereas groupthink syndrome characterized the decision-making process of the US-led coalition's decision to attack Raqqa, it was polythink that

characterized the decision-making dynamics surrounding the implementation of that policy within both the broader US-led coalition and the inner circle of President Obama's foreign policy advisors in implementing this decision (Barr & Mintz 2019). Thus, polythink in both the US administration and in the international coalition (where Turkey, for example, expressed serious opposition to the involvement of the Kurds in the coalition on Raqqa), essentially paralyzed and greatly delayed the attack. Those in the US administration who were in favor of arming the Syrian Kurds directly included Secretary of Defense Ashton Carter as well as General Joseph F. Dunford, Chairman of the Joint Chiefs of Staff. In contrast, National Security Advisor Susan Rice, Ambassador to the UN Samantha Power, and Ambassador to Turkey John Bass opposed this move "because of the impact it would have on US-Turkish relations" (Barr & Mintz 2019). They proposed utilizing Arab forces backed by the soldiers that Turkey was offering to send. These subgroups "broke down along two distinct institutional lines, the Pentagon and the State department" (Barr & Mintz 2021). This case study demonstrates the effect of intragroup dynamics and the effect of leaders on decisions on the use of force. The authors provided further support for a broader theoretical hypothesis whereby groupthink is more likely in overall strategic decisions, whereas polythink is more likely in lower-level tactical choices (Barr & Mintz 2021; Barr 2019).

16. www.telegraph.co.uk/news/2019/01/11/us-begins-withdrawing-troops-syria/
17. www.telegraph.co.uk/news/2019/01/11/us-begins-withdrawing-troops-syria/
18. www.telegraph.co.uk/news/2019/01/11/us-begins-withdrawing-troops-syria/

6 FEELING POLITICS

1. In this way, AIT is more similar to a valence approach to the study of emotions.
2. www.axios.com/trump-politicization-coronavirus-response-eb06ee87-8c29-499d-8451-295649fa8c95.html
3. www.pewresearch.org/politics/2020/06/25/republicans-democrats-move-even-further-apart-in-coronavirus-concerns/
4. www.cbsnews.com/news/covid-november-cases-united-states/
5. https://onlinelibrary.wiley.com/toc/14679221/2012/33/3
6. A caveat is required here: though these approaches are indeed innovative and exciting, with the potential to provide a window into previously invisible factors that might impact human behavior, it is important not to overstate the deterministic nature of biology in humans' decision-making. Just because a biological variable is correlated with social or political behavior does not mean that one's behavior is predetermined or predestined at birth. In other words, there is no gene for being a Republican or Democrat, despite what some catchy headlines might claim!
7. Motivated reasoning is discussed at length in Chapter 8.
8. www.washingtonpost.com/graphics/2020/elections/voter-turnout/
9. www.bbc.com/news/world-middle-east-13134956
10. The conviction was reversed in 2017 and he was released from prison, after General al-Sisi's successful coup against the Egyptian President Mohamed Morsi.
11. www.apmreports.org/story/2018/10/19/georgia-voter-purge
12. https://apnews.com/article/5dca86cf28114b23b94e4a3891da1d64
13. www.nytimes.com/2020/11/06/us/politics/stacey-abrams-georgia.html
14. www.washingtonpost.com/opinions/the-enemy-below-why-hamas-tunnels-scare-israel-so-much/2014/07/25/c7ef0902-1281-11e4-9285-4243a40ddc97_story.html?utm_term=.0b018a72b88a
15. Ibid.
16. This was explained by poliheuristic theory (discussed at length in Chapter 4), in Mintz and DeRouen (2010).

7 THE ORIGINS OF POLITICAL PREFERENCES

1. Much of the recent work on behavioral formal models of politics discussed in Chapter 2 explicitly incorporates so-called non-standard or behavioral preferences.
2. https://medium.com/s/trustissues/the-lifespan-of-a-lie-d869212b1f62
3. A tautology is saying the same thing twice, using different words. For example, predicting partisan identification based on whether you identify as a Republican or Democrat would be a tautology.
4. The authoritarian predisposition is only one example of research that examines how variations in ex ante dispositions shape political attitudes. For example, one particularly notable research program highlights individual differences in levels of "social dominance orientation," the degree to which individuals feel like their group should dominate, in a hierarchical fashion, other groups. In other words, individuals high in social dominance (SDO) will tend to espouse beliefs justifying relative inequality between groups. A vast array of studies in this program have demonstrated that levels of SDO correlate strongly with a host of political attitudes from support for war, to civil rights and social programs (see, e.g., Pratto et al. 1994).
5. www.theatlantic.com/magazine/archive/2016/06/the-mind-of-donald-trump/480771/
6. See, for example, the open letter to Donald Trump published by GOP foreign policy advisors in March 2016: https://warontherocks.com/2016/03/open-letter-on-donald-trump-from-gop-national-security-leaders/
7. http://thehill.com/policy/defense/326020-reports-of-civilian-deaths-raise-questions-about-trumps-airstrike-policy
8. www.washingtonpost.com/blogs/federal-eye/wp/2013/10/18/how-much-did-the-shutdown-cost-the-economy/
9. On the other hand, these norms are not necessarily universally followed. For example, there have been reports of Bashar al-Assad's regime in Syria gassing civilian populations sympathetic to Syrian rebels in the ongoing civil war there. The responses of Western states to these reports, however, demonstrate the power of norms: the response from the international community to Syrians being killed by mustard gas is much more forceful than the response to the many more that have been killed by "traditional" bombs and artillery.
10. Other scholars disagree with these normative explanations, arguing that institutional constraints are a more important driver of state foreign policy than are norms. This school of thought is known as neoliberal institutionalism. Neoliberalism differs from liberalism in that it does not rely solely on the normative importance of democratic ideals (or the lack thereof) in structuring international relations, but the instrumental importance of the institutions put in place by democracies. In other words, democracies behave differently than autocracies not necessarily because of some normative dedication to nonviolence, but because of institutional structures that limit their freedom of action in certain ways (see, for example, Bueno de Mesquita et al. 1999).
11. Though outside the purview of this book, the constructivist research program has greatly contributed to our understanding of the origins of identity, preferences and norms (see, for example, Alexander Wendt, 1992).

8 BETTER TO BE RIGHT OR TO BELONG?

1. One potential explanation for these findings that fits within the RCT tradition involves the different information environments these types of events create (Ashworth, Bueno de Mesquita & Friedenberg 2018). For example, the damage caused by an earthquake may be at least partially due to the quality of government preparedness in place prior (eg., regulations for building quality, disaster response plans in place). When a natural disaster strikes, voters can thus learn how well the politician planned for such a crisis.

2. www.washingtonpost.com/politics/former-trump-aide-rex-tillerson-says-alternative-realities-are-a-threat-to-democracy/2018/05/16/4d0353f0-594b-11e8-8836-a4a123c359ab_story.html

3. www.washingtonpost.com/news/monkey-cage/wp/2016/12/18/a-new-poll-shows-an-astonishing-52-of-republicans-think-trump-won-the-popular-vote/

4. http://robertreich.org/post/156777888615

5. www.washingtonpost.com/blogs/the-fix/post/a-double-standard-on-gas-prices/2012/03/29/gIQAVMHRjS_blog.html?utm_term=.7c1a58620a61

6. These "memory-based" psychological models are derived, in part, from the Bayesian approach we discussed in Chapter 2.

7. South Carolina senator Lindsey Graham is a notable example: www.washingtonpost.com/outlook/2019/10/11/history-behind-lindsey-grahams-about-face-president-trump/

8. https://news.gallup.com/poll/245996/trump-job-approval-sets-new-record-polarization.aspx

9. https://misinforeview.hks.harvard.edu/article/the-causes-and-consequences-of-covid-19-misperceptions-understanding-the-role-of-news-and-social-media/

10. www.latimes.com/politics/la-na-pol-trump-south-korea-20171106-story.html

11. www.washingtonpost.com/politics/hes-a-tough-guy-trump-downplays-the-human-rights-record-of-kim-jong-un/2018/06/14/90ed487e-6fbb-11e8-bf86-a2351b5ece99_story.html?utm_term=.7ce5b4f478ce

9 LOOKING FORWARD

1. See, for example, the many behavioral formal models of political phenomena described in Chapter 2.

2. https://obamawhitehouse.archives.gov/the-press-office/2015/09/15/executive-order-using-behavioral-science-insights-better-serve-american

3. https://obamawhitehouse.archives.gov/the-press-office/2015/09/15/executive-order-using-behavioral-science-insights-better-serve-american

4. https://cpl.hks.harvard.edu/behavioral-insights-group

5. www.bi.team/our-work/publications/

6. www.bi.team/wp-content/uploads/2016/09/BIT_Update_Report_2015-16-.pdf

7. www.theguardian.com/commentisfree/2020/mar/13/why-is-the-government-relying-on-nudge-theory-to-tackle-coronavirus

Glossary of Terms

Acceptability Threshold: According to the school of Bounded Rationality, most decision makers engage in a "satisficing" strategy, making a choice that reaches some minimum level of viability that is considered "good enough," rather than optimal.

Accuracy Motivation: The motivation to form accurate perceptions about the world, regardless of whether they contradict previous beliefs. Accuracy motives are often compared to directional motives, the desire to believe things about the world that conform to cherished group norms, even if invalid. These concepts play important roles in the theory of Motivated Reasoning.

Accountability Models: A common class of formal models that incorporates domestic political considerations into theories of state foreign policy-making. Often an elected official must formulate a policy while anticipating reactions from the electorate in a future round of the game. These models use a rational choice framework that deconstructs the billiard-ball model of states used in structural theories of international relations, assessing how domestic electoral considerations may structure leaders' policy-making.

Advisory Systems: Systems of advisors with three distinct types – formal, collegial, or competitive – all of which are hypothesized to distinctly affect the character of policy decision-making.

Affective Heuristic: A decision-making shortcut that relies on immediate, emotion-driven impressions of a political candidate, issue, or event. It is a quick judgment about whether a political object makes one feel positive or negative.

Affective Intelligence Theory: A theory arguing that the traditional conception of emotions – as an evolutionarily antiquated cognitive "defect" that impedes rational decision-making – is misguided. Affective Intelligence argues that emotions are a crucial component of human decision-making, without which people would be unable to reason. AIT characterizes emotions as immediate, preconscious reactions to stimuli that affect how we process information – whether we rely on the less cognitively demanding dispositional system, or whether we engage our surveillance system – leading us to engage in deeper information search and processing.

226

Affective Polarization: A term used to describe intense dislike that has developed between members of major parties, especially in the United States. Affective polarization is often measured by subtracting the positive feelings one possesses toward one's own party from the negative feelings one has toward the other party.

Agenda Setting: The creation of common concerns and public attention toward particular issues by opinion leaders and political elites. Via the media, elites can make certain issues more salient than others, subsequently influencing the priorities people use when evaluating candidates and issues.

Alternative-Based Search: An information acquisition search that focuses on each potential choice, considering it holistically along dimensions before moving on to the next option. This form of information search is often contrasted with a dimension-based search, where alternatives are compared to each other dimension by dimension.

Anchoring Heuristic: A heuristic whereby individuals use information from a previous task or experience to help make a second choice (e.g., as an "anchor"), even if the two decisions are completely unrelated. This heuristic can lead to biases that trigger suboptimal decision-making.

Applied Decision Analysis: An analytical approach that reproduces an individual's decisions allowing the analyst to trace back the strategy of decision-making and the decision rule of that individual.

Audience Costs: The reputational costs, both domestic and international, of a leader's decision to back down from publicly announced threats or promises. Generating these costs can be one way in which leaders signal commitment to allies and adversaries.

Availability Heuristic: A cognitive shortcut whereby individuals make judgments concerning the frequency of an event based on how easily similar instances are recalled. This leads more memorable events to be judged as occurring more frequently than mundane ones, even if they are equally likely.

Backlash/Contrast Effect: An effect that occurs when those who are invested in one side of an argument react to contradictory information not just by counterarguing or rejecting the message, but by taking an even more extreme position than they previously held.

Bargaining Theory: A subset of game theory that concerns individuals strategically bargaining for the division of items. Equilibria outcomes are influenced by the strategic settings of the interaction – how much information is known, the relative power distribution between the parties, what options are available to each party, who moves first, and what preferences they each possess.

Bayes' Rule: A simple algorithm that describes the relationship between prior probabilities and conditional probabilities. Bayesian updating is a canonical RCT assumption about the way individuals process information, learn, and change their behavior as a result.

Belief Persistence: The tendency for one to hold tight to a belief about the world even when it is demonstrably false. Belief persistence is a consequence of motivated reasoning.

Big Five Personality Inventory: An approach to describing the main independent dimensions of personality: (1) openness to experience; (2) conscientiousness; (3) extraversion; (4) agreeableness; and (5) emotional stability. These predispositions have, to a variety of degrees, been found to influence policy preferences, partisan identity, and electoral behavior.

Black Utility Heuristic: The view that one's personal economic fate is tied closely to that of an ethnic group. What is determined to be good for the group can be used as a mental shortcut for individuals attempting to maximize their own material interests.

Blind Spot Bias: A phenomenon where one recognizes biased reasoning in others but not in oneself. This concept is similar to naïve realism – the belief that one sees the world correctly, while others do not.

Bounded Rationality: The notion that limitless cognitive processing capacity is not possible for human brains. The approach recognizes that people are susceptible to a variety of limits on their cognitive abilities and, because information search is costly, they accept a satisfactory outcome instead of a maximizing one.

Bureaucratic Model of Policy-Making: A model of policy-making that assumes leaders are rational actors, but that they hold preferences that do not necessarily align with the interests of the "state" writ large. For example, bureaucrats' interests could depend on which particular department of government they represent, meaning that "where they stand" on issues could depend on "where they sit" in government. As such, government policies are the result of the push and pull between bureaucratic agents with various individual interests.

Cheerleading: When individuals state beliefs that are simply expressive and do not actually shape their behavior.

Choice Architect: An individual who packages policy alternatives in a way that pushes the target audience toward one outcome over another. In so doing, choice architects can shape people's contexts for decision-making. Central to the theory of "nudging," choice architects are thought to play a key role in shaping decision outcomes based on the way they design the choice set.

Cognitive Appraisal Theories: Theories positing that specific emotions like fear, anger, pride, disgust, and others are the result of specific considerations such as what caused an event to occur, who is to blame, and how one might react most effectively. As such, cognitive appraisal theories posit that cognitive feedback loops are important in the generation of emotional reactions to stimuli. In contrast to valence approaches, cognitive appraisal theories argue that each emotion stems from a unique combination of appraisals regarding an event or actor and that specific emotions lead to distinct behavioral outcomes.

Cognitive Bias: A systematic, subconscious error in reasoning that deviates from what is considered rational judgment. This bias could lead individuals to make suboptimal choices. Cognitive biases are often caused by the use of heuristics.

Cognitive Dissonance Theory: A theory postulating that the discomfort people experience when their behavior contradicts their beliefs will lead them to change their beliefs more often than their behavior. By bringing their beliefs into line with their behavior, the individual may reduce mental discomfort, but they will also hold increasingly false beliefs that could harm their well-being.

Cognitive Hierarchy Equilibrium: An equilibrium that occurs when players naively believe that their strategy must be the best or most sophisticated (e.g., that other players will make a variety of mistakes in choosing their strategy, but that they never will). This equilibrium outcome is an example of how behavioral concepts can be incorporated into formal models of strategic decision-making.

Cognitive Incommensurability: The lack of a common basis of knowledge between two parties to relate a value or concept to the same measure. Incommensurability can make it difficult to compare two outcomes that have no common scale (e.g., love and money).

Collective Action Problem: A dilemma in which all parties would benefit most by working together but fail to do so because they are not punished for acting selfishly. The collective action problem is a generalization of the Prisoners' Dilemma.

Compensatory Decision-Making: A compensatory pattern is a decision-making model where a low score on a dimension of an alternative can be compensated for by a high score on another dimension (or on multiple other dimensions).

Conditional Probabilities: New probabilities arrived at after updating initial positions based on new information. Conditional probabilities are central to Bayesian updating.

Confirmation Bias: A bias in which individuals seek out evidence that confirms their preexisting views but reject evidence that potentially disconfirms them. Confirmation bias is postulated to be a consequence of motivated reasoning.

Conjunctive Decision Rule: A rule in which the decision maker sets a minimum acceptable value for each dimension of a decision. To be accepted, an alternative has to be above the minimum acceptable value on all dimensions. An alternative is rejected if it fails to exceed any minimum value, even if its overall sum is highest.

Constructivist School: A school of political science that argues many aspects of society and, specifically, relationships between states, are in fact socially constructed, rather than inevitable, stable consequences of international structure or human nature. Much of the research on the importance of norms in shaping behavior is conducted in the constructivist school, which is less concerned with quantitative measurement and explicit hypothesis testing than either behavioral political science or rational choice theory.

Counterarguing: The manufacture of contradictory arguments when presented with opposing views. The tendency to counterargue, rather than carefully listening to one's opponent in a debate and considering the strengths and weaknesses of their argument. Counterarguing helps to maintain stable belief systems and is a feature of motivated reasoning.

D-Term: A factor in the citizen's decision to vote that incorporates motivations of civic duty and the ethical satisfaction of voting. This concept helps understand why citizens may turn out to vote despite there being almost no chance they can change the outcome of an election.

Decision-Theoretic Problem: A problem that can be solved by understanding how various choices affect the interests of a single individual. This is in contrast to a game-theoretic problem, which can only be solved by understanding the strategic interaction of two or more actors who are simultaneously trying to maximize their interests.

Deductive Reasoning: A deductive approach to theorizing considers past knowledge or theory in order to propose new hypotheses. These hypotheses can then be tested using data. Deductive reasoning is often contrasted with an inductive approach. Rational Choice Theories are well-known for their deductive approaches to politics, one of their great strengths, though many behavioral researchers also engage in deductive, if not formal, reasoning.

Democratic Dilemma: A dilemma that asks how democracy functions in the context of uninformed or misinformed citizens. Democracies are founded on the normative idea that citizens are able to hold their leaders accountable for their actions and, if they do not pursue the public good, can vote them out of office. However, many citizens are uninformed, inaccurately assessing the performance of their leaders. This may fundamentally challenge the concept of self-governance in democracy.

Democratic Peace Theory: A theory that posits that democracies are less likely to fight wars against other democracies than against nondemocratic regimes. The reasons for this empirical pattern are debated, but are due to a variety of factors, include values, norms, or the signaling power of democratic institutions.

Deterrence Theory: The idea that coercion rests in holding the ability to do harm in reserve. Deterrence relies on the threat of punishment if an adversary takes an undesired action, as well as the promise that the adversary can avoid punishment if they comply with the demand. Central to academic and policy theorizing during the Cold War was the role that nuclear weapons could play in deterrence – that the power to hurt from nuclear weapons was so high, that no action could be worth the consequences.

Dimension-Based Search: A method of information acquisition whereby an individual considers alternatives across a dimension, and then moves on to the next dimension where they do the same.

Directional Motivations: A core component of motivated reasoning theory, directional motives lead the individual to hold beliefs that are consistent with their sense of belonging to a valued group, regardless of their validity. These motivations can be consequential, especially when the beliefs they cause directly endanger the person's well-being.

Dispositional System: One of two information processing systems postulated by affective intelligence theory. Individuals rely on previous dispositions and habits of mind when they are not confronted with novel, threatening information in the environment. In these situations, people act on standing assumptions about how the world works that could be based on stereotypes and strongly held group identities.

Diversionary Tactics: When a person intends to distract attention away from one issue by creating a new problem demanding government action. Diversionary tactics are often attempts to shift public opinion, whereby elected leaders facing flagging domestic political support may create new crises or conflicts in order to shift attention from their unpopularity.

Dual Cognitive Systems: Recent findings in cognitive neuroscience suggest there exist two parallel systems in the mind. System 1 describes the predominant set of cognitive processes that operate quickly, easily, automatically, and outside of our conscious awareness but nonetheless have very significant effects on our behavior. System 2 represents the more effortful, deliberate, and controlled processes which require access to working memory, but which is actually only a small proportion of all human cognition. Examples of dual systems approaches include affective intelligence theory, the elaboration likelihood model, and many others.

Economic Man: The theory that political choices are driven mostly by material self-interests, that individuals are capable of reliably and consistently calculating using all available information relevant to the choice. The assumptions underlying the ideal of Economic Man are central to many Rational Choice models of politics.

Elimination by Aspects: A decision rule whereby individuals will eliminate alternatives sequentially based on dimensions they judge to be most important, and then moving sequentially to less important dimensions.

Elite Framing: When leaders craft messages to highlight the benefits and downplay the costs of their preferred policies, seeking to shape public opinion in favor of their policy agenda.

Emotional Leadership: The idea that political elites' actions are often guided by their emotions, just as the mass public is. This concept pushes back on the RCT idea that elites are less reliant on their emotions in decision-making compared to the average citizen.

Endowment Effect: A cognitive bias whereby individuals place higher value on things they already possess compared to things that they do not. The endowment effect is one explanation for loss aversion in prospect theory.

Episodic and Thematic Frames: In an episodic frame, the news focuses on specific individuals, events, or cases in order to illustrate the more abstract issue a story addresses. In a thematic frame, the news places a problem in a broad and general context, mostly free of specific examples or people. The public's attributions of responsibility for problems facing the nation are influenced by the news media's framing choices.

Ethnocentrism: The belief in the inherent superiority of one's own ethnic or cultural group.

Equilibrium: A term in game theory that describes the outcome(s) where every player makes the choice that maximizes their utility, given the structural constraints of the game.

Equivalency Framing: Statements that are logically equivalent, describing precisely the same outcomes but in slightly different ways. For example, one might describe a policy outcome in terms of how much is lost or how much is gained. According to rational choice theory, these types of frames should not impact choices, as they do not present different information or alter underlying calculations of utility.

Evolutionary Approaches: Evolutionary approaches to politics drawing on what we know about adaptive strategies in early human societies to explain patterns in contemporary politics. According to evolutionary theory, the challenges facing our earliest ancestors over thousands of years shape key attributes of human reasoning even today. Notably, strategies optimal for our ancestors may not be in modern contexts.

Expected Utility Theory: Expected utility is at the core of rational choice approaches to politics. The theory posits that individuals choose actions that maximize their net gain: expected benefits minus expected costs. Expected utility for each potential strategy is calculated by summing the potential value (or cost) of each outcome multiplied by the probability that the outcome will occur.

F-Scale: A measure of "authoritarian personality" originally proposed by Theodor Adorno and his colleagues. It purportedly taps a cluster of stable traits that can predict support for fascist leaders and policies. The F-Scale was based on nine key traits: conventionalism, authoritarian submission, aggression, anti-intellectualism, anti-intraception, superstitiousness, proneness to stereotypes, sensitivity to levels of power, and toughness. Though the concept of authoritarianism has persisted in modern research on political attitudes, this measure has largely fallen out of favor as a result of conceptual and methodological problems.

Formal Advisory System: An advisory group structure designed to reduce the effects of human error via the implementation of a management system that is hierarchical, focused on issues rather than personalities, nonconfrontational, and oriented toward evaluating rather than generating options and making the "best" decision.

Formal Modeling: A tool for building and testing social science theories that involves the mathematical formalization of assumptions about strategic interactions, the attributes of the actors involved, and their preferences. The mathematical formalization and deductive reasoning used in formal modeling is valued for its commitment to precision and transparency and is a hallmark of many rational choice models of political behavior. Increasingly, the tools of formal modeling have been used to test behavioral theories of politics as well.

Frame Blindness: Setting out to solve the wrong problem because your framework causes you to overlook attractive options or lose sight of important objectives.

Framing: The process in which very subtle differences in the way information is presented can dramatically alter behavior, even if they do not change the fundamental argument or choice in any substantive way.

Fundamental Attribution Error: A bias whereby individuals rely on a heuristic that attributes others' negative actions to stable personality characteristics rather than to situational constraints, but their own negative actions to the specifics of the situation.

Gain-Loss Framing: A type of framing that describes a decision problem, choice or outcome using different reference points in order to emphasize potential gains or losses. Central to prospect theory, these frames are logically equivalent, but still produce very different reaction and distributions of public approval in reaction.

Game-Theoretic Decision: The study of mathematical models of strategic interactions among multiple decision makers who are simultaneously trying to maximize their own interests. Game theoretic tools are frequently used by rational choice theorists, but can also be used in behavioral research.

Group Decision-Making: When individuals make a collective decision as part of a larger group, rather than individually. Decision-making dynamics in this group can vary broadly. Groupthink, Polythink, and Con-Div are some examples of different configurations of intra-group dynamics.

Group-Based Emotions: Emotions that individuals experience as a result of identifying with their fellow group members. Essentially, emotions are felt on behalf of some larger social group.

Groupthink: A mode of thinking that people engage in when the members' strivings for unanimity override their motivation to realistically appraise alternative courses of action.

Halo Effect: A bias whereby people assume that physically attractive individuals are more likely to have other socially desirable traits.

Heuristic: Shortcuts and coarse rules of thumb that sacrifice some decision-making accuracy for a corresponding increase in simplicity and speed. While they may be adaptive in many situations, such shortcuts can lead to costly mistakes and biases as well.

Hot Cognition: A theory that recognizes that reason and emotion are not distinct or inconsistent forces in human decision-making, but rather that we reason from our emotions. As individuals are repeatedly exposed to a political object such as a candidate or policy, each experience gets tagged with an affective label – positive or negative. Subsequent judgments about that stimulus are then based on the cumulative weight of positive versus negative affective tags, rather than more detailed, substantive information.

If-Then Conception of Traits: When stable personality differences emerge in distinct ways depending on the context. This approach recognizes that it is not only the person or the situation that shapes behavior, but the interaction between the two.

Illusion of Control: A bias whereby individuals overestimate the amount of control they have to affect outcomes in their own lives, disregarding the role of luck, context, and the actions of others.

Inductive Theorizing: An approach where one begins with a set of observations, seeks patterns in those observations and then theorizes about them. Inductive theorizing is often contrasted with deductive theorizing.

Information Costs: The time and money required to obtain information. The idea that information is costly is a central component of bounded rationality theory and explains why individuals rely on heuristics or engage in satisficing decision-making.

Instrumental Rationality: A less cognitively demanding definition of rationality than procedural rationality, instrumental rationality assumes that individuals make decisions "as if" they were processing all relevant information for a decision, even if they are not. In other words, instrumental rationality presumes decision makers can use less effort and still arrive at choices that would have resulted from a more comprehensive reasoning process.

Integrative Complexity: A measure of the thought complexity of an individual, including how much one engages both sides of an issue and takes the perspective of others. Variations in integrative complexity among political leaders has been linked to different patterns in foreign policy decision-making.

Intergroup Emotions Theory: A theory that posits that cherished group identities become integral extensions of the self. This leads individuals to react emotionally to events, threats, and opportunities that impact the group even if they do not affect the individual directly.

Intergroup Threat Theory: A theory explaining the phenomena when members of one group believe that another group is in a position to cause harm to them either physically or symbolically. This perceived threat can cause members of a group to experience intense emotions, even if they are not personally at risk.

Invariance Assumption: A rational choice assumption that the order of information presented or processed should not affect the choice.

Issue Indivisibility: A situation in which a contested issue cannot be easily shared or split.

Levels of Analysis: Refers to different levels of explanation for political phenomena, such as the individual, group, coalition, or state. Different schools of thought presume different levels are most crucial for structuring political outcomes. Realists focus on the structure of the international system as a key driver of leader behavior, while liberals and institutionalists tend to focus on domestic and international institutions. Behavioral theories of international relations, in contrast, emphasize the roles of individuals and groups in shaping international outcomes.

Lexicographic Decision Rule: A rule that requires individuals to make a decision based only on the single dimension that is most important to them.

Likeability Heuristic: A heuristic in which individuals make decisions (such as when choosing among political candidates), based simply on the likeability of each choice rather than their issue positions, experience, or performance in office.

Likely Voter Model: A polling model used to enhance the accuracy of election predictions by adjusting the weights respondents have on the outcome based on their likelihood of actually casting a ballot.

Loss Aversion: The tendency to prefer avoiding losses. A central finding of prospect theory, loss aversion also implies that framing a choice as a loss (rather than a gain) will lead individuals to be more risk-accepting even when the two alternatives are actually equivalent in terms of expected utility. One speculation is that people hope to avoid losses because they are more painful than the satisfaction resulting from equal sized gains.

Materialism: A rational choice assumption that believes individuals are primarily focused on the maximization of individual material wealth and other concrete resources.

Mental Accounting: A cognitive bias that occurs when people think of money differently depending on where it came from or what it was used to purchase.

Milgram Experiment: A psychological experiment conducted by Stanley Milgram in 1963, in which he attempted to investigate the power of situational constraints to determine behavior. In particular, Milgram was interested in the power of authority to influence "normal" people to commit immoral acts. Participants in the study were required to administer ever-increasing levels of a shock to a student (unbeknownst to them, a confederate of the experimenters). Milgram ultimately concluded that there was nothing innately authoritarian about these particular individuals, but that many individuals may be induced by an authority figure to inflict extreme harm on others.

Minimal Group Paradigm: The discovery that even completely imaginary group distinctions can trigger group conflict, prejudice, and hostility. While early theories of intergroup conflict suggested that intergroup hostility would increase with real resource competition, subsequent studies have found that negative intergroup attitudes can form even in the absence of competition.

Moral Foundations Theory: A theory that suggests that there may be as few as five key dimensions on which values are grounded in all human groups across cultures: harm/care, fairness/reciprocity, in-group/loyalty, authority/respect, and purity/sanctity. The theory argues that those who ascribe importance to all five moral dimensions are much more likely to hold conservative belief systems, while those who score lower on the last three (in-group loyalty, respect for authority, and purity) are much more likely to be liberal.

Moral Hazard: The absence of an incentive for a leader or citizen to guard against serious risks because they are protected from the consequences of failure. For example, bailing out banks with taxpayer dollars during the Great Recession of 2008 after they made billions of dollars in risky home loans removes the incentive to avoid risky loans in the future.

Moral Values: Concepts or beliefs that pertain to desirable end states or behaviors, transcend specific situations, guide the selection or evaluation of behavior and events, and are ordered by relative importance.

Motivated Reasoning Theory: A theory that suggests that people have both accuracy and directional motives which shape their beliefs about the world. Directional motives, often designed to preserve self- or group-esteem, can motivate people to reject new information and defend their preexisting attitudes, even when they would benefit materially by changing their beliefs and thus adopting new attitudes. In the language of the theory, people often reason from their preexisting attitudes to their beliefs, rather than the other way around.

Naïve Realism: The biased but pervasive view that anyone who disagrees with us is uninformed, biased, or irrational while we perceive reality objectively.

Narrative Framing: A particular way in which a message weaves facts together; the way it lays out a persuasive narrative about why a particular problem occurred, who is to blame, and therefore who should fix it. Narrative-based framing produces much broader effects than frames which simply alter the salience of specific pieces of information.

New Institutionalism: An approach that argues that political institutions are neither a mirror of society nor strictly the realization of individual preferences, but rather autonomous factors that provide meaning and context to interactions. This theory argues that institutions could be thought of as political actors themselves that structure the scope of "appropriate" actions through their norms and formal rules, fundamentally constraining the freedom of choice of individuals.

Non-Common Priors: Differing beliefs at the outset of an interaction. This nonstandard assumption is sometimes incorporated into RCT models of political behavior to explain why beliefs may not converge at the end of a game.

(Non-)Compensatory Decision-Making: A non-compensatory pattern in decision-making is where a low score on one dimension cannot be compensated for by a higher score along another dimension (or multiple dimensions). Non-compensatory search patterns are a key feature of poliheuristic theory.

Non-Holistic Information Search: Decision-making processes where individuals do not consider all the relevant information and dimensions of a choice, often using the minimal amount of information they deem necessary to make an educated choice.

Norm Cascades: The process of how common conjectures change over time. Norm cascades occur when there is a rapid decline in the acceptability of a previously popular course of action.

Normativism: An approach to the study of politics that includes opinions or views involving the moral desirability of a policy outcome. Normativism is contrasted with positivist approaches, which seek to determine what *is* rather than what *ought to be*.

Nudging: The purposeful structuring of the architecture of a given choice that alters individuals' behavior *without* forbidding any options or significantly altering material incentives. Nudging has become an increasingly popular tool for policy-makers seeking ways to help citizens make better decisions without restricting choice.

Optimistic Overconfidence: A cognitive bias whereby individuals are overconfident in their own abilities, prospects, and control over their future, even if they know the general odds of success are much lower.

Operational Code: An individual's fundamental beliefs about the nature of politics and political conflict, their views regarding the extent to which historical developments can be shaped, and their notions of correct strategies and tactics.

Optimizing: A concept central to rational choice theory, whereby individuals use careful and exhaustive information search to make choices that provide the best possible payoff, given the structural constraints of the context.

Organizational Politics Models: An approach to the study of policy-making which emphasizes policies as "outputs" generated by standard operating procedures (SOPs) and other constraints and compromises inherent in the institutional structure, rather than as strictly conscious choices by individuals.

Over-Precision: A bias in which the decision maker underestimates uncertainty about the payoff of a specific outcome.

Paradox of Persuasion: A dilemma in which actors have an incentive to misrepresent their true capabilities or intentions in order to gain an advantage in bargaining. This means, many statements made by opposing sides in a dispute cannot be trusted on their face, since each has an incentive to lie. These incentives to misrepresent are hypothesized to be a central reason for violent conflict according to rationalist theories of war.

Paradox of Voting: The paradox that people expend resources to turn out to vote even when they have almost no chance of altering the outcome of an election. In almost every election with more than a few voters, casting a ballot seems individually suboptimal in terms of material utility.

Partisan Identification/Partisanship: Partisan identification is a deep emotional attachment to a party that can shape perceptions, attitudes, and behavior independent of social demographics, issue preferences, and political ideology. The strength of partisan identification challenges notions of democracy that depend on citizens remaining open-minded to new information and choosing candidates who support their issue preferences rather than simply bear the party standard.

Path Dependence: The dependence of future decisions on past decisions. Path dependence can have both rational and behavioral foundations. On the one hand, it may be costly to change course once a policy decision has been made. However, on the other, path dependence may be caused by cognitive biases such as sensitivity to sunk costs, leading individuals to continue pursuing strategies that are suboptimal.

Person–Situation Debate: A prominent scholarly debate in psychology about whether a person's character and personality or attributes of the specific situation are more influential causes of their behavior.

Poliheuristic Theory: A theory that suggests that when making decisions, leaders engage in a two-stage process. First, they use heuristics to reject any alternative that would result in a major loss on a key dimension (the *non-compensatory principle*), especially one that would damage them politically. Second, leaders maximize utility in choosing among the remaining alternatives or by using a lexicographic decision rule.

Poliheuristic Voting Rule: The process by which political candidates are first considered on a crucial, non-compensatory dimension. For example, an individual would first explore whether their favorite candidate can beat their political opponent in the general election. Candidates that fall short on this non-compensatory dimension will be removed from consideration, regardless of how well they match the voter's preferences. In the second stage of the voter's decision, remaining candidates will be assessed based on their overall score on all dimensions, or by using a lexicographic rule.

Polythink: A group decision-making dynamic in which members in a decision-making unit espouse a plurality of opinions and offer divergent policy prescriptions. This approach is the opposite of groupthink on the continuum of decision-making from "completely cohesive" (groupthink) to "completely fragmented" (polythink). It can result in a deadlock or in a suboptimal decision.

Positivism: An approach to the study of politics that seeks to objectively verify *facts* about the world – how the world *is* – without making claims about how the world *ought to be*. As such, positivism is often contrasted with normative approaches, which hold a particular opinion of viewpoint on what the state of the world should be.

Priming: A tactic to elevate the prominence of a certain issue or dimension of a choice. For example, when the news focuses on one issue at the expense of others, voters will often rank candidates on the salient issue dimension rather than other equally important issues. Because the first stimulus is not materially related to the second, it should not affect subsequent decision-making according to traditional RCT assumptions, but it nonetheless often does.

Principal-Agent Problem: Also known as the agency dilemma, principal-agent problems occur when an individual (the agent) is able to make decisions on behalf of another individual (the principal). The dilemma emerges when the interests of the principal and agent diverge, which can lead agents to act in their own best interests rather than the principal's. This leads to problems such as moral hazard.

Procedural Rationality: A strict interpretation of rationality in which an individual must hold complete and transitive preferences and process *all* available information relevant to a decision in order to calculate an optimal choice.

Prospect Theory: A theory which describes how individual choices are affected by the framing of a choice in terms of losses or gains. The central finding of prospect theory is that individuals will make decisions based on deviations from a reference point (e.g., the status quo) rather than based on absolute outcomes. Specifically, when a reference point frames a choice as a loss, individuals will be risk-accepting to attempt to avoid losing utility; however, when the same outcome is framed as a gain, individuals will be risk-averse and will hold on to what they have.

Pseudo-Environment: A term coined by Walter Lippman to describe human behavior as responding to the "imagined reality" created by the mass media rather than events in the real world. He speculated, quite presciently, that these mental pictures of the world may bear only limited resemblance to the real world, but nonetheless can powerfully shape political behavior.

Quantal Response Equilibrium: A solution concept in game theory that incorporates bounded rationality. In this equilibrium, individuals are assumed to make systematic errors in selecting their optimal strategies, and this affects the modal outcomes of their strategic interaction.

Rational Comprehensive Model: Lindblom's "rational" model in which decision makers analyze the costs and benefits from all possible approaches to solving the problem. This is contrasted with a subrational decision-making model of "successive limited comparisons," which Lindblom argues more accurately reflects the policy-making process.

Rational Egoism: The idea that individuals will try to do what is in their immediate self-interest by making choices that maximize pleasure and reduce pain.

Reactive Devaluation: A cognitive bias whereby a preferred proposal is devalued, or underrated, simply because it gets proposed by an adversary, even if it is identical in terms to a proposal offered by one's own side.

Realistic Group Conflict Theory: A theory that argues that conflicting group-level goals and competition for scarce resources are more likely to cause prejudice and intergroup hostility than unmet individual needs and wants. As such, negative intergroup attitudes should vary with the level of competition over resources in general, not whether the individual is doing well or poorly.

Realism: A foundational international relations theory that argues that (1) the nation state is the principal actor in international relations, (2) the state can be treated as unitary, (3) decision makers rationally pursue their states' interests and, (4) they make decisions in the context of international anarchy (e.g., no superordinate enforcement authority), which leads states to be fundamentally preoccupied with security.

Receive-Accept-Sample (RAS) Model: A model of public opinion and change in which an individual's opinions are response to cues from news media and trusted public officials. Individuals receive information from political elites according to how much attention they pay to the media and accept arguments that are consistent with prior beliefs or if they are one sided in a partisan sense. When making a decision about a novel stimulus, people sample from these existing considerations to arrive at a choice based on which seem most relevant or important in that moment.

Retrospective Voting: A form of voting in which voters punish or reward elected officials for past performance, even if it is unlikely to be related to future performance.

Reference Point: The benchmark or baseline against which individuals evaluate an alternative. Reference points, similar to anchoring heuristics, are centrally important in prospect theory.

Representativeness Heuristic: A rule of thumb whereby individuals assess the probability an object or person fits in a given category based on the degree to which they descriptively resemble a typical category member. This heuristic can lead to a bias whereby individuals ignore low base-rate probabilities that *any* individual belongs to a rare category, even if they look like those that do. For example, the likelihood that *anyone* is a criminal is quite low, even if they appear descriptively similar to one's stereotype of that category.

Revolving Framing: This refers to the introduction of different frames by political elites in order to identify the frame that is most effective in shaping public opinion to their advantage.

Right Wing Authoritarianism (RWA):   A measure of authoritarianism, a concept thought to explain prejudice and discrimination. Individuals higher in RWA tend to be more willing to submit to authority, adhere to societal conventions and norms, and express hostility toward people who break these norms.

Risky Shift: A phenomenon where individuals working in groups tend to take greater risks than they would have when making decisions individually. The reason this happens is contested, though there are a few plausible hypotheses: (1) Groups may diffuse responsibility and provide reassurance to each member so that risk is perceived to be shared; (2) High risk takers in the group tend to be more confident, and therefore more persuasive to others; (3) Social status is related to risk taking, so more cautious group members will fail to speak up against risky strategies.

Salami Tactics: A strategy that policy-makers use to set a new reference point in each key step in the negotiation process to gain more in the negotiation. Each "salami slice" incrementally and gradually moves the negotiator closer to his or her goal.

Satisficing: A decision-making strategy central to bounded rationality where individuals make choices that net them an outcome that is good enough – a minimum acceptability standard, but not necessarily the best they could have gotten with even more careful deliberation. The reason people satisfice is that information seeking is costly, and considering all relevant information is cognitively challenging.

Self-Confirming Equilibrium: A behavioral solution concept for game theoretic models that addresses the limitations of human processing abilities discovered by behavioral researchers. The self-confirming equilibrium explains that players' strategies can be best responses to their *beliefs* about other players, even if those beliefs are wrong. As a result, players may never observe behavior that contradicts their beliefs, even if their "off-equilibrium" beliefs (e.g., beliefs about things that never end up happening) are in fact wrong.

Sentiment Analysis: A content analytic technique that is used to assess the tone or emotions expressed in textual data. One could, for example, map changes and infer trends in negativity in the news media's coverage of politics over time using this technique.

Single Issue Voter: A voter who focuses on their most important issue, while immediately disqualifying candidates who do not come close to their preference on this issue, regardless of how much they approve of the candidate on other issues.

Social Dominance Orientation (SDO):   A measure of the degree to which society is naturally organized in a hierarchy where some groups dominate others. Individuals high in SDO therefore tend to espouse beliefs justifying inequality between groups, and approve of policies that maintain the status quo group hierarchy in their society.

Social Identity Theory (SIT):   SIT argues that social identities provide positive self-esteem such that individuals will feel better about themselves when their group is viewed favorably. In addition, the theory predicts that discriminatory or prejudicial behavior toward outgroups emerges spontaneously as soon as social categories are made salient, even in the absence of material competition.

Societal Norms: These capture conduct or opinions that a collective – its individual members and its entirety – consider acceptable within the group. The study of norms and how they change is frequently explored by researchers working in the constructivist approach to politics.

Source Credibility: The degree of trust different individuals place in various institutions and leaders. Information is more likely to be believed when it comes from a trusted source, especially when it contradicts the interests of the group to which the speaker belongs.

Spinning: A manipulative framing technique that works via the repetition of a particular consideration and the selective presentation of facts. This may lead voters to use that frame rather than others to understand a given problem, candidate, or issue.

Spiral Theories of Deterrence: These theories highlight the dangers of traditional deterrence theories that rely on adversaries properly interpreting the actions of an adversary in order to avoid conflict. They posit that, because states seeking to maintain their own security may seem like they are in fact aggressive, leaders will incorrectly assume opponents with "status quo" preferences are aggressively expansionist. This leads to a spiral of arms building and threats that increasingly risks a catastrophic conflict.

Standard Operating Procedures (SOPs):   A set of routines that different organizations develop to govern their day-to-day workflow. SOPs are typically most useful during periods of stability and familiarity, but can lead to suboptimal decisions during periods of upheaval or novel crises. This concept is key to the organizational politics model of decision-making.

Stanford Prison Experiment: A controversial study led by Philip Zimbardo at Stanford University in 1971, in which researchers tested the hypothesis that authority leads individuals to be cruel. Those participants assigned to be jailors were documented as behaving cruelly toward those randomly chosen to be inmates. The study's results have been questioned in recent years and raised various ethical concerns, but its insights on the role of situation rather than individual personality in augmenting behavior were considerable.

Statistical Discrimination: A term economists have developed to explain individuals' tendencies to stereotype based on differential base likelihoods of groups engaging in a given activity. This term is often contrasted with "taste-based" discrimination.

Stereotypes: An often normatively problematic heuristic in which people characterize individual cases based on superficial rather than detailed individual information. The most common example is group stereotypes, where an individual's behavior is judged based on (often false) beliefs about the group as a whole.

Structural Determinacy: An approach central to realist theories of politics that suggest that overarching features of the international structure will have a larger impact on the decisions of states than will individual differences between leaders. The "burning house" analogy is often used to characterize this idea – that anyone would run from a burning house – so there is no reason to learn about characteristics of individuals in these situations.

Sunk Costs Bias: When individuals rationalize subsequent decisions based on costs already paid, even though these can have no influence on the maximization of future utility.

Surveillance System: One of two information processing systems postulated by affective intelligence theory, the surveillance system is triggered during times of negative uncertainty. In these times, individuals might feel anxious, and this emotional reaction leads them to seek out new information and question standing assumptions about how the world works.

Symbolic Politics: Nonmaterial interests such as abstract values and identities that strongly influence an individual's political preferences. Often contrasted with explanations for political behavior that rely on material interests.

Taboo Trade-offs: Taboo trade-offs occur when an individual must compare the worth of two competing values that feel wholly incomparable, where even the consideration of trading off one for the other is inconceivable. For example, being asked how much money you would accept in return for a loved one would be considered a taboo trade-off, since the value of money and family are not comparable.

Taste-Based Discrimination: A term used to describe "real" prejudice, whereby individuals have an intrinsic animus against individuals of other racial backgrounds that structures their behavior toward these groups, regardless of the base likelihood the out-group member is a threat.

Thin Slicing: A decision-making process whereby individuals quickly and easily elaborate on very scant pieces of information about a person (e.g., a candidate for office), or object to make important decisions. The common example of this phenomenon is the saying "you never have a second chance to make a first impression."

Threat Framing: A framing tactic that highlights the danger of a situation in order to focus decision-making on that dimension and not on any positive opportunities associated with the situation or on other issues.

Top-Down Processing: A method of processing information by which an individual's existing beliefs will affect how they view new information, rather than new information changing their existing beliefs.

Trait Theory: The idea that people are born with innate tendencies to react to the world around them in consistent ways across situations. People with different traits may also react differently to the same situation.

Transitive Preferences: A key element of procedural rationality that characterizes an individual's preferences as logically ordered. Transitive preferences guarantee that individuals who prefer a to b and b to c, will prefer a to c.

Two Presidencies Theory: The theory that presidents have much more autonomy and freedom of action in the making of foreign policy than domestic policy and, as such, essentially have two distinct presidencies.

Type 1/Type 2 Error: A Type 1 Error occurs when an individual believes something happened when it did not, often referred to as a false positive test. Type 2 occurs when an individual does not believe something has happened when it did, often referred to as a false negative test.

Ultimatum Game: A canonical model used in game theory in which two parties interact only once. One party proposes an offer of how to divide a sum of money and the other party must decide whether to accept. If the second party does not accept the offer, neither party gets anything. The RCT equilibrium of this game is that the proposing party offers the smallest non-zero amount possible to the other party. However, experimental tests of this game often find that offers are often much closer to 50–50, illustrating how internalized norms govern individual behavior. Individuals appear to assign values to abstract ideas like fairness, which is usually considered beyond the scope of direct material interests.

Unitary Actor: An individual with a single and invariant set of preferences. The simplifying assumption of a "unitary actor" is often made in the subfield of international relations when theorists discuss the behavior of states.

Utility Function: A mathematical representation of the expected benefits/costs for each potential strategy. This function includes the potential value (or cost) of each of the outcomes to which a strategy may lead, multiplied by the probability that each of those outcomes occurs.

Valence Theory: An approach to the study of emotion that classifies emotions broadly as positive or negative. A valence approach to emotions typically assumes that emotions are immediate reactions to stimuli that occur prior to deeper, conscious awareness.

Valence-Arousal Model: A variation of valence theory that captures two dimensions of emotion, their valence (positive-negative), and their arousal (high-low) into an affective circumplex.

References

Abrahms, M. (2006). Why terrorism does not work. *International Security*, *31*(2), 42–78.

Acharya, A, Blackwell, M., & Sen, M. (2018). Explaining preferences from behavior: A cognitive dissonance approach. *The Journal of Politics*, *80*(2), 400–411.

Achen, C. H., & Bartels, L. M. (2017). *Democracy for Realists: Why Elections Do Not Produce Responsive Government* (vol. 4). Princeton, NJ: Princeton University Press.

Adorno, T. W., Frenkel-Brunswik, E., Levinson, D. J., & Sanford, R. N. (1950). *The Authoritarian Personality*. London: Verso Books.

Akerlof, G. A., & Kranton, R. E. (2000). Economics and identity. *The Quarterly Journal of Economics*, *115*(3), 715–753.

Aldrich, J. H. (1993). Rational choice and turnout. *American Journal of Political Science*, *37*(1), 246–278.

Alford, J. R., Funk, C. L., & Hibbing, J. R. (2005). Are political orientations genetically transmitted? *American Political Science Review*, *99*(2), 153–167.

Aliotta, J. M. (1988). Social backgrounds, social motives and participation on the US Supreme Court. *Political Behavior*, *10*(3), 267–284.

Allison, G. T., & Zelikow, P. (1971). *Essence of Decision: Explaining the Cuban Missile Crisis* (vol. 327, no. 729.1). Boston: Little, Brown.

Allison, G. T., & Zelikow, P. (1999). *Essence of Decision: Explaining the Cuban Missile Crisis*. New York: Longman.

Allport, G. W. (1937). *Personality: A Psychological Interpretation*. New York: Holt.

Altemeyer, B. (1981). *Right-Wing Authoritarianism*. Winnipeg, MB: University of Manitoba Press.

Althaus, S. L. (2003). *Collective Preferences in Democratic Politics: Opinion Surveys and the Will of the People*. Cambridge, UK: Cambridge University Press.

Ambady, N., & Rosenthal, R. (1992). Thin slices of expressive behavior as predictors of interpersonal consequences: A meta-analysis. *Psychological Bulletin*, *111*(2), 256–274.

Anderson, B. (1983). 1991. *Imagined Communities: Reflections on the Origin and Spread of Nationalism*. London: Verso.

Arendt, H. (1963). *Eichmann in Jerusalem*. London: Penguin.

Ariely, D., & Jones, S. (2008). *Predictably Irrational*. New York: Harper Audio.

Aronow, P. M., & Miller, B. T. (2016). Policy misperceptions and support for gun control legislation. *The Lancet*, *387*(10015), 223.

Arrow, K. (1973). The theory of discrimination. In O. Ashenfelter and A. Rees (eds.), *Discrimination in Labor Markets* (pp. 3–33). Princeton, NJ: Princeton University Press.

Ashworth, S. (2012). Electoral accountability: Recent theoretical and empirical work. *Annual Review of Political Science*, *15*, 183–201.

Ashworth, S., & Bueno de Mesquita, E. (2014). Is voter competence good for voters? Information, rationality, and democratic performance. *American Political Science Review*, 108(3), 565–587.

Ashworth, S., Bueno de Mesquita, E., & Friedenberg, A. (2018). Learning about voter rationality. *American Journal of Political Science*, 62(1), 37–54.

Astorino-Courtois, A., & Trusty, B. (2003). Degrees of difficulty: The effect of Israeli policy shifts on Syrian peace decisions. In A. Mintz (ed.), *Integrating Cognitive and Rational Theories of Foreign Policy Decision Making* (pp. 29–53). New York: Palgrave Macmillan.

Atran, S., Axelrod, R., & Davis, R. (2007). Sacred barriers to conflict resolution. *Science*, 317 (5841), 1039–1040.

Axelrod, R. (1986). An evolutionary approach to norms. *American Political Science Review*, 80 (04), 1095–1111.

Axelrod, R., & Hamilton, W. D. (1981). The naked emperor: Seeking a more plausible genetic basis for psychological altruism. *Science*, 211, 1390–1396.

Aytac, S. E., & Stokes, S. C. (2019). *Why Bother? Rethinking Participation in Elections and Protests*. Cambridge, UK: Cambridge University Press.

Baekgaard, M., Christensen, J., Dahlmann, C. M., Mathiasen, A., & Petersen, N. B. G. (2019). The role of evidence in politics: Motivated reasoning and persuasion among politicians. *British Journal of Political Science*, 49(3), 1117–1140.

Bali, V. A. (2007). Terror and elections: Lessons from Spain. *Electoral Studies*, 26(3), 669–687.

Ballew, C. C., & Todorov, A. (2007). Predicting political elections from rapid and unreflective face judgments. *Proceedings of the National Academy of Sciences*, 104(46), 17948–17953.

Banks, A. J. (2014). *Anger and Racial Politics: The Emotional Foundation of Racial Attitudes in America*. Cambridge, UK: Cambridge University Press.

Banks, A. J., & Valentino, N. A. (2012). Emotional substrates of white racial attitudes. *American Journal of Political Science*, 56(2), 286–297.

Bar-Hillel, M. (1980). The base-rate fallacy in probability judgments. *Acta Psychologica*, 44(3), 211–233.

Bar-Joseph, Uri & Levy, J. S. (2009). Conscious action and intelligence failure. *Political Science Quarterly*, 124(3), 461–488.

Baron, J., & Spranca, M. (1997). Protected values. *Organizational Behavior and Human Decision Processes*, 70(1), 1–16.

Barr, K. (2019). Change and continuity in Obama's Middle East Policy: An analysis of groupthink and polythink in Obama's Advisory Team. Paper presented at the annual meeting of the International Studies Association, Toronto, Canada. March 27.

Barr, K., & Mintz, A. (2021). Did groupthink or polythink derail the 2016 Raqqa offensive? The impact of group dynamics on strategic and tactical decision making. In A. Mintz & L. Terris (eds.), *The Oxford Handbook of Behavioral Political Science*. Oxford: Oxford University Press.

Bartels, L. M. (1996). Uninformed votes: Information effects in presidential elections. *American Journal of Political Science*, 40(1), 194–230.

Bartels, L. M. (2002). Beyond the running tally: Partisan bias in political perceptions. *Political Behavior*, 24(2), 117–150.

Bayes, R., Druckman, J. N., Goods, A., & Molden, D. C. (2020). When and how different motives can drive motivated political reasoning. *Political Psychology*, 41(5), 1031–1052

Bazerman, M. H., & Chugh, D. (2006). Decisions without blinders. *Harvard Business Review*, 84 (1), 88–97.

Bechara, A. (2004). The role of emotion in decision-making: evidence from neurological patients with orbitofrontal damage. *Brain and Cognition*, 55(1), 30–40.

Bendor, J. (2010). *Bounded Rationality and Politics*. Berkeley: University of California Press.

Bendor, J., Diermeier, D., Siegel, D. A., & Ting, M. M. (2011). *A Behavioral Theory of Elections*. Princeton, NJ: Princeton University Press.

Bendor, J., Kumar, S., & Siegel, D. A. (2010). Adaptively rational retrospective voting. *Journal of Theoretical Politics*, 22(1), 26–63.

Bennett, A., & Checkel, J. T. (eds.). (2014). *Process Tracing*. Cambridge, UK: Cambridge University Press.

Berezin, M. (2001). Emotions and political identity: Mobilizing affection for the polity. In J. Goodwin, J. M. Jasper, & F. Polletta (eds.), *Passionate Politics: Emotions and Social Movements* (pp. 83–98). Chicago: University of Chicago Press.

Berinsky, A. J. (2017). Rumors and health care reform: Experiments in political misinformation. *British Journal of Political Science*, 47(2), 241–262.

Berinsky, A. J., & Kinder, D. R. (2006). Making sense of issues through media frames: Understanding the Kosovo crisis. *Journal of Politics*, 68(3), 640–656.

Berkowitz, L. (1990). On the formation and regulation of anger and aggression: A cognitive-neoassociationistic analysis. *American Psychologist*, 45(4), 494–503.

BI Team (2011). Behavioural Insights Team Annual Report 2010–2011. Cabinet Office, ed. London, UK: Crown.

BIT Annual Report 2015–2016. www.bi.team/blogs/the-behavioural-insights-teams-update-report-2015-16/

Bloom, M. M. (2004). Palestinian suicide bombing: Public support, market share, and outbidding. *Political Science Quarterly*, 119(1), 61–88.

Bode, L., Budak, C. Ladd, J. M. et al. (2020). *Words that Matter: How the News and Social Media Shaped the 2016 Presidential Campaign*. Washington, DC: Brookings.

Bodenhausen, G. V., Sheppard, L. A., & Kramer, G. P. (1994). Negative affect and social judgment: The differential impact of anger and sadness. *European Journal of Social Psychology*, 24(1), 45–62.

Bolsen, T., & Druckman, J. N. (2018). Do partisanship and politicization undermine the impact of a scientific consensus message about climate change? *Group Processes & Intergroup Relations*, 21(3), 389–402.

Bowles, S. (2009). *Microeconomics: Behavior, Institutions, and Evolution*. Princeton, NJ: Princeton University Press.

Brader, T. (2005). Striking a responsive chord: How political ads motivate and persuade voters by appealing to emotions. *American Journal of Political Science*, 49(2), 388–405.

Brader, T., Valentino, N. A., & Suhay, E. (2008). What triggers public opposition to immigration? Anxiety, group cues, and immigration threat. *American Journal of Political Science*, 52(4), 959–978.

Brady, H. E., & Sniderman, P. M. (1985). Attitude attribution: A group basis for political reasoning. *American Political Science Review*, 79(4), 1061–1078.

Brannick, M. T., & Brannick, J. P. (1989). Nonlinear and noncompensatory processes in performance evaluation. *Organizational Behavior and Human Decision Processes*, 44(1), 97–122.

Brooks, S. M., Cunha, R., & Mosley, L. (2015). Categories, creditworthiness, and contagion: how investors' shortcuts affect sovereign debt markets. *International Studies Quarterly*, 59(3), 587–601.

Brulé, D. J. (2005). Explaining and forecasting leaders' decisions: A poliheuristic analysis of the Iran hostage rescue decision. *International Studies Perspectives*, 6(1), 99–113.

Brulé, D., & Mintz, A. (2006). Blank check or marching orders? Public opinion and the presidential use of force. In H. Starr (ed.), *Approaches, Levels, and Methods of Analysis in International Politics* (pp. 157–172). New York: Palgrave Macmillan.

Bueno De Mesquita, E. (2005). The quality of terror. *American Journal of Political Science*, 49(3), 515–530.

Bueno De Mesquita, E., Morrow, J. D., Siverson, R. M., & Smith, A. (1999). An institutional explanation of the democratic peace. *American Political Science Review*, 93(4), 791–807.

Bullock, J. G. (2009). Partisan bias and the Bayesian ideal in the study of public opinion. *The Journal of Politics*, 71(3), 1109–1124.

Bullock, J. G., & Lenz, G. (2019). Partisan bias in surveys. *Annual Review of Political Science*, 22, 325–342.

Burke, J. P. (2005). The contemporary presidency: Condoleezza Rice as NSC Advisor: A case study of the honest broker role. *Presidential Studies Quarterly, 35*(3), 554–575.

Cacioppo, J. T., Petty, R. E., Kao, C. F., & Rodriguez, R. (1986). Central and peripheral routes to persuasion: An individual difference perspective. *Journal of Personality and Social Psychology, 51*(5), 1032–1043.

Cahill, L., Weinberger, N. M., Roozendaal, B., & McGaugh, J. L. (1999). Is the amygdala a locus of "conditioned fear"? Some questions and caveats. *Neuron, 23*(2), 227–228.

Camerer, C. (1995). *Individual decision making.* In J. H. Kagel and A. E. Roth (eds.), *Handbook of Experimental Economics* (pp. 587–704). Princeton: Princeton University Press.

Camerer, C. F., Ho, T. H., & Chong, J. K. (2004). A cognitive hierarchy model of games. *The Quarterly Journal of Economics, 119*(3), 861–898.

Campbell, A., Converse, P. E., Miller, W. E., & Stokes, D. E. (1960). *The American Voter.* New York: John Wiley & Sons.

Campbell, D. T. (1965). Ethnocentric and other altruistic motives. In *Nebraska Symposium on Motivation* (vol. 13, pp. 283–311). Lincoln: University of Nebraska Press.

Canes-Wrone, B., Herron, M. C., & Shotts, K. W. (2001). Leadership and pandering: A theory of executive policymaking. *American Journal of Political Science, 45*(3), 532–550.

Canetti, D., Gross, M., Waismel-Manor, I., Levanon, A., & Cohen, H. (2017). How cyberattacks terrorize: cortisol and personal insecurity jump in the wake of cyberattacks. *Cyberpsychology, Behavior, and Social Networking, 20*(2), 72–77.

Capraro, V., & Barcelo, H. (2020). The effect of messaging and gender on intentions to wear a face covering to slow down COVID-19 transmission. *arXiv preprint arXiv:2005.05467.*

Carlyle, T. (1993). *On Heroes, Hero-Worship, and the Heroic in History* (vol. 1). Berkeley: University of California Press.

Carmen, I. H. (2007). Genetic configurations of political phenomena: New theories, new methods. *The Annals of the American Academy of Political and Social Science, 614*(1), 34–55.

Carney, D. R., Jost, J. T., Gosling, S. D., & Potter, J. (2008). The secret lives of liberals and conservatives: Personality profiles, interaction styles, and the things they leave behind. *Political Psychology, 29*(6), 807–840.

Casscells, W., Schoenberger, A., & Graboys, T. B. (1978). Interpretation by physicians of clinical laboratory results. *New England Journal of Medicine, 299*(18), 999–1001.

Ceron, A., L. Curini, S. M. Iacus, and G. Porro. (2014). "Every tweet counts? How sentiment analysis of social media can improve our knowledge of citizens' political preferences with an application to Italy and France." *New Media & Society, 16*(2), 340–358.

Cesarini, D., Dawes, C. T., Fowler, J. H., Johannesson, M., Lichtenstein, P., & Wallace, B. (2008). Heritability of cooperative behavior in the trust game. *Proceedings of the National Academy of Sciences, 105*(10), 3721–3726.

Cesarini, D., Dawes, C. T., Johannesson, M., Lichtenstein, P., & Wallace, B. (2009). Genetic variation in preferences for giving and risk taking. *The Quarterly Journal of Economics, 124*(2), 809–842.

Chatagnier, J. T., Mintz, A., & Samban, Y. (2012). The decision calculus of terrorist leaders. *Perspectives on Terrorism, 6*(4/5), 125–144.

Cheung-Blunden, V., & Blunden, B. (2008). The emotional construal of war: Anger, fear, and other negative emotions. *Peace and Conflict, 14*(2), 123–150.

Chong, D. (2000). *Rational Lives: Norms and Values in Politics and Society.* Chicago: University of Chicago Press.

Chong, D. (2013). Degrees of rationality in politics. In L. Huddy, D. O. Sears, & J. S. Levy (eds.), *The Oxford Handbook of Political Psychology* (2nd ed., pp. 96–129). Oxford, UK: Oxford University Press.

Chong, D., & Druckman, J. N. (2007). A theory of framing and opinion formation in competitive elite environments. *Journal of Communication, 57*(1), 99–118.

Christensen, T. J., & Snyder, J. (1997). Progressive research on degenerate alliances. *American Political Science Review*, 91(4), 919–922.

Collins, B. E., & Guetzkow, H. S. (1964). *A Social Psychology of Group Processes for Decision-Making*. New York: Wiley & Sons.

Collins, R. (1990). Stratification, emotional energy, and the transient emotions. In T. D. Kemper (ed.), *Research Agendas in the Sociology of Emotions* (pp. 27–57). Albany: State University of New York Press.

Comte, A. (1853). *The Positive Philosophy of Auguste Comte*. London: Chapman.

Conover, P. J. (1985). The impact of group economic interests on political evaluations. *American Politics Quarterly*, 13(2), 139–166.

Converse, P. E. (1964).The nature of belief systems in mass publics. In D. Apter (ed.), *Ideology and Discontent* (pp. 206–261). New York: Free Press.

Costa, P. T. Jr., & McCrae, R. R. (1992). Four ways five factors are basic. *Personality and Individual Differences*, 13, 653–665.

Craemer, T. (2008). Nonconscious feelings of closeness toward African Americans and support for pro-Black policies. *Political Psychology*, 29(3), 407–436.

Crawford, N. C. (2000). The passion of world politics: Propositions on emotion and emotional relationships. *International Security*, 24(4), 116–156.

Crenshaw, M. (1992). Current research on terrorism: The academic perspective. *Studies in Conflict & Terrorism*, 15(1), 1–11.

Cyert, R. M., & March, J. G. (1963). *A Behavioral Theory of the Firm*. Englewood Cliffs, NJ: Prentice-Hall.

Damasio, A. R. (1994). *Descartes' Error: Emotion, Reason, and the Human Brain*. New York: G. P. Putnam.

Davison, G., Roll, S. P., Grinstein-Weiss, M., Despard, M. R., & Bufe, S. (2018). *Refund to Savings 2015–2016: Field Experiments to Promote Tax-Time Saving in Low- and Moderate-Income Households (CSD Research Report No. 18–28)*. St. Louis, MO: Washington University, Center for Social Development.

Dawson, M. C. (1995). *Behind the Mule: Race and Class in African-American Politics*. Princeton, NJ: Princeton University Press.

Delli Carpini, M. X., & Keeter, S. (1996). *What Americans Know about Politics and Why It Matters*. Yale University Press.

DeRouen Jr., K. (2003). The decision not to use force at Dien Bien Phu: A poliheuristic perspective. In A. Mintz (ed.), *Integrating Cognitive and Rational Theories of Foreign Policy Decision Making* (pp. 11–28). New York: Palgrave Macmillan.

DeRouen Jr., K. R. (1995). The indirect link: Politics, the economy, and the use of force. *Journal of Conflict Resolution*, 39(4), 671–695.

DeRouen, K. (2000). Presidents and the diversionary use of force: A research note. *International Studies Quarterly*, 44(2), 317–328.

DeSteno, D., Petty, R. E., Rucker, D. D., Wegener, D. T., & Braverman, J. (2004). Discrete emotions and persuasion: The role of emotion-induced expectancies. *Journal of Personality and Social Psychology*, 86(1), 43.

DeSteno, D., Petty, R. E., Wegener, D. T., & Rucker, D. D. (2000). Beyond valence in the perception of likelihood: the role of emotion specificity. *Journal of Personality and Social Psychology*, 78(3), 397.

Devine, P. G. (1989). Stereotypes and prejudice: Their automatic and controlled components. *Journal of Personality and Social Psychology*, 56(1), 5.

Downs, A. (1957). *An Economic Theory of Democracy*. New York: Harper & Row.

Downs, A. (1957). An economic theory of political action in a democracy. *The Journal of Political Economy*, 65(2), 135–150.

Downs, G. W., & Rocke, D. M. (1994). Conflict, agency, and gambling for resurrection: The principal-agent problem goes to war. *American Journal of Political Science*, 38(2), 362–380.

Doyle, M. W. (1986). Liberalism and world politics. *American Political Science Review, 80*(4), 1151–1169.

Drew, E. (1991). Washington prepares for war. In M. L. Sifry & C. Cerf (eds.), *The Gulf War Reader: History, Documents, Opinions* (pp. 227–220). New York: Times Books.

Druckman, J. N. (2001). The implications of framing effects for citizen competence. *Political Behavior 23*(3), 225–256.

Druckman, J. N. (2004). Political preference formation: Competition, deliberation, and the (ir) relevance of framing effects. *American Political Science Review 98*(4), 761–86.

Druckman, J. N., & McDermott, R. (2008). Emotion and the framing of risky choice. *Political Behavior, 30*(3), 297–321.

Druckman, J. N., & McGrath, M. C. (2019). The evidence for motivated reasoning in climate change preference formation. *Nature Climate Change, 9*(2), 111–119.

Durkheim, E. (1973). *Emile Durkheim on Morality and Society*. Chicago: University of Chicago Press.

Eddy, D. M., & Clanton, C. H. (1982). The art of diagnosis: Solving the clinicopathological exercise. *New England Journal of Medicine, 306*(21), 1263–1268.

Efrat, A. (2016). Global efforts against human trafficking: The misguided conflation of sex, labor, and organ trafficking. *International Studies Perspectives, 17*(1), 34–54.

Einhorn, H. J. (1970). The use of nonlinear, noncompensatory models in decision making. *Psychological Bulletin, 73*(3), 221–230.

Einhorn, H. J. (1971). Use of nonlinear, noncompensatory models as a function of task and amount of information. *Organizational Behavior and Human Performance, 6*(1), 1–27.

Eisenband, D. (2003). Application of the poliheuristic theory of decision to the political negotiation process. Paper presented at the Nexus Between Domestic and International Relations conference, March, Texas A&M University, College Station, TX.

Enos, R. D. (2014). Causal effect of intergroup contact on exclusionary attitudes. *Proceedings of the National Academy of Sciences, 111*(10), 3699–3704.

Entine, J., & Randall, R. (2015). Scientific consensus on GMO safety stronger than for global warming. *Genetic Literacy Project,* January, 29.

Entman, R. M. (1993). Framing: Toward clarification of a fractured paradigm. *Journal of Communication, 43*(4), 51–58.

Erikson, R. S., MacKuen, M. B., & Stimson, J. A. (2002). *The Macro Polity*. Cambridge, UK: Cambridge University Press.

Erisen, C., Lodge, M., & Taber, C. S. (2014). Affective contagion in effortful political thinking. *Political Psychology, 35*(2), 187–206.

Farrell, J., & Rabin, M. (1996). Cheap talk. *The Journal of Economic Perspectives, 10*(3), 103–118.

Fearon, J. D. (1994). Domestic political audiences and the escalation of international disputes. *American Political Science Review, 88*(3), 577–592.

Fearon, J. D. (1995). Rationalist explanations for war. *International Organization, 49*(3), 379–414.

Fearon, J. D. (1997). Signaling foreign policy interests tying hands versus sinking costs. *Journal of Conflict Resolution, 41*(1), 68–90.

Fearon, J. D. (1994). Domestic political audiences and the escalation of international disputes. *The American Political Science Review, 88*(3), 577–592.

Feddersen, T., Gailmard, S., & Sandroni, A. (2009). Moral bias in large elections: Theory and experimental evidence. *American Political Science Review, 103*(2), 175–192.

Federico, C. M., & Deason, G. (2012). Uncertainty, insecurity, and ideological defense of the status quo: The extremitizing role of political expertise. In M. A. Hogg & D. L. Blaylock (ed.), *Extremism and the Psychology of Uncertainty* (pp. 197–211). Boston: Wiley-Blackwell.

Feldman, S. (1982). Economic self-interest and political behavior. *American Journal of Political Science, 103*(2), 446–466.

Feldman, S., & Stenner, K. (1997). Perceived threat and authoritarianism. *Political Psychology*, *18*(4), 741–770.

Feldman, S., Huddy, L., & Marcus, G. E. (2015). *Going to War in Iraq: When Citizens and the Press Matter*. Chicago: University of Chicago Press.

Festinger, L. (1956). *When Prophecy Fails: A Social and Psychological Study of a Modern Group that Predicted the Destination of the World*. New York: Harper & Row.

Festinger, L. (1962). *A Theory of Cognitive Dissonance* (vol. 2). Palo Alto, CA: Stanford University Press.

Fiorina, M. (1981). *Retrospective Voting in American National Elections*. New Haven, CT: Yale University Press.

Fisk, K., Merolla, J. L. , & Ramos, J. M. (2019). Emotions, terrorist threat, and drones: Anger drives support for drone strikes. *Journal of Conflict Resolution*, *63*(4), 976–1000.

Fiske, A. P., & Tetlock, P. E. (1997). Taboo tradeoffs: Reactions to transactions that transgress the spheres of justice. *Political Psychology*, *18*(2), 255–297.

Fiske, S. T. (1998). Stereotyping, prejudice, and dis-crimination. In D. T. Gilbert, S. T. Fiske, & G. Lindzey (eds.), *Handbook of Social Psychology* (4th ed., vol. 2, pp. 357–411). New York: McGraw-Hill.

Fiske, S. T. (2002). What we know now about bias and intergroup conflict: The problem of the century. *Current Directions in Psychological Science*, *11*(4), 123–128.

Fiske, S. T., Kinder, D. R., & Larter, W. M. (1983). The novice and the expert: Knowledge-based strategies in political cognition. *Journal of Experimental Social Psychology*, *19*(4), 381–400.

Flynn, D. J., Nyhan, B., & Reifler, J. (2017). The nature and origins of misperceptions: Understanding false and unsupported beliefs about politics. *Political Psychology*, *38*(S1), 127–150.

Fordham, B. (1998). Partisanship, macroeconomic policy, and US uses of force, 1949–1994. *Journal of Conflict Resolution*, *42*(4), 418–439.

Forman, E. H., & Selly, M. A. (2001). *Decision by Objectives: How to Convince Others that You Are Right*. Hackensack, NJ: World Scientific.

Fortna, V. P. (2015). Do terrorists win? Rebels' use of terrorism and civil war outcomes. *International Organization*, *69*(3), 519–556.

Fowler, J. H., & Schreiber, D. (2008a). Biology, politics, and the emerging science of human nature. *Science*, *322*(5903), 912–914.

Fowler, J. H., Baker, L. A., & Dawes, C. T. (2008b). Genetic variation in political participation. *American Political Science Review*, *102*(2), 233–248.

Fraga, B. L. (2018). *The Turnout Gap: Race, Ethnicity, and Political Inequality in a Diversifying America*. Cambridge, UK: Cambridge University Press.

Freed, G. L., Clark, S. J., Butchart, A. T., Singer, D. C., & Davis, M. M. (2010). Parental vaccine safety concerns in 2009. *Pediatrics*, *125*(4), 654–659.

Friedman, J. A. (2019). Priorities for preventive action: Explaining Americans' divergent reactions to 100 public risks. *American Journal of Political Science*, *63*(1), 181–196.

Friedman, M. (1953). The methodology of positive economics. *Essays in Positive Economics*, *3* (3), 145–178.

Friedman, M., & Savage, L. J. (1948). The utility analysis of choices involving risk. *Journal of Political Economy*, *56*(4), 279–304.

Frijda, N. H. (1986). *The Emotions: Studies in Emotion and Social Interaction*. Paris: Maison de Sciences de l'Homme.

Fudenberg, D., & Levine, D. K. (1993). Self-confirming equilibrium. *Econometrica: Journal of the Econometric Society*, *61*(3), 523–545.

Gabbat, A. (2017). How Trump undercuts his staff again and again. *The Guardian*, May 16.

Gadarian, S. K. (2010). The politics of threat: How terrorism news shapes foreign policy attitudes. *Journal of Politics*, *72*(2),469–483.

Gadarian, S. K., & Albertson, B. (2014). Anxiety, immigration, and the search for information. *Political Psychology*, *35*(2), 133–164.

Gaddis, J. L. (2002). Strategic Surprise. *Hoover Digest* (Issue 2): The Hoover Institution. www.hoover.org/research/strategic-surprise.

Galinsky, A. D., & Mussweiler, T. (2001). First offers as anchors: The role of perspective-taking and negotiator focus. *Journal of Personality and Social Psychology*, *81*(4), 657–669.

Gamson, W. A., & Modigliani, A. (1987). The changing culture of affirmative action. In R. A. Braumgart (ed.), *Research in Political Sociology* (pp. 137–77). Greenwich: JAI 3.

George, A. L. (1969). The "operational code": A neglected approach to the study of political leaders and decision-making. *International Studies Quarterly*, *13*(2), 190–222.

Getmansky, A. & T. Zeitzoff. (2014). Terrorism and voting: The effect of rocket threat on voting in Israeli elections. *American Political Science Review 108*(3), 588–604.

Geva, N., & Mintz, A. (eds.). (1997). *Decisionmaking on War and Peace: The Cognitive-Rational Debate*. Boulder, CO: Lynne Rienner Publishers.

Geva, N., DeRouen, K. R., & Mintz, A. (1993). The political incentive explanation of "democratic peace": Evidence from experimental research. *International Interactions*, *18*(3), 215–229.

Gifford, R. (2011). The dragons of inaction: Psychological barriers that limit climate change mitigation and adaptation. *American Psychologist*, *66*(4), 290–302.

Gigerenzer, G., & Hoffrage, U. (1995). How to improve Bayesian reasoning without instruction: Frequency formats. *Psychological Review*, *102*(4), 684–704.

Gilens, M. (2001). Political ignorance and collective policy preferences. *American Political Science Review*, *95*(2), 379–396.

Goldberg, L. R. (1990). An alternative "description of personality": The big-five factor structure. *Journal of Personality and Social Psychology*, *59*(6), 1216–1229.

Goldgeier, J. M., & Tetlock, P. E. (2001). Psychology and international relations theory. *Annual Review of Political Science*, *4*(1), 67–92.

Gould, E. D., & Klor, E. (2010). Does terrorism work? *Quarterly Journal of Economics 125*(4), 1459–1510.

Graham, J., Haidt, J., & Nosek, B. A. (2009). Liberals and conservatives rely on different sets of moral foundations. *Journal of Personality and Social Psychology*, *96*(5), 1029–1046.

Gray, J. A. (1990). Brain systems that mediate both emotion and cognition. *Cognition & Emotion*, *4*(3), 269–288.

Greenstein, F. I. (1967). The impact of personality on politics: An attempt to clear away underbrush. *American Political Science Review*, *61*(3), 629–641.

Greenstein, F. I. (1969). *Personality and Politics: Problems of Evidence, Inference, and Conceptualization*. Chicago: Markham Publishing Company.

Grinstein-Weiss, M., Cryder, C., Despard, M., Perantie, D., Oliphant, J., & Ariely, D. (2017a). The role of choice architecture in promoting saving at tax time: Evidence from a large-scale field experiment. *Behavioral Science & Policy*, *3*(2), 21–38.

Grinstein-Weiss, M., Roll, S. P., Pinto, O., Barkali, N., Gottlieb, D., & Gal, J. (2017b, December). Israeli Savings for Every Child Program (SECP). Presentation at the International Symposium on Inclusion in Asset Building: Policy Innovation and Social Impacts, Singapore.

Grinstein-Weiss, M., Russell, B. D., Gale, W. G., Key, C., & Ariely, D. (2017c). Behavioral interventions to increase tax-time saving: Evidence from a national randomized trial. *Journal of Consumer Affairs*, *51*(1), 3–26. http://doi.org/10.1111/joca.12114

Groenendyk, E. W., & Banks, A. J. (2014). Emotional rescue: How affect helps partisans overcome collective action problems. *Political Psychology*, *35*(3), 359–378.

Gross, J. J. (2014). *Emotion regulation: Conceptual and empirical foundations*. In J. J. Gross (ed.), *Handbook of Emotion Regulation* (pp. 3–20). New York: The Guilford Press.

Gruszczynski, M. W., Balzer, A., Jacobs, C. M., Smith, K. B., & Hibbing, J. R. (2013). The physiology of political participation. *Political Behavior*, *35*(1), 135–152.

Guess, A., & Coppock, A. (2020). Does counter-attitudinal information cause backlash? Results from three large survey experiments. *British Journal of Political Science, 50*(4), 1497–1515.

Gul, F., & Pesendorfer, W. (2001). Temptation and self-control. *Econometrica, 69*(6), 1403–1435.

Gul, F., & Pesendorfer, W. (2004). Self-control and the theory of consumption. *Econometrica, 72* (1), 119–158.

Gul, F., & Pesendorfer, W. (2016). Interdependent preference models as a theory of intentions. *Journal of Economic Theory, 165*, 179–208.

Gul, F., Pesendorfer, W., & Strzalecki, T. (2017). Coarse competitive equilibrium and extreme prices. *American Economic Review, 107*(1), 109–137.

Gunaratna, R. (2002). *Inside al Qaeda: Global network of Terror*. New York: Columbia University Press.

Gvosdev, N. K., Blankshain, J. D., & Cooper, D. A. (2019). *Decision-Making in American Foreign Policy*. Cambridge, UK: Cambridge University Press.

Hafner-Burton, E. M., Haggard, S., Lake, D. A., & Victr, D. G. (2017). The behavioral revolution and international relations. *International Organization, 71*(S1), S1–S31.

Hainmueller, J., & Hiscox, M. J. (2010). Attitudes toward highly skilled and low-skilled immigration: Evidence from a survey experiment. *American Political Science Review, 104*(1), 61–84.

Hainmueller, J., and D. J. Hopkins. (2014). Public attitudes toward immigration. *Annual Review of Political Science, 17*, 225–249.

Hall, T. H. (2011). We will not swallow this bitter fruit: Theorizing a diplomacy of anger. *Security Studies, 20*(4), 521–555.

Hall, T., & Yarhi-Milo, K. (2012). The personal touch: Leaders' impressions, costly signaling, and assessments of sincerity in international affairs. *International Studies Quarterly, 56*(3), 560–573.

Halperin, E., Porat, R., Tamir, M., & Gross, J. J. (2013). Can emotion regulation change political attitudes in intractable conflicts? From the laboratory to the field. *Psychological Science, 24*(1), 106–111.

Halperin, M. H., & Clapp, P. (2007). *Bureaucratic Politics and Foreign Policy*. Washington, DC: Brookings Institution Press.

Hammond, R. A., & Axelrod, R. (2006). The evolution of ethnocentrism. *Journal of Conflict Resolution, 50*(6), 926–936.

Hart, P. S., & Nisbet, E. C. (2012). Boomerang effects in science communication: How motivated reasoning and identity cues amplify opinion polarization about climate mitigation policies. *Communication Research, 39*(6), 701–723.

Hatemi, P. K., & McDermott, R. (eds.). (2011). *Man Is by Nature a Political Animal: Evolution, Biology, and Politics*. Chicago: University of Chicago Press.

Hatemi, P. K., Alford, J. R., Hibbing, J. R., Martin, N. G., & Eaves, L. J. (2009). Is there a "party" in your genes? *Political Research Quarterly, 62*(3), 584–600.

Healy, A. J., Malhotra, N., & Mo, C. H. (2010). Irrelevant events affect voters' evaluations of government performance. *Proceedings of the National Academy of Sciences, 107*(29), 12804–12809.

Herda, D. (2010). How many immigrants? Foreign-born population innumeracy in Europe. *Public Opinion Quarterly, 74*(4), 674–695.

Hermann, M. G. (1980). Explaining foreign policy behavior using the personal characteristics of political leaders. *International Studies Quarterly, 24*(1), 7–46.

Hermann, M. G. (2001). How decision units shape foreign policy: A theoretical framework. *International Studies Review, 3*(2), 47–81.

Hermann, M. G., & Preston, T. (1994). Presidents, advisers, and foreign policy: The effect of leadership style on executive arrangements. *Political Psychology, 15*(1), 75–96.

Herrmann, R. K., & M. P. Fischerkeller. (1995). Beyond the enemy image and spiral model: cognitive–strategic research after the cold war. *International Organization*, 49(3), 415–450.

Hetherington, M. J., & Weiler, J. D. (2009). *Authoritarianism and Polarization in American Politics*. Cambridge, UK: Cambridge University Press.

Hetherington, M., & Suhay, E. (2011). Authoritarianism, threat, and Americans' support for the war on terror. *American Journal of Political Science*, 55(3), 546–560.

Horowitz, M. C., Stam, A. C., & Ellis, C. M. (2015). *Why Leaders Fight*. Cambridge, UK: Cambridge University Press.

Huber, G. A., Hill, S. J., & Lenz, G. S. (2012). Sources of bias in retrospective decision making: Experimental evidence on voters' limitations in controlling incumbents. *American Political Science Review*, 106(4), 720–741.

Huddy, L., Feldman, S., & Cassese, E. (2007). On the distinct political effects of anxiety and anger. In G. E. Marcus, W. R. Neuman, & M. MacKuen (eds.), *The Affect Effect: Dynamics of Emotion in Political Thinking and Behavior* (pp. 202–230). Chicago: Chicago University Press.

Huddy, L., Feldman, S., Capelos, T., & Provost, C. (2002). The consequences of terrorism: Disentangling the effects of personal and national threat. *Political Psychology*, 23(3), 485–509.

Huddy, L., Feldman, S., Taber, C., & Lahav, G. (2005). Threat, anxiety, and support of antiterrorism policies. *American Journal of Political Science*, 49(3), 593–608.

Immelman, A. (2017). The leadership style of US President Donald J. Trump. *Working Paper*.

Iyengar, S. (1991). *Is Anyone Responsible? How Television Frames Political Issues*. Chicago: University of Chicago Press

Iyengar, S., & Westwood, S. J. (2015). Fear and loathing across party lines: New evidence on group polarization. *American Journal of Political Science*, 59(3), 690–707.

Iyengar, S., Sood, G., & Lelkes, Y. (2012). Affect, not ideology a social identity perspective on polarization. *Public Opinion Quarterly*, 76(3), 405–431.

James, P., & Oneal, J. R. (1991). The influence of domestic and international politics on the president's use of force. *Journal of Conflict Resolution*, 35(2), 307–332.

Janis, I. L. (1982). *Groupthink: Psychological Studies of Policy Decisions and Fiascoes* (vol. 349). Boston: Houghton Mifflin.

Jasper, J. M. (1998). The emotions of protest: Affective and reactive emotions in and around social movements. *Sociological Forum*, 13(3), 397–424.

Jefferson, H. J., Neuner, F. G., & Pasek, J. (2020). Seeing blue in black and white: Race and perceptions of officer-involved shootings. *Perspectives on Politics*. DOI: https://doi.org/10.1017/S1537592720003618

Jensen, M. C., & Meckling, W. H. (1976). Theory of the firm: Managerial behavior, agency costs and ownership structure. *Journal of Financial Economics*, 3(4), 305–360.

Jervis, R. (1976). *Perception and Misperception in International Politics* (vol. 49). Princeton, NJ: Princeton University Press.

Jervis, R. (1978). Cooperation under the security dilemma. *World politics*, 30(2), 167–214.

Jervis, R. (2009). Unipolarity: A structural perspective. *World Politics*, 61(1), 188–213.

Jervis, R., Lebow, R. N., & Stein, J. G. (1989). *Psychology and Deterrence*. Baltimore: Johns Hopkins University Press.

Johnson-Laird, P. N., & Oatley, K. (1992). Basic emotions, rationality, and folk theory. *Cognition & Emotion*, 6(3–4), 201–223.

Johnson, D. D. (2009). *Overconfidence and War*. Cambridge, MA: Harvard University Press.

Johnson, D. D., McDermott, R., Barrett, E. S., et al. (2006). Overconfidence in wargames: experimental evidence on expectations, aggression, gender and testosterone. *Proceedings of the Royal Society of London B: Biological Sciences*, 273(1600), 2513–2520.

Johnson, E. J., & Meyer, R. J. (1984). Compensatory choice models of noncompensatory processes: The effect of varying context. *Journal of Consumer Research*, 11(1), 528–541.

Johnson, R. T. (1974). *Managing the White House: An Intimate Study of the Presidency*. New York: HarperCollins Publishers.

Jones, B. D. (1994). *Reconceiving Decision-Making in Democratic Politics: Attention, Choice, and Public Policy*. Chicago: University of Chicago Press.

Jones, E. E., & Harris, V. A. (1967). The attribution of attitudes. *Journal of Experimental Social Psychology, 3*(1), 1–24.

Jost, J. T., & Amodio, D. M. (2012). Political ideology as motivated social cognition: Behavioral and neuroscientific evidence. *Motivation and Emotion, 36*(1), 55–64.

Jost, J. T., Glaser, J., Kruglanski, A. W., & Sulloway, F. J. (2003). Political conservatism as motivated social cognition. *Psychological Bulletin, 129*(3), 339–375.

Kahan, D. M. (2012). Ideology, motivated reasoning, and cognitive reflection: An experimental study. *Judgment and Decision Making, 8,* 407–424.

Kahneman, D. (2003). A perspective on judgment and choice: Mapping bounded rationality. *American Psychologist, 58*(9), 697–720.

Kahneman, D. (2011). *Thinking, Fast and Slow*. New York: Macmillan.

Kahneman, D., & Renshon, J. (2007). Why hawks win. *Foreign Policy, 158,* 34–38.

Kahneman, D., & Tversky, A. (1979). Prospect theory: An analysis of decision under risk. *Econometrica: Journal of the Econometric Society, 47*(278), 263–291.

Kahneman, D., & Tversky, A. (1984). Choices, values, and frames. *American Psychologist, 39*(4), 341–350.

Kalkan, K. O., Layman, G. C., & Uslaner, E. M. (2009). "Bands of others"? Attitudes toward Muslims in contemporary American society. *The Journal of Politics, 71*(3), 847–862.

Kant, I. (2015). *On Perpetual Peace*. Peterborough, ON: Broadview Press.

Keltner, D., Ellsworth, P. C., & Edwards, K. (1993). Beyond simple pessimism: Effects of sadness and anger on social perception. *Journal of Personality and Social Psychology, 64*(5), 740–752.

Kertzer, J. D. (2017). Microfoundations in international relations. *Conflict Management and Peace Science, 34*(1), 81–97.

Kertzer, J. D. (2020). Re-assessing elite public gaps in political behavior. *American Journal of Political Science. Early View.* https://doi.org/10.1111/ajps.12583

Kertzer, J. D., Holmes, M., LeVeck, B., Wayne, C. (n.d.). *Hawkish Biases and Group Decision Making*. Presented at The Weidenbaum Center Frontiers Virtual Workshop on Political Violence, Washington University in St. Louis. St. Louis: March 11, 2021.

Kertzer, J. D., Rathbun, B. C., & Rathbun, N. S. (2020). The price of peace: Motivated reasoning and costly signaling in international relations. *International Organization, 74*(1), 95–118.

Key Jr., V. O. (1949). *Southern Politics*. New York: Alfred A. Knopf.

Key, V. O. (1966). *The Responsible Electorate: Rationality in Presidential Voting 1936–1960.* Cambridge, MA: Belknap Press.

Kinder, D. R., & Kiewiet, D. R. (1979). Economic discontent and political behavior: The role of personal grievances and collective economic judgments in congressional voting. *American Journal of Political Science, 23*(3), 495–527.

Kinne, B. J. (2005). Decision making in autocratic regimes: A poliheuristic perspective. *International Studies Perspectives, 6*(1), 114–128.

Kissinger, H. A. (1984). *Nuclear Weapons and Foreign Policy*. Milton Park, UK: Routledge.

Kivetz, R. (1999). Advances in research on mental accounting and reason-based choice. *Marketing Letters, 10*(3), 249–266.

Koh, H. H., Chayes, A., Chayes, A. H., & Franck, T. M. (1997). Why do nations obey international law? *The Yale Law Journal, 106*(8), 2599–2659.

Kosfeld, M., Heinrichs, M., Zak, P. J., Fischbacher, U., & Fehr, E. (2005). Oxytocin increases trust in humans. *Nature, 435*(7042), 673–676.

Kraus, S. (1996). Winners of the first 1960 televised presidential debate between Kennedy and Nixon. *Journal of Communication, 46*(4), 78–96.

Kruger, D. J. (2003). Evolution and altruism: Combining psychological mediators with naturally selected tendencies. *Evolution and Human Behavior, 24*(2), 118–125.

Kuklinski, J. H., Quirk, P. J., Jerit, J., Schwieder, D., & Rich, R. F. (2000). Misinformation and the currency of democratic citizenship. *Journal of Politics*, 62(3), 790–816.

Kull, S., Ramsay C., & Lewis, E. (2003). Misperceptions, the media, and the Iraq war. *Political Science Quarterly*, 118(4), 569–598.

Kunda, Z. (1990). The case for motivated reasoning. *Psychological Bulletin*, 108(3), 480–498.

Kuru, O., Pasek, J., & Traugott, M. W. (2017). Motivated reasoning in the perceived credibility of public opinion polls. *Public Opinion Quarterly*, 81(2), 422–446.

Kurzban, R., DeScioli, P., & O'Brien, E. (2007). Audience effects on moralistic punishment. *Evolution and Human Behavior*, 28(2), 75–84.

Kurzban, R., Tooby, J., & Cosmides, L. (2001). Can race be erased? Coalitional computation and social categorization. *Proceedings of the National Academy of Sciences*, 98(26), 15387–15392.

Kydd, A. H., & Walter, B. F. (2006). The strategies of terrorism. *International Security*, 31(1), 49–80.

Lake, D. A., & Powell, R. (eds.). (1999). *Strategic Choice and International Relations*. Princeton, NJ: Princeton University Press.

Landau-Wells, M., & Saxe, R. (2020). Political preferences and threat perception: opportunities for neuroimaging and developmental research. *Current Opinion in Behavioral Sciences*, 34, 58–63.

Lasswell H. D. (1930). *Psychopathology and Politics*. Chicago: University of Chicago Press.

Lau, R., & Redlawsk, D. (2001). Advantages and disadvantages of cognitive heuristics in political decision making. *American Journal of Political Science*, 45(4), 951–971.

Lavine, H. G., Johnston, C. D., & Steenbergen, M. R. (2012). *The Ambivalent Partisan: How Critical Loyalty Promotes Democracy*. Oxford: Oxford University Press.

Lavine, H., Lodge, M., & Freitas, K. (2005). Threat, authoritarianism, and selective exposure to information. *Political Psychology*, 26(2), 219–244.

Lazarus, R. S. (1991). Cognition and motivation in emotion. *American Psychologist*, 46(4), 352–367.

LeDoux, J. (2003). The emotional brain, fear, and the amygdala. *Cellular and Molecular Neurobiology*, 23(4–5), 727–738.

Lerner, J. S., & Keltner, D. (2000). Beyond valence: Toward a model of emotion-specific influences on judgement and choice. *Cognition & Emotion*, 14(4), 473–493.

Lerner, J. S., & Keltner, D. (2001). Fear, anger, and risk. *Journal of Personality and Social Psychology*, 81(1), 146–159.

Lerner, J. S., & Tiedens, L. Z. (2006). Portrait of the angry decision maker: How appraisal tendencies shape anger's influence on cognition. *Journal of Behavioral Decision Making*, 19 (2), 115–137.

Lerner, J. S., Goldberg, J. H., & Tetlock, P. E. (1998). Sober second thought: The effects of accountability, anger, and authoritarianism on attributions of responsibility. *Personality and Social Psychology Bulletin*, 24(6), 563–574.

Lerner, J. S., Gonzalez, R. M., Small, D. A., & Fischhoff, B. (2003). Effects of fear and anger on perceived risks of terrorism a national field experiment. *Psychological Science*, 14(2), 144–150.

LeVeck, B. L., & Narang, N. (2017). The democratic peace and the wisdom of crowds. *International Studies Quarterly*, 61(4), 867–880.

LeVeck, B. L., Hughes, D. A., Fowler, J. H., Hafner-Burton, E., & Victor, D. G. (2014). The role of self-interest in elite bargaining. *Proceedings of the National Academy of Sciences*, 111(52), 18536–18541.

Levendusky, M. S. (2013). Why do partisan media polarize viewers? *American Journal of Political Science*, 57(3), 611–623.

Levy, J. S. (1992). An introduction to prospect theory. *Political Psychology*, 13(2), 171–186.

Levy, J. S. (1996). Loss aversion, framing, and bargaining: The implications of prospect theory for international conflict. *International Political Science Review*, 17(2), 179–195.

Levy, J. S. (1997a). Prospect theory and the cognitive-rational debate. In N. Geva & A. Mintz (eds.), *Decisionmaking on War and Peace: The Cognitive-Rational Debate* (pp. 33–50). Boulder, CO: Lynne Rienner.

Levy, J. S. (1997b). Prospect theory, rational choice, and international relations. *International Studies Quarterly*, 41(1), 87–112.

Levy J. S. (2013). The psychology of foreign policy decision-making. In Huddy, L., Sears, D. O., & Levy, J. S. (eds.), *The Oxford Handbook of Political Psychology* (pp. 301–333). Oxford: Oxford University Press,

Lewis-Beck, M. S., Norpoth, H., Jacoby, W., & Weisberg, H. F. (2008). *The American Voter Revisited*. Ann Arbor: University of Michigan Press.

Liberman, P., & Skitka, L. (2019). Vicarious retribution in US public support for war against Iraq. *Security Studies*, 28(2), 189–215.

Lieberfeld, D. (2005). Theories of conflict and the Iraq war. *International Journal of Peace Studies*, 10(2), 1–21.

Lindblom, C. E. (1959). The science of "muddling through." *Public Administration Review*, 19 (2), 79–88.

Lippmann, W. (1922). *Public Opinion*. New York: Free Press

Little, A. T. (2019). The distortion of related beliefs. *American Journal of Political Science*, 63(3), 675–689.

Little, A. T., Schnakenberg, K., & Turner, I. R. (2020). Motivated reasoning and democratic accountability. SocArXiv. June, 30.

Locksley, A., Hepburn, C., & Ortiz, V. (1982). Social stereotypes and judgments of individuals: An instance of the base-rate fallacy. *Journal of Experimental Social Psychology*, 18(1), 23–42.

Lodge, M., & Taber, C. S. (2005). The automaticity of affect for political leaders, groups, and issues: An experimental test of the hot cognition hypothesis. *Political Psychology*, 26(3), 455–482.

Lodge, M., & Taber, C. S. (2013). *The Rationalizing Voter*. Cambridge, UK: Cambridge University Press.

Lodge, M., McGraw, K. M., & Stroh, P. (1989). An impression-driven model of candidate evaluation. *American Political Science Review*, 83(2), 399–419.

Lucas, R. E., & Donnellan, M. B. (2009). If the person–situation debate is really over, why does it still generate so much negative affect? *Journal of Research in Personality*, 43(2), 146–149.

Luce, R. D., & Raiffa, H. (1958). *Games and Decisions: Introduction and Critical Survey*. New York: Wiley.

Lupia, A. (1994). Shortcuts versus encyclopedias: Information and voting behavior in California insurance reform elections. *American Political Science Review*, 88(1), 63–76.

Lupia, A., & Menning, J. O. (2009). When can politicians scare citizens into supporting bad policies? *American Journal of Political Science*, 53(1), 90–106.

Lupia, A., Levine, A. S., & Zharinova, N. (2010). When should political scientists use the self-confirming equilibrium concept? Benefits, costs, and an application to jury theorems. *Political Analysis*, 18(1), 103–123.

Lupia, A., McCubbins, M. D. , & Arthur, L. (1998). *The Democratic Dilemma: Can Citizens Learn What They Need to Know?* Cambridge, UK: Cambridge University Press.

Mackie, D. M., Devos, T., & Smith, E. R. (2000). Intergroup emotions: explaining offensive action tendencies in an intergroup context. *Journal of Personality and Social Psychology*, 79(4), 602–616.

Macrae, C. N., & Bodenhausen, G. V. (2000). Social cognition: Thinking categorically about others. *Annual Review of Psychology*, 51(1), 93–120.

MacWilliams, M. C. (2016). Who decides when the party doesn't? Authoritarian voters and the rise of Donald Trump. *PS: Political Science & Politics*, 49(4), 716–721.

Maoz, I., Ward, A., Katz, M., & Ross, L. (2002). Reactive devaluation of an "Israeli" vs. Palestinian" peace proposal. *Journal of Conflict Resolution*, 46(4), 515–546.

Maoz, Z. (1990). Framing the national interest: The manipulation of foreign policy decisions in group settings. *World Politics*, 43(1), 77–110.

Maoz, Z., & Russett, B. (1993). Normative and structural causes of the decentralized peace, 1946–1986. *American Political Science Review, 87*(3), 624–638.

March, J. G., & Olsen, J. P. (1983). The new institutionalism: Organizational factors in political life. *American Political Science Review, 78*(3), 734–749.

Marcus, G. E. (1988). The structure of emotional response: 1984 presidential candidates. *American Political Science Review, 82*(3), 737–761.

Marcus, G. E. (2002). *The Sentimental Citizen: Emotion in Democratic Politics.* University Park: Pennsylvania State University Press.

Marcus, G. E., & MacKuen, M. B. (1993). Anxiety, enthusiasm, and the vote: the emotional underpinnings of learning and involvement during presidential campaigns. *American Political Science Review, 87*(3), 672–685.

Marcus, G. E., Neuman, W. R., & MacKuen, M. (2000). *Affective Intelligence and Political Judgment.* Chicago: University of Chicago Press.

Marcus, G. E., Valentino, N. A., Vasilopoulos, P., & Foucault, M. (2019). Applying the theory of affective intelligence to support for authoritarian policies and parties. *Political Psychology, 40*(S1), 109–139.

Mason, L. (2015). "I disrespectfully agree": The differential effects of partisan sorting on social and issue polarization. *American Journal of Political Science, 59*(1), 128–145.

Matthews, G., Deary, I. J., & Whiteman, M.C. (2009). *Personality Traits.* Cambridge, UK: Cambridge University Press.

McAdams, D. P., & Pals, J. L. (2006). A new Big Five: Fundamental principles for an integrative science of personality. *American Psychologist, 61*(3), 204–217.

McCrae, R. R., & Costa, P. T. (1987). Validation of the five-factor model of personality across instruments and observers. *Journal of Personality and Social Psychology, 52*(1), 81–90.

McCright, A. M., & Dunlap, R. E. (2011). Cool dudes: The denial of climate change among conservative white males in the United States. *Global Environmental Change, 21*(4), 1163–1172.

McDermott, R. (2001). *Risk-Taking in International Politics: Prospect Theory in American Foreign Policy.* Ann Arbor: University of Michigan Press.

McDermott, R. (2004). Prospect theory in political science: Gains and losses from the first decade. *Political Psychology, 25*(2), 289–312.

McDermott, R. (2014). The biological bases for aggressiveness and nonaggressiveness in presidents. *Foreign Policy Analysis, 10*(4), 313–327.

McDermott, R., Johnson, D., Cowden, J., & Rosen, S. (2007). Testosterone and aggression in a simulated crisis game. *The ANNALS of the American Academy of Political and Social Science, 614*(1), 15–33.

McDermott, R., Tingley, D., Cowden, J., Frazzetto, G., & Johnson, D. D. (2009). Monoamine oxidase A gene (MAOA) predicts behavioral aggression following provocation. *Proceedings of the National Academy of Sciences, 106*(7), 2118–2123.

McKelvey, R. D., & Palfrey, T. R. (1995). Quantal response equilibria for normal form games. *Games and Economic Behavior, 10*(1), 6–38.

McMaster, C., & Lee, C. (1991). Cognitive dissonance in tobacco smokers. *Addictive Behaviors, 16*(5), 349–353.

Mearsheimer, J. J. (1995). A realist reply. *International Security, 20*(1), 82–93.

Mearsheimer, J. J. (2001). *The Tragedy of Great Power Politics.* New York: W. W. Norton & Company.

Mearsheimer, J. (2017). *Conventional Deterrence.* Ithaca, NY: Cornell University Press.

Miles, R. E. (1978). The origin and meaning of Miles' Law. *Public Administration Review, 38*(5), 399–403.

Milgram, S. (1963). Behavioral study of obedience. *The Journal of Abnormal and Social Psychology, 67*(4), 371–378.

Milgram, S. (1973). The perils of obedience. *Harper's Magazine, 247*(1483), 62–77.

Milner, H. V. (1997). *Interests, Institutions, and Information: Domestic Politics and International Relations.* Princeton, NJ: Princeton University Press.

Minozzi, W. (2013). Endogenous beliefs in models of politics. *American Journal of Political Science, 57*(3), 566–581.

Mintz, A. (1993). The decision to attack Iraq: A noncompensatory theory of decision making. *Journal of Conflict Resolution, 37*(4), 595–618.

Mintz, A. (2004). How do leaders make decisions? A poliheuristic perspective. *Journal of Conflict Resolution, 48*(1), 3–13.

Mintz, A. (2005). Are leaders susceptible to negative political advice? An experimental study of high-ranking military officers. In A. Mintz & B. M. Russett (eds.), *New Directions for International Relations: Confronting the Method of Analysis Problem* (pp. 223–238). Lahman, MD: Lexington Books.

Mintz, A. (2007). Why behavioral IR? *International Studies Review, 9*(1), 157–162.

Mintz, A., & Chatagnier, J. T. (2020). Poliheuristic theory: A middle ground between rational and cognitive decision theories. *Oxford Research Encyclopedia of Politics.* Oxford, UK: Oxford University Press.

Mintz, A., & Sofrin, A (2017). Decision making theories in foreign policy analysis. In *Oxford Encyclopedia of Foreign Politics.* Oxford, UK: Oxford University Press.

Mintz, A., & DeRouen Jr., K. (2010). *Understanding Foreign Policy Decision Making.* Cambridge, UK: Cambridge University Press.

Mintz, A., & Geva, N. (1993). Why don't democracies fight each other? An experimental study. *Journal of Conflict Resolution, 37*(3), 484–503.

Mintz, A., & Redd, S. B. (2003). Framing effects in international relations. *Synthese, 135*(2), 193–213.

Mintz, A., & Wayne, C. (2014). Group decision making in conflict: From Groupthink to Polythink in the war in Iraq. In P. T. Coleman, M. Deutsch, & E. C. Marcus, *The Handbook of Conflict Resolution: Theory and Practice* (pp. 331–352). San Francisco: Jossey-Bass.

Mintz, A., & Wayne, C. (2016). *The Polythink Syndrome: US Foreign Policy Decisions on 9/11, Afghanistan, Iraq, Iran, Syria, and ISIS.* Stanford, CA: Stanford University Press.

Mintz, A., Chatagnier, J. T., & Brulé, D. J. (2006). Being Bin Laden: An applied decision analysis procedure for analyzing and predicting terrorists' decisions. In A. Pedahzur (ed.), *Root Causes of Suicide Terrorism: The Globalization of Martyrdom* (pp. 172–198). Milton Park, UK: Routledge.

Mintz, A., Chatagnier, T., & Samban, Y. (2020). *Terrorist Decision-Making: A Leader-Centric Approach.* Milton Park, UK: Routledge.

Mintz, A., Geva, N., Redd, S. B., & Carnes, A. (1997). The effect of dynamic and static choice sets on political decision making: An analysis using the decision board platform. *American Political Science Review, 91*(3), 553–566.

Mintz, A., Mishal, S., & Morag, N. (2005). Victims of Polythink? The Israeli Delegation to Camp David 2000. Unpublished manuscript. *UN studies, Yale University.*

Mintz, A., Redd, S. B., & Vedlitz, A. (2006). Can we generalize from student experiments to the real world in political science, military affairs, and international relations? *Journal of Conflict Resolution, 50*(5), 757–776.

Mischel, W. (1973). Toward a cognitive social learning reconceptualization of personality. *Psychological Review, 80*(4), 252–283.

Mischel, W., & Shoda, Y. (1995). A cognitive-affective system theory of personality: reconceptualizing situations, dispositions, dynamics, and invariance in personality structure. *Psychological Review, 102*(2), 246–268.

Mishal, S., & Sela, A. (2006). *The Palestinian Hamas: Vision, Violence, and Coexistence.* New York: Columbia University Press.

Mondak, J. J. (2010). *Personality and the Foundations of Political Behavior.* Cambridge, UK: Cambridge University Press.

Morgan, T. C., & Bickers, K. N. (1992). Domestic discontent and the external use of force. *Journal of Conflict Resolution, 36*(1), 25–52.

Morrow, J. D. (1993). Arms versus allies: Trade-offs in the search for security. *International Organization, 47*(02), 207–233.

Morrow, J. D. (1999). The strategic setting of choices: Signaling, commitment, and negotiation in international politics. In D. A. Lake & R. Powell (eds.), *Strategic Choice and International Relations* (pp. 77–114). Princeton, NJ: Princeton University Press.

Morrow, J. D. (2002). The laws of war, common conjectures, and legal systems in international politics. *The Journal of Legal Studies, 31*(S1), S41–S60.

Morrow, J. D. (2007). When do states follow the laws of war? *American Political Science Review, 101*(3), 559–572.

Morton, R. (1991). Groups in rational turnout models. *American Journal of Political Science, 35*(3), 758–776.

Mueller, J. E. (1973). *War, Presidents, and Public Opinion.* New York: Wiley.

Mueller, J., & M. G. Stewart. (2012). The terrorism delusion: America's overwrought response to September 11. *International Security, 37*(1), 81–110.

Myerson, R. B. (1992). On the value of game theory in social science. *Rationality and Society, 4*(1), 62–73.

Nadeau, R., Niemi, R. G., & Levine, J. (1993). Innumeracy about minority populations. *Public Opinion Quarterly, 57*(3), 332–347.

Nelson, T. E., Clawson, R. A., & Oxley, Z. (1997). Media framing of a civil liberties controversy and its effect on tolerance. *American Political Science Review, 91*(3), 567–584.

Nelson, T. E., Oxley, Z. M., & Clawson, R. A. (1997). Toward a psychology of framing effects. *Political Behavior, 19*(3), 221–246.

Neuner, F. (2018). Elite Framing and the Legitimacy of Global Governance. Ph.D. thesis. University of Michigan.

Nincic, M. (1997). Loss aversion and the domestic context of military intervention. *Political Research Quarterly, 50*(1), 97–120.

Nyhan, B., & Reifler, J. (2010). When corrections fail: The persistence of political misperceptions. *Political Behavior, 32*(2), 303–330.

O'Curry, S. (1997). Income source effects. Unpublished working paper, DePaul University.

Ostrom C. W. (1978). A reactive linkage model of the US defense expenditure policymaking process. *The American Political Science Review, 72*(3), 941–957.

Ostrom, C. W., & Job, B. L. (1986). The president and the political use of force. *American Political Science Review, 80*(2), 541–566.

Oxley, D. R., Smith, K. B., Alford et al. (2008). Political attitudes vary with physiological traits. *Science, 321*(5896), 1667–1670.

Page, B. I., & Shapiro, R. Y. (1992). *The Rational Public: Fifty Years of Trends in Americans' Policy Preferences.* Chicago: University of Chicago Press.

Patel, M. (2021). Test behavioural nudges to boost COVID immunization. *Nature, 590*(7845), 185.

Payne, J. W. (1976). Task complexity and contingent processing in decision making: An information search and protocol analysis. *Organizational Behavior and Human Performance, 16*(2), 366–387.

Payne, J. W., Bettman, J. R., & Johnson, E. J. (1988). Adaptive strategy selection in decision making. *Journal of Experimental Psychology: Learning, Memory, and Cognition, 14*(3), 534–552.

Payne, J. W., Bettman, J. R., & Johnson, E. J. (1993). *The Adaptive Decision Maker.* Cambridge, UK: University Press.

Payne, R. A. (2014). Thinking the unthinkable about national security narratives. International Security and Arms Control Section of the American Political Science Association; Springfield, MA; October 9–10, 2014.

Pearlman, W. (2013). Emotions and the microfoundations of the Arab uprisings. *Perspectives on Politics*, 11(2), 387–409.

Penn, E. M. (2008). Citizenship versus ethnicity: The role of institutions in shaping identity choice. *The Journal of Politics*, 70(4), 956–973.

Peterson, E., & Iyengar, S. (2021). Partisan gaps in political information and information-seeking behavior: Motivated reasoning or cheerleading? *American Journal of Political Science*, 65(1), 133–147.

Phelps, E. S. (1972). The statistical theory of racism and sexism. *The American Economic Review*, 62(4), 659–661.

Phoenix, D. L. (2019). *The Anger Gap: How Race Shapes Emotion in Politics*. Cambridge, UK: Cambridge University Press.

Pierson, P. (2000). Increasing returns, path dependence, and the study of politics. *American Political Science Review*, 94(2), 251–267.

Posner, J., Russell, J. A., & Peterson, B. S. (2005). The circumplex model of affect: An integrative approach to affective neuroscience, cognitive development, and psychopathology. *Development and Psychopathology*, 17(3), 715–734.

Post, J. M. (2005). *The Psychological Assessment of Political Leaders: With Profiles of Saddam Hussein and Bill Clinton*. Ann Arbor: The University of Michigan Press.

Poulsen, L. N. S., & Aisbett, E. (2013). When the claim hits: Bilateral investment treaties and bounded rational learning. *World Politics*, 65(2), 273–313.

Powell, R. (2017). Research bets and behavioral IR. *International Organization*, 71(S1), S265–S277.

Pratto, F., Sidanius, J., Stallworth, L. M., & Malle, B. F. (1994). Social dominance orientation: A personality variable predicting social and political attitudes. *Journal of Personality and Social Psychology*, 67(4), 741–763.

Price, V., & Tewksbury, D. (1997). News values and public opinion: A theoretical account of media priming and framing. In G. A. Barnett & F. J. Boster (eds.), *Progress in Communication Sciences* (vol. 13, pp. 173–212). New York: Ablex.

Prior, M. (2007). *Post-Broadcast Democracy: How Media Choice Increases Inequality in Political Involvement and Polarizes Elections*. Cambridge, UK: Cambridge University Press.

Prior, M., Sood, G., & Khanna, K. (2015). You cannot be serious: The impact of accuracy incentives on partisan bias in reports of economic perceptions. *Quarterly Journal of Political Science*, 10(4), 489–518.

Pronin, E., Gilovich, T., & Ross, L. (2004). Objectivity in the eye of the beholder: divergent perceptions of bias in self versus others. *Psychological Review*, 111(3), 781–799.

Putnam, R. D. (1988). Diplomacy and domestic politics: The logic of two-level games. *International organization*, 42(3), 427–460.

Redd, S. B. (2002). The influence of advisers on foreign policy decision making: An experimental study. *Journal of Conflict Resolution*, 46(3), 335–364.

Redd, S. B. (2005). The influence of advisers and decision strategies on foreign policy choices: President Clinton's decision to use force in Kosovo. *International Studies Perspectives*, 6(1), 129–150.

Redlawsk, D. P. (2002). Hot cognition or cool consideration? Testing the effects of motivated reasoning on political decision making. *The Journal of Politics*, 64(4), 1021–1044.

Reicher, S., & Haslam, S. A. (2006). Rethinking the psychology of tyranny: The BBC prison study. *British Journal of Social Psychology*, 45(1), 1–40.

Renshon, J., & Kahneman, D. (2017). Hawkish biases and the interdisciplinary study of conflict decision-making. In S. A. Yetiv & P. James (eds.), *Advancing Interdisciplinary Approaches to International Relations* (pp. 51–81). London: Palgrave Macmillan.

Renshon, J., & Lerner, J. S. (2012). The role of emotions in foreign policy decision making. In D. J. Christie (ed.), *Encyclopedia of Peace Psychology* (pp. 313–317). Hoboken, NJ: Wiley-Blackwell.

Renshon, J., Lee, J. J., & Tingley, D. (2015). Physiological arousal and political beliefs. *Political Psychology*, 36(5), 569–585.

Riker, W. H., & Ordeshook, P. C. (1968). A theory of the calculus of voting. *American Political Science Review*, 62(1), 25–42.

Risse, T., & Sikkink, K. (1999). The socialization of international human rights norms into domestic practices: introduction. In T. Risse, K. Sikkink, & S. C. Ropp (eds.), *The Power of Human Rights: International Norms and Domestic Change* (pp. 1–38). Cambridge, UK: Cambriddge University Press.

Rokeach, M. (1973). *The Nature of Human Values*. New York: Free Press.

Roseman, I. J. (1984). Cognitive determinants of emotion: A structural theory. *Review of Personality & Social Psychology*, 5, 11–36.

Roseman, I. J. (1996). Appraisal determinants of emotions: Constructing a more accurate and comprehensive theory. *Cognition & Emotion*, 10(3), 241–278.

Rosenstone, S. J. H., Rosenstone, J. M. J., & Hansen, J. M. (1993). *Mobilization, Participation, and Democracy in America*. New York: Macmillan Publishing Company.

Ross, L. (1977). The intuitive psychologist and his shortcomings. In L. Berkowitz (ed.), *Advances in Experimental Social Psychology* (pp. 173–220). New York: Academic Press.

Rubin, J. Z., & Brown, B. R. (2013). *The Social Psychology of Bargaining and Negotiation*. New York: Academic Press.

Russett, B. (1993a). Can a democratic peace be built? *International Interactions*, 18(3), 277–282.

Russett, B. (1993b). *Grasping the Democratic Peace: Principles for a Post-Cold War World*. Princeton, NJ: Princeton University Press.

Russett, B. & Graham, T. (1989). Public opinion and national security policy. In M. I. Midlarsky. (ed.), *The Handbook of War Studies* (pp. 239–258). Ann Arbor: Michigan University Press.

Ryan, T. J. (2017). No compromise: Political consequences of moralized attitudes. *American Journal of Political Science*, 61(2), 409–423.

Sage, A. P., & Palmer, J. D. (1990). *Software Systems Engineering*. Hoboken, NJ: Wiley-Interscience.

Sartori, A. E. (2002). The might of the pen: A reputational theory of communication in international disputes. *International Organization*, 56(1), 121–149.

Saunders, E. N. (2017). No substitute for experience: Presidents, advisers, and information in group decision making. *International Organization*, 71(S1), S219-S247.

Scherer, K. R. (1999). Appraisal theory. In T. Dalgleish & M. J. Power (eds.), *Handbook of Cognition and Emotion* (pp. 637–663). Hoboken, NJ: John Wiley & Sons.

Schultz, K. A., & Weingast, B. R. (2003). The democratic advantage: institutional foundations of financial power in international competition. *International Organization*, 57(1), 3–42.

Schwartz, S. H. (1992). Universals in the content and structure of values: Theoretical advances and empirical tests in 20 countries. *Advances in Experimental Social Psychology*, 25, 1–65.

Schwartz, S. H., & Bilsky, W. (1987). Toward a universal psychological structure of human values. *Journal of Personality and Social Psychology*, 53(3), 550–562.

Schwartz, S. H., & Bilsky, W. (1990). Toward a theory of the universal content and structure of values: Extensions and cross-cultural replications. *Journal of Personality and Social Psychology*, 58(5), 878–891.

Sears, D. O., & Citrin, J. (1985). *Tax Revolt: Something for Nothing in California*. Cambridge, MA: Harvard University Press.

Sears, D. O., & Funk, C. L. (1990). The limited effect of economic self-interest on the political attitudes of the mass public. *Journal of Behavioral Economics*, 19(3), 247–271.

Sears, D. O., & Lau, R. R. (1983). Inducing apparently self-interested political preferences. *American Journal of Political Science*, 27(2), 223–252.

Sears, D. O., Hensler, C.P., & Speer, L. K. (1979). "Whites' opposition to "busing": Self-interest or symbolic politics? *American Political Science Review* 73(2), 369–384.

Sears, D. O., Lau, R. R., Tyler, T. R., & Allen, Jr., H. M. (1980). Self-interest vs. symbolic politics in policy attitudes and presidential voting. *American Political Science Review*, 74(3), 670–684.

Sell, A., Tooby, J., & Cosmides, L. (2009). Formidability and the logic of human anger. *Proceedings of the National Academy of Sciences*, 106(35), 15073–15078.

Seul, J. R. (1999). "Ours is the way of god": Religion, identity, and intergroup conflict. *Journal of Peace Research*, 36(5), 553–569.

Shay, S. (2017). *The Globalization of Terror: The Challenge of Al-Qaida and the Response of the International Community*. Milton Park, UK: Routledge.

Sheffer, L., Loewen, P. J., Soroka, S., Walgrave, S., & Sheafer, T. (2018). Nonrepresentative representatives: An experimental study of the decision making of elected politicians. *American Political Science Review*, 112(2), 302–321.

Sherif, M., Harvey, O. J., White, B. J., Hood, W. R., & Sherif, C. W. (1961). *Intergroup Cooperation and Competition: The Robbers Cave experiment* (Vol. 10). Norman, OK: The University Book Exchange.

Sibley, C. G., & Duckitt, J. (2008). Personality and prejudice: A meta-analysis and theoretical review. *Personality and Social Psychology Review*, 12(3), 248–279.

Sidanius, J. (1993). The psychology of group conflict and the dynamics of oppression: A social dominance perspective. In S. Iyengar & W. J. McGuire (eds.), *Duke Studies in Political Psychology: Explorations in Political Psychology* (pp. 183–219). Durham, NC: Duke University Press.

Sides, J., & Citrin, J. (2007). European opinion about immigration: The role of identities, interests and information. *British Journal of Political Science*, 37(03), 477–504.

Sigelman, L., & Niemi, R. G. (2001). Innumeracy about minority populations: African Americans and whites compared. *The Public Opinion Quarterly*, 65(1), 86–94.

Simon, H. A. (1955). A behavioral model of rational choice. *The Quarterly Journal of Economics*, 69(1), 99–118.

Simon, H. A. (1956). Rational choice and the structure of the environment. *Psychological Review*, 63(2), 129–138.

Simon, H. A. (1967). Motivational and emotional controls of cognition. *Psychological Review*, 74 (1), 29–39.

Sinclair, S, & Antonius, D. (eds.). (2013). *The Political Psychology of Terrorism Fears*. Oxford: Oxford University Press.

Singer, J. D. (1972). The "Correlates of War" Project: Interim report and rationale. *World Politics*, 24(2), 243–270.

Sivak, M., & Flannagan, M. J. (2004). Consequences for road traffic fatalities of the reduction in flying following September 11, 2001. *Transportation Research Part F: Traffic Psychology and Behaviour*, 7(4), 301–305.

Skitka, L. J, Bauman, C. W., Aramovich, N. P & Morgan, G. S. (2006). Confrontational and preventative policy responses to terrorism: Anger wants a fight and fear wants "them" to go away. *Basic and Applied Social Psychology*, 28(4), 375–384.

Slantchev, B. L., & Tarar, A. (2011). Mutual optimism as a rationalist explanation of war." *American Journal of Political Science*, 55(1), 135–148.

Smirnov, O., Arrow, H., Kennett, D. , & Orbell, J. (2007). Ancestral war and the evolutionary origins of "heroism." *The Journal of Politics*, 69(4), 927–940.

Smith, A., & Stam, A. C. (2004). Bargaining and the nature of war. *Journal of Conflict Resolution*, 48(6), 783–813.

Smith, E. R., Seger, C. R., & Mackie, D. M. (2007). Can emotions be truly group level? Evidence regarding four conceptual criteria. *Journal of Personality and Social Psychology*, 93(3), 431–446.

Smith, K. & Hibbing, A. (2011). The mind-body connection. In P. K. Hatemi & R. McDermott (eds.), *Man Is by Nature a Political Animal: Evolution, Biology, and Politics* (pp. 224–246). Chicago: University of Chicago Press.

Smith, K. B., Alford, J. R., Hibbing, J. R., Martin, N. G., & Hatemi, P. K. (2016). Intuitive ethics and political orientations: Testing moral foundations as a theory of political ideology. *American Journal of Political Science*, *61*(2), 424–437.

Smith, K. B., Oxley, D., Hibbing, M. V., Alford, J. R., & Hibbing, J. R. (2011). Disgust sensitivity and the neurophysiology of left-right political orientations. *PloS one*, *6*(10), e25552.

Sniderman, P. M., & Theriault, S. M. (2004). The structure of political argument and the logic of issue framing. In W. E. Saris & P. M. Sniderman, *Studies in Public Opinion: Attitudes, Nonattitudes, Measurement Error, and Change* (pp. 133–165). Princeton, NJ: Princeton University Press.

Sofrin, A. (2019). A Two-Group Decision Making Model on Military Intervention. Ph.D. dissertation. Hebrew University of Jerusalem.

Soroka, S. N. (2006). Good news and bad news: Asymmetric responses to economic information. *Journal of Politics*, *68*(2), 372–385.

Spencer, H. (1898). *The Principles of Sociology* (vol. 1). New York: D. Appleton and Company.

Spezio, M. L., Rangel, A., Alvarez, R. M., et al. (2008). A neural basis for the effect of candidate appearance on election outcomes. *Social Cognitive and Affective Neuroscience*, *3* (4), 344–352.

Stein, A. (2019). America's almost withdrawal from Syria. *War on Rocks, Texas National Security Review*, Jan 29.

Stenner, K. (2005). *The Authoritarian Dynamic*. Cambridge, UK: Cambridge University Press.

Stephan, W. G., & Stephan, C. W. (2000). An integrated threat theory of prejudice. In S. Oskamp (ed.), *Reducing Prejudice and Discrimination* (pp. 23–45). Mahwah, NJ: Lawrence Erlbaum Associates Publishers.

Stephan, W. G., Ybarra, O., Morrison, K. R. (2009). Intergroup threat theory. In T. D. Nelson (ed.), *Handbook of Prejudice, Stereotyping, and Discrimination* (pp. 43–59). London: Psychology Press.

Stimson, J. A., MacKuen, M. B., & Erikson, R. S. (1995). Dynamic representation. *American Political Science Review*, *89*(03), 543–565.

Stone, W. F., & Schaffner, P. E. (1988). *The Psychology of Politics*. New York: Springer-Verlag

Stoner, J. A. (1968). Risky and cautious shifts in group decisions: The influence of widely held values. *Journal of Experimental Social Psychology*, *4*(4), 442–459.

Stoner, J. A. F. (1961). *A Comparison of Individual and Group Decisions Involving Risk*, Ph.D. dissertation, Massachusetts Institute of Technology.

Suedfeld, P., & Tetlock, P. (1977). Integrative complexity of communications in international crises. *Journal of Conflict Resolution*, *21*(1), 169–184.

Suedfeld, P., Tetlock, P. E., & Ramirez, C. (1977). War, peace, and integrative complexity UN Speeches on the Middle East Problem, 1947–1976. *Journal of Conflict Resolution*, *21*(3), 427–442.

Sullivan, C. R., & Muetze, A. (2007). Simulation model of common-mode chokes for high-power applications. In *Industry Applications Conference, 2007. 42nd IAS Annual Meeting. Conference Record of the 2007 IEEE* (pp. 1810–1815). IEEE.

Sunstein, C. R. (1996). Social norms and social roles. *Columbia Law Review*, *96*(4), 903–968.

Sunstein, C. R. (1997). Behavioral analysis of law. *The University of Chicago Law Review*, *64*(4), 1175–1195.

Svensson, I. (2007). Fighting with faith: Religion and conflict resolution in civil wars. *Journal of Conflict Resolution*, *51*(6), 930–949.

Taber, C. S., & Lodge, M. (2006). Motivated skepticism in the evaluation of political beliefs. *American Journal of Political Science*, *50*(3), 755–769.

Tajfel, H., & Turner, J. C. (1986). The social identity theory of inter group behavior. In S. Worchel & W. G. Austin (eds.), *Psychology of Intergroup Relations* (pp. 7–24). Chicago: Hall Publishers.

Tajfel, H., Turner, J. C., Austin, W. G., & Worchel, S. (1979). An integrative theory of intergroup conflict. In M. J. Hatch & M. Schultz (eds.), *Organizational Identity: A Reader* (pp. 56–65). Oxford: Oxford University Press.

Taylor, S. E., & Brown, J. D. (1988). Illusion and well-being: A social psychological perspective on mental health. *Psychological Bulletin, 103*(2), 193–210.

Tetlock, P. (2005). *Expert Political Judgment: How Good Is It? How Can We Know?* Princeton, NJ: Princeton University Press.

Tetlock, P. E., Kristel, O. V., Elson, S. B., Green, M. C., & Lerner, J. S. (2000). The psychology of the unthinkable: taboo trade-offs, forbidden base rates, and heretical counterfactuals. *Journal of Personality and Social Psychology, 78*(5), 853–870.

Thaler, R. H. (1985). Mental accounting and consumer choice. *Marketing Science, 4*(3), 199–214.

Thaler, R. H. (1999). Mental accounting matters. *Journal of Behavioral Decision Making, 12*(3), 183–206.

Thaler, R. H. (2008). Mental accounting and consumer choice. *Marketing Science, 27*(1), 15–25.

Thaler, R. H., & Sunstein, C. R. (2008). *Nudge: Improving Decisions about Health, Wealth, and Happiness.* New Haven, CT: Yale University Press.

't Hart, P. T., Stern, E. K., & Sundelius, B. (1997). *Beyond Groupthink: Political Group Dynamics and Foreign Policymaking.* Ann Arbor: University of Michigan Press.

Thayer, B. A. (2004). *Darwin and International Relations: On the Evolutionary Origins of War and Ethnic Conflict.* Lexington: The University Press of Kentucky.

Thomas, J. (2014). Rewarding bad behavior: How governments respond to terrorism in civil war. *American Journal of Political Science, 58*(4), 804–818.

Tiedens, L. Z. (2001). Anger and advancement versus sadness and subjugation: The effect of negative emotion expressions on social status conferral. *Journal of Personality and Social Psychology, 80*(1), 86–94.

Tiedens, L. Z., & Linton, S. (2001). Judgment under emotional certainty and uncertainty: The effects of specific emotions on information processing. *Journal of Personality and Social Psychology, 81*(6), 973–988.

Tingley, D. H., & Walter, B. F. (2011a). The effect of repeated play on reputation building: An experimental approach. *International Organization, 65*(02), 343–365.

Tingley, D. H., & Walter, B. F. (2011b). Can cheap talk deter? An experimental analysis. *Journal of Conflict Resolution, 55*(6), 996–1020.

Todorov, A., Mandisodza, A. N., Goren, A., & Hall, C. C. (2005). Inferences of competence from faces predict election outcomes. *Science, 308*(5728), 1623–1626.

Tooby, J., & Cosmides, L. (1990). The past explains the present: Emotional adaptations and the structure of ancestral environments. *Ethology and Sociobiology, 11*(4–5), 375–424.

Trivers, R. L. (1971). The evolution of reciprocal altruism. *The Quarterly Review of Biology, 46* (1), 35–57.

Tumasjan, A., Sprenger, T. O., Sandner, P. G., & Welpe, I. M. (2010). Predicting elections with twitter: What 140 characters reveal about political sentiment. In *Fourth international AAAI conference on weblogs and social media.*

Tversky, A. (1972). Elimination by aspects: A theory of choice. *Psychological Review, 79*(4), 281–299.

Tversky, A., & Kahneman, D. (1973). Availability: A heuristic for judging frequency and probability. *Cognitive Psychology, 5*(2), 207–232.

Tversky, A., & Kahneman, D. (1974). Judgment under uncertainty: Heuristics and biases. *Science, 185*(4157), 1124–1131.

Valentino, N. A. and F. G. Neuner. (2017). Why the sky didn't fall: Mobilizing anger in reaction to voter id laws. *Political Psychology, 38*(2), 331–350.

Valentino, N. A., Brader, T., Groenendyk, E. W., Gregorowicz, K., & Hutchings, V. L. (2011). Election night's alright for fighting: The role of emotions in political participation. *The Journal of Politics, 73*(1), 156–170.

Valentino, N. A., Wayne, C., & Oceno, M. (2018). Mobilizing sexism: The interaction of emotion and gender attitudes in the 2016 US presidential election. *Public Opinion Quarterly, 82*(S1), 213–235.

Vasilopoulos, P., Marcus, G. E., & Foucault, M. (2018). Emotional responses to the Charlie Hebdo attacks: Addressing the authoritarianism puzzle. *Political Psychology*, 39(3), 557–575.

Von Neumann, J. (1953). A certain zero-sum two-person game equivalent to the optimal assignment problem. In H. Kuhn & A. W. Tucker (eds.), *Contributions to the Theory of Games* (vol. 2, pp. 5–12). Princeton, NJ: *Princeton University Press.*

Waismel-Manor, I., Ifergane, G., & Cohen, H. (2011). When endocrinology and democracy collide: Emotions, cortisol and voting at national elections. *European Neuropsychopharmacology*, 21(11), 789–795.

Walker, S. G. (1977). The interface between beliefs and behavior: Henry Kissinger's operational code and the Vietnam War. *Journal of Conflict Resolution*, 21(1), 129–168.

Walker, S. G., Schafer, M., & Young, M. D. (1998). Systematic procedures for operational code analysis: Measuring and modeling Jimmy Carter's operational code. *International Studies Quarterly*, 42(1), 175–189.

Walker, S. G., Schafer, M., & Young, M. D. (1999). Presidential operational codes and foreign policy conflicts in the post-cold war world. *Journal of Conflict Resolution*, 43(5), 610–625.

Wallach, M. A., Kogan, N., & Bem, D. J. (1964). Diffusion of responsibility and level of risk taking in groups. *The Journal of Abnormal and Social Psychology*, 68(3), 263–274.

Waltz, K. N. (1964). The stability of a bipolar world. *Daedalus*, 93(3), 881–909.

Waltz, K. N. (2000). Structural realism after the Cold War. *International Security*, 25(1), 5–41.

Waltz, K. N. (2010). *Theory of International Politics*. Long Grove, IL: Waveland Press.

Ward, A., Ross, L., Reed, E., Turiel, E., & Brown, T. (1997). Naive realism in everyday life: Implications for social conflict and misunderstanding. In E. S. Reed, E. Turiel & T. Brown (eds.), *Values and Knowledge* (pp. 103–135). New York: Psychology Press.

Wayne, C. (2019). Risk or Retribution: The Micro-Foundations of State Responses to Terror. Ph.D. dissertation, University of Michigan.

Weeden, J. & Kurzban, R. (2014). *The Hidden Agenda of the Political Mind: How Self-Interest Shapes Our Opinions and Why We Won't Admit It*. Princeton, NJ: Princeton University Press.

Weeden, J. & Kurzban, R. (2017). Self-interest is often a major determinant of issue attitudes. *Political Psychology*, 38(S1), 67–90.

Wendt, A. (1992). Anarchy is what states make of it: the social construction of power politics. *International Organization*, 46(2), 391–425.

Westen, D., Blagov, P. S., Harenski, K., Kilts, C., & Hamann, S. (2006). Neural bases of motivated reasoning: An fMRI study of emotional constraints on partisan political judgment in the 2004 US presidential election. *Journal of Cognitive Neuroscience*, 18(11), 1947–1958.

Whitmarsh, L. (2011). Scepticism and uncertainty about climate change: Dimensions, determinants and change over time. *Global Environmental Change*, 21(2), 690–700.

Wildavsky, A. (1998). The two presidencies. *Society*, 35(2), 23–31.

Winter, D. G. (1973). *The Power Motive*. New York: Free Press.

Winter, D. G. (1982). Motivation and performance in presidential candidates. In A. J. Stewart (ed.), *Motivation and Society* (pp. 244–273). San Francisco: Jossey-Bass.

Winter, D. G. (1993a). Measuring personality at a distance: Development of an integrated system for scoring motives in running text. In D. J. Ozer, J. M. Healy, Jr., &A. J. Stewart (eds.), *Perspectives in Personality, Vol. 3. Part A: Self and emotion; Part B: Approaches to understanding lives* (pp. 59–89). Philadelphia, PA: Jessica Kingsley Publishers.

Winter, D. G. (1993b). Power, affiliation, and war: Three tests of a motivational model. *Journal of Personality and Social Psychology*, 65(3), 532–545.

Wolfers, A. (1965). *Discord and Collaboration: Essays on International Politics*. Baltimore, MD: Johns Hopkins University Press.

Wolpert, R. M., & Gimpel, J. G. (1998). Self-interest, symbolic politics, and public attitudes toward gun control. *Political Behavior*, 20(3), 241–262.

Wong, C. J. (2007). "Little" and "big" pictures in our heads race, local context, and innumeracy about racial groups in the United States. *Public Opinion Quarterly*, 71(3), 392–412.

Woon, J. (2012). Democratic accountability and retrospective voting: A laboratory experiment. *American Journal of Political Science*, 56(4), 913–930.

Yunis, H. (ed.). (2011). *Plato: Phaedrus*. Cambridge, UK: Cambridge University Press.

Yzerbyt, V., Dumont, M., Wigboldus, D., & Gordijn, E. (2003). I feel for us: The impact of categorization and identification on emotions and action tendencies. *British Journal of Social Psychology*, 42(4), 533–549.

Zagare, F. C. (1990). Rationality and deterrence. *World Politics*, 42(2), 238–260.

Zaller, J. (1992). *The Nature and Origins of Mass Opinion*. Cambridge, UK: Cambridge University Press.

Zimbardo, P. G. (1971). The power and pathology of imprisonment. *Congressional Record*, 15, 110–121.

Index